Teaching Mathematics in Grades K–8

TEACHING MATHEMATICS IN GRADES K–8

Research Based Methods

EDITED BY

THOMAS R. POST

University of Minnesota

ALLYN AND BACON, INC.

BOSTON • LONDON • SYDNEY • TORONTO

Series Editor: Susanne F. Canavan
Senior Editoral Assistant: Elizabeth Brooks
Cover Administrator: Linda Dickinson
Composition Buyer: Linda Cox
Manufacturing Buyer: Bill Alberti
Editorial-Production Service: Editing, Design & Production, Inc.
Cover Designer: Design Ad Cetera

Copyright © 1988, by Allyn and Bacon, Inc.
A Division of Simon & Schuster
7 Wells Avenue, Newton, Massachusetts, 02159

Library of Congress Cataloging-in-Publication Data

Teaching mathematics in grades K−8.

  Includes bibliographies and index.
  1. Mathematics—Study and teaching (Elementary)
I. Post, Thomas Richard.
QA135.5.T399   1987   372.7   87-12380
ISBN   0-205-11076-2

Printed in the United States of America.
10 9 8 7 6 5 4 3 2 1 92 91 90 89 88 87

Brief Contents

Contents

3 Problem Solving
Richard Lesh, Judith S. Zawojewski

4 Foundational Ideas in Teaching About Measure
Patricia S. Wilson, Alan Osborne

5 Arithmetic Operations on Whole Numbers: Addition and Subtraction

James M. Moser

6 Arithmetic Operations on Whole Numbers: Multiplication and Division
Julie Anghileri, David C. Johnson

7 Teaching Rational Number and Decimal Concepts
Merlyn J. Behr, Thomas R. Post

8 Geometry and Visual Thinking
Alan R. Hoffer

9 Estimation
Barbara Reys

10 Ratios and Proportional Thinking
Alan R. Hoffer

11 Developing Relationships Among Mathematics and Other Subjects: An Interdisciplinary Approach
Alan H. Humphreys, Thomas R. Post, Arthur K. Ellis

12 Calculators and Computers
Richard J. Shumway

13   Moving to Algebraic Thought
Alan Osborne, Patricia S. Wilson

14 Girls, Boys, and Mathematics
Margaret R., Meyer, Elizabeth Fennema

15 Mathematical Evaluation and Remediation
Robert Underhill

Preface

All is not well in the mathematics classrooms of the nation's schools. International comparisons of the United States and leading industrial nations consistently rank the United States in the lower half in nearly every major mathematical category. For example, in the Second International Mathematics Study[1] eighth grade children in the United States ranked below students from Japan and Canada in every mathematical category assessed. In the areas of measurement and geometry these students scored in the bottom quarter of 20 developed countries. The 1980 National Assessment of Educational Progress revealed that less than one-fourth of this nation's 13-year-old children could correctly estimate the sum of 7/8 and 12/13. In a study reported in 1986[2] the highest average score for any American fifth-grade classroom assessed was below the average score of the lowest Japanese fifth-grade classroom. In that same study only 1 of 40 Chinese classrooms showed an average score lower than the highest American classroom.

These examples of very major differences in achievement patterns of school children have raised many eyebrows and in fact have been the impetus for much concern and a series of major reports, each decrying the overall quality of American education. Mathematics was not the only discipline under attack, but because of its importance to the physical and biological sciences it has received a disproportionate amount of attention.

Why do these discrepancies occur? Is it because our children are less able? Are our teachers less prepared? Is it because our schools are not committed to improving mathematics education? Are there differences among countries in

1. International Association for the Evaluation of Educational Achievement 1984. *Second study of mathematics—summary report.* Champaign, Ill.: U. S. National Coordinating Center, Univ. of Illinois.
2. Stevenson, H., Shin-Ling, L., Stigler, J. 1986. Mathematics achievement of Chinese, Japanese and American children. *Science* 231:693–698.

the importance attributed to educational achievement? Are there societal factors that influence childrens' attitudes toward school and the pursuit of excellence?

Since 1980 there have been no less than six major reports commenting on the adequacy (or inadequacy) of American education. Every one of these reports singled out mathematics as an area of greatest need. One report in 1983 described American education as a "rising tide of mediocrity."[3] This single phrase captured the attention of the news media for a time, then faded from sight and apparently also from mind. More current reports have sounded a similar alarm. As of this writing there continues to be a good deal of talk with relatively little action. This is true at the local, state, and federal levels.

During the early to mid 1970s a new movement known as "back to the basics" enveloped American education. In many situations this movement intentionally restricted attention to the development of higher order cognitive skills and higher order thinking processes. Textbook companies responded with new textbook series that were relatively devoid of topics other than developing paper-and-pencil skill and accuracy with addition, subtraction, multiplication, and division. At least part of the result is reflected in the studies cited above.

This back to basics movement was inspired perhaps by discontent with an earlier movement known as "the new mathematics," which never captured the interest and imagination of the people it was to have influenced. The new math of the late 1960s and early 1970s attempted to improve the quality of mathematics instruction from both a content and a method perspective. Although well intentioned and conceptualized the new mathematics was poorly packaged and was never used in schools on a large scale because it did not pay enough attention to the re-education of the parents and teachers who would also be affected by it. The resulting discontent paved the way for a return to the known and to the comfortable, those basic skills that had always been the focus of American education.

The back to basics movement was a curious phenomenon because it represented a negative national statement about one large-scale attempt to improve the state of the art. It was also curious in that it was launched by laypersons not professionally linked with the formal education of children. It was not endorsed by individual professional mathematics educators or professional organizations, nor was it endorsed by the groups and individuals who were best equipped to lead in this area. It is a commonly held belief among such professionals that the back to basics movement has significantly retarded progress in mathematics education. Many feel that five years from now we may be where we were ten years ago. A sample of those professionals are represented as authors in this book. Happily, things are beginning to reverse as evidence continues to emerge suggesting the shortsightedness of the back to basics approach. Attention is now being focused on more appropriate mathematical content and teaching methods. Unhappily, we have lost much valuable time.

3. National Commission on Excellence in Education 1983. *A nation at risk: the imperatives for educational reform.* (GPO #065-000-001772-2) Washington, D. C.: U. S. Govt. Printing Office.

Concurrent with the back to basics period the research community in mathematics education was undergoing changes that will significantly affect school mathematics programs in the years to come.

In the early 1970s The National Science Foundation funded a research center at the University of Georgia for the teaching and learning of mathematics. The Georgia Center was instrumental in organizing individuals from many different universities having common research interests and expertise into coordinated units capable of addressing important issues at a level far more penetrating than was possible by individuals working alone. Research prior to 1970 had been generally quite fragmented. Cooperative efforts were rare, and themes in research were difficult to identify. The large-scale cooperative effort begun at the University of Georgia has spread to many other locations and continues to this day. As a result, the literature dealing with teaching and learning of mathematics underwent enormous changes. Professional researchers, mathematics teachers, cognitive psychologists, and mathematicians working together produced more and better quality research. Much of this research was highly focused and represented coordinated attacks on areas of common interest. Out of such efforts new organizations were formed. Their primary purpose was to promote research. As a result, of these interdisciplinary cooperative efforts we know much more about children's learning of mathematics today than we did just a few short years ago.

Most of the themes that have received attention from these groups revolve around children's conceptual development in selected mathematical domains. For example, there have been large-scale and long-term projects dealing with childrens' learning of early number concepts, geometry, and rational number concepts; childrens' development of concepts of multiplication and division; the development of estimation strategies and processes; the influence of sex-related variables on mathematics performance; the impact of calculators and computers; and other aspects of childrens' thinking and concept development. There is still much that is not fully understood, but real progress has been made.

A large percentage of these projects were funded by the National Science Foundation and the U.S. Department of Education. Because of the expenses involved it is clear that large-scale efforts to revise school mathematics curricula or to mount substantive research programs cannot occur without external financial support. This is a most appropriate role for the federal government. Renewed interest in mathematics achievement in the press and in schools, coupled with a more highly refined research-related knowledge base, has raised optimistic projections as to what is possible. We now know children are capable of learning far more than we have expected of them. Educators can look ahead to a period of increased activity and large scale changes in the ways we conduct the business of education.

This book integrates many of those major research findings with a multitude of ideas and activities for the prospective and in-service teacher of elementary and junior high school mathematics. The authors of this book are all experts in the mathematical domains that they represent. The vast majority of these authors have been involved in research for many years. Combined, they have published over thirty books and several hundred research reports and journal articles. As of this writing several are involved in large-scale curriculum development or federally sponsored research programs. It has been a stimulating experience for me to have worked with them in the production of this book.

The ideas presented here are timely and appropriate. I feel confident that they will benefit the children with whom you work. The mathematics programs in the nation's schools are on the verge of yet another revolution—one that will be progressive rather than regressive. I trust that this book will assist with this important process.

T.R.P.

Teaching Mathematics in Grades K–8

Some Notes on the Nature of Mathematics Learning

1

THOMAS R. POST

University of Minnesota

INTRODUCTION

The process of learning has been a source of amazement, fascination, and study for centuries. Investigators have continually attempted to describe both animal and human learning in a wide variety of interactions and contexts. More recently, large numbers of actual experiments have been conducted. It is perhaps ironic, given the sheer magnitude of the learning research that has been undertaken, that we still do not know precisely how human beings learn. Numerous theories have emerged, many describing in minute detail both the learner and the manner in which learning can be enhanced. Others have chosen to adopt a comparatively broad interpretation of the learner and have satisfied themselves with a rather general description of the kinds of activities that will most effectively promote learning.

Some theories have portrayed the learner as a passive recipient in the learning process, almost as if her or his mind were a blank slate that could be written on at will by some outside source. Others have contended that children must be actively involved, both mentally and physically, if they are to truly benefit from a given experience.

Some theorists have depicted the role of the teacher as the prime exposer of knowledge, as the person primarily responsible for children's learning, almost as if the children were not intimately involved! Others view the role of the teacher primarily as a guide or facilitator of learning, one who effectively organizes the conditions under which the learning can take place and then exposes children to those conditions. The latter position tends to place more of the responsibility for learning on the individual rather than on the teacher.

The way the learner and the teacher perceive their roles in the actual learning process has a profound effect on the learning environment. The behavioral and cognitive theories are two broad theoretical umbrellas under which the vast majority of learning theories can be classified. In this chapter we shall examine the implications that these two major types of theories have for the teacher in the mathematics classroom.

BEHAVIORIAL PSYCHOLOGY

Two basic schools of learning theories have dominated educational psychology since the beginning of the twentieth century. One of these is behaviorial psychology. Individuals such as Edward L. Thorndike (1898), B. F. Skinner (1938), and Robert Gagné (1985) have contributed enormously to this perspective. The stimulus-response (S-R) theories of Thorndike were basically overhauled by Skinner, and the concept of operant conditioning emerged in the 1950s and 1960s. You have probably read about pigeons being trained to play table tennis, rats being trained to run mazes, or babies being trained to hold a bottle correctly. These are examples of operant conditioning. In each case the appropriate behavior is gradually "shaped" into the desired outcome. This notion appealed to psychologists at the time because of the precision with which it attempted to describe the learning process. The conditioning (behaviorial) theories worked particularly well in the animal laboratory. They were severely criticized by some psychologists who suggested that conceptual learning in human beings does not necessarily parallel the learning of lower life forms and that operant conditioning is a more appropriate model for rats and pigeons than it is for young girls and boys. A modified version of behaviorism, one more closely concerned with human beings, emerged in the 1960s.

THE NEO-BEHAVIORIAL POSITION OF ROBERT GAGNÉ

Robert Gagné emerged in the 1960s as the spokesperson for neo-behavorism. Gagné's primary concern is the *behaviorial* response of the learner following some form of instruction. In his latest book (Gagné, 1985) he identifies the general types of human capabilities that are learned. He suggests that human capabilities "are the behavioral changes that a truly comprehensive learning theory must explain (and which no theory as yet does encompass)." Gagné has been largely concerned with an attempt to clarify the relationships between the psychology of learning and instruction, that is, of arranging the conditions to bring about the most effective learning of intellectual skills, cognitive strategies, verbal information, motor skills, and attitudes. These five areas are defined by Gagné as "categories of capabilities."

The central question of the behaviorial tradition and therefore also for Gagné is what do you want the individual to be able to do?

> A learning occurrence, then, takes place when the stimulus situation together with the contents of memory affect the learner in such a way that his or her performance changes from a time before being in that situation to a time after being in it. The change in performance (behavior) is what leads to the conclusion that learning has occurred. (Gagné, 1985, p. 4)

To answer the question "What do you want students to be able to do?", behaviorists rely on task analysis (see Fig. 1–1), the process of breaking concepts down into smaller bits and pieces. Underlying the procedure of analyzing tasks into their component parts is the assumption (belief) that it is possible to subdivide a desired learning goal into its constituent parts and that once these parts have been learned, they will be synthesized by the learner in such a way that the larger goal is understood.

This is in essence a belief that the whole (the desired goal) is equal to the sum of its parts (the identified component parts). This belief has distinguished

FIGURE 1-1
A simplified example of task analysis

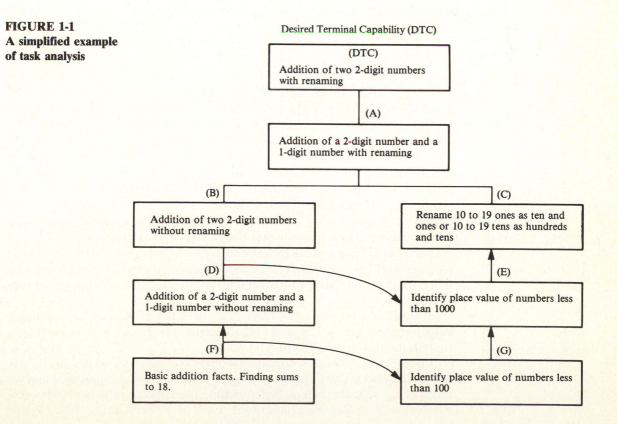

behavioral theories of learning from the cognitive approaches, which will be discussed in the next section.

Gagné believes that teaching and learning should be very specific or goal directed. They should be based on task analyses so as to have "the level of specificity needed in the planning of learning conditions. Broad goal statements must be subjected to additional analysis to make clear the components of what is to be learned" (Gagné, 1985, p. 261).

Once the learning objective has been established, it must then be broken into component parts. Students' understandings are then assessed to determine which students possess which prerequisite behaviors. Pupils lacking one or more of these must be specifically taught them before the desired learning goal (desired terminal capability) can be reached.

In a paper comparing the teaching–learning strategies of Robert Gagné and Jerome Bruner, Shulman (1968) depicted the Gagné strategy diagrammatically (see Fig. 1–1).

Gagné suggests that the behaviors prerequisite to a desired capability—in this case the addition of two 2-digit numbers with renaming—be assessed by answering the question, What needs to known before an individual can do that? (the desired terminal capability [DTC]). When it is determined that A (see Fig. 1–1) is needed to be able to do the DTC, the question is repeated with reference to A. This procedure continues until all relevant prerequisite behaviors (B through G in Fig. 1–1) have been identified. Instruction then proceeds upward from the prerequisite skill(s) the learner has not mastered.

It is interesting to note that Gagné, true to the behaviorist tradition, is not concerned with how the desired capabilities and prerequisite behaviors are taught. Lecture, discussion, guided discovery, or true discovery techniques may be utilized. For example, to teach the skill, in Box F of Fig. 1–1, the teacher could start by using manipulative materials and proceed to examples in symbolic form as given in textbooks. The final evaluative criterion is not how something was learned, but rather what was learned. If the learner was able to master the desired capability, the instructional strategy was successful; if he did not, the strategy used was unsuccessful. Variables other than the product or final content outcome of instruction tend to be overlooked and relegated to a position of insignificance. Thus, such factors as student motivation, positive attitudinal development, and student–teacher characteristics receive little direct consideration. It is not that Gagné is totally unconcerned with these matters, but rather that they gain attention only as they relate to the promotion of the desired behavior. In all cases, this criterion is identified as the product or outcome of the educative process and is specified in terms of what the learner can do.

It is not difficult to see that Gagné's model lends itself to the programming of learning sequences. The parts of the sequence are the sub-behaviors thought to underlie the larger objective.

Gagné's insistence that educational objectives be stated in specific behavioral terms and his resulting knowledge hierarchies have formed the basis for much of the school mathematics curricula. The concept of behavioral objectives is based on Gagné's task analysis. Each of the prerequisite behaviors or subskills (boxes in Fig. 1–1) is normally the sum and substance of a single behavioral objective. When an educational program is completely defined in terms of desired capabilities, and the attainment of those capabilities becomes the major goal of the educational process, there is the temptation to involve students in those (and perhaps only those) activities that promise to have direct payoff. Payoff is always defined in terms of student achievement. Mathematical excursions not directly relevant to the content at hand can become unacceptable.

Consequently, the child's activities are in effect completely determined by the objectives (capabilities) that have been established as program goals. Such an environment often results in very limited opportunities for deviation from the development of the desired capabilities. A danger inherent in this approach is the possible elimination of informal kinds of learning activities, which may not directly contribute to the attainment of a specific capability, but ultimately may prove vital in the overall learning process. Indeed, there is much evidence that this has happened in the majority of the nation's elementary schools where calculations with paper and pencil have dominated the mathematics curriculum, and exploratory and more loosely structured activities are almost nonexistent.

A second danger relates to the probability that important capabilities are often overlooked, and a third relates to the notion that some very desirable higher order capabilities, for example, problem solving, simply do not lend themselves to task analytic procedures. Gagné himself has suggested that task analysis is more appropriate to lower level objectives (R. Gagné, personal communication, November 20, 1979).

Gagné is primarily concerned with the what of the learning process. He is not particularly concerned with how it is that the child actually learns or with the behavior of the teacher. It does not follow that teachers using this approach use the lecture or expository approach as the sole teaching technique. The child may be taught by lecture, or discussion, or even discovery. The child is not necessarily passive (listening) and, in fact, may be quite active in the learning process. The rate at which a child progresses through the activities is not fixed. The teacher determines the pace as well as the activities and remains accountable for the program objectives. Consequently, the pupil's actions are somewhat confined under the very strict goal-directed procedures.

Using Gagné's approach to instruction, one can expect students to develop only a limited capability for transfer of training. Because specific knowledges are taught directly, transfer of training is also assumed to be quite specific. Gagné believes that individuals learn what they have been taught and do not effectively apply knowledge to new situations, unless these modes of transfer have been taught to them directly. It has been hypothesized by Shulman (1968) that this approach inhibits transfer of training because students learn specific knowledges well and these specifics in turn act as a source of inference (negative transfer) for new and different situations. To the degree that specific learning is done well, transfer is restricted. Although the research is inconclusive, it would appear that teaching for specific knowledges, using programmed learning, lecture method, exposition, and so forth, is most effective in short-term specific learning situations, such as the development of computational skills.

Although Gagné shares ideas with behaviorists before him, his views are decidedly contemporary. He has had and will continue to have significant impact on curriculum development in the area of school mathematics because there is a certain undeniable logic in his arguments. His position can perhaps be best summarized by his own words: "There are many, many specific sets of 'readinesses to learn.' If these are present, learning is at least highly probable. If they are absent, learning is impossible. So is we wish to find out how learning takes place, we must address ourselves to these specific readinessess" (Gagné, 1963, p. 626).

To Gagné, instruction forms the backbone of the educational process. Learning is not to be left to the vagaries of unattended or unanticipated occurrences. Guided instruction, as contrasted with discovery-oriented instruction, is the preferred model. He states:

> In the most general sense, instruction is intended to promote learning. This means that the external situation needs to be arranged to activate, support, and maintain the internal processing that constitutes each learning event. At one point, instruction may support the process of attending, which is an early phase of learning. At another point, the external stimulation provided by instruction may activate an internal strategy for encoding a mass of facts. And at still another point, instruction may primarily function to provide cues that make a newly learned skill memorable or readily applicable to a novel problem encountered by the student. Whether instruction is given by a teacher, or is in some fashion provided by the student, it has several important functions in influencing the ongoing processes of learning. (Gagné, 1985, p. 20)

THE COGNITIVE PSYCHOLOGICAL PERSPECTIVE

The second basic school of learning theories that have dominated educational psychology in recent decades is cognitive psychology. This theory provides the major theoretical rationale for the promotion of active student involvement in the learning process. The works of Jean Piaget, Jerome Bruner, and Zoltan Dienes are especially noteworthy. Each represents the cognitive viewpoint of learning, a position that differs substantially from the neo-behavioral approach.

Modern cognitive psychology places great emphasis on the process dimension of the learning process and is at least as concerned with how children learn as with what it is that they learn. Note the major difference in the orientation between this and neo-behaviorism. The objective of true understanding is given highest priority in the teaching/learning process. Cognitive psychologists believe that learning is a very personal matter and that true understanding involves an internalization of concepts and relationships by the individual involved and involves far more than mere observable behaviors. Emphasis is placed, therefore, on the interrelationships between parts as well as the relationship between parts and the whole.

Cognitive psychology assumes that the whole is greater than the sum of its parts and that the learning of large conceptual structures is more important than the mastery of large collections of isolated bits of information. Learning is thought to be intrinsic to the individual and, therefore, intensely personal in nature. It is the meaning that each individual attaches to an experience that is important. It is generally felt that the degree of meaning is maximized when individuals are encouraged to interact personally with various aspects of their environment. This, of course, includes other people. It is the physical action on the part of the child that contributes to his or her understanding of the ideas encountered. Proper use of manipulative materials should be used to promote these broad goals.

In this section, the theories of Piaget, Bruner, and Dienes will each be discussed because each person has made distinct contributions to our understanding of the process of learning mathematical concepts. As you will see, effective learning of mathematics often involves the use of manipulative materials and the opportunity to interact with other students.

Jean Piaget

Jean Piaget was a Swiss psychologist who was professionally active from the 1930s until his death in 1980. His contribution to the psychology of intelligence has often been compared to Freud's contributions to the psychology of human personality. Piaget has provided numerous insights into the development of human intelligence, ranging from the random responses of the young infant to the highly complex mental operations inherent in adult abstract reasoning.

In his book *The Psychology of Intelligence* (1960), Piaget formally develops the stages of intellectual development and the way they are related to the development of cognitive intellectual structures. His theory of intellectual development views intelligence as an evolving phenomenon occurring in identifiable stages that have a constant order. The age at which children attain and progress through these stages is variable and depends on factors such as physiological maturation, the degree of meaningful social and educational transmission, and the nature and degree of relevant intellectual and psychological experiences.

Piaget regards intelligence as effective adaptation to one's environment. The evolution of intelligence involves the continuous organization and reorganization of one's perceptions of, and reactions to, the environment. This involves the complementary processes of assimilation (fitting new situations into existing psychological frameworks) and accommodation (modification of behavior by developing or evolving new cognitive structures). The effective use of the assimilation–accommodation cycle continually restores equilibrium to an individual's cognitive framework. Thus the development of intelligence is viewed by Piaget as a dynamic, nonstatic evolution of newer and more complex mental structures.

Piaget's now famous four stages of intellectual development (sensorimotor, preoperational, concrete operational, and formal operational) are useful to educators because they emphasize the fact that children's modes of thought, language, and action differ both in quantity and in quality from those of the adult. Piaget has argued persuasively that children are not little adults and therefore cannot be treated as such in learning situations.

"Perhaps the most important single proposition that the educator can derive from Piaget's work, and its use in the classroom, is that children, especially young ones, learn best from concrete activities" (Ginsburg and Opper, 1969, p. 221). This proposition, if implemented in schools, would substantially alter the role of the teacher and the nature of the learning environment. The teacher would become less of an expositor and more of a facilitator. A facilitator is one who promotes and guides children's learning rather than teaching everything directly.

While it is true that when children reach adolescence their need for concrete experiences is somewhat reduced because of the evolution of new and more sophisticated intellectual systems of concepts, it is not true that this dependence is eliminated. The kinds of thought processes so characteristic of the stage of concrete operations (hands-on experience) are in fact utilized at all developmental levels. Piaget has emphasized the important role that student-to-student interaction plays in both the rate and the quality with which intelligence develops. The opportunity to exchange, discuss, and evaluate one's own ideas and the ideas of others promotes in children a more critical and realistic view of self and others. Piaget has called this decentration, the ability to step outside of one's self and view matters from another's perspective, and it is a very important ability that must be nurtured and encouraged in the classroom. Contrast this perspective with the reality that school children rarely if ever talk about mathematics with their classmates.

It would be impossible to find the essence of these ideas in a mathematics program that relies primarily (or exclusively) on the textbook for its direction or one in which the teacher is always responsible for "teaching" the subject to children. It is unfortunate indeed that the majority of the nation's classrooms rely almost exclusively on the mathematics textbook.

Piaget speaks to much more than just the learning of mathematics. Intellectual development cannot be separated from the social and psychological development of children. Mathematics and science, with their wide diveristy of ideas and concepts, are especially well suited to helping children develop intellectually, socially, and psychologically.

Zoltan Dienes and Jerome Bruner, while generally espousing the views of Piaget, have made contributions to the cognitive view of mathematics learning that are distinctly their own. Their work lends additional support to this point of view.

Zoltan P. Dienes

Unlike Piaget, Zoltan Dienes has concerned himself exclusively with mathematics learning; yet like Piaget, his major message is also concerned with encouraging active student involvement in the learning process. Such involvement routinely employs a vast amount of concrete material.

Rejecting the position that mathematics is to be learned primarily for utilitarian or materialistic reasons (because it is useful or because it helps one get a better job), Dienes (1960) sees mathematics as an art form to be studied for the intrinsic value of the subject itself. He believes that learning mathematics should ultimately be integrated into one's personality and thereby become a means of genuine personal fulfillment. Dienes has expressed concern with many aspects of the status quo, including the restricted nature of the mathematical content considered, the narrow focus of program objectives, the overuse of large-group instruction, the debilitating nature of the punishment—reward system of grading, and the limited nature of the instructional methodology used in most classrooms.

Dienes' theory of mathematics learning has four basic components or principles. The reader will notice large-scale similarities to the work of Piaget.

The Dynamic Principle

The dynamic principle suggests that true understanding of a new concept is an evolutionary process involving the learner in three temporally ordered stages. The first stage is the preliminary or play stage. The learner here experiences the concept in a relatively unstructured but not random manner. For example, when children are exposed to a new type of manipulative material, they characteristically "play" with their newfound "toy." Dienes suggests that such informal activity is a natural and important part of the learning process and should therefore be provided by the classroom teacher. Following the informal exposure afforded by the play stage, more structured activities are then appropriate. This is the second stage. It is here that the child is given experiences that are structurally similar (isomorphic) to the concepts to be learned. The third stage is characterized by the emergence of the mathematical concept with ample provision for reapplication to the real world.

The completion of this cycle is necessary before any new mathematical concept can become operational for the learner. Dienes referred to the process as a learning cycle (Dienes and Golding, 1971). The dynamic principle establishes a general framework within which learning of mathematics can occur. The remaining components should be considered as existing within this framework.

The Perceptual Variability Principle

The perceptual variability principle suggests that conceptual learning is maximized when children are exposed to a concept through a variety of physical contexts or embodiments. The experiences provided should differ in outward appearance while retaining the same basic conceptual structure. The provision of multiple experiences (not the same experience many times), using a variety of materials, is designed to promote abstraction of the mathematical concept. When children are given opportunities to see a concept in different ways and under different conditions, they are more likely to perceive that concept irrespective of its concrete embodiment. For example, the regrouping procedures (ten ones exchanged for one ten, ten tens for one hundred, and so forth) used in the process of adding two numbers is independent of the type of materials used. The teacher could therefore use tongue depressors, rubber bands, chips, an abacus, or multibase arithmetic blocks to illustrate the regrouping process. When exposed to a number of seemingly different tasks that are identical in structure, children will tend to abstract the similar elements from their experiences. It is not the performance of any one of the individual tasks that is the mathematical abstraction but the ultimate realization of their similarity. Children thus will realize that it is not the particular material that is important but the exchange process because that is the variable common to all embodiments. This process is known as mathematical *abstraction*.

The Mathematical Variability Principle

This third principle suggests that the *generalization* of a mathematical concept is enhanced when variables irrelevant to that concept are systematically varied while keeping the relevant variables constant. For example, if one is interested in promoting an understanding of the term "parallelogram," this principle suggests that it is desirable to vary as many of the irrelevant attributes as possible. In this instance, the size of angles, the length of sides, and the position on the paper should be varied while keeping the only crucial attributes—a four-sided figure with opposite sides parallel—intact. Many persons erroneously believe that squares and rectangles are *not* parallelograms. This misconception has resulted because the appropriate mathematical variables had not been manipulated when they were taught the concept. There are many other similar examples. Each is an endorsement of the arguments made by Dienes to consciously provide for this variable in our instruction. Dienes suggests that the two variability principles be used in concert with one another. They are intended to promote the complementary processes of abstraction and generalization, both of which are crucial aspects of conceptual development.

The Constructivity Principle

Dienes identifies two kinds of thinkers: the constructive thinker and the analytical thinker. He roughly equates the constructive thinker with Piaget's concrete operational stage and the analytical thinker with Piaget's formal operational stage of cognitive development.

The constructivity principles states simply that "construction should always precede analysis." It is analogous to the assertion that children should be allowed to develop their concepts in a global intuitive manner beginning with their own experiences. According to Dienes, these constructive experiences should form the cornerstone on which all mathematics learning is based. At some future time, attention can be directed toward the analysis of what has been constructed; however, Dienes points out that it is not possible to analyze what is not yet there in some concrete form.

One major problem in schools is the fact that many children are asked to abstract mathematical ideas before they have the opportunity to experience them in concrete form. A common result is rote learning. The constructivity principle, although simplistic in concept, if implemented, would have profound implications for change in mathematics classrooms.

Summary and Implications

The unifying theme of these four principles is undoubtedly that of stressing the importance of learning mathematics by means of direct interaction with the environment. Dienes is continually implying that mathematics learning is not a spectator sport and, as such, requires a very active type of physical and mental involvement on the part of the learner. In addition to stressing the environmental role in effective conceptual learning, Dienes addresses in his two variability principles the problem of providing for individualized learning rates and learning styles. His constructivity principle aligns itself closely with the work of Piaget and suggests a developmental approach to the learning of mathematics that is ordered so as to coincide with the various stages of intellectual development. The following are some implications of Dienes' work:

1. The whole-class (or large-group) lesson would be greatly de-emphasized in order to accommodate individual differences in ability and interests.
2. Individual and small-group activities would be used concomitantly because it is not likely that more than two to four children would be ready for the same experience at the same point in time.
3. The role of the teacher would include exposition as well as being a facilitator.
4. The role of students would be expanded. They would assume a greater degree of responsibility for their own learning.
5. The newly defined learning environment would create new demands for additional sources of information and direction. The creation of a learning laboratory containing a large assortment of materials and other conceptual amplifiers such as computers would be a natural result of serious consideration of Dienes' ideas (Reys and Post, 1973).

Jerome Bruner

Jerome Bruner was greatly influenced by the work of Piaget, worked for some time with Zoltan Dienes at Harvard, and shares many of their views. Interested in the general nature of cognition (conceptual development), Bruner has provided additional evidence suggesting the need for firsthand student interaction with the environment. His widely quoted (and hotly debated) view that "any subject can be taught effectively in some intellectually honest form to any child at any stage of development" (Bruner, 1966) has encouraged curriculum developers in some disciplines, especially the social studies, to explore new avenues of both content and method. Bruner has become widely known in the field of curriculum development through his controversial elementary social studies program, *Man: A Course of Study* (1969).

Bruner's instructional model is based on four key concepts: structure, readiness, intuition, and motivation. These constructs are developed in detail in his classic book, *The Process of Education* (Bruner, 1960).

Bruner suggests that teaching students the structure of a discipline leads to greater intellectual involvement as they discover basic principles for themselves. This, of course, is very different from the learning model, which suggests students be receivers rather than developers of information. Bruner states that learning the structure of knowledge facilitates comprehension, memory, and transfer of learning. The idea of structure in learning leads naturally to a process approach in which the very process of learning (how one learns) becomes as important as the content of learning (*what* one learns). Bruner never said that learning content is unimportant, as some have inferred from his writing. Rather, he is arguing for a greater balance between process- and product-oriented experiences for children.

Bruner (1966) suggests an important model for depicting levels of or ways things can be represented. One can experience and subsequently think about a particular idea or concept on three different levels: enactive, iconic, and symbolic. At the enactive level, learning involves hands-on or direct experience. The strength of enactive learning is its sense of immediacy. The mode of learning Bruner terms iconic is based on the use of the visual medium: films, pictures, diagrams, and the like. Symbolic learning is that stage in which one uses abstract symbols to represent reality.

For example, consider the operation "two plus three." From the child's perspective this idea is experienced *enactively* if the child joins a set of two objects with a set of three objects and determines that there are five objects altogether. This same notion is experienced *iconically* if the child views a series of pictures. The first might have two objects (birds, children), which are joined with a set of three objects in a second picture. The third picture might show that here are five altogether. Note that at the iconic level the determination of the result, five, is actually made by the developer of the diagram or photo, not by the child. The relationship is *symbolically* encountered when the child writes $2 + 3 = 5$. Bruner contends that all three types of interpretations or modes are important and that there is a common sense order implied by three levels because each requires familiarity with the earlier modes of representation.

Implicit in his and later work (Lesh, 1979) is the fact that these modes should be interactive in nature, the child freely moving from one mode to another. For example, given the equation $2 + 3 = 5$, the child could be asked to draw a picture of this situation. This would in effect be a translation from the symbolic ($2 + 3 = 5$) to the iconic mode (pictures). Other mode translations are possible.

Bruner feels that a key to readiness for learning is intellectual development, or an enlarging perspective of how a child views the world. To make this point, Bruner refers to the work of Piaget, stating that "what is most important for teaching basic concepts is that the child be helped to pass progressively from concrete thinking to the utilization of more conceptually adequate modes of thought'' (Bruner, 1960).

Bruner suggests that readiness depends more on an effective mix of these three learning modes than on waiting until children are capable of learning certain ideas. Throughout his writing is the notion that the key to readiness is a rich and meaningful learning environment, coupled with an exciting teacher who involves children in learning as a process that creates its own excitement. (This sounds very much like Piaget and Dienes, doesn't it?) Bruner clings to the idea of intrinsic motivation—learning as its own reward. This continues to be a refreshing thought.

Implications of Bruner's Work

Most commercial textbook series are concerned with essentially the same mathematical topics. These topics are important and should be maintained in the school program. However, the mode in which these ideas are presented is essentially inconsistent with the psychological composition of the intended consumer. A textbook can never provide inactive experiences. By its very nature it is exclusively iconic and symbolic. That is, it contains pictures of things (physical objects and situational problems or tasks), and it contains the symbols to be associated with those things. It does not contain the things themselves. A textbook is simply not (nor can it ever be) designed to do this.

Mathematics programs that are dominated by textbooks are inadvertently creating a mismatch between the nature of the learner's needs and the mode in which mathematical content is to be assimilated or learned. This view is supported by cognitive psychologists who have indicated that (1) knowing is a process, not a product (Bruner, 1960); (2) concepts are formed by children through a reconstruction of reality, not through an imitation of it (Piaget, 1958); and (3) children need to build or construct their own concepts from within rather than have those concepts imposed by some external force (Dienes, 1960).

This evidence suggests that children's concepts basically evolve from direct interaction with the environment. This is equivalent to saying that children need a large variety of enactive experiences. Yet textbooks, because of their very nature, cannot provide these. Hence, a mathematics program that does not make use of the environment to develop mathematical concepts eliminates the first and perhaps the most crucial of the three levels, or modes, of the representation of an idea (see Fig. 1–2).

FIGURE 1-2
Bruner's Modes of
Representational
Thought

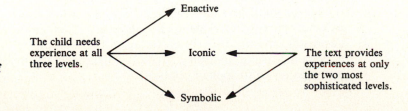

Clearly an enactive void is created unless textbook activities are supplemented with real-world experiences. Mathematics interacts with the real world to the extent that attempts are made to reduce or eliminate this enactive void. An argument for a mathematics program more compatible with the nature of the learner is therefore an argument for including more manipulative materials and more experiences in applying mathematical ideas in the real world.

It does not follow that paper-and-pencil activities should be eliminated from the school curricula. However, such activities alone can never constitute a necessary and sufficient condition for effective learning. Activities approached solely at the iconic and symbolic levels need to be restricted considerably, and more appropriate modes of instruction should be considered. This approach will naturally result in greater attention to mathematical application and environmental embodiments of mathematical concepts.

Some Recent Extensions to Bruner's Modes of Representation

Manipulative aids help learners move from concrete situations and problems to abstract ideas. Psychological analyses, however, show that manipulative aids are just one part of the development of mathematical concepts. Other modes of representation, for example, pictorial, verbal, symbolic, and real-world situations, also play a role (Lesh, Landau, & Hamilton, 1980). When learning a new concept, it is important that students "see" the concept from a variety of perspectives or interpretations.

How learners translate the various ways of representing mathematical ideas is important to the teacher and the researcher. These modes, shown in Figure 1–3, represent an extension of Bruner's early work in representational modes (Bruner, 1966). The term "manipulative aids" in this figure relates to Bruner's enactive level, "pictures" relates to Bruner's iconic level, and "written symbols" relates to Bruner's symbolic level. Lesh (1979) added verbalization ("spoken symbols") and "real-world situations" to Bruner's model and stressed the interdependence of these modes. Stressing the various translations within and among these modes of representation is the most important contribution of this model.

Asking a child to draw a picture given a manipulative display is a translation from the manipulative mode to the pictorial mode. Likewise, asking a child to construct a manipulative display given a verbal description is a translation from the oral mode to the manipulative mode. It is also possible to encourage within-mode translations. For example, if a child were given a display of chips showing the concept one-half with counters (Fig. 1–4a) and asked to show the same idea using paper folding (Fig. 1–4b), she would be making a translation from one manipulative aid to another. This is within-mode translation and is an extremely important translation for students to make. Many other translations are possible and are also to be encouraged. For example, when asked to explain the idea in a pictorial display, a child is making a translation from the iconic mode (pictures) to spoken symbols.

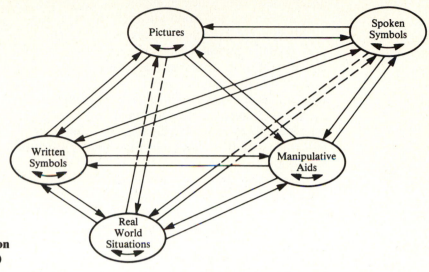

**FIGURE 1-3
Lesh's Model for
Translations Between
Modes of Representation
(adapted from Bruner)**

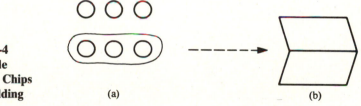

**FIGURE 1-4
Within-mode
translation: Chips
to paper folding**

(a)   (b)

A bit of reflection will indicate that these translations cannot be made unless the child understands the concept under consideration in the given mode. Further, the child must reinterpret that concept in order to display it in another mode or with another material in the same mode. This understanding and reinterpreting are important cognitive (intellectual) processes and need to be encouraged in the teaching/learning process. It is for this reason that the Lesh model is such a powerful tool for the classroom teacher.

Future research will determine which of the many paths through the model are crucial, necessary, or important to mathematical learning. For instance, two triads through the model involving manipulative aids follow the paths manipulative aids → spoken symbols → written symbols and real-world situations → manipulative aids → written symbols. Research may establish how manipulative aids facilitate concept development and problem solving.

For example, Gagné and White (1978) found that students who made oral observations about their manipulative aid experiences solidified the experience in memory and could retrieve it for later use.

Mathematical problem solving requires a move from the real-world situation to mathematical symbolism. Manipulative aids are in a sense halfway between the concrete real world of problem situations and the world of abstract ideas and mathematical symbols (written or oral). They are symbols in that they are made of physical materials, which in turn represent real-world situations. For example, chips could be used to replace automobiles in a problem asking a child to determine the total of six autos and five trucks. Manipulative aids, then, can be used to move the learner from the real-world level to the symbolic level.

That move, however, may not be a simple one. Behr (1976) found a significant gap between manipulative aids and symbols. He suggested the mental bridge to cross this gap is complex. Further research should help identify that gap and determine pieces of the bridge necessary to span it.

In the meantime, research has translated the theories into useful classroom teaching techniques [strategies] that can be used by teachers. The model in Fig. 1−3 predicts that mathematical learning, retention, and transfer will be enhanced when teachers provide for interaction among the various modes of representation.

Implications

A general overhaul of existing pedagogical practices, teacher−pupil interaction patterns, mathematical content, mode of presentation, and general aspects of classroom climate would be called for if the views of Piaget, Dienes, and Bruner were to be taken seriously. Each in his own way would promote a revolution in school curricula, one whose major focus would be method as well as content. It is important to note that even though the framework of the cognitive position was developed in the 1960s and 1970s, it remains as contemporary and important today as it was when originally conceived. More recent research has corroborated the vast majority of these theoretical underpinnings. Schools are still a long way from truly internalizing and implementing these ideas, despite the fact that we now have the research base and the know-how necessary to do it. At a recent meeting someone said, "What is new is what is old." It is still appropriate for us to review these important principles for guidance as we attempt to improve the mathematics program in the nation's schools.

CHAPTER 1 SUMMARY

The cognitive and behaviorist theories differ in their view of how children learn. One way to view the differences is to realize that the behavioral perspective is primarily concerned with *what* children learn. The cognitive view stresses the importance of *how* a child learns, often focusing on the physical conditions surrounding the learning process.

To the strict behaviorist, learning takes place best in tightly controlled situations. There may not be a great amount of student chance or variation from the "charted course." Very explicit objectives (behavioral objectives) expressed in behavioral terms accompany each activity or lesson in which the student is involved. Teaching and learning success is dependent on how well the student has mastered specific, precisely defined content material. That is, success in the learning process is defined with an emphasis on knowing. The criterion for success is *what* the student has learned as a result of instruction. There is an assumption that if a person knows the prerequisite behaviors for a task then she also has the ability to assemble or apply these behaviors to higher order tasks such as problem solving.

In the behaviorist tradition, transfer of what is learned is thought to be very specific. If certain skills or knowledge are required, then it is believed they should be taught directly. Involvement in activities not directly related to the attainment of an identified goal (behavioral objective) is often thought to be superfluous and therefore not encouraged. Most studies attempting to contrast the results of expository teaching and the more loosely defined discovery learning situation conclude that very tightly controlled expository teaching sequences are superior to discovery techniques when immediate learning is the goal. Neither method appears to be significantly better when long-term retention is considered.

Adherents to the cognitive viewpoint subscribe to a very different kind of environmental and teaching model. Although specific knowledge is not ignored, the major objectives of the cognitive position are more global and more general in nature. Whereas the behaviorist continually asks "*What* do you want the child to know?" or "*How* do you want the child to behave?", an equally important question from the cognitive viewpoint is "*How* do you want the child to learn?" Success is as much (or more) dependent on the attainment of process-oriented goals as it is on the mastery of specific content (product-oriented) competencies. The criteria by which success is determined are, therefore, quite different. Shulman (1968) comments on some possible results of involving students with process-oriented objectives.

> . . . by loosening up the objectives, we lower the probability of non-reinforcing error, while increasing the likelihood of profitable, non-threatening exploratory behavior. The error concept is irrelevant when the goal is exploration. There are goodies at every turn.

Cognitive-oriented learning tends to be both present and future oriented. Learning activities are selected partially because they are of interest at the moment, and not solely because they fit neatly into the predetermined logical pattern of content development. As a result, students can find themselves immersed in problem situations for which they do not possess all of the necessary understandings. Children are encouraged to obtain information in order to solve a problem at hand, rather than because it happens to be the next topic in the textbook. We thus find pupils learning because of present relevance, here and now, rather than the "learn now it will pay later" approach so often found in the mathematics classroom. The cognitive viewpoint contends that children have broad transfer capabilities, provided they are exposed to appropriate structural ideas in meaningful learning situations. The "meaningful learning situations" usually involve active involvement, both mental and physical. Learning contexts often contain a wide variety of manipulative forms of learning materials such as field trips, museums, and field work.

Evaluation of the cognitive-oriented learning sequence is often not as clear-cut and precise as in the situation where precise behavioral objectives have been predetermined. The cognitive viewpoint does not assume that the whole is equal to the sum of its parts. One must therefore not conclude that global objectives (i.e., problem solving, inferential thinking, and ability to make valid conclusions) have been accomplished merely because students can do a specific task. The larger objectives cannot be as easily evaluated. For example, being able to add two-digit numbers does not imply that a child understands addition, because the procedures used could be rote and devoid of any understanding. Unfortunately many adults have learned much arithmetic in this way. "Invert and multiply" is another example.

Because there are different criteria for success, it is not possible to conduct a comparative evaluation of behavioral and cognitive approaches to instruction. If one's primary intent is the immediate learning of very specific information, current research indicates that the most effective way to ensure this is to teach this material directly in a tightly controlled expository teaching sequence. If, on the other hand, the major objective is exploratory and investigatory in nature, then the tightly controlled expository teaching sequence is surely inappropriate. Teaching and learning sequences must be designed to promote the attainment of the established objectives.

Both types of objectives are important, and both can coexist. Unfortunately, most classrooms use too much exposition and not enough discovery, investigation, and problem solving.

It is time that the nation's schools involve students in a new and different type of learning environment that permits flexibility and active student involvement, contains a plethora of manipulative and other learning aids, and considers a much broader spectrum of topical areas. This is not to suggest a complete abandonment of behavioral objectives, for they are useful in limited situations. Rather this is an argument for a more balanced approach to providing for children's learning of mathematical concepts.

Postscript

The following chapters include repeated references to the way in which mathematics should be taught and to an expanded definition of the type of mathematics to be taught and learned. One study (Post, Ward, & Willson, 1977) determined that the vast majority (96%) of professional mathematics educators describe their primary philosophical orientation as belonging squarely in the cognitive camp. The authors here are no exception. As you read about and ponder the comments and suggestions made, it would be well to keep in mind the general philosophical framework that is being espoused. The experts really are agreed!

REFERENCES

Behr, M. 1976. *The effect of manipulatives in second graders' learning of mathematics.* (Technical Report Vol. 1, No. 11). Tallahassee, FL: PMDC.

Bruner, J. S. 1960. *The process of education.* Cambridge, MA: Harvard University Press.

————. 1966. *Toward a theory of instruction.* New York: W. W. Norton & Company, Inc.

————. 1969. Man: A course of study. Cambridge, MA: Education Department Center, Inc.

Dienes, Z. P. 1960. *Building up mathematics.* London: Hutchinson Educational Ltd.

Dienes, Z. P., & Golding, E. W. 1971. *Approach to modern mathematics.* New York: Herder and Herder.

Gagné, R. M. 1963, December. Learning and proficiency in mathematics. *The Mathematics Teacher,* 51(8), 620–626.

Gagné, R. & White, R. 1978. Memory strategy and learning. *Review of Educational Research,* 48(2):187–222.

Gagné, R. M. 1985. *The conditions of learning and theory of instruction* (4th ed.). New York: Holt, Rinehart & Winston.

Ginsburg, H., & Opper, S. 1969. *Piaget's theory of intellectual development: An introduction.* Englewood Cliffs, New Jersey: Prentice-Hall.

Lesh, R. 1979. Mathematical learning disabilities: Considerations for identification, diagnosis, and remediation. In R. Lesh, D. Mierkiewicz, & M. G. Kantowski (Eds.), *Applied mathematical problem solving.* Columbus, OH: ERIC/SMEAR.

Lesh, R., Landau, M, & Hamilton, E. 1980. Rational number ideas and the role of representational systems. In R. Karplus (Ed.), *Proceedings of the Fourth International Conference for the Psychology of Mathematics Education.* Berkeley, CA: Lawrence Hall of Science.

Piaget, J. 1960. *The psychology of intelligence.* Littlefield, NJ: Adams.

Piaget, J., & Inhelder, B. 1958. *The growth of logical thinking from childhood to adolescence* (A. Parsons and S. Seagrin, Trans.). New York: Basic Books.

Post, T., Ward, W., & Willson, V. 1977. Teachers, principals and university faculties: views of mathematics learning and instruction as measured by a mathematics inventory. *Journal for Research in Mathematics Education,* 8(5).

Reys, R. E., & Post, T. R. 1973. *The mathematics laboratory: Theory to practice.* Boston, MA: Prindle, Weber & Schmidt, Inc.

Shulman, L. S. 1968. Psychological controversies in the teaching of science and mathematics. *Science Teacher,* 38:34–38.

Skinner, B. F. 1938. *The behavior of organisms.* New York: Appleton.

Thorndike, E. L. 1898. Animal intelligence: An experimental study of the associative processes in animals. *Psychological Review Monograph Supplements,* 2(4).

2 Planning for Mathematics Instruction

ARTHUR K. ELLIS

Seattle Pacific University

INTRODUCTION

No two teachers will teach the same material in exactly the same way. When a teacher successfully motivates students and promotes their academic achievement to exemplary levels, all of us applaud his or her performance. Success in the mathematics classroom is the result of a number of factors, but the planning stage can be the most crucial. Teaching works best when it is viewed as having practical outcomes based on a theory or theories of instruction. Most theories of instruction include provisions for (1) planning, (2) method, and (3) evaluation. Effective teaching in mathematics, as in other curricular areas, begins with thoughtful planning.

   The goal of this chapter is to prepare you, the teacher, to decide what skills will be learned, which goal structure will be applied to convey that learning, and what mode of instruction, direct or indirect, will be used. Included are a step-by-step guide to planning a lesson and a unit, as well as a survey of the resources available to help you plan effectively.

THE TEACHER AS DECISION MAKER

Madeline Hunter (1978) suggests that teachers need to make three basic decisions as they plan for instruction. Those decisions are about (1) content,

(2) behavior of the learners, and (3) behavior of the teacher. These decisions will set the course of your long-term strategy as well as your day-to-day routine and, ultimately, will determine your level of success as a mathematics teacher.

Hunter advocates a developmental approach to the teaching of *content*. This means that your instruction should proceed from what students already know toward knowledge and skills beyond their present understanding. This is hardly a new idea. Socrates employed the same method centuries ago. Thus, you will want to sequence your instruction from simple to complex. Such sequencing is known as a developmental approach to teaching. The key to effective instruction depends on the teacher's ability to enable students to make connections between what they already know and what they must learn. Simple skills, such as measuring distances, can become part of more complex skills such as the application of measurements of distance and size with accuracy in solving complex problems.

Decisions about content have another dimension as well. Suppose two fifth-grade teachers were each assigned to teach multiplication as a component of their mathematics curriculum. One teacher might give more emphasis to computation, while the other might choose to emphasize applications of multiplication to problem-solving situations. One might spend more time on drill and practice while another might spend more time emphasizing the use of the hand-held calculator. And so on. The point is, of course, that teachers have a great deal of autonomy within the prescribed curriculum. While this autonomy permits you a range of freedom, it can be abused if you do not have a comprehensive plan for your instruction.

A second instructional decision that you must make has to do with the *behavior of the learners*. What will your students actually do during mathematics class? Will they work problems: orally? silently? together? alone? What will be the source of the problems they work: textbooks? problem cards? worksheets? the world around them? Will they engage in discussion? If so, with whom? Will you lead class discussions or will students discuss ideas in small groups? Will your students be expected to listen to you as you lecture and demonstrate to them? Will they take notes? Will you have your students apply what they learn? Will they work competitively? cooperatively? Whatever your students eventually do in mathematics, however they spend their time, will be because of decisions that you have made. And one thing is a certainty: *how* you have students spend their time will have a great effect on both their attitudes and achievement in mathematics.

The third decision is about your conduct, the *behavior of the teacher*. As you plan for your behavior in the instructional process, you will need to keep in mind several principles of learning, namely motivation, reinforcement, retention, and transfer.

As Jerome Bruner (1966) has pointed out, *motivation* is a powerful tool in the process of learning. How motivated are you to be the best teacher possible? It is probably true that the level of your motivation will dictate the extent to which you succeed, assuming, of course, that you possess the basic knowledge and abilities in the first place.

According to Walberg (1984), *reinforcement* is the single most important factor affecting instructional quality. A teacher's ability and willingness to provide both cognitive and affective reinforcement to learners are of paramount importance in the teaching of mathematics, an area of the curriculum often singled out (fairly or not) for its anxiety-producing effects, its failure to produce higher achievement scores, and its lack of appeal to many students. Reinforcement of key skills, attitudes, and ideas is crucial because of the cumulative, increasingly complex nature of mathematics. Perhaps the most crucial decision a teacher can make is to clarify to himself and to students the strategies he will use to reinforce mathematics learning.

Retention is a measure of how well you remember what you hear, see, and experience. There is the old saying, "I hear and I forget, I see and I remember, I do and I understand." The key to the old proverb's truth is, of course, level of involvement in the learning process.

Few of us retain all or even very much of what we learn. Our memories are less than perfect, and we may not have fully understood what we were taught in the first place. As a teacher, your responsibility is to attempt to maximize the understanding and retention of key concepts and skills. Number facts, taught as items of specific knowledge are, for most of us, short-term memory items at best. The keys to retention relate to appropriate usage and understanding the connections between these bits of knowledge and the real world.

Transfer means that something learned in one situation can be used in new situations. A straightforward question to ask students is, "Can you think of any ways you can use this?" If the answer is "yes" then transfer is probably occurring. Obviously, specific facts taught without any meaningful context have very little potential for transfer. On the other hand, processes such as observing, recording, measuring, and estimating have unlimited transfer value because they can be used in so many unforeseen circumstances. Generalized concepts also transfer well. The child who has learned about size and distance, estimating, and problem solving has learned about ideas that will transfer to a variety of situations, now and in the future.

One other thing you can do to promote the transfer of learning is to make connections among the subjects you teach. Challenge yourself, for example, to use ideas from mathematics in science. If your students are learning to make graphs in math, give them the opportunity to graph some science data such as high and low temperature readings for a week from the newspaper or television. If your students are learning to write letters in language arts, have them send real letters to cities around the country asking for information about climate, commerce, recreation, and agriculture, which they can use, among other things, as sources of quantifiable data.

You are responsible for what you teach and how you teach it. Your level of success will depend on such factors as your ability to make mathematics appealing, useful, and understandable.

ACTIVITIES

1. With a partner list at least ten ways to motivate students to learn mathematics.

2. Why do you think some students fear or dislike mathematics? What things could a teacher do to make math less threatening and more appealing?
3. The content, concepts, and skills of mathematics should be sequenced from simple to increasingly complex. Choose a math text from any grade level and try to document how this is done by the authors of that textbook.
4. We stated that a teacher's behavior is a crucial factor in mathematics learning. Write a paragraph in which you identify at least three positive classroom teacher behaviors.

GOALS OF MATHEMATICS LEARNING: TEN BASIC SKILL AREAS

As you plan activities for mathematics instruction, it is well to keep in mind the range of basic skill areas identified by the National Council of Supervisors of Mathematics and endorsed by the National Council of Teachers of Mathematics (NCTM) in 1977.

These skill areas broaden the scope of what is considered basic in the mathematics curriculum. As you examine them, try to expand your own thoughts about teaching mathematics. Your instructional planning should include a balanced coverage of the ten skill areas.

1. *Problem solving.* The principal reason for studying mathematics is to solve problems by applying previously acquired knowledge to new situations. Problem-solving strategies include: posing questions, analyzing situations, translating results, illustrating results, drawing diagrams, making models, and using trial and error. Students must be able to apply logical thought patterns to arrive at correct conclusions, to determine relevant data, and to draw inferences from their information base. Solving word or story problems is only one form of problem solving. (This will be discussed in more detail in Chapter 3, Problem Solving.) Students should be given real-life problems and a variety of other types of problems.
2. *Applying mathematics to everyday situations.* The use of mathematics is interrelated with all computation activities. Have students take everyday situations, translate them into mathematical expressions, solve the equations, and interpret the results.
3. *Alertness to the reasonableness of results.* Sometimes mistakes are made in computational work. Students should learn to check for the reasonableness of their answer in relation to the original problem. With the increased use of electronic calculating devices, this skill is particularly important.
4. *Estimation and approximation.* Students should have the ability to work out rapid approximate calculations by first rounding off numbers.

They should be skilled in estimating quantity, length, distance, and weight. They also must be able to decide when a particular estimate is precise enough for the situation at hand.

5. *Appropriate computational skills.*   Students must have skills in single digit (decimal and whole number) addition, subtraction, multiplication, and division. They must be able to recognize and manipulate common fractions and percentages. Mental arithmetic is a valuable skill for students to have even though in today's world long, complicated calculations are generally done with a calculator.

6. *Geometry.*   Students should learn the geometric concepts necessary to function in a three-dimensional world. Concepts such as point, line, plane, parallel, and perpendicular are important to know. Students should know the basic measurement and problem-solving properties of simple geometric figures, and they should be able to apply those properties to real-life situations.

7. *Measurement.*   As a minimum skill, students should be able to measure distance, weight, time, capacity, and temperature. Measurement of angles and calculations of simple areas and volumes are also essential. Students should have knowledge in both the metric and customary systems.

8. *Reading, interpreting, and constructing tables, charts, and graphs.*   Students should know how to read and draw conclusions from simple tables, charts, maps, and graphs. They should be able to condense numerical information into more meaningful terms by creating tables, charts, and graphs.

9. *Using mathematics to predict.*   Students should know how future events, such as election results, are predicted by the use of probability. They should be able to identify situations in which an immediate past experience would or would not affect the likelihood of a future event.

10. *Computer literacy.*   Students should be aware of the many uses of computers in society, such as in teaching/learning situations, financial transactions, and information storage and retrieval. The increased use of computers by government, industry, and business demands an awareness of computer uses and limitations.

These ten basic skill areas, presented here in an introductory fashion, are pursued in depth in later chapters. They represent the abiding concerns of mathematics instruction, and in that respect they form a structure for your planning, teaching and evaluating. No planning that you do should ignore these goals.

ACTIVITIES

1. Become an investigator. Examine any two elementary math textbook series and compare and contrast their respective coverage of the ten basic skill areas.

2. See how well you understand the implications of instruction in the ten basic skill areas. Write a sample application problem for children in each area.
3. Try some role play. Choose one or more of the ten basic skill areas and play the role of a teacher who tries to convince his or her fellow teachers of their importance in the mathematics curriculum.

VARIETY IN TEACHING MATHEMATICS

Research in effective teaching supports the use of a variety of teaching strategies (Goodlad, 1983). There are, perhaps, two reasons why it is useful for you to employ variety in the way you teach mathematics. First, we know that students respond differently to various ways of teaching. Some students learn effectively through silent reading, others do not. Some students benefit from direct instruction, others seem to learn more from inquiry methods. These comments are not made to typecast learners or to imply that anyone cannot learn in a variety of ways. Rather, it indicates a degree of sensitivity on your part when you are willing to make provisions for a wide range of learning styles. Second, just as we prefer to vary our diet and other routines, we gain from variety in instruction. A class is simply more interesting and appealing when students can look forward to discussions, hands-on projects, games, demonstrations, and other strategies. A monotonous, predictable routine reduces motivation and retention of ideas.

STRUCTURED LEARNING IN THE MATHEMATICS CURRICULUM

The teaching and learning of mathematics are too important to be left to random, unstructured encounters. Mathematics must often be taught in a systematic, sequential, and structured manner if students are to gain an ability to solve problems, to estimate and approximate, and to apply math to everyday situations. For instructional purposes, this means that there must be formal time allotments for the development of specific content, concepts, and skills.

Research findings tend to support high academic learning time, teacher-centered classrooms, an orderly, well-disciplined learning climate, and monitored assignments, including homework (Bossert, 1985). Let us look, in turn, at each of these variables.

Structured learning refers to time spent by the teacher with the whole class, during which time the teacher performs such functions as explaining, checking for pupil understanding, giving instructions, and conducting discussions. A high degree of correlation exists between the amount of time the teacher keeps the students on task (academic learning time) and the levels of academic achievement those pupils attain in various mathematics competencies. This is sometimes referred to as the opportunity to learn variable.

Structured Learning Strategies

We will examine three structured learning strategies: lecture or teacher presentation, class discussion, and demonstration. In each, the teacher is directly in charge of the instructional process and the students are challenged to acquire information and skills.

Lecture or Teacher Presentation

The idea of lecturing to young children may seem at first glance to be preposterous, particularly in light of the things we have learned about elementary school students from developmental psychology. Of course, long, didactic presentations would be inappropriate. But, a mini-lecture or brief teacher presentation makes a lot of sense if it is done in the context of a felt need on the part of the students. For example, in a lesson on consumer research, students were going to investigate several brands of a certain product. The teacher spent the first ten minutes of the class telling the students how a group of professional researchers had investigated the same product. The teacher's presentation or brief lecture was given in the context of a highly motivating activity, and the information was of significance to the students. The same information, presented out of context or in the absence of a related activity, would probably have gone right over the children's heads. Instead, because they had a need to know, the students were paying close attention to and taking crude notes on the teacher's lecture. There are several things to bear in mind when you lecture to children.

1. Is the idea or content I am presenting related to a meaningful context?
2. Do I have a clear outline of my talk so that the students can follow along?
3. Have I prepared any visual or other aids to accompany my presentation?
4. Am I teaching my students to become active listeners by having them take notes?
5. Do I check for understanding by asking questions at appropriate points?

Class Discussion

Class discussion can be a very meaningful mathematics teaching/learning strategy. It is a direct teaching strategy because the teacher is responsible for structuring the flow of the interaction and for directing the students' involvement and participation. The secret to effective class discussion is organization. A well-organized discussion has four basic components: a base of information, a central focus, effective questions, and a supportive classroom environment.

Information or content is essential to a purposeful exchange of ideas and points of view. It is well for you to get that point across with your students. Even good questions will not rescue a floundering discussion that is rendered empty simply because time was not taken to give students sufficient information on which to build answers.

In a whole class discussion, it is the teacher's responsibility to ensure that there is a central focus of discussion and that the questions keep coming back to the key issues. You can facilitate this by writing out your questions in advance and by gently reminding students that extraneous information, while often interesting, is not useful in the process of examining ideas in depth.

The next two issues, effective questions and a supportive environment, are somewhat complex. As you develop your questions for discussion, use Bloom's *Taxonomy of Educational Objectives* (1956) (see "How to Develop a Unit" in this chapter) to ensure that you will have a range of questions that includes the *knowledge* and *understanding* of the issue, questions that allow for *applications* to the real world, and higher level questions that ask students to *analyze, synthesize,* and *evaluate.* The level of the questions that you ask sets the tone for the level of thinking by the students. The pacing of your questions is also important. Casual observation in elementary classrooms would lead one to the obvious conclusion that teachers are trying to teach students to be impulsive in their answers. Budd-Rowe (1978) found that teachers generally wait less than one second after posing a question before they give the answer, ask another question, ask another student, or rephrase the original question. She found that students could be "trained" to wait a full three seconds before changing directions. When teachers did wait longer, students' responses were qualitatively better. Seldom does one see a teacher encouraging a student to take the time to fully explain his or her idea. Also, the classroom environment must be "safe" for students to answer questions. That is, the students need to feel that there will be an encouraging response to their participation during the questioning session.

Demonstration

A demonstration lesson is a structured teaching strategy in which the teacher models the behaviors of presentation, analysis, and synthesis. The role of the student is that of observer, recorder, and evaluator of information and/or skills. Demonstrations are most effective when they are followed by a corresponding student activity. Demonstrations, often wrongly called experiments, are, in fact, carefully rehearsed situations in which the outcome is fully known by the teacher. Thus, a teacher who demonstrates a measuring technique for determining distances on maps would reasonably expect the class to use the same technique in a follow-up activity. Or if the class were going to conduct a probability experiment by tossing dice, the teacher might be expected beforehand to demonstrate the appropriate techniques for recording data and summarizing the results. Application is the key to a demonstration's ultimate worth. If something is worth demonstrating to students, it is also worth the time to engage students in a direct application of the skill or activity. Demonstration is an efficient strategy because it allows the teacher to illustrate procedures and to communicate information at the same time. The danger of the demonstration strategy lies with the passive role of the students who may not understand the concept or skill the teacher is demonstrating. The demonstration should be followed by an application to be completed by the students, which, in turn, could be followed by a discussion of similarities and differences between the demonstration and the application.

Structured learning classrooms are characterized by a high teacher profile. The teacher in such rooms does little sitting at a desk. Rather he or she moves about the room while students are at work in their seats. And during discussions, the teacher plays the guiding role. This is not to say that you won't use small group discussion and nondirective approaches to teaching and learning, but they must be carefully planned and used for clear instructional purposes. It is, after all, to be assumed that you know the skills and content of the mathematics curriculum and that you will arrange for children to learn them. Teaching them directly and systematically is one way to do this.

Order and discipline are crucial to improved achievement in mathematics. Your classroom should have a firm, friendly, businesslike atmosphere. There should be no doubt as to who is in charge (you are) and it should be clear in everyone's mind that the classroom is a workplace. Only those who wish purposely to create a oversimplified dichotomy between a grim, overbearing prisonlike workplace and a noisy, cheerful, fun-loving atmosphere where the joys of childhood are celebrated daily ought to argue this point. As a teacher, you were not elected to serve in your position; you were appointed because it was decided that you have the authority and the ability to teach children about the world in which they live.

INDIRECT INSTRUCTIONAL MATH STRATEGIES

There are four indirect instructional strategies: inquiry, reflective thinking, creative expression, and values analysis. In each the teacher plays the role of *facilitator* of learning, the *process* of learning is emphasized, and students are *actively engaged* in learning.

Inquiry

Inquiry is a process of framing questions, gathering and processing data relevant to those questions, and drawing inferences or conclusions about the data. In mathematics, the inquirer emulates the behavior of the mathematician. The inquirer learns to value evidence, to think rationally, and to produce new (at least to the inquirer) knowledge. The responsibility of the teacher in inquiry learning is to help students frame meaningful, researchable questions, to help students find ways to gather and evaluate evidence, and to help them interpret, generalize, or infer from their data. An inquiry classroom is one in which students are free to take risks, to try out new ideas, and to expand their powers of rational thought. Inquiry takes students and teachers beyond the textbook into problem-solving investigations which may also involve the classroom, the school, and the community.

There are at least two areas of confusion regarding inquiry teaching and learning. Inquiry is not a "do your own thing" approach to teaching. Inquiry is a process that follows rather systematic procedures. It demands a great deal of self-discipline and perseverance on the part of students. Another point of confusion regarding inquiry relates to the issue of classroom management. Some teachers are convinced that students who are engaged in inquiry will be more difficult to control than are students who are sitting quietly in rows working from a textbook. There is no evidence to support this. Discipline problems occur when students are bored, frustrated, or confused. This often occurs as a result of teachers who are unorganized and ill-prepared. Management problems should not be automatically associated with any one particular teaching style.

Reflective Thinking

Reflective thinking is designed to give learners the opportunity to be philosophical, that is, to consider, discuss, and argue issues. The mathematics teacher can strive to make the classroom a "safe" environment where students feel free to speculate, hypothesize, and question ideas. Reflective thinking sessions give students the opportunity to analyze tasks that they have performed, or to speculate about how a certain chain of events might take place under certain conditions. Reflective thinking and inquiry share the idea of active student involvement in problems and questions. They differ in that inquiry asks the student to look for sufficient data to solve the problem, and reflective thinking deals with questions that require the student to go beyond the data.

Creative Expression

Mathamatics offers students a great opportunity to express themselves creatively. They can build, draw, paint, graph, chart, photograph, and so on, as a means of demonstrating what they have learned in math class.

Values Analysis

Values analysis as an alternative for learning in the math class is directed toward enabling students to develop a conscious awareness of their values and ideas.

In an age where there is so much "math anxiety," it is very important to take time to discuss children's feelings, the choices they make, and so on. The role of the teacher is to help students clarify their values and their point of view; to suggest alternatives, and to model; not to simply supply "right answers" to higher level questions and issues.

EXTENDING THE TIME FOR LEARNING

Everyone wants to know how well he or she is doing. Knowledge of results provides learners with the necessary stimulus for continued improvement. In this context, it is well for you to bear in mind that not all formal mathematics learning can possibly take place during the time alloted in the curriculum. This raises the issue of homework.

Homework

Studies of effective teachers and effective schools support the idea of systematic homework assignments in the basic skills areas from about third grade onward (Walberg, 1985). Whether younger children should be given homework in mathematics lies outside the range of demonstrated research evidence. Students should, however, become responsible for their own learning. Homework is an important step in this direction.

Homework assignments in mathematics are most useful when a few simple guidelines are followed. First, homework is not a type of punishment. It should be presented by you to students as a matter-of-fact, logical extension of the school day. In most cases, it is wise to avoid the introduction of new skills or concepts in homework assignments. You introduce, teach, and reinforce new skills and concepts during class time. Homework is a part of the process of completing assignments. Keep in mind that it is unfair to both your students and their parents (who may be trying to help them!) for you to assign material that has not been explained in class.

To summarize these points of effective instruction, let us urge you to keep in mind that there is ample opportunity over the course of a school year for both structured and indirect instruction in mathematics. Both are necessary, and both will succeed when they are carefully planned. Good management is based on firm, friendly leadership which emphasizes attention to task-oriented behavior in a disciplined atmosphere. And, of course, the amount of time students spend on various tasks, homework, classroom order, and so forth are meaningful learning variables only when the work you give to students is purposeful to begin with.

ACTIVITIES

1. Search through an elementary math textbook and find examples of lessons that lend themselves to structured learning. Then look for examples of lessons that lend themselves to indirect instruction. Which are easier to find?

2. It could be argued that a mathematics teacher is too busy trying to teach the basics in math and that there really is no time to digress into discussions of questions of values and feelings about mathematics. How do you respond?

3. How important is creativity in children's mathematics learning? Discuss this issue with one or two experienced teachers and then formulate a written position on creativity and mathematics learning.

HOW TO PLAN A LESSON

Effective teaching is based on careful planning. Planning is important to the beginning teacher and to the veteran teacher. Good planning is one of the keys to improved achievement. Let us examine eight planning criteria[1] for the conduct of successful mathematics lessons.

1. *Set the stage.* At the beginning of the lesson you want to arouse students' attention, capture their imagination, or possibly, just indicate how today's lesson is connected to yesterday's lesson. In any event, you are putting the activity into context and making it meaningful to your students. Motivation is a crucial issue early in the lesson because this is the stage at which you create an appropriate mental set and an accompanying desire to learn.

    If you were going to teach a problem-solving lesson on the topic of consumer research, you might want to motivate the class by asking students if they had ever purchased something that proved to be unsatisfactory. Such a question should lead to a discussion of product satisfaction based on students' own experiences.

2. *Tell students your objective(s).* Students need to know the intended purpose of the lesson. What will your students know or be able to do as a result of the lesson?

3. *Give directions.* Students must understand specifically what they will be doing during the lesson. Clear directions are crucial to the success of a lesson. Will students work together or alone? Will they make things? Do

[1]Adapted from Gagné, Robert M. 1965. Events of a lesson. In *The Conditions of Learning*. New York: Holt, Rinehart and Winston.

seatwork? Do they know how they will communicate their results? How much time do they have to complete the activity?

4. *Provide a context for learning.*   To provide some sense of continuity in learning and to help students see that learning has a cumulative effect, it is necessary to build a frame of reference based on past learning and projected toward future learning. Whether you teach from the textbook or you use hands-on strategies, you really do have to be aware that it is extremely easy to fall into a routine of doing an unrelated series of activities or assignments. It is absolutely critical that you make connections between lessons. Always work toward building bridges. One way to ensure that this will happen is to continuously reexamine your objectives.

    You will need to refer to yesterday's lesson, which we can assume was a precursor to today's activity. And you will need to point out (perhaps at the lesson's close) how today's content, concepts, skills, and values lead to tomorrow's lesson.

5. *Illustrate the key concept or skill.*   Try to decide ahead of time exactly what your students will need to know or do in order to carry out the assignment. Demonstrate or illustrate the material until you feel the students have grasped the idea and are ready to work on their own.

6. *Help your students to carry out the assignment.*   Don't return to your desk and sit down at this point. Rather, move around the room providing assistance. Ask questions, probe, clarify, maintain order, reassure. If teaching means changing students' knowledge, skills, and values, it follows that your support is necessary. Otherwise, there would be no need for the teacher's presence. Of course, the nature and amount of guidance will vary with such factors as student age, ability, motivation, and with the nature of the task itself.

7. *Promote reflective thinking.*   Whatever the assignment, it will need some pulling together, some summarizing, or some means of looking back. In some cases, a brief discussion will be adequate. In other cases, you will need to analyze the students' work. In perhaps another instance, you may give a quiz or test. You do need, as part of your instructional strategy, to allow time for students to look reflectively on their work. If you don't do this, you may seriously inhibit your students' chances of retaining key ideas, and you may limit the lesson's potential to achieve transfer of learning. Chapter 15 explores measurement and evaluation issues in more detail.

8. *Clarify any extended expectations.*   Many times you will conduct an assignment by explaining it and then having the students work on it in class. But there will also be times when you assign homework. When you do, be certain that you are clear about what students are to do at home and what they will be expected to turn in. Remember that they are "on their own" so it isn't fair to expect them to develop new skills. Rather, they will continue or build on their classwork.

These eight steps are meant to give you a framework for lesson planning. Don't fall into the trap of thinking that this is a lock-step recipe and that every point has to be thoroughly accounted for every time you work with students.

But remember that the steps are based on known principles of effective teaching.

ACTIVITIES

1. Select a lesson from an elementary math textbook and develop a plan for teaching it to students. Use the seven steps presented in this chapter as a basis of your plan.
2. It could be argued (and often is) that there is no reason to plan mathematics lessons because you just proceed from page to page throughout the textbook, and the teacher's guide tells you what to do and say. How do you respond?

List the lesson topic you intend to teach. *Beginning LOGO: Geometric Designs*

List your instructional objectives. *Using an Apple IIe computer, the student will use the "edit mode" to draw and define geometric designs.*

List the key idea, skill, or major concept you intend to teach. *LOGO is a sequential, concrete approach to understanding geometry.*

Identify the teaching strategies you intend to use. *"Hands on" learning. teacher models skills and students work in teams of two to develop their definitions of geometric designs in the LOGO edit mode.*

List the materials and resources you will need. *Apple LOGO disk, manual, blank disks.*

What motivational strategy will you use? *demonstration of capabilities of LOGO language. review of fundamental commands.*

What provisions will you make for individual differences? *peer helper approach with students working in pairs.*

How will you bring the lesson to a close? *Discuss problems students may have had. Talk about how these geometric shapes are found in the built environment.*

How will you determine whether your lesson objectives have been met? *the graphics mode will show any errors students make in the edit mode therefore giving them immediate feedback.*

HOW TO DEVELOP A UNIT

Planning a unit of instruction has many of the aspects of lesson planning, but on a larger scale. It is a useful approach to most teaching and learning situations because it concentrates your efforts and those of your students on a central theme, organizing idea, or set of concepts. The effect of such a focus is to promote systematic learning toward clearly defined objectives, thus keeping you from falling into the trap of teaching nothing more than activities or pages from a textbook.

What is a unit?   A unit is a sequential progression of lessons directed toward the development of a theme. Unit themes are developed through an articulation of content, concepts, skills, and values. The term "unit" implies oneness or wholeness as opposed to fragmentation. Thus a unit title will describe its sense of coherence and oneness. In mathematics, common unit titles might include "Addition/Subtraction," "The Measurement of Length, Area, Volume," "Geometry and the Geoboard," or "Number Patterns in the Real World." Of course, the textbook and district or state guides are major sources of information regarding appropriate topics at your grade level. Most elementary school mathematics textbooks are divided into units. Often a chapter constitutes a unit.

Time allotments.   How long should a unit be? How many days of instruction should be allocated to each unit? There is no predetermined amount of time that must be allocated for any given unit. You need to make those decisions on the basis of what topics must be addressed in the course of the school year.

How to begin.   The first step in the development of a unit is to think of it in terms of your objectives for the entire year. You will need to answer such long-range planning questions as "Where does this topic logically fit in the flow of my instruction?" and "What skills and knowledge are prerequisite to the skills and knowledge of this unit?" The second step in the development of a unit is to develop an overview that contains the rationale and a brief statement of contents. The purpose of a written rationale is to state why you are teaching a particular unit. How is the unit important to the process of students' learning? Your statement of contents can be written in paragraph or a table of contents format.

Unit objectives.   Objectives for the unit can be global or very specific. Specifically stated behavioral objectives specify exactly what performance is expected of students. Thus, while a more global statement such as "Students need to develop greater skill development in the area of addition," is an important part of your overall goal, it is not acceptable as a behaviorally stated objective. Here are some examples of behavioral objectives. Note that they specify *who* (the student), does *what* (solves, computes, graphs, demonstrates), *under what conditions* (paper and pencil, using a computer tutorial), and *mastery criteria* (for example, nine out of ten times):

1. Given ten 2-digit addition problems in which no regrouping is necessary, students compute sums and will enter answers into a computer-based management system with 90% accuracy.

2. Given a worksheet with 25 single-digit addition and subtraction facts, students will write answers to the problems with no more than two errors.

3. During class discussion, students will demonstrate understanding of the application of measurement to real-life activities by listing three uses of the skill and then demonstrating those uses to the class.

When you develop your set of unit objectives, it is important that you consider the range of intellectual endeavor from knowledge and comprehension through such higher thought levels as application, analysis, and evaluation. As you will see, not all worthwhile objectives can be written in precisely stated behavioral form.

Bloom's *Taxonomy of Educational Objectives* (1956) is a useful guide to help you conceptualize your unit objectives. The taxonomy (cognitive domain) is a hierarchy divided into six increasingly complex levels. Take a few moments to consider each level. Remember that your unit objectives should reflect a representative distribution of each level.

1. *Knowledge.* The issue is recall of information. This level is crucial because if students do not possess knowledge of basic factual information, they cannot carry out the operational processes necessary in the computational skills area.

2. *Comprehension.* Your objective at this level is to ensure that students can recall concepts, translate or interpret the processes, and extrapolate necessary information. In other words, the emphasis is on demonstrating an understanding of concepts and their relationships, not on producing the solution. It is one thing, for example, to be able to recall the answers to basic addition facts from zero to nine (knowledge) and quite another to be able to explain (comprehension) when to use the concept of addition.

3. *Application.* Objectives developed at the application level have as their purpose something practical—usage. The issue at this level is whether students can use skills and concepts in new situations. For example, in counting, a child needs to be able to recite numbers in the correct order (knowledge), and he or she needs to understand one-to-one correspondence (comprehension). The child also has to be able to construct a one-to-one matchup between the objects being counted and the numbers being recited (application). Therefore, the application of a child's counting skills rests heavily on his or her understanding of one-to-one correspondence.

4. *Analysis.* Objectives written at the analysis level are designed to enable students to see relationships, make comparisons and contrasts, and look for patterns. Analysis, as the term implies, is an attempt to break down whole entities into their component parts. For example, in the study of story problems, you might wish to present the following problem to your students:

The number of lily pads on a pond doubles each day. On the thirtieth day, the pond is completely covered. On which day will the pond be half covered with lily pads?

Activities at the analysis level require a nonroutine application of concepts in order to arrive at the correct answer (which is the twenty-ninth day).

5. *Synthesis.*   Synthesis represents a pulling together or combining of elements. As a synthesis level objective, you might ask your students to locate and record or draw the various ways that the community uses measurement, geometry, and other mathematics skills that they have studied or to create their own problems utilizing a combination of the math skills that they have learned.
6. *Evaluation.*   Evaluation level objectives encourage your students to take their own points of view or to somehow express their ideas on issues. A class debate or written papers that include students' individual opinions or judgments are examples of evaluation. At the evaluation level, divergent thinking is encouraged and differences of opinion are to be expected.

Although you need to develop unit objectives at all six levels, you will write more knowledge and comprehension objectives than you will write for the higher categories. There are two reasons for this. Knowledge and comprehension represent the most basic skills and are, therefore, fundamental to the learning enterprise. And the complexity of tasks at such levels as synthesis and evaluation means that those assignments will usually be of longer duration.

It is important that you recognize the necessity of developing your unit objectives using all the levels of Bloom's *Taxonomy of Educational Objectives*. These objectives will serve to guide your day-to-day instruction, and they can form the basis for your test items or other means of evaluating student progress. Thus, there is a natural axis that runs from planning through instruction to evaluation. Developing an understanding of appropriate connections among these three important factors of instruction is one of most important things you will learn as a teacher.

Unit Resources

It is quite possible that the majority of the units you develop and teach will depend heavily on your students' textbooks and your own accompanying teacher's guide for both content and direction. When this is the case, the textbook and teacher's guide are, of course, your primary resources. But even the teacher who takes a textbook-oriented approach to instruction will need to look for additional source material.

As you consider the development of a unit, particularly one that goes beyond a series of textbook assignments, you will find it necessary and helpful to seek resources that will help you to strengthen your own background on the topic in question (rational numbers, geometry, or whatever) and resource material for your students to use as they study the topic throughout the course of the unit.

At the elementary level, concrete materials, hands-on learning, and real-world applications are essential. The textbook alone is inadequate. You simply must make certain that your students are actively engaged in learning.

Teacher resources such as books, journal articles, and other materials, will strengthen your own understanding of the unit topic in question. If, for example, you are preparing a unit on measurement, you will want to ask a reference librarian to identify some appropriate sources. In all likelihood, you will want to seek material that deals with both content and methods of instruction. (See the list of professional journals at the end of this chapter.)

REVIEW

Careful planning is the foundation of successful mathematics instruction. Use the checklist below to review your own understanding of the planning process.

- What are the crucial planning decisions a teacher must make? How do those decisions affect the quality of mathematics instruction?
- What are the ten basic skill areas of mathematics instruction? How can an awareness and application of them improve your teaching?
- What do you think are the differences between structured and indirect teaching strategies in mathematics? What is an appropriate balance between the two?
- What is the role of homework in elementary mathematics? List some reasons for and against assigning homework to students.
- Identify the seven criteria for planning a lesson in mathematics. Why is it not necessary that the seven criteria be followed in lock-step fashion when you teach each lesson?
- The planning guide in this chapter covers such "nuts and bolts" as lesson topic, instructional objective, key idea, strategy, and materials. Use the planning guide to illustrate how you would teach a lesson on the topic, "An Introduction to Fractions."
- The portion of the chapter to unit planning placed emphasis on a working knowledge of Bloom's *Taxonomy of Educational Objectives*. Demonstrate your understanding of the taxonomy by writing a mathematics objective for a particular topic at each level.
- Many teachers simply follow the textbook page by page in their teaching. List examples of teaching/learning resources that you could employ to make mathematics more appealing and understandable to your students. (You may want to skim through the text for help with this item.)

CHAPTER 2 SUMMARY

In this chapter, you have been given ideas for planning instruction in mathematics. Planning is the essential first step toward effective teaching.

There are many reasons why mathematics instruction succeeds or fails. Some are obvious: a teacher's knowledge of the subject matter, a teacher's ability to communicate ideas to students, the match between student ability and the level of difficulty of that which is taught, student motivation and desire to learn, and the extent to which the teacher makes meaningful applications of the material taught.

Math is a powerful intellectual tool. Tools are to be used. The ability of a teacher to effectively use mathematical skills throughout the curriculum sets a student free to investigate and solve problems independently, not only in mathematics area, but in other areas as well. Remember, good planning does not ensure good teaching, but poor planning does ensure poor teaching.

REFERENCES

Walberg, H. J. 1984, May. Improving the productivity of American schools. *Educational Leadership*, 41:19−27.

SUGGESTED READINGS

Barnett, C. S., & Young, S. 1982. *Teaching kids math: Problem-solving activities to help young children learn and enjoy mathematics.* Englewood Cliffs, NJ: Prentice-Hall.

Barratta-Lorton, M. 1976. *Mathematics their way: An activity-centered mathematics program for early childhood education.* Menlo Park, CA: Addison-Wesley.

Bloom, B. 1956. *Taxonomy of educational objectives: cognitive domain.* New York: David O. McKay Co.

Bossert, S. 1985. Effective elementary schools. In R. Kyle (ed.) *Reaching for Excellence: An effective schools sourcebook.* Washington, D.C.: U.S. Government Printing Office.

Brainerd, C. J. (Ed.) 1982. *Children's logical and mathematical cognition.* New York: Springer-Verlag.

Bruner, J. 1966. *Toward a theory of instruction.* New York: Norton Books.

Budd-Rowe, M. B. 1978. *Teaching science as continuous inquiry: A basic 2-e.* New York: McGraw-Hill.

Dienes, Z. P. 1973. *Mathematics through the senses, games, dance, and art.* United Kingdom: NFER Ltd.

Ginsberg, H. P. (ed.) 1983. *The development of mathematical thinking.* New York: Academic Press.

Goodlad, J. 1983. *A place called school.* New York: Wiley.

Grady, T., & Gawronski, J. D. 1983. *Computers in curriculum and instruction.* Alexandria, VA: ASCD.

Hargreaves, D. H. 1984, February. Teachers' questions: Open, closed, half-open. *Journal of Educational Research,* 26:46−51.

Heimer, R. T., & Trueblood, C. R. 1977. *Strategies for teaching children mathematics.* Reading, MA: Addison-Wesley.

Hunter, M. 1978. *Theory into practice publications (motivation, reinforcement, retention, transfer).* El Segundo: TIP Publications.

Johnson, D. W., & Johnson, R. T. 1984. *Circles of learning: Cooperation in the classroom.* Alexandria, VA: ASCD.

Olugokinski, E. 1984, February. Developing cooperative school environments for children. *Elementary School Guidance Counselor,* 18:209−215.

Papert, S. 1980. *Mindstorms: Children, computers, and powerful ideas*. New York: Basic Books.

Position paper on basic mathematical skills. 1977. Reston VA: National Council of Supervisors of Mathematics.

Silbert, J., Carnine, D., & Stein, M. 1981. *Direct instruction mathematics*. Columbus, OH: Charles E. Merrill, Inc.

Stoner, W. F., & Pukala, D. R. 1984, January. How to teach by asking questions. *Instructional Innovator,* 29:52.

Walberg, H. J. 1985. Homework's powerful effects on learning, *Educational Leadership,* 42(7):76−79.

Webb, N. M. 1984, April. Stability of small group interaction and achievement over time. *Education Psychology,* 76:211−224.

SUGGESTED JOURNALS FOR THE ELEMENTARY MATHEMATICS TEACHER

Arithmetic Teacher

Classroom Computer Learning

Creative Computing

Computer Education

Educational Studies in Mathematics

Journal of Computers in Mathematics and Science Teaching

Journal for Research in Mathematics Education

Mathematics in School

School Science and Mathematics

Learning Magazine

3 Problem Solving

RICHARD LESH

WICAT Systems
Provo, Utah

JUDITH S. ZAWOJEWSKI

National College of Education
Chicago, Illinois

INTRODUCTION

Because of our increasingly technological society, more people than ever must use mathematics to solve problems in daily situations, for career entry, or just for informed citizenship. Solving everyday problems requires skills that go beyond applying arithmetic to textbook-type word problems. A person must be able to interpret and analyze problem settings, develop ways of organizing and filtering large amounts of data, generate information relevant to particular problems or decisions, and analyze assumptions underlying the results and conclusions generated by others. Yet, results from recent testing programs, like the National Assessment of Educational Progress (Carpenter, Corbitt, Kepner, Lindquist, & Reys, 1981; Lindquist, Carpenter, Silver, & Matthews, 1983) or the Second International Mathematics Study (Crosswhite, Dossey, Swafford, McKnight, & Cooney, 1985) indicate that students across the country continue to have difficulty with all but the simplest one-step word problems.

Poor performance is especially apparent on nonroutine problems that require multiple steps, or that have extra information, or that require students to use mathematics to make nonmathematical decisions.

The purpose of this chapter is to acquaint the reader with recent research on problem solving, to provide some sample problems to try, and to facilitate teachers' understanding so they can begin to integrate a comprehensive problem-solving component into their own curricula.

THE ROLE OF PROBLEM SOLVING IN SCHOOL MATHEMATICS PROGRAMS

In the past decade, problem solving has been one of the most important areas of research and instructional development in mathematics education. For example, the National Council of Teachers of Mathematics cited problem solving as one of the major goals in their *Agenda for Action* (1980). Resources using a variety of teaching methods and problem types are available. They include Bell and Usiskin (1983), Brown and Walter (1983), Burkhardt (1981), Butts (1973), Freudenthal (1968), Gardner (1978), Goodstein (1983), Hughes, Huntley and McDonald (1982), Krulik and Reys (1980), Lesh (1985), Mason, Burton, and Stacey (1982), Schoenfeld (1986), the NCTM/MAA *Sourcebook of Applications of School Mathematics* (1980), Usiskin (1978), and Whimbey and Lochhead (1984). However, even though some excellent problem-solving resources are available, the task remains for teachers to integrate these curriculum supplements into existing mathematics programs.

PROBLEM-SOLVING HEURISTICS

Research on mathematical problem solving often has been based on the work of the famous mathematician and master teacher, George Polya (1957, 1962, 1965) who advocated that students use self-generated questions to help themselves when they are "stuck" during solution attempts. These strategies, or *heuristics,* were intended to help students think about their own thinking strategies so they could discover useful solution paths.

The heuristics Polya stressed were based on his own and other experts' problem-solving processes. He believed that the questions and hints an expert problem solver consciously uses could be modeled by teachers as they give suggestions to students during problem-solving attempts. Just as expert problem solvers often carry on internal dialogues with themselves during solution processes, Polya believed that, with guidance from a teacher or role-model, students could eventually internalize these questioning processes and use them without external guidance.

Among the heuristics identified by Polya, one involved considering problems similar to the given problem (for example, a simpler situation or a special case). Another involved introducing useful symbols or representations (for example, by drawing pictures or diagrams or by making a chart or graph). Other heuristics involved a variety of "means-ends analysis techniques" to reduce the gap between what was known and what was wanted. Such techniques included clearly identifying knowns and unknowns, working backwards from desired results to the givens, setting intermediate goals which can be addressed one step at a time, or breaking up complex situations into distinct sets of simpler problems.

General Problem-Solving Heuristics

Try using some of the preceding heuristics to solve the problem below. Then think back about your solution process.

PROBLEM-SOLVING ACTIVITY 3−1

Two glass jars were sitting on a table. One contained 1,000 blue beads and the other contained 500 yellow beads. A teacher took 20 beads out of the blue bead jar and put them into the yellow bead jar. Then she shook the yellow bead jar until the yellow and blue beads were thoroughly mixed. Next, she randomly selected 20 beads from the yellow bead jar and put them into the blue bead jar.

Are there more blue beads in the yellow bead jar than there are yellow beads in the blue bead jar? (Bell, Fuson, & Lesh, 1976)

Exercise Set 3−1

1. The correct answer is that there are the same number in each jar at the end. If you did not get the answer correct, try the problem again using the heuristic, "consider a simpler problem," and/or "use a representation." For example, consider jars with smaller numbers of beads or act it out.
2. Watch someone else try to solve the problem. Describe their solution process, including any heuristics they used or hints you have.

Figure 3−1 shows a diagram of a simpler case—the jars contain only a small number of beads at the start, and only five beads from Jar B (the blue bead jar) are mixed with the beads in Jar Y (the yellow bead jar). Figure 3−2 shows a particular case when five beads are then returned to Jar B—it focuses on the special case when two of the returned beads are yellow. The result is that two blue beads would remain in Jar Y, and two yellow beads would be in Jar B.

Try some other combinations. For example, what happens if you select one

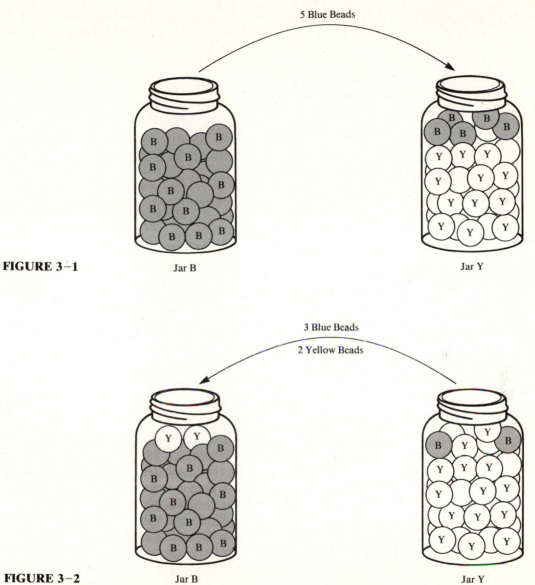

FIGURE 3–1   Jar B   Jar Y

FIGURE 3–2   Jar B   Jar Y

blue bead and four yellow beads from Jar Y? Will you always end up with the same number of blue beads and yellow beads in opposite jars?

General heuristics, like "draw a picture," "consider a simpler problem," and "consider a special case," can be useful in a wide variety of problem situations. But, there are other problems in which these heuristics are not especially useful, or in which other heuristics are far more helpful. Try to think of several possible examples of your own; then try solving the problem below. Notice any heuristics that you use naturally.

PROBLEM-SOLVING ACTIVITY 3–2

Three men who are sharing a room in a motel pay $10 each, or $30 in all. Later, the proprietor feels that he charged too much. He gives the bellboy $5 to return to them. The bellboy decides that since there is no way to divide the $5 evenly among the three men, he will give each man $1, and keep the other $2 for himself. That makes the room cost $9 per man, or $27 in all. The $27 paid for the room plus $2 that the bellboy kept makes $29. But the men paid $30 originally. What happened to the other dollar? (Bell, Fuson, & Lesh, 1976)

Exercise Set 3–2

1. How can these heuristics be used on the problem: "identify the knowns and unknowns," "weed out irrelevant information," "consider a similar or simpler problem" (for example, with smaller numbers), or "introduce a useful representation" (draw a picture or use concrete materials)? Identify some other strategies that you think might be useful.
2. What "key difficulty" needs to be resolved in this problem? Paraphrase the problem in your own words, emphasizing the "key difficulty" in a way that might help someone else who was trying to solve it.

The "key difficulty" in the hotel problem is to explain why the trick that seemed to happen (that is, $27 plus $2 equals $30) did not really happen. The hotel problem, like many everyday problems, requires that a situation be explained rather than that an answer be found to a specific question. So, heuristics that are especially helpful for explanation problems tend to focus on various ways to understand the problem. Once the situation is clearly understood, the explanation is obvious. For example, consider the following re-description of the problem.

Each customer originally paid $10, making a total of $30. Then, each received $1 from the bellboy, which makes a total price of $27. Of the $27, $25 was for the room and $2 was for the bellboy. So, the statement, "The $27 paid for the room plus $2 that the bellboy kept," is misleading. The $27 actually includes the amount kept by the bellboy.

The first two problems were of the "puzzle" variety. Such problems are interesting and motivating to many students, but they are not really the kind that are likely to occur in everyday situations. Also, the problems require few substantive mathematical understandings. So, perhaps different kinds of heuristics are needed for realistic problems solving sophisticated content understandings.

Content-Dependent Heuristics

The word problem below is similar to a situation that might really occur in everyday life.

PROBLEM-SOLVING ACTIVITY 3–3

Al has an afterschool job. He earns $6 per hour if he works 15 hours per week. If he works more than 15 hours, he gets paid time and a half for overtime. How may hours must Al work to earn $135 during one week?

Exercise Set 3–3

1. Unlike children, the reader may have solved this problem using algebra as well as arithmetic. If so, watch a youngster solve this problem using only a series of arithmetic computations. How did the child decide which operation to use at each step? Note the noncomputational phases of the solution attempt. Note the ways in which the child broke the problem into a collection of simpler parts.

2. When algebra is used to solve the problem, the first step is to translate the given situation into an algebraic description:

$$(6 \times 15) + 9(x - 15) = 135$$

Then the algebraic sentence can be translated to an arithmetic expression:

$$x = \frac{135 - (6 \times 15)}{9} + 15 = 20$$

Finally, the individual computations can be made and the answer can be translated back into the original problem to see if it makes sense.

The possibility of first describing and then calculating is one of the key features that makes algebra different from arithmetic.

In what ways does the first algebraic expression require understandings similar to those needed to "paraphrase the problem in your own words," "act out the situation using concrete materials," or "draw a picture or diagram to describe the situation?"

If only arithmetic procedures are used in the solution to Al's problem, the situation has to be paraphrased; and heuristics that ask you to "describe the problem in your own words" usually depend on specific content understandings. The strategies used are not simply general heuristics that can be carried out regardless of mathematical ideas that are known.

The next problem again illustrates the content-related nature of useful heuristics, like "draw a diagram" and "break up the problem into several simpler problems."

PROBLEM-SOLVING ACTIVITY 3–4

A goat is tied to the corner of a 20 foot by 40 foot barn with a 50-foot rope. If it can graze everywhere outside of the barn that its rope allows it to reach, what is the size of its grazing area? (LeBlanc, Kerr, Hudson, & Thompson, 1975)

Exercise Set 3–4

1. In what ways did the heuristics you used depend on specific mathematical knowledge?
2. Watch a youngster trying to solve the problem; if you give any heuristic hints, note whether the student's ability to use your hint depended on some specific mathematical understandings.

Figure 3–3 might be helpful in solving this problem. The grazing area is divided into several smaller parts so the solution can be found by calculating the areas of each of the parts.

Figure 3–3 illustrates the use of two heuristics: "break up the problem into simpler problems" and "draw pictures." But the type of drawings and subdivi-

FIGURE 3–3

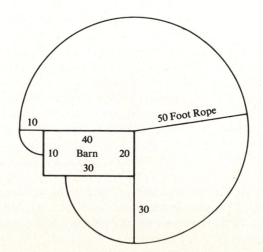

sions that are useful for both of these general strategies depend on specific ideas about areas of basic geometric figures. Unfortunately, Fig. 3−3 would be of little help if you weren't reasonably proficient at finding the areas of circles and other basic geometric shapes. In fact, without such understandings, it is unlikely that it would have occurred to you to draw a diagram like Fig. 3−3.

THE RELATIONSHIP BETWEEN GENERAL AND CONTENT-DEPENDENT HEURISTICS

The four problems considered so far vary greatly in the amount of prerequisite mathematical knowledge needed in their solutions. In fact, the first two problems were chosen partly because they allowed us to illustrate heuristics without having to be concerned about differences in content understanding among readers. For similar reasons, such problems often have been popular as vehicles for teaching heuristics in problem-solving instruction. However, as later examples in this chapter will show, heuristics that are useful for problems with little mathematical content may need to be modified and refined significantly to be useful for problems in which nontrivial mathematical ideas are needed.

The relationship between general heuristics and specific content understandings has been a longstanding issue that cuts across nearly all forms of learning research. The fundamental dilemma is: if a learned idea (or heuristic) is too specific, then it cannot be expected to transfer easily to other situations; yet if it is presented in too general a form, then it tends to be unclear what "mastering it" really means. For example, the heuristic "draw a picture" can be helpful in a wide range of problem-solving situations, but no one ever really masters this skill in a general sense (that is, in a way that is not restricted by context or content).

The ability to recognize and generate relevant pictures and diagrams is linked to fundamental content understandings throughout virtually every topic in this book: counting numbers, rational numbers, proportional reasoning, algebraic equations, geometry, and so forth. In these other chapters, you will see that the kinds of pictures that are insightful, and not misleading, are closely tied to specific content understanding. So, drawing conceptually illuminating pictures tends to be a very content-related ability. On the other hand, common experience tells us that if we suggest that students draw a picture, they often discover keys to the solutions of problems that they otherwise would have had difficulty solving. So, the general heuristic seems to have power, even though mastering the skill is very content- and context-dependent.

The central issue being raised here is, "What do we mean when we identify a given heuristic as a goal for instruction?" Other chapters in this book discuss what it means to understand *ideas* like fractions, *rules* like the Pythagorean theorem, and *procedures* like long division. Teachers also should have reasonably clear notions about what it means to understand *heuristics* like "look for a similar problem," "work backwards," or "draw a picture."

As we discuss some research-based conclusions about heuristic understandings, the distinction between general heuristics and content-specific heuristics will be important to keep in mind. Another important distinction is the one between problems that require only general knowledge and those that require students to use nontrivial mathematical ideas.

RESEARCH RELATED TO PROBLEM-SOLVING HEURISTICS

Hatfield's (1978) review of early research on problem-solving heuristics noted that many of the most useful general heuristics (for example, trial and error, successive approximations, working backward, and pattern searching) seemed to be simply qualities of common sense. That is, knowing *how* to do them seemed less important than knowing *when* to use them. But what kind of knowledge is needed to make judgments about when to use a given general heuristic? Before addressing this question, several related issues also should be considered.

Hatfield's review classified research on heuristics into two categories: research aimed at teaching selected heuristics and research aimed at identifying the heuristics used by successful problem solvers. Therefore, this section will begin with a brief summary of major conclusions in each of these two categories.

RESEARCH ON TEACHING HEURISTICS

One major conclusion from the teaching studies has been that it is possible to teach students to use general heuristics within a restricted category of problems. However, this learning seldom transfers well to other categories of problems. As Begle's (1979) literature review stated, ". . . simplistic efforts to improve students' problem solving abilities will not be enough (p. 144). . . . hopes of finding one (or a few) strategies which should be taught to all (or most) students are far too simplistic" (p. 145).

While many studies have successfully taught students to use specific heuristics in restricted content/context domains, it seems likely that increases in problem-solving performance resulted primarily from increased understandings about relevant underlying concepts, which in turn resulted from activities like drawing pictures or searching for patterns. So the improved performance in problem solving was likely due more to increased mathematical knowledge than to general heuristic understanding.

Not only are general heuristics difficult to teach in a meaningful and generalizable way, there is also growing skepticism that critical differences between successful and less successful problem solvers really have to do with students learning a manageably short list of heuristics (Lester, 1978; Schoenfield, 1986). Research into the processes that experts use in problem solving has revealed some of the complexities involved.

RESEARCH ON HEURISTICS USED BY PROBLEM-SOLVING EXPERTS

A substantial amount of research has been done to compare the behaviors of "successful" versus "less successful" problem solvers. Results indicate that, for problem-solving situations in which only general knowledge is needed, successful problem solvers do indeed appear to use general heuristics more often than less successful problem solvers. However, for problems in which a substantial amount of knowledge and experience is needed, a growing body of research suggests that critical differences between successful and less successful problem solvers are not attributable to the use of some small number of general heuristics. We will use three examples to illustrate the point.

Experts in chess, physics, and other domains require substantial amounts of knowledge and experience. Simon's (1981) artificial intelligence based research suggests that successful problem solvers tend to use powerful content-related processes rather than general heuristics. These content-related processes are based on complex systems of knowledge and experience (Larkin, McDermott, Simon, & Simon, 1980).

Krutetskii's (1976) research with gifted mathematics students in the Soviet Union suggests that gifted mathematical problem solvers use qualitatively different systems of thought than average students. They do not simply learn a few additional ideas and heuristics. Furthermore, the most important heuristics that gifted students use appear to be largely inaccessible to students with less elaborate conceptual networks.

Bloom's (1985) research documenting the life-long development of virtuosos in the arts, sports, or academic fields, suggests that Krutetskii's "qualitatively different systems of knowledge" and Simon's "powerful, content-related processes" are based on the gradual acquisition of complex networks of ideas and processes. These knowledge networks typically take years to acquire. They are not simply the result of a combination of innate talent plus a few general heuristics, skills, or pieces of information.

Similar conclusions have emerged from research in other knowledge-intensive problem-solving domains, such as medical decision making (Elstein, Shulman, & Sprafka, 1978) and teacher decision making (Shavelson, Caldwell, & Izu, 1978). For example, in medical problem solving, Elstein and co-workers concluded:

> With increasing frequency medical educators were told that their objective was to produce problem solvers, inquirers, individuals skilled in gathering and interpreting information for the purpose of rendering judgements, making decisions, and taking action. As dissatisfaction with the lockstep curriculum and with a sharp distinction between basic and clinical education grew, it was at times argued that mastery of specific content was less important than mastery of process, particularly since the content was likely to be obsolete in a relatively short time (say five to ten years). . . .
> The most startling and controversial aspects of our results have been the findings of case specificity and the lack of intraindividual consistency over problems, with the accompanying implication that knowledge of content is more critical than mastery of

generic problem solving processes. . . . In our opinion there are general mental processes common to all medical problem solving. . . . However, the effectiveness with which this process is mobilized in any particular case depends on knowledge in a particular domain (Elstein et al., 1978, p. 292).

Two themes stand out in problem-solving studies in knowledge-intensive domains. First, the most significant processes, heuristics, and strategies tend to be very content-dependent. Second, beyond the amount of information one knows, the organization of that knowledge is critical.

RESEARCH ON KNOWLEDGE ORGANIZATION AND HEURISTICS

Krutetskii (1976) has argued that the qualitatively different systems of thought used by experts or gifted problem solvers enable them to use capabilities that are inaccessible to those who do not have highly organized knowledge. Inaccessible abilities identified by Krutetskii included generalizing broadly and rapidly, often from a single instance; curtailing normal chains of reasoning by skipping intermediate steps and moving rapidly from problems to solutions; perceiving and remembering the underlying mathematical structure of problem situations. Novice problem solvers, on the other hand, tend to notice and remember relatively superficial problem characteristics.

Krutetskii's "inaccessible capabilities" cannot easily be "lifted" in isolation and used as instructional goals for average ability students who have relatively unstable and unorganized systems of knowledge. For example, "step skipping" and "premature generalizations" are common sources of errors for average ability students. "Structure identification," which is elusive to the novice problem solver, is a critical prerequisite for heuristics like "look for a similar problem." So, the meanings that experts have for various heuristics may be qualitatively different from those that novices acquire.

The qualitatively distinct systems of thought used by expert or gifted problem solvers are unlikely to be learned through the teaching of a few isolated skills, abilities, heuristics, or strategies. Heuristic understandings that depend on higher order networks of knowledge may be just as inaccessible to novice problem solvers as Piaget's formal operational reasoning strategies are to most seven-year-old children. This is not to say that such heuristic understandings cannot be achieved, but they may require students to develop whole new modes of thinking, analogous to the qualitative reorganization of knowledge that distinguishes Piaget's concrete operational level of reasoning from formal operational levels.

Fortunately, teachers do not have to choose between teaching "content independent processes" and "process independent content." Instead, examples throughout this book illustrate why some of the most important problem-solving processes contribute significantly to the underlying meaning of basic mathematical ideas, and why these ideas in turn serve as "cues" for processes that will be useful in particular situations.

Students do not become better problem solvers by first learning some basic mathematical ideas, then learning some general problem-solving processes and strategies, and finally, learning to apply these ideas and processes in problem situations. Rather than applications and problem solving coming after basic content ideas are learned, they should play important roles on the way to learning these ideas. Later sections of this chapter will give examples of how problem solving can help students go beyond the learning of isolated ideas to develop stable and well-organized systems of knowledge.

Disorganized clusters of ideas are not knowledge any more than disorganized piles of books are libraries, and organization cannot be imposed on students from external sources; it must be constructed by students themselves. So, problem-solving experiences can contribute to knowledge development as much as knowledge development contributes to problem-solving ability. In fact, the most important reason for integrating problem solving into instruction may be the contribution such experiences make to students' understandings of basic mathematical ideas, as well as to increasing general problem-solving ability.

THINKING ABOUT THINKING IN PROBLEM SOLVING

The research of Krutetskii (1976), Simon (1981), and Bloom (1985) had to do with experts, gifted students, and virtuosos. But what about garden variety problem solvers? If two average students of comparable ability have acquired equivalent systems of knowledge, can heuristics make a significant difference in their problem-solving capabilities?

Hatfield (1978), Lester and Garofalo (1982), and Schoenfeld (1986) are among those who would, in general, answer "yes" to the preceding question. However, the kind of heuristic instruction that these researchers have found effective is different, in a subtle way, from most of the earlier studies reviewed by Hatfield (1978). The difference has to do with the distinction between a heuristic being a "means to an end" versus an "end in itself." To understand the importance of this distinction, solve the following set of problems, which were used in Lesh's (1985) research investigating ways in which students solve new problems by using or modifying knowledge and information from earlier problems.

PROBLEM-SOLVING ACTIVITY 3–5

1. John is constructing a recreation room in his basement. He has put up the walls and put down a floor. He needs to buy baseboard to put along the walls. The room is 21 feet by 28 feet. The baseboards come in 10-foot and 16-foot lengths. How many of each kind should he buy?

2. If John wants to have as few seams as possible, how many of each size baseboards should he buy?

3. If John wants to have as little waste as possible, how many of each size should he buy?
4. If the 16-foot boards cost $1.25 per foot and the 10-foot baseboards cost $1.10 per foot, how many of each kind should he buy if he wants to spend the least amount of money?
5. There is a sale on the 16-foot baseboards. They now cost $.85 per foot while the 10-foot baseboards still cost $1.10 per foot. How many of each should he buy if he wants to spend the least amount of money?

Exercise Set 3—5

1. Read the accounts that follow about how two upper-grade students began solution attempts to the carpentry problems. Notice the students' uses of the heuristics, "draw a picture" and "look for a similar problem." Describe what you think about the distinction between a heuristic as an "end in itself" versus a "means to an end."

One student began working on the first carpentry problem by drawing a picture like the one in Fig. 3—4. This picture led him to notice that the problem was similar to some problems about finding areas that he had been doing in his science course. Unfortunately, rather than using information about similar area problem to better understand the given perimeter problem, the student (unconsciously) *replaced* the given perimeter problem with the similar area problem. He spent the next ten minutes on a wild goose chase, trying to find some combinations of 10 and 16 to equal the product of 21 and 28 (that is, 588).

Another student began working on the first carpentry problem by drawing a picture like the one in Fig. 3—5. After drawing the picture, however, he looked at it and said, "No, it's more like this" (Fig. 3—6). Then, he corrected himself again saying, "No, that's only half of it; it's really more like this" (Fig. 3—7), and proceeded to solve the problem correctly by marking off 10- and 16-foot lengths on each of the four sides of the room.

FIGURE 3—4

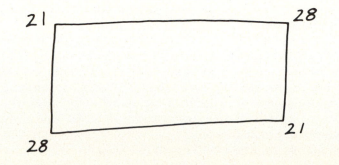

FIGURE 3–5

FIGURE 3–6

FIGURE 3–7

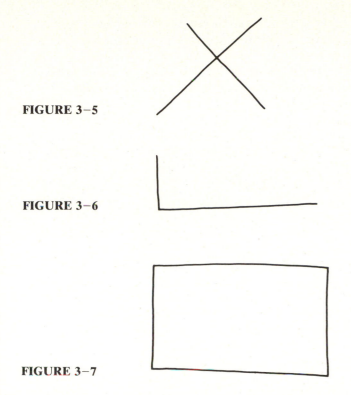

In the preceding examples, both students began by (implicitly) using the heuristic "draw a picture" and "look for a similar problem." The first student's similar problem was borrowed from his science course; the second student partitioned the situation into four simpler problems (one for each side of the room). Yet, the outcomes were very different. The second student was successful, even though his picture did not appear to be a good one; whereas the first student's picture led to a wild goose chase even though it appeared to be a good drawing. An apparently "good" picture led to a bad result, and an apparently "bad" picture led to a good result.

A picture is neither "good" nor "bad" in and of itself. Instead, its value depends on the *function* it serves. Similarly, other heuristics like "look for a similar problem" are neither good nor bad as ends in themselves. They are "means to an end," and their worth depends on whether they really contribute to beneficial ends.

Most teachers believe that students will think better if they think intelligently; and thinking intelligently means *thinking about thinking*. For example, the first student above was unsuccessful partly because he was so caught up in thinking (that is, working busily to get from his perception of the givens to goals) that he did not pause to ask himself:

1. What (exactly) am I doing? (Can I describe it in such a way that a friend, in another room, could do the step for me?)

2. Why am I doing it? (How does this step fit into my solution plan?)
3. How will it help? (What will I do with the outcome if I get it?)

Schoenfeld (1986) has used the preceding three questions to help his students better become problem solvers in algebra and geometry courses. He sorted solution-step decisions into two categories: implementation decisions and managerial decisions. *Implementation decisions* have to do with *"How* will I do the next step?" *Managerial decisions* have to do with *"Why* and *when* should I do the next step?" and "How will the result be helpful?" Managerial decisions involve planning, monitoring, and assessing the solution process as a whole.

Problem solving is like many domains in that becoming educated means acquiring the ability to "look beyond the end of your nose." Students often do poorly if they become too preoccupied with "What do I do next?" to get from givens to goals, and consequently fail to notice that their early perceptions of the problem and its components often are distorted and simplistic.

To help students think about their thinking, Garofalo and Lester (1985) sorted managerial behaviors into four functional groups: (1) orientation behaviors, which help assess the nature of the givens and goals); (2) organizational behaviors, which help plan and choose general paths for getting from givens to goals; (3) execution behaviors, which regulate behaviors to conform to plans; and (4) verification behaviors, which evaluate decisions made and outcomes of executed plans.

Heuristics, according to the preceding point of view, are "means to ends" rather than "ends in themselves." The goal of heuristic instruction is not to "learn" some short list of general strategies; instead it is to learn to think thoughtfully (think about thinking) during solution attempts.

TEACHING ABOUT PROBLEM SOLVING

Problem Solving and Mathematical Knowledge

Earlier parts of this chapter have emphasized ways that mathematical knowledge influences problem-solving abilities. This section focuses on ways that problem-solving activities can contribute to knowledge acquisition. To begin, spend 20 to 30 minutes working on the camp replacement problem below. As you work on the problem, try talking aloud into a tape recorder. Then, after arriving at an answer that you believe is "good enough" (many levels of correctness are possible), think back over the solution process that you went through, and make notes for future reference.

PROBLEM-SOLVING ACTIVITY 3–6

Imagine that you are a counselor at a sports camp specializing in track and field. In preliminary events held the first day of camp, the 12-year-old boys performed as follows:

Name	50-yd Run (sec.)	100-yd Run (sec.)	High Jump	Long Jump	Swim Level
Andy	7.9	14.6	4'2"	10'9"	Bass
Brian	9.4	16.5	3'4"	10'0"	Sunfish
Charles	7.0	13.5	4'4"	11'6"	Shark
Doug	7.8	14.4	4'7"	12'0"	Bass
Eric	6.8	12.6	4'8"	12'2"	Shark
Fred	8.0	14.5	4'1"	10'9"	Trout
Greg	8.1	15.0	4'3"	10'6"	Trout
Herb	7.2	13.8	4'3"	9'6"	Shark
John	7.7	14.0	4'4"	10'11"	Trout
Kevin	7.4	14.0	3'8"	11'2"	Bass
Larry	7.7	14.2	4'6"	11'0"	Bass
Mike	8.0	15.0	4'0"	10'2"	Trout

(Swim levels, from highest to lowest, are Shark, Bass, Trout, Sunfish)

Based on the preceding information, and the following comments from their school coaches, you are to assign these twelve campers to three groups.

Coaches' comments:

ANDY: Tremendous effort has helped Andy make some good gains this season, but his performance is not consistent.

BRIAN: Poor attendance at practice, an unwillingness to follow team rules, and goofing around during practice have surely contributed to Brian's deplorable performance.

CHARLES: Charles has consistently worked hard.

DOUG: Doug has good endurance in most running events but tends to be sloppy about his performance in some throwing events.

ERIC: Eric is a dedicated and motivated team member.

FRED: Fred's fair ability in most events does not offset a poor attitude toward practice.

GREG: Greg's immature behavior has interfered with his progress this year and has occasionally disrupted the whole group. He seems to do the least work required to stay on our track team.

HERB: Herb has shown tremendous improvement this year, but his previous training had been rather weak so he still has a lot to learn.

JOHN: John has a lot of natural athletic ability but hasn't worked up to his potential because of missed practices and failure to pay attention to advice from the coaches.

KEVIN: Keven is a natural athlete who hasn't worked up to his potential. I think he needs more of a challenge—more competition—to make him work harder.

LARRY: Larry is a rather shy boy who doesn't care to be in the spotlight. He just doesn't seem comfortable with heavy competition.

MIKE: Although Mike's ability in jumping events is not outstanding, he has made good progress this year in sprinting.

Exercise Set 3-6

1. Make a list of some ways that you think the camp placement problem is different from the other problems given so far in this chapter.
2. Identify any heuristics that you used and describe the functions that they played—positive, neutral, or negative.
3. Identify the ways in which you refined or reorganized your number, arithmetic, and measurement ideas during your solution process.

The camp placement problem illustrates a number of problem characteristics that are typical of realistic situations. Many of the problem characteristics actually encourage students to extend or refine their mathematical knowledge as well as their understandings about the nature of mathematics and mathematical problem solving in ways described below.

Refining or Extending Known Concepts

Adequate solutions to this problem involve only straightforward uses of easy-to-identify arithmetic, number, or measurement ideas. No "tricks" are needed. Unlike situations in which students can't think of any ideas that might be helpful, they usually are aware of a number of relevant ideas that could apply to this problem. However, these ideas need to be refined or put together in new ways to fit the situation. So, the most useful problem-solving heuristics are those that help students combine or refine ideas that they already know, not those designed to help them find relevant ideas when none seem relevant.

Organizing Related but Distinct Mathematical Topics

Relevant ideas and procedures do not fall into a single topic area, the way they are organized in textbooks. For example, the information given in the camp placement problem involves several distinct measurement systems such as length and time. Further, some of the information is qualitative (for example, coaches, comments, swimming levels) and may need to be quantified. Solutions to this problem usually involve several arithmetic operations, as well as several distinct number systems (for example, rational numbers, negative numbers, decimals), especially if electronic calculators are used.

Such problems force students to think about familiar idea in unfamiliar contexts, and they require students to go beyond the learning of isolated facts to (re)organize their knowledge into integrated systems. Students need to notice similarities and differences among related ideas that may never before have been considered in the same context.

A New Perspective on "Right Answers"

Real problems tend to have no single "right answer." For example, in the camp placement problem, no criteria are given about what makes a "good" group at the sports camp. Nowhere is it stipulated whether the groups are supposed to be equal in size, equal according to the abilities of their members, or the same throughout the entire camp day. Only implicit clues are given about the purpose of the group formations (for example, the camp is a track and field camp).

In a real sports camp, one criterion that an experienced counselor uses to make assignments is that it can be justified to angry parents who complain, "Why is my Freddy in the 'slow' group?" Answer *justification* is as important as answer *giving*. The quality of solutions depends on the amount of information on which answers are based, the assumptions that are made, the awareness or consideration of possible sources of error, and so forth—all of which emphasize non-answer-giving (or beyond-answer quiz) phases of problem solving.

Underlying Problem Conceptualizations

In real-world problem solving, mathematical answer giving is usually a tool rather than an end in itself. So, good solutions tend to focus on non-answer-giving stages of problem solving (for example, question refinement and trial solution evaluation). Finding a useful way to think about the problem tends to be far more important than simply finding a way to arrive at an answer quickly. In fact, research has shown that, in problems like the camp placement problem, students who produce the best solutions rarely spent more than one-fourth of their time in "getting from givens to goals" behaviors (Lesh, 1985). Once the problem situations were thought about in useful ways, solutions tended to be produced rather quickly. On the other hand, students who spent large portions of their time on answer-giving activities (without thinking about the nature of givens and goals) usually produced inferior solutions. These weaker solutions generally took into account less information, recognized fewer or less complex relationships or trends in the data, and failed to compensate for sources of uncertainty.

Selecting, Organizing, and "Filling In" Information

Unlike most textbook word problems which have either too much or not enough information, problems like camp placement often have both too much and not enough information. Yet, a solution that can be defended must be given anyway. Therefore, solutions require that the most important information be selected, the least useful information be filtered out, and missing information be "filled in" or compensated for in some way. The relative importance of information is based on interpretations that students impose on the problem-solving situation. The process is more complex than simply sorting out relevant and irrelevant information.

Interpreting "Given" Information

Information in realistic everyday problems often is not given in a form that is useful; some data preparation or interpretation may be needed. For example, in the camp placement problem, most successful solutions somehow assign weights (implicitly perhaps) to the running scores, jumping scores, coaches' comments, swim levels, and so forth.

Lesh's research (1985) has shown what happens when these data interpretation phases of problem solving are ignored. Students solving the camp placement problem often simply added (or averaged) the four running and jumping scores for a given camper (for example, for Andy, 7.9 seconds + 14.6 seconds + 4 feet 2 inches + 10 feet 9 inches). They often noticed and then ignored the unit labels and other relevant facts, such as: low numbers are good for running scores, whereas high numbers are good for jumping scores; distances and times cannot be added together sensibly. Discussions following the problem-solving sessions nearly always showed that students recognized that 4'11" (for example) represented 4 feet and 11 inches. Nonetheless, during solution attempts, 4'11" often was read as "4 (pause) 11", or as "4 point 11"—and was then written on paper or keystroked into a calculator as 4.11, or as two separate numbers, 4 and 11.

Students who are quite skillful at the arithmetic of numbers still often encounter difficulties when unit labels also are important. In addition to doing things like adding times and distances, as mentioned above, students often have difficulty reading and writing quantities like 4'11", especially when calculators are used. Such quantities often are entered incorrectly, and students typically are not proficient at enter−check−process−check procedures that are needed to accurately use a calculator. In these and other simple situations, students tend to have difficulty when they must both do and also monitor, record, and check what they are doing. Few have had experience in problem-solving situations in which it is important to record or even remember elements of solutions.

Beliefs about the Nature of Mathematical Problem Solving

Because problems like camp placement often have several alternative solution routes, student perceptions about the legitimacy of alternatives are important. Otherwise capable students are often restricted by a belief that doing math should always involve one right way and one right answer. They usually search for a rule that must be remembered and executed, rather than trying to combine several basic principles in some new way. For example, students who did not do well on the camp placement problem often had difficulties because they rejected any solution that did not fit the single idea of summing or averaging the given information to the problem. Better answers usually resulted from a gradual refinement process in which an initial trial answer was based on only a subset of the given information (for example, the campers were ranked using only the scores from the running events). The first trial answer was then modified using some additional information (for example, the initial ranking was modified using the jumping scores). The modified answer was again fine tuned using still more information (for example, the ranking was again modified using the coaches' comments as additional information).

What was remarkable about the preceding "multiple (re)conceptualization cycle" approach was that the students definitely had not learned it in school. In fact, their school experiences generally had led them to believe that such approaches were not acceptable solution strategies.

Because of extensive experiences with restricted types of problems (for example, one-rule, one-step word problems), many students conclude that mathematics problems should always be answered in less than 30 seconds; a solution procedure should involve only a single idea, equation, or computation (which you must know, not construct); and the best procedure is one based on the most abstract and general concept known that seems to be related to the problem. These beliefs pose major obstacles for many students when they face more realistic multiple-concept, multiple-step problems like the camp placement problem.

Because these counterproductive beliefs are learned, they often have particularly negative influences on the real-world problem-solving capabilities of students who learn quickly and who are especially concerned about winning the approval of misguided role models. Such students frequently have histories of performing well in mathematics courses and on standardized tests (where knowing the answer and giving quick responses are rewarded); yet, they may be relatively unsuccessful on more complex and "realistic" problems. Perhaps many talented students are being inhibited in their problem-solving capabilities, not because they have failed to learn, but because they have learned a number of (incorrect) generalizations that their teachers (implicitly) model and instill. Research has shown, for example, that the average amount of time that students are given to respond to questions in class is about one second (Budd-Rowe, 1978).

Students' problem-solving experiences should include some problems in which an adequate solution should take at least 30 minutes. They should

encounter problems in which solutions involve a number of qualitatively different ideas and several distinct solution steps. Whether students use a "modify a
single all-inclusive idea" approach or a "piece together several simpler ideas
and procedures" approach, both methods involve gradually refining problem
conceptualizations.

The tailoring (or modeling) that is required to make a basic problem
conceptualization fit a real situation is one of the most useful kinds of general
techniques for using mathematics and solving problems in everyday situations.
Unfortunately, many students' school experiences have convinced them that
this sort of "tinkering" is equivalent to not knowing the answer, and it is wrong
to do in mathematics.

Providing Problem-Solving Experiences

Situational Problems

Rather than generating an entire problem set based on a single concept or skill,
a teacher can start with a realistic situation and then discuss a number of
different kinds of problems that arise naturally, using any ideas that are
relevant. If the goal is for students to recognize many situations in which a
single idea is useful, then the former technique is useful; but the latter may be
more useful for helping students become better able to use mathematics to
solve everyday problems. In real problem-solving situations, you seldom start
with an idea and then look for situations to which it applies; instead, you start
with a situation and look for relevant ideas.

The problem, considered earlier, about the grazing area for a goat, can be
used to illustrate the nature of situational problems. The goat problem also
illustrates another important point, that is, it often is difficult to predict which
problems students will find realistic and motivating. To some extent, reality is
in the eye of the beholder.

The first time one of the authors used the goat problem in a class, it was
chosen with the hope that it would seem relevant to students in a farming
community where a demonstration class on problem solving was being taught.
Ironically, because the students really were familiar with goats (and the author
wasn't), the problem turned out to be not as realistic as hoped. Yet, precisely
because the students didn't think it was very realistic, the problem turned out to
be both fun and interesting.

One group of students pointed out that a goat tied by the neck would eat the
rope immediately, so the correct answer would be that the goat would eat
wherever it pleased. In reality goats are tied by a hind leg so that the chances
are less that the rope will be eaten (goats are not good problem solvers). But, if
a goat is tied by a hind leg, this will extend the perimeter of the grazing area by
at least 3 feet on all sides, and significantly change the correct answer to the
question.

Another group sarcastically pointed out that the real answer should be that the goat would graze anywhere he wanted because no matter how a rope is tied, the goat would eat through it. Their conclusion was to use a chain to tie the goat, and this in turn led to a discussion about relative costs of keeping farm animals and pets.

If the preceding kinds of realistic discussions are used wisely and sparingly, they can serve very important instructional functions. Answers given in books may be less realistic, less interesting, and even less mathematically sophisticated, than those students may suggest. So occasionally, encouraging students to pursue their own interpretations of problems may have more instructional value than limiting answers to narrow views of correctness. Problem posing can be just as important a skill in problem solving as answer giving. Some good examples of problem-posing activities can be found in Brown and Walter (1982).

Focusing on Individual Stages in the Problem-Solving Process

The rule of thumb that "the best way to learn to solve problems is to solve lots of problems" can be overused. Usually, there is a trade-off between the number of problem situations students will be able to consider, and the depth with which they will be able to examine any one of the problems. So, for some instructional goals, it is better to focus on many problems requiring a small number of solution steps rather than a few problems with complete solutions. For example, if the instructional goal is to point out the usefulness of school mathematics in everyday situations, then it may be unnecessary for students to carry out all steps of solving all of the problems given.

Solutions to word problems often involve the following three steps: (1) describe the situation using relevant mathematical ideas; (2) carry out the computation, simplify the description, or solve the equation; and (3) evaluate the answer.

To save time, as well as to focus attention on especially critical solution steps, students can be assigned to go through an entire problem set, doing only one or two of these steps. That is, rather than solving the problems, students can simply write equations to describe each problem situation; then, the relevant calculations can be carried out for them (by another student using a calculator), and they can check to see whether the answers they are given make sense.

Representational Systems and Word Problems

There are five representation systems that are particularly critical to solving textbook word problems, and to using mathematics in everyday situations. Also, to diagnose students' difficulties in solving a particular class of problems, teachers can generate a variety of useful questions by presenting a problem situation in one mode and asking students to translate (illustrate, describe, or

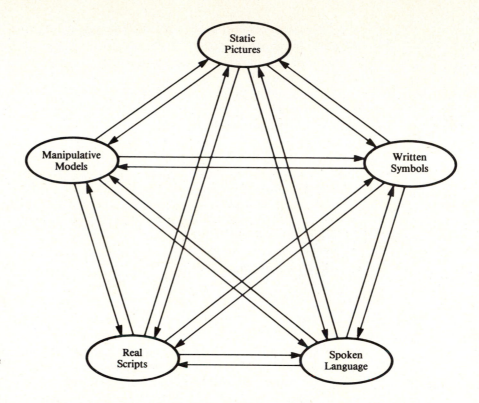

FIGURE 3–8
A Scheme for Mode
Translations

represent) to another representational system. Students are often surprisingly inept at such seemingly simple tasks. Yet, these translation processes are important components of what it means to *understand* a given mathematical idea.

The five types of representational systems are included in Fig. 3–8. Scripts are based on experience and knowledge organized around real-world events. These events serve as general prototypes for interpreting and solving a variety of different kinds of problem situations.

Manipulative models refer to concrete materials such as Cuisenaire rods, fraction bars, arithmetic blocks, or balance scales. These materials can be used to act out different kinds of problem situations. The built-in relationships in the models focus attention on the underlying structure of problem situations.

Static figural models refer to pictures, diagrams, or graphs. These representations can be used to clarify and illustrate important relationships in many different kinds of real situations.

Spoken language occurs in specialized sublanguages related to domains like logic or geometry. Often everyday words like "and" and "or" may take on meanings that differ slightly from their usual meanings.

Written symbols, like spoken language, involve specialized sentences and phrases ($X + 3 = 7$, $A'UB' = (AUB)'$) as well as normal English sentences and phrases.

The use of various representational systems can be illustrated by completing Problem-Solving Activity 3–7.

PROBLEM-SOLVING ACTIVITY 3–7

1. Which picture in Fig. 3–9 is 1/3 shaded?
2. The ratio of boys to girls in a class is 3 to 8. How many girls are in the class if there are 9 boys?
      a. 17   b. 14   c. 24   d. not given   e. I don't know.
3. Without using a pencil and paper or a calculator, how much is 725 plus 356?
4. Again, without using a pencil and paper or calculator, how much is $17.25 plus 23.56?
5. Answer this question using any method you like: 2725
                                                    +1356

FIGURE 3–9
What picture is 1/3 shaded?

Item 31. What picture shows 1/3 shaded?

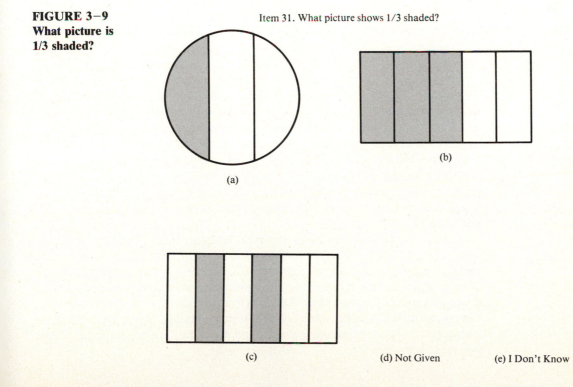

(a)

(b)

(c)

(d) Not Given   (e) I Don't Know

Exercise Set 3—7

1. Compare problems 1 and 2 above. Which do you think would be more difficult? At what grade level would you guess each is mastered by at least 75% of the students?
2. What representational systems would a student be likely to use in the solution of each of these problems?
3. List the processes that you used to solve Problems 3, 4, and 5. Were they the same in each case?

Problems 1 and 2 were taken from a written test about rational number relations and proportions, which was given to several thousand students throughout the United States (Lesh, Post, & Behr, 1985). Problem 1 required a translation from written symbols (that is, 1/3) to pictures. The success rates were only 4% for fourth graders, 8% for fifth graders, 19% for sixth graders, 21% for seventh graders, and 24% for eighth graders. Only one in four eighth graders answered the question correctly! Forty-three percent selected answer choice a; 4% selected b; 15% selected c; 34% selected d; 3% selected e; and 2% did not give a response.

Problem 2 was adapted from a recent National Assessment examination (Carpenter et al., 1981). The students' primary task was to translate the problem (which is given using normal English sentences) into an algebraic equation, and then to perform the necessary computation. The success rates for Problem 2 were 11% for fourth graders, 13% for fifth graders, 30% for sixth graders, 29% for seventh graders, and 51% for eighth graders.

Unfortunately, as the relative performance levels on Problems 1 and 2 illustrate, many students not only have seriously deficient understandings of word problems and pencil-and-paper computations, but many have equally deficient understandings of the models, diagrams, and languages needed to describe, illustrate, and manipulate these ideas. Such poor performance by American students on problems similar to these led to a report called *A Nation at Risk* (National Commission on Excellence in Education, 1983), and other reports from a number of federal agencies and professional organizations, which called for new efforts to increase the quality of school mathematics instruction.

Other chapters in this book describe techniques for building students' understandings of basic mathematical ideas by associating these ideas with a variety of different kinds of representation systems. For example, in the domain of proportional reasoning and rational number concepts, part of what it means to understand an idea like 1/3 is to recognize the idea embedded in a variety of different representational systems, flexibly manipulate the idea within given representational systems, and accurately translate the idea from one system to another.

Schemata for Thinking about Mathematical Ideas and Problems

Students do not always organize their knowledge around abstract ideas; knowledge is also organized around real-world experiences and events, with the result that separate mathematical understandings may be formed for distinct situations. For example, Lawler (1981, p. 4) reported three analogous questions from an interview with his 6-year-old daughter, Miriam:

1. "How much is seventy-five plus twenty-six?" Miriam answered, "Seventy, ninety, ninety-six, ninety-seven, ninety-eight, ninety-nine, one hundred, one-oh-one" (counting up the last five numbers on her fingers).
2. Later: "How much is seventy-five cents and twenty-six cents?" Miriam said, "That's three quarters, four and a penny, a dollar one."
3. Later, he presented Miriam with the same problem in written vertical form. She added right to left with carries.

In these three different situations, Miriam used three different knowledge systems, or schemata, even though the underlying problem was the same. Miriam's first solution was based on a counting schema; she interpreted the problem as a counting numbers problem. The second solution used a money schema that provided her with information about the values of coins and their various equivalencies. Her third solution was derived from a paper sums schema in which she used the standard algorithm for addition.

The fact that a student's knowledge may be organized around "events" as much as around abstract ideas gives a second very important role for using word problems in instruction. Not only do mathematical ideas bring greater understanding to problem situations, but problem situations can bring increased meaning to abstract ideas. Recent research in educational anthropology illustrates the importance of this fact. Lave, Murtaugh, and de la Rocha (1984) compared the arithmetic capabilities of "expert grocery shoppers" on pencil-and-paper computations versus the use of arithmetic during shopping. Like Lawler, they found that, in different contexts, shoppers used different procedures for equivalent problems. In grocery store settings, prices, totals, and so forth were calculated almost flawlessly using mental arithmetic. The shoppers paid attention to units, and they used accurate methods for recognizing errors. However, on paper-and-pencil tests, and in interview situations resembling school settings, these experts' performance levels often dropped to around 60%; exclusively algorithmic processes were used.

Although the depth of the thinking underlying experts' "grocery store mathematics" often was considerably more sophisticated and effective than their "school mathematics," many apologized for the type of mathematics they used in the grocery store, thinking it was not *real* mathematics.

Because "everyday mathematics" sometimes is both more effective and more sophisticated than "school mathematics," word problems can be a vehicle to help students transfer everyday understandings to school understandings, as well as helping them transfer school understandings to everyday situations. Certainly one of the reasons we want students to learn mathematics is to make them better equipped to deal with real-world problems. However, it is equally true that real-world problem-solving experiences can help bring meaning to the mathematical ideas we hope to teach. The relationships between real experience and school mathematics should be reciprocal.

Expert problem solvers often transform problems from the forms in which they are given into interpretations that are easier or more familiar. For example, for Problems 3 to 5 in Activity 3–7, you could have applied a money schema to all of the problems. Or, you could have converted all of them to a paper-and-pencil format. It also is possible to use three completely different schemes to solve each of the problems, or to switch schemes midway during individual solutions.

Successful problem solvers apply a variety of different kinds of representation systems to given problems or ideas, and they flexibly switch from one to another in a way that best serves their purposes. For example, consider the following two "realistic" pizza problems.

Show a sixth grader one-fourth of a real pizza, and then ask, "If I eat this much pizza, and then eat one-third of another pizza, how much will I have eaten altogether?"

Show a sixth grader one-third of a real pizza, and then ask, "If I already ate one-fourth of a pizza, and now I plan to eat this much, how much will I have eaten already?"

Rather than giving two symbols (or two spoken words, or two concrete objects), which are to be added, both of these problems involve mixed representatons for the givens. They each involve a real object (the pizza) and a spoken word (representing a past or future event). Realistic versions of word problems often occur naturally in this sort of multimode form. So, one difficulty in solving them is to convert the items to a single representation system, so they can be combined (or operated on) in some sensible way. In fact, skillful problem solvers may flexibly switch from one representational system to another several times during the course of a single problem's solution. In the pizza problem, an experienced problem solver may begin by drawing pictures to represent the pizzas and then switch to spoken language to describe the dynamic aspects of the situation (that is, the combining process). Another alternative is to use spoken language as an intermediate form to help introduce appropriate written symbols, which are then added using a paper-and-pencil solution routine (without any reference to either pictures or spoken language).

Skillful problem solvers are sufficiently flexible in their use of a variety of relevant schemata and representational systems that they instinctively switch to the most convenient system at given points in solution processes.

PROBLEM-SOLVING ACTIVITY 3–8

Imagine that you are watching "The A Team" on television. In the first scene, you see a crook running out of a bank carrying a bag over his shoulder. You are told that he has stolen one million dollars in small bills. Could this really have happened?

Exercise Set 3–8

1. What pictures, diagrams, concrete objects, mental images, spoken language, written symbols, or schemes did you use to solve the problem?
2. Describe how multiple representations may be use simultaneously during the solution process. Describe how one may switch from one representation to another in order to solve the problem. What might prompt these changes?

One student solved the "million dollar" problem in the following way. She began by using sheets of typewriter paper to represent several dollar bills. She used a box of typewriter paper to find how many $1 bills such a box could hold, and she considered how large the box would need to be to hold one million $1 bills. While holding the box of paper, she was reminded to think about *weight* rather than *volume*. This allowed her to switch to a new representation, that is, stacks of books. She soon concluded that, if each bill was worth no more than $10, then the bag would be far too large and heavy for a single person to carry.

Conceptual flexibility was one of the main factors that distinguished the preceding student's rapid and elegant solution to the "million dollar" problem. Even though her solution was based on available concrete materials, and even though the symbolic systems she used involved little more than arithmetic, her solution was quite sophisticated.

Thinking about Thinking

This chapter has emphasized the close relationship between problem-solving ability and mathematical concept understanding. Multiple-step and multiple-idea problems like the camp placement problem and the million dollar problem illustrate yet another important aspect of this relationship. That is, in many everyday problem-solving situations, problem solving is really "local conceptual development." During the 20 to 40 minutes it takes to solve such problems, students' ideas often can actually be seen to evolve. For example, while trying to solve the camp placement problem, students frequently invented for themselves procedures needed to combine rankings or use weighted averages. Or, in the million dollar problem, students often dramatically extended their conceptions of large quantities.

To understand the nature of problem solving in local conceptual development sessions, it is important to notice that mathematical concepts do not go from "not understood" to "understood" in a single step. *Ideas develop!* Students first understand them only in a restricted range of situations. Then, meanings grow as the idea becomes usable in more different kinds of situations, as it is embedded in progressively more complex networks of ideas, as well as in progressively more powerful and economical symbol systems (for example, specialized technical languages, graphs and diagrams, or written symbols).

The local conceptual development view of problem solving has important and wide-ranging implications. First and foremost, it means that problem solving is not restricted to situations in which a solver is stuck in the sense of not being aware of any substantive ideas to apply to the situation. Often, for the kinds of everyday situations in which mathematics is useful, students are aware of a number of relevant ideas. Yet, these ideas still need to be modified, refined, or extended to deal with the given problem. Second, success in local conceptual development types of problem-solving sessions proves that even average ability students are capable of inventing (or at least dramatically extending) some significant mathematical ideas.

The Activity 3–9 shows how students' ideas may evolve during a single problem-solving session. Try the problem with a group of two or three junior high school students, and take notes on the problem-solving skills, processes, and understandings that seem to affect solutions either positively or negatively. Put yourself in the role of the researcher, observing and recording students behaviors, rather than in the role of a teacher, trying to influence their solutions. Give as little guidance as possible. If hints are needed, use only general heuristics.

Make sure the students realize that it may take them 20 to 40 minutes to solve the problem, and that a number of solutions to the problem are acceptable, depending on the amount (and types) of information taken into account, the restrictions and assumptions that are imposed on the problem, and the extent to which possible errors and sources of errors are considered.

You should anticipate that students often arrive at final solutions by gradually refining series of trial solutions, which differ according to the preceding kinds of factors. This gradual conceptualization refinement process is exactly what is meant by local conceptual development. Thinking about thinking is critical in such a process because students must think about their own conceptualizations of problem situations.

PROBLEM-SOLVING ACTIVITY 3–9

Modify this problem to be appropriate to your local situation. Try it with a group of students in grades 6, 7, and 8.

Materials: calculator, Sears catalog from ten years ago, current Sears catalog, newspaper from ten years ago, and current newspaper.

Fred Findley began teaching ten years ago in Centerville. He and his new bride rented an apartment at 3188 Main Street for $250 per month. He also bought a new VW Rabbit for $4500. His starting salary was $14,000. This year, Fred's younger brother, Tom, also began teaching in Centerville. He and his new bride rented the very same apartment that Fred had rented ten years earlier, only now the rent was $430 per month. He too bought a new VW Rabbit; the price was now $8900. Other price differences can be found in the catalogs and newspapers that you have been given. What should Tom's starting salary be to be equivalent to Fred's from ten years earlier?

Exercise Set 3–9

1. Describe the group's problem-solving process. Did they produce more than one trial solution? How did the underlying problem conceptualizations differ (for example, amount of information accounted for, the assumptions made)?
2. How did the group decide which information to consider and exclude?
3. Compare the problem characteristics for this inflation problem to those that were described for the camp placement problem. Was there too much information? Not enough information?

Hopefully, the things that you have learned in this chapter will help you notice more different kinds of things about your students' problem-solving abilities. This ability to recognize many aspects of students' problem solving behaviors is needed to help students become better problem solvers.

Compare the solution that your students produced with the one described below from Lesh's 1985 research session, which involved five distinct (re)conceptualization cycles.

Conceptualization 1: The group subtracted to find price differences for pairs of (presumably comparable) old and new items. But, only a few items were considered, which were simply the items noticed first (that is, the car and two items from the catalog). No apparent thought was given to how these subtracted differences would allow a new salary to be determined.

(Note: At this point, one student went off on "wild goose chases" by spending the next 30 minutes calculating weekly budgets for a family. He never asked himself, "Why am I doing this?" or "How will this information help me answer the question?")

Conceptualization 2: Because it was tedious to carry out the first approach, other ways to think about the problem were considered. But, whereas the first conceptualization had lost sight of the overall goal while focusing on details (that is, price differences for individual items), the second conceptualization "brainstormed" by tolling out wild ideas, ignoring details, and temporarily postponing assessment or criticism. The group made a wild guess: because ten years had passed, perhaps the new salary should be ten times the old salary.

Although this guess was quickly recognized as foolish, it did serve a very positive function; it introduced a productive new way to think about the relationships among old prices, old salaries, new prices, and new salaries— *multiplicative relations.*

Conceptualization 3: The third conceptualization was based on *multiplicative* proportions (that is, A is to B as C is to D) rather than on *additive* differences.

$$\frac{\text{new prices}}{\text{old prices}} = \frac{\text{new salary}}{\text{old salary}}$$

The students also began to explicitly consider the basis for selecting data; after calculating price increase ratios for five or six items, they noticed that the ratios had very different values for different items. They then began to argue about which increase was most typical. As a result, the new salary estimate was based on only one item, the car. Yet, there were disagreements about which item was really typical (for example, it was noted that the price of calculators and tape recorders actually decreased), so conceptualization 3 was not satisfactory.

Conceptualization 4: In conceptualization 3, the students had referred to the "price increase ratios" as "percent increases," even though percents were never calculated. Conceptualization 4 was based on real percent increases. Also, a second important idea also was added: finding an *average* percent increase. That is, for the first time, information from several items was combined to find an answer. Unfortunately, this clarity of thought enabled the students to notice that simple averages assign just as much importance to candy bar increases as to car increases; so this again seemed unsatisfactory.

Conceptualization 5: The students' final conceptualization was similar to the fourth, but instead of averaging percent increases, they (1) found the sum of the old prices for a list of "important" items, (2) found the sum of the current prices for the same list of items, and (3) calculated the percent increase for these two sums. That is, weights were implicitly assigned to the items (based on their price). Expensive items influenced the result more than inexpensive items. In fact, the group even noticed that estimates based on sums of high cost items were not changed much by adding small numbers of low cost items. So, they began to think about possible sources of error built into their way of combining data.

The preceding solution has a number of characteristics that are typical of "local conceptual development" sessions. First, the solution involved several reconceptualization cycles. So, *thinking about thinking* was essential. Furthermore, the students' first conceptualization of the problem distorted and over-filtered the given information; only a few of the most obvious facts and relationships were noticed, and unnecessary or inaccurate restrictions were assumed to apply. Just as eyewitness reports of accidents or robberies often are biased by what observers expect to see, students frequently distort given problem information to fit prior understandings and expectations. When they focus on details, they lose cognizance of their overall way of thinking about the problem; or when they focus on overall conceptualization or goals, they ignore details or distort facts.

Students' early conceptualizations of problem situations often consist of several half-formulated (often logically incompatible) ways of thinking about the problem. Each conceptualization may suggest half-formulated solution procedures and alternative ways to select, filter, interpret, relate, organize, or combine information. In fact, differentiating or integrating these unstable conceptualizations is often the main difficulty underlying such problem-solving sessions.

Solutions often are constructed in somewhat the following way. An initial conceptualization of a problem selects, organizes, and interprets certain information. This interpreted information then requires certain aspects of the conceptualization to be refined or elaborated. The refined or elaborated model allows new information and relationships to be noticed, giving rise to a new reconceptualization cycle.

Other chapters in this book describe stages in the development of students' conceptualizations of a variety of mathematical ideas. The developmental transitions referred to in these other chapters, in general, take place over several years. Yet, these evolutionary stages often are strikingly similar to those that occur within 40-minute "local conceptual development" problem-solving sessions. For example, in the chapters of this book about rational number concepts (Chapter 7) and proportional reasoning concepts (Chapter 10), the stages that students typically go through are amazingly similar to those described in the preceding solution to the inflation problem. Students' early proportional reasoning concepts tend to be based on additive or subtractive relationships, rather than on multiplicative relationships or ratios. Their early proportional reasoning judgments tend to take into account only the most obvious facts and relationships and tend to impose inappropriate biases. Such students often do not notice mismatches between their conceptualizations and reality. These characteristics of novice problem solvers were all evident in the description of the solution process to the inflation problem.

HEURISTICS: A DEVELOPMENTAL PERSPECTIVE

What roles might heuristics play in local conceptual development sessions? Keep in mind that the solutions involve several reconceptualization cycles and the first conceptualizations tend to be barren and distorted. For example, if a student's conception of a problem is barren and distorted, then premature attempts to "identify the givens and goals" may lock thinking into a distorted interpretation of the problem. In these cases, the perceived problem may effectively replace the given problem in the consciousness of the student—as it did for the student working on the inflation problem who went on the wild goose chase of working on a weekly family budget, or as it did for those students in the carpentry problem who drew a picture that reminded them of a familiar (area) problem. In such instances, a heuristic may actually derail productive thinking if it serves to trigger some borrowed solution procedure that should have been modified to be appropriate.

Heuristics like "look for a similar problem" or "identify the givens and goals" could either hinder or help problem-solving attempts, depending on the functions that they serve. In local conceptual development sessions, the important functions have to do with facilitating conceptual evolution and minimizing the effects of early inadequate conceptualizations.

Just as behaviors that are generally considered to be good can actually be counterproductive, depending on the functions they serve, behaviors that are generally considered to be hindrances to good problem solving sometimes actually help produce beneficial results. For example, brainstorming is a well-known group problem-solving technique based on the tactic of spewing out "wild ideas" and temporarily agreeing not to monitor and assess—even though careful monitoring and assessing of solution steps are (in general) thought to be important.

The primary goals of brainstorming are to help problem solvers avoid being a victim of their own early conceptualizations of problems by thinking about problems in a variety of ways before settling on one conceptualization. So, not monitoring and not assessing can actually be helpful at some stages in solution attempts, even though these behaviors may later become counterproductive.

Teaching problem solving is not reducible to teaching a set of cookbooklike rules so that students can avoid thinking. If students' problem-solving capabilities are to be improved, they must think about thinking. They must learn not only to think *with* mathematical ideas, but also to think *about* their conceptualizations of problem situations. So, they must acquire better understandings about the nature of different kinds of problems and problem-solving experiences, and also about their own conceptual characteristics in different kinds of problem-solving situations. For example, it is very helpful to understand that, in certain real-word problem-solving situations, your first conceptualizations are likely to be barren and distorted. Then at least you can take actions to guard against being a victim of your own conceptualizations.

In the same way that students' mathematical ideas evolve, their understandings about the nature of problem solving also evolve. So, even understandings about heuristics can be thought about as developing. The concluding section of this chapter takes a developmental view of the three heuristics that were considered at the beginning of the chapter: "look for a similar problem," "draw a picture" (or more generally, "introduce a useful notation"), and "identify the knowns and unknowns." We will describe how barren and distorted conceptualizations interact with the use of these heuristics and then will suggest several ways to use group problem-solving experiences to help students gradually acquire more sophisticated problem-solving understandings.

Look for a Similar Problem

For novice problem solvers, initial ways of thinking about problems tend to take into account only a few superficial (or especially striking) characteristics of problem situations. So, if a similar problem is suggested, novices may tend to either notice only superficial similarities or differences and treat the new situation as a replacement for the original problem. This can be recalled in one student's solution to the carpentry problem, in which the given perimeter problem was replaced with a similar area problem.

A more elementary version of "look for a similar problem" may be to "look at the same problem from a different point of view." However, even this capability is often difficult for novice problem solvers because of their inability to let go of their own initial biased ways of viewing problem situations. When a group of novice problem solvers begin to work on a problem, each one may conceptualize the problem in a different way, unconscious of their own misleading biases and misconceptions.

Teachers can help novice problem solvers become aware of their own barren and distorted ways of thinking about problem solving by providing experience in group problem-solving sessions. As students have to confront one another's biases, they also have to confront mismatches between reality and their own conceptualizations.

Piaget (1928), a famous Swiss psychologist, referred to these kinds of conceptual confrontations (with reality or with colleagues) as "cognitive conflict" situations. He described how such conflicts can be important stimulants to conceptual growth—whether we are concerned about general conceptual development over several years or about local conceptual development within individual problem-solving sessions. By having students work in groups, teachers can help novice problem solvers internalize the kind of external conflicts that occur naturally in group settings. That is, expert problem solvers gradually learn to behave as though they were, within themselves, a group of people sitting around a table, working cooperatively to solve the problem. A variety of biases and views are represented, so the expert is able to avoid being a victim of his or her own initial interpretations of problems.

Introduce a Useful Representation or Notation

Drawing diagrams, making tables, and recording information may all be ways of "introducing a useful representation or notation" to describe a problem. But, the term "useful" here raises the question, "Useful to what?" The answer often has to do with communication. For example, expert problem solvers often seem to carry on internal dialogues. They record and justify their work to an "internal observer," and they also realize that their solution paths are one of many that could be taken. Isolated problem situations are treated as part of larger implicitly "social" contexts, which presuppose interactions with other people, oneself at a later time or oneself in similar situations.

When a picture is drawn, or other representations are introduced, the purpose may be to help oneself keep an eye on the "big picture" while details are being worked out; it may be to reduce the memory load; it may be to communicate with others; it may be to clarify an argument for or against some other point of view; or it may be to make it easier to retrieve information at a later time. In any case, the purpose for which the representation or notation is used influences the nature of the picture that is drawn, the chart that is used, or the steps that are recorded. Unfortunately, most students have not had much experience with problems in which it is important to record, diagram, or even remember accurately the information they used to arrive at answers. Furthermore, students often are unable to simultaneously think and think about thinking, or work and also monitor/plan/assess their work.

Again, group problem-solving experiences can play an important role in the development of individual problem-solving abilities. By working in a group, students first assess and monitor each other. This can eventually help them detect errors and omissions in their own reasoning. Gradually the external monitoring techniques can become internal.

Research based on the theories of the famous Soviet psychologist, Vygotsky, helps to explain a second role that group activities may play in problem-solving instruction (see, for example, Vygotsky, 1978; Wertsch, 1980). Whereas Piaget emphasized concrete-to-abstract dimensions of conceptual development and the role of cognitive conflict in conceptual growth, Vygotsky emphasized external-to-internal (interpersonal to intrapersonal) dimensions of conceptual evolution. Vygotsky was especially interested in ways that adults could enhance childrens' problem-solving capabilities by modeling heuristic suggestions that would gradually be internalized by the novice.

Providing group problem-solving experiences maximizes the opportunity for communication during the problem-solving process. The interpersonal interaction may provide both a purpose for creating and using pictures, diagrams, charts, and so forth, and may eventually be internalized by the student for intrapersonal communication.

Identify the Knowns and Unknowns

Problem-solving strategies like "identify the givens," "identify the unknowns," "eliminate irrelevant information," or "organize the information given" all fall under the general heading "understand the problem." Unfortunately, the suggestion to understand the problem seems rather useless to novice problem solvers who start off with inaccurate understandings of the problem. On the other hand, advising students to identify knowns and unknowns when they have no stable way of thinking about the problem is often not helpful and may even be counterproductive. Before a student can identify the knowns and unknowns, he must first understand the problem.

Group problem-solving activities can again be used to reconcile the above dilemma. Elementary versions of the preceding strategies may be "use your own words to describe the problem to a friend" or "describe the problem in such a way that a friend could give you the answer." Poor problem solvers sometimes flounder with a problem for a long time before even noticing (if asked) that they are unable to give a clear description of the problem. By trying to describe a problem to a friend, students often are forced to consider their own problem conceptualizations, to eliminate irrelevant information, to identify knowns and unknowns, and to organize the information given. As students gain experience from external dialogues about a problem, they gradually become able to internalize the process; in group sessions where the communicative purposes of conceptual clarification are made as concrete as possible, they gradually develop more abstract understandings about these functions.

CHAPTER 3 SUMMARY

A variety of problem-solving situations can be used to address several different types of instructional objectives. Several problem solving heuristics were identified and explored. The review of the research indicated a shift over the years from a view of successful problem solving as a simple application of general heuristics to a more complex picture that takes into account students' content understandings, beliefs, and ability to think about their own thinking. Instruction in problem solving was presented as a complex topic that requires varied and integrated experiences.

As you work through other chapters of this book, remember that problem solving and concept formation cannot really be separated. An idea is of little value if a student is unable to use it.

In the same way that it is simplistic to imagine that we could make students better problem solvers by simply teaching them a short list of rules or facts, it would be naive to imagine that we could make you a better teacher of problem solving by simply presenting facts and rules. Neither we nor anyone else can give you a foolproof set of things to do in a classroom, but we can help you create better ways to think about what you are doing when you teach. Just as students gradually need to acquire the ability to "think about thinking," we hope that you have begun to "think about thinking about thinking"—and that your conceptualizations of problem-solving processes will be a bit less barren and distorted than before you began working in this chapter.

REFERENCES

Agenda for action. 1980. Reston, VA: National Council of Teachers of Mathematics.

Begle, E. G. 1979. *Critical variables in mathematics education: Findings from a survey of the empirical literature.* Washington, D.C.: Mathematical Association of America.

Bell, M. S., Fuson, K. C., & Lesh, R. A. 1976. *Algebraic and arithmetic structures: A concrete approach for elementary school teachers.* New York: The Free Press.

Bell, M. S., & Usiskin, Z. P. 1983. *Applying arithmetic: A handbook of applications of arithmetic.* (Parts 1—3). Chicago: University of Chicago Press.

Bloom, B. S. 1985. *The development of talent in young people.* New York: Balentine.

Brown, S., & Walter, M. I. 1982. *The art of problem posing.* Philadelphia: Franklin Institute Press.

Budd-Rowe, M. 1978. *Teaching science as continuous inquiry.* New York: McGraw-Hill.

Burkhardt, H. 1981. *The real world and mathematics.* Bishopbriggs, Glasgow: Blackie and Son Limited.

Butts, T. 1973. *Problem solving in mathematics.* Glenview, IL: Scott Foresman.

Carpenter, T., Corbitt, M., Kepner, H., Lindquist, M., & Reys, R. 1981. *Results from the second mathematics assessment of the national assessment of educational progress.* Reston, VA: National Council of Teachers of Mathematics.

Crosswhite, J., Dossey, J., Swafford, J., McKnight, C., & Cooney, T. 1985. *Second international mathematics study summary report for the United States.* Champaign, IL: Stripes Publishing.

Elstein, A. S., Shulman, L. S., & Sprafka, S. A. 1978. *Medical problem solving: An analysis of clinical reasoning.* Cambridge, MA: Harvard Univerity Press.

Freudenthal, H. 1968. Why to teach mathematics so as to be useful. *Educational Studies in Mathematics,* 1(1):2, 38−67.

Gardner, M. 1978. *Aha! Insight.* New York: Scientific American/W. H. Freeman.

Garofalo, J., & Lester, F. K. 1985. Metacognition and mathematical performance. *Journal for Research in Mathematics Education.* 16:163−176.

Goodstein, M. 1983. *Sci-math: Applications in proportional problem solving* (Modules 1−2). Menlo Park, CA: Addison-Wesley.

Hatfield, L. 1978. Heuristical emphases in the instruction of mathematical problem solving: Rationales and research. In L. Hatfield (Ed.), *Mathematical problem solving.* Columubus, OH: ERIC/SMEAC.

Hughes, D., Huntley, I., & McDonald, J. 1982. *Applying mathematics.* Chichester, England: Ellis Horwood Limited.

Krulik, S., & Reys, R. (Eds.). 1980. *Problem solving in school mathematics.* Reston, VA: National Council of Teachers of Mathematics.

Krutetskii, V. 1976. *The psychology of mathematical abilities in school children.* Chicago: University of Chicago Press.

Larkin, J. G., McDermott, J., Simon, D. P., & Simon, H. J. 1980. Models of competence in solving physics problems. *Cognitive Science,* 4:317−345.

Lave, J., Murtaugh, M., & de la Rocha, O. 1984. The dialectics of arithmetic in grocery shopping. In B. Rogoff and J. Lave (Eds.), *Everyday cognition: Its development in social context.* Cambridge, MA: Harvard University Press.

Lawler, R. 1981. The progressive construction of mind. *Cognitive Science,* 5:1−30.

LeBlanc, J., Kerr, D., Hudson, T., & Thompson, M. 1975. *Experiences in problem solving.* Bloomington, IN: Indiana University.

Lesh, R. 1985. *Applied mathematical problem solving,* unpublished manuscript.

Lesh, R., Post, T., & Behr, M. 1985. Representations, and translations among representations, in mathematics learning and problem solving, in Claude Janvier (Ed.), *Toward a theory of mathematical representation.* Hillsdale, NJ: Lawrence Erlbaum Associates.

Lester, F. 1978. Mathematical problem solving in the elementary school: Some educational and psychological considerations. In L. Hatfield (Ed.), *Mathematical problem solving.* Columbus, OH: ERIC/SMEAC.

Lester, F. K., & Garofalo, J. 1982. (Eds.). *Mathematical problem solving: Issues in research.* Philadelphia: Franklin Institute Press.

Lindquist, M., Carpenter, T., Silver, E., & Matthews, W. 1983. The third national mathematics assessment: Results and implications for elementary and middle schools. *Arithmetic Teacher,* 31(4):14−19.

Mason, J., Burton, L., & Stacey, K. 1982. *Thinking mathematically*. London: Addison-Wesley.

National Commission on Excellence in Education 1983. *A nation at risk: The imperatives for educational reform* (GPO #065-000-001772-2). Washington, DC: U. S. Government Printing Office.

Piaget, J. 1928. *Judgment and reasoning in the child*. London: Routledge and Kegan Paul.

Polya, G. 1957. *How to solve it*. Princeton: Princeton University Press.

Polya, G. 1962. *Mathematical discovery: On understanding, learning and teaching problem solving*. (Vol. 1). New York: Wiley.

Polya, G. 1965. *Mathematical discovery: On understanding, learning and teaching problem solving*. (Vol. 2). New York: Wiley.

Schoenfeld, A. 1986. *Mathematical problem solving*. New York: Academic Press.

Shavelson, R. J. , Caldwell, J., & Izu, T. 1978. Teachers' sensitivity to the reliability of information in making pedagogical decisions. *American Educational Research Journal* 14:(21):83−97.

Simon, H. 1981. Studying human intelligence by creating artificial intelligence. *American Scientist*. 69:300−309.

A Sourcebook of applications of school mathematics. 1980. Reston, VA: National Council of Teachers in Mathematics.

Usiskin, Z. 1978. *Algebra through applications with probability and statistics* (Parts 1−2). Reston, VA: National Council of Teachers of Mathematics.

Vygotsky, L. S. 1978. *Mind in society: The development of higher psychological processes*. Cambridge, MA: Harvard University Press.

Wertsch, J. 1980. The adult-child diad as a problem solving system. *Child Development* 51:1215−1221.

Whimbey, A., & Lochhead, J. 1984. *Beyond problem solving and comprehension: An exploration of quantitative reasoning*. Philadelphia: Franklin Institute Press.

4 Foundational Ideas in Teaching about Measure

PATRICIA S. WILSON

Univerity of Georgia

ALAN OSBORNE

The Ohio State University

INTRODUCTION

Using rulers, reading dials on instruments, noting volume, and inferring whether clothing will fit are examples of measuring in everyday life. Measuring is such a familiar task for adults that it is difficult to identify the misconceptions about measure that cause children to perform poorly on measurement tasks. In order to teach measurement, a teacher must understand the foundational ideas of measure and incorporate these ideas at all levels of instruction. Good instruction in measurement should not only teach skills but should expand a child's ability to learn and understand mathematics and science. Many teachers are surprised by students' lack of understanding about measurement. The data indicate traditional approaches to measurement found in many textbooks do not address the misconceptions of students.

The goal of this chapter is to present and develop the foundations of the concepts of measurement. These foundational ideas are illustrated in the measurement systems of length and area. An instructional sequence is presented to help the teacher incorporate these ideas into classroom instruction.

and a step-by-step plan for teaching angle measure is offered as an example. Related research is provided on children's abilities to learn measurement concepts and on test results reporting the measurement skills of students. Also included are innovative activities to help children avoid some common misconceptions.

In a single chapter, or at a single grade level for that matter, it is not possible to teach all of the measurement systems necessary for everyday life, and for mathematics and science. By consistently incorporating the foundational ideas of measure in instruction a teacher gives the students the basis for learning new measurement systems whenever necessary.

THE ROLE OF MEASURE

Understanding measure provides knowledge that goes far beyond the use of measure in everyday life. Knowing and using science to understand the environment is difficult without measurement. Much of the learning yet to come in high school and college mathematics is developed using ideas of measurement.

It is important to distinguish between measure in mathematics and measuring in science. The distinction concerns the differences in doing science and doing mathematics. Science is at its heart an observational process. If your task is to find the length of segment AB by using a ruler, you do several acts that affect the precision and accuracy of the measurement (see Fig. 4−1).

First, you need to place the ruler next to segment AB. The endpoint A needs to be placed accurately next to a point on the ruler; for convenience, say at the zero point at the end of the ruler. Then it must be decided whether the B endpoint falls closer to the point of the ruler labeled with 10 or 11. Judgment and perception enter at this point. A decision must be made. Accuracy can be improved by having additional points of subdivision on the ruler but at some point either the limitations of how finely divided the scale is or how well the observer can see enters the picture. Observation characterizes doing science. Necessarily, error is involved.

Inaccuracy in measurement cannot be escaped in the observational processes of science. If you use protractors, thermometers, or any observational measurement tool, you must deal with error. Although activities in using measurement tools are—and should be—in mathematics textbooks, you are teaching observational aspects of science.

The mathematics of length is different; observational error is not involved. In studying geometry, you encountered the idea that corresponding to a pair of distinct points A and B there is exactly one number that is the length of the line

FIGURE 4−1
Finding the length of AB

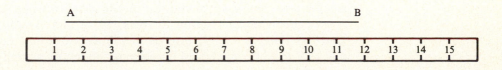

segment connecting the points or the distance from A to B. This is in the ideal world of mathematics free from observational error.

Mathematical measure is clean, precise, and not subject to observational error. Scientific measure necessarily has error and judgment stemming from observation. For most teaching and learning activities concerning measure, a bit of both is involved because you often find you must use activities based on manipulation of materials (observation) to make the mathematical points. Similarly, when measuring in science, the mathematical structure of the system cannot be ignored. However, as a teacher you must keep in mind whether your primary goals are the mathematical ideas or the observational processes of science.

Assignment

1. Select a mathematics textbook for a grade level. Classify each lesson directly concerned with measurement as being primarily concerned with measure from a scientific or from a mathematical point of view.
2. Design a lesson that stresses reading the scale on a ruler accurately.
3. Identify the specific subskills children should acquire.
4. Design an evaluation activity to indicate whether a child has acquired each subskill.

Students need to learn about several systems of measure. Length, area, angle size, and volume are among those encountered in elementary school mathematics, but the systems students encounter throughout schooling extend to measurement systems such as density, temperature, force, work, and the like.

In addition to different systems of measure, students will meet different standard units such as the English system used in the United States and the metric system used in other countries. *A Metric Handbook for Teachers* (Higgins, 1974) explains the many advantages of the metric system. Because the metric system consists of units related by powers of ten, comparison of units and calculations is much easier than in the English system. For example there are ten centimeters in a decimeter, ten decimeters in a meter, and ten meters in a kilometer. The U.S. movement toward adopting the metric system in the 1970s lost momentum, and the U.S. Metric Commission was abolished in 1984. It is still important for students to be able to work successfully in the metric system because most countries, industries, and many sciences do use metric measure. Conversion between metric units and English units is not a wise use of student time, but understanding the metric system is valuable. *Measurement in School Mathematics* (Nelson & Reys, 1976) and *A Metric Handbook for Teachers* (Higgins, 1974) provide ample activities and extensive bibliographies for teachers interested in teaching the metric system.

FOUNDATIONAL IDEAS OF MEASURE

The presence or absence of a few foundational ideas serves to characterize each measurement system and to distinguish it from others. Many of the foundational ideas work in several different measurement systems. Most of the foundational ideas are obvious to adults. They are such an integral part of adult use of measure that they are thought about separately. If you watch children as they encounter new measurement concepts, you can be more helpful if you think of separate foundational ideas.

As an example, the measurement system of length is examined in terms of these foundational ideas.

FOUNDATIONAL IDEA 1: *Number Assignment:* Given a pair of points A and B, there is exactly one nonnegative number, $d(A,B) > O$, that is length of segment AB.

Foundational Idea 1 contains several important features. The d in $d(A,B)$ indicates the statement is about distance. The (A,B) in $d(A,B)$ indicates the distance is from point A to point B. Of course, we want the distance from point A to point B to be the same as the distance from point B to point A or $d(A,B) = d(B,A)$. The most important feature is that for every segment there is a number that is its length. The second most important feature is that there is only one such number assignment to the segment. Finally, measure of length should be a positive number. The case in which $d(A,B) = 0$ indicates that A and B are the same point.

FOUNDATIONAL IDEA 2: *Comparison:* If segment AB is contained by segment AC, then $d(A,B) < d(A,C)$.

Figure 4−2 illustrates the comparison in Foundational Idea 2. Intuitively, it appears clear that because B is between A and C, the distance from A to B should be less than from A to C.

FOUNDATIONAL IDEA 3: *Congruence:* Segment AB congruent to segment CD means that $d(A,B) = d(C,D)$.

FIGURE 4−2
Comparison

If one segment can be picked up and put down on another so that the endpoints correspond exactly, then the segments have the same length.

FOUNDATIONAL IDEA 4:   *Unit:* There is a line segment that can be assigned the length one.

In order to work with rulers, a specific segment needs to have a distance measure of one. A unit for measuring length may be a common one used in a standard measurement system such as an inch, a meter, or a light year, or the unit may be arbitrary such as the length of a particular book.

FOUNDATIONAL IDEA 5:   *Additivity:* A line segment made by joining two distinct line segments has a length equal to the sum of the lengths of the joined segments.

Figure 4−3 illustrates that if line segment AB is joined to line segment BC, then the length of line segment AC is equal to the length of AB added to the length of BC. This foundational idea is extremely important. It assures that dealing with length is like dealing with numbers. Joining segments in a line segment behaves like adding numbers. It means that the structure of addition can guide children's thinking about measurement, and vice versa.

The idea of additivity is difficult for many children initially. A failure to conserve is bound up with whether children can use additivity to construct new concepts about measure.

FOUNDATIONAL IDEA 6:   *Archimedean Iteration:* If a point B is between points A and C on a line, then a counting number *n* can be found so that

$$n \times d(A,B) > d(A,C)$$

Foundational Idea 6, as represented by the diagram in Fig. 4−4, says that in this case of segments AB and AC in which B is between A and C, 13 copies or

FIGURE 4−3
Additivity

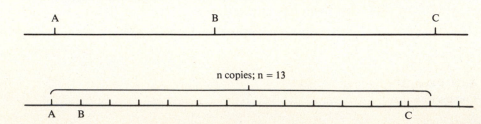

FIGURE 4−4
Archemedian
iteration

iterations of AB laid end-to-end are all that are needed to get beyond point C. This notion is the basis for developing number lines and ruler use.

The above six foundational ideas are sufficient to describe measurement of a line. The formal language used to describe the ideas is inappropriate to use with children but is sparse and lean in getting to the heart of thinking about length or distance. A teacher's responsibility in planning instruction for the foundational ideas is to find activities to ensure every idea is encountered in an informal, significant setting.

FOUNDATIONAL IDEAS IN AREA

Distance is typically the first measurement system taught in school. The foundational ideas of length are helpful in thinking about any new measurement systems such as area. The first foundational idea was that of number assignment. For area, this foundational idea has an exact analogue: to a region R, a number (again, nonnegative) is assigned called the area. There is a parallel comparison property. If one region R can be covered with another region Q, then the area of Q is greater than or equal to the area of R. Congruence is strictly paralleled also; that is, if two regions are congruent, then they have the same area. We can define a unit, such as a square mile, a hectare, or a square centimeter, for area measurement or simply use an arbitrary unit.

The additivity property for area of regions is an analogue of that for length. For rectangles it can be shown pictorially as in Fig. 4–5.

Assignment

A geoboard (see Fig. 4–6) is a useful device in teaching about area. It is a board with nails or pegs in a square lattice pattern. Regions can be indicated by stretching rubber bands around the pegs. Many teachers find it useful in working with area to give each child several unit squares cut from paper to cover exactly the region between four pegs. Teachers can also provide children with paper and scissors to cut out figures to match those constructed with rubber bands.

FIGURE 4–5
Area additivity— the area of the union of non-over-lapping Regions I and II is the same as the sum of the areas of Regions I and II

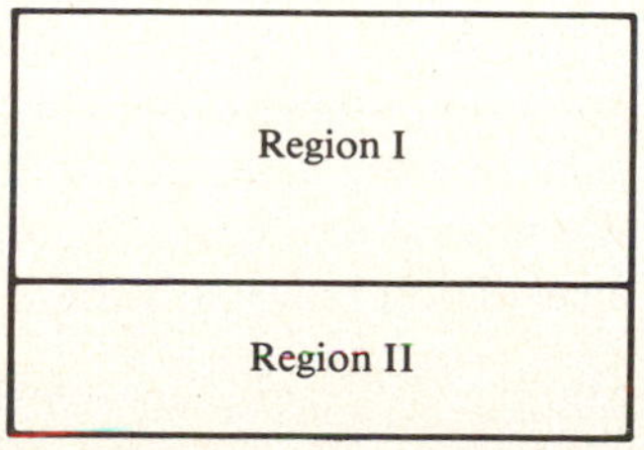

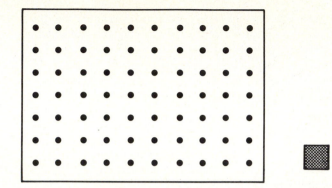

FIGURE 4–6
Geoboard

1. Make a geoboard.
2. Design a problem or a demonstration for geoboard work on area measure specific to each of the foundational ideas except Archimedean iteration.

Area and length measurement systems are similar; the foundational ideas work in both systems. This is true for many but not all measurement systems. Considerable instructional time can be saved if children can be led to look for a transfer of the foundational ideas from one system of measure to another. By the time the child has become a student in twelfth-grade physics, typically two dozen different measurement systems have been encountered. If the importance and significance of ideas such as unit and additivity do not have to be relearned on each encounter with a new measurement system, then the elementary school curriculum in measurement will have been successful.

FOUNDATIONAL IDEAS IN OTHER MEASUREMENT SYSTEMS

Not all measurement systems have all of the foundational ideas. For example, consider additivity and temperature. If 65°F cream is mixed with 155°F coffee in equal parts to produce café au lait, the mixture does not boil! In fact, the temperature becomes about 110°F rather than the 220°F additivity would predict. Particularly in the upper elementary school mathematics and science programs, students should begin to expect the foundational ideas to apply when they encounter new mathematical and scientific measurement systems, but they should also develop a suspicion that leads them to verify each of the ideas.

PROVISIONS FOR INDIVIDUAL DIFFERENCES

Students must be actively involved in measuring if they are to learn about measurement. Certainly, the teacher can explain the foundational ideas and can demonstrate measuring techniques, but it is not until the students actually measure and use measurements in problem-solving situations that they can achieve the measurement objectives they need to function in today's world. Each student will bring a slightly different background and physical ability to an activity. Each student will exhibit strengths and disabilities in dealing with the activities. The teacher needs to be sensitive to the individual differences in planning activities and in observing what each student is learning from the activity.

The following sections offer instructional suggestions, research findings on student misconceptions and learning patterns, and activities to help avoid misconceptions and build on learning capabilities. Each section discusses individual differences you will find in your classroom.

The following guidelines will help the teacher become aware of what students are doing and thinking.

1. Get students involved in measurement activities.
2. Observe and interact with individual students and small groups.
3. Allow students to work in pairs. When physical disabilities interfere with a student's ability to perform an activity, a partner can explain or demonstrate the activity.
4. Assess misconceptions.
5. Assign follow-up activities to address the problem.
6. Use class discussion to highlight insights developed by individuals.

Good classroom management is the key to accomplishing successful activities. For example, it is difficult for the whole class to measure the teacher's desk, but pairs of students could easily measure different items around the classroom at the same time. Small group work allows the teacher to observe more closely. By planning time for students to report on their activities, the teacher can uncover misconceptions that were not observed.

SEQUENCING INSTRUCTION FOR A NEW MEASUREMENT SYSTEM

The following instructional sequence of four steps for establishing a new measurement system has been suggested by both research and the experiences of many teachers:

Step 1: Do number-free comparison activities to focus attention on the attribute being measured.
Step 2: Develop and use non-standard, arbitrary units.

Step 3: Examine the measurement system in terms of whether each foundational idea works within the system.

Step 4: Move instruction to the standard units used by many people in order to communicate.

Instruction developed around these four steps should span an extended period of time rather than simply happening in one or two lessons. Lessons late in the sequence should contain a quick review or reinforcement of prior steps to begin each lesson.

The instructional sequence is valuable for all measurement systems. As an example, we shall examine teaching about angle measure in terms of this four-step sequence.

Step 1: Do number-free comparison activities to focus attention on the attribute being measured.

Children should know what an angle is and different ways of naming and identifying angles. Comparing angles to see which is bigger can be accomplished by placing one angle on top of another with the vertex of one on the vertex of the other. If you have access to acetate for use with the overhead projector, it is good to draw and label several angles of different sizes on separate sheets of acetate. Ask children to compare two angles for which you have been careful to keep the drawing quite similar except for size. Begin with two acute angles, represent the rays with line segments of the same length, label the vertices similarly, and have one ray of each angle horizontal and pointing in the same direction. Children will contrast the angles and focus on the important attribute to decide one angle is larger than the other because it has more "spread" between the rays. They will tend to observe the excess such as marked in Fig. 4−7.

A next venture might be to ask the children how to best place angles for comparison to decide which is bigger. Try several different arrangements of the acetates. Most children conclude it is helpful to have a ray of one angle falling on the ray of the other with the interior of one angle containing the interior of the other. Three possible arrangements for comparing angle A with angle B are shown in Fig. 4−8.

FIGURE 4−7
Angle BCD is larger than angle ACD

m ∡ BCD > m ∡ ACD

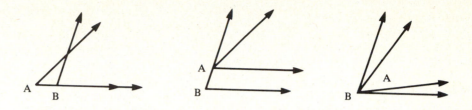

FIGURE 4–8
Comparing angles

At this point it is necessary to expose students to a set of angles with equal measures but diverse characteristics (see Fig. 4–9). Show a wide variety of angles with the same measure. The only attribute that does *not* change is the "spread" of the rays. All of the characteristics held constant in the first comparison situation have changed. The rays look different, the angles are labeled differently, and the angles have different orientations.

Students develop many misconceptions because teachers fail to vary the characteristics not relevant to the concept being taught (Wilson, 1986). For example, suppose angle A and angle B have the same measure but the rays are drawn so that those of A appear longer than those of B (see Fig. 4–10). Some children compare on the basis of the apparent length of the rays rather than the attribute of spread. You want children to conclude that angles A and B are congruent and the same size. Illustrating a related misconception, the National Assessment of Educational Progress (NAEP) (1979) found some children would indicate that in the equilateral triangles shown in Fig. 4–11 angle A was smaller than angle X. One should conclude the children were responding to the length of the sides or the areas rather than angle size.

FIGURE 4–9
Angles with equal
measures

FIGURE 4–10
Misconception:
angle B is larger
than angle A

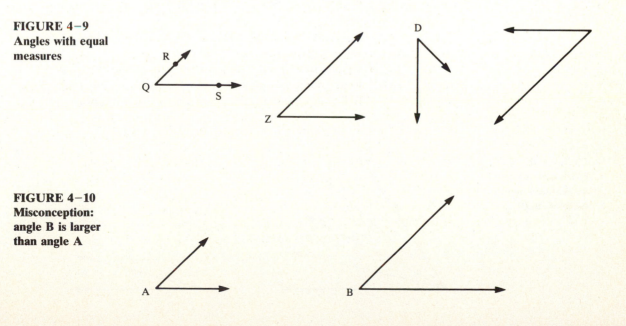

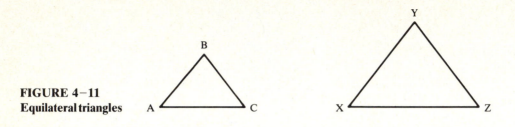

FIGURE 4–11
Equilateral triangles

Step 2: Develop and use non-standard arbitrary units

Children need to move from making nonnumerical comparisons of angle sizes to developing a numerical approach. At first children should work with arbitrary units rather than standard units. Select a unit like one of the standard units but of a different size. Figure 4–12 demonstrates using a set of wedges of about 15°. Counting how many it takes to measure a variety of angles is a sensible approach.

There is nothing magic about the measure of 15°; almost any angle would work for initial activities with a non-standard unit. If you select 15°, do *not* label it with 15° or even mention 15°. The intent is to have children use the wedge as the angle with measure 1, a unit measure. By measuring several angles with this unit wedge, they will develop a readiness for moving on to the use of protractors with an understanding and feeling for what the standard unit of degree represents.

Do note that children bring to initial measurement different geometric experiences, which affect how they think when encountering a new measurement system. In the case of angle measure, children who have had experience with Logo language on computers have moved turtles on the computer screen, and in some cases have walked through analogous moves on the floor. These experiences may make them behave differently than you might predict. If they have been programming the LOGO turtle with commands such as RT 37, FD 25 or LT 45, FD 25, they have been telling the turtle to rotate clockwise 37, go forward 25 units or turn counterclockwise 45, go forward 25 units, respectively (see Fig. 4–13). Will children accept the spread between the rays as the angle

FIGURE 4–12
Using a wedge as an arbitrary angle measure unit

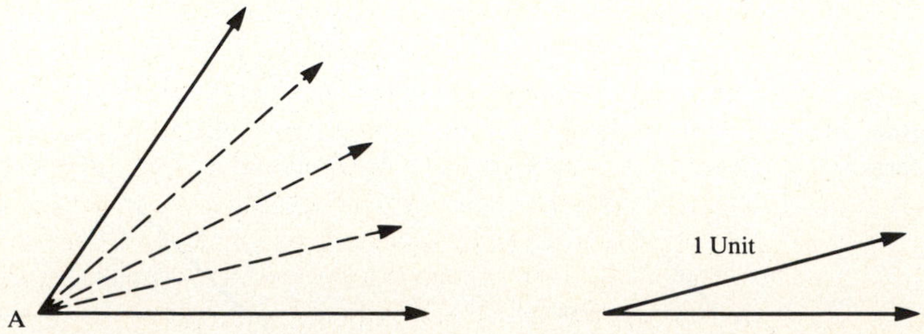

1 Unit

RT 37 FD 25   LT 45 FD 25

FIGURE 4–13
LOGO turtle
moves

measure as readily or will they be thinking in terms of a turn from a line or even an arc? You will need to listen carefully to ascertain the conceptual base from which the children operate.

Step 3: Examine the measurement system in terms of whether each Foundational Idea works within the system

The third step in the instructional sequence is to examine each of the foundational ideas to see how it applies in the angle measurement system. Does additivity work? How? Do congruent angles have the same measure? Find problem settings and geometric situations to serve as test cases for each of the foundational ideas. Do take the time to make comparisons with other measurement systems. For example, lead children to observe that the comparison property works in the same way for angle measure as for length.

Step 4: Move instruction to the standard units used by many people in order to communicate

This final step focuses the learner's attention on a standard unit of measure for angles. The standard unit is important because it represents what many other people in the world use and thereby assures a basis for communication. Typically, you will stress using degree measure and introduce the protractor as a measurement device. Children need to be shown how the unit is used in constructing and labeling the protractor.

Attention will need to be given to placing the protractor appropriately to find the measure of an angle. Children have trouble placing the zero point of the scale correctly on a ray of the angle and frequently are confused about where to place the protractor relative to the vertex of the angle being measured. This was one reason for stressing how to place one angle on another in the initial step of non-numerical comparison.

RESEARCH ON READINESS FOR LEARNING FOUNDATIONAL IDEAS

The majority of research concerning children and the foundational ideas for measurement systems concerns readiness to learn (Anderson & Cuneo, 1978; Hart, 1984; Piaget, Inhelder, & Szeminska, 1960). Many of the studies are conducted in the style of Piaget and examine questions of the intellectual maturity of the child. Carpenter (1976) provides a thorough examination of the literature concerning readiness for measure learning. We examine three of the areas of controversy: transitivity, conservation, and unit. Each is directly related to the foundational ideas children need to acquire. Given the mathematical nature of measurement, failure to attain any of the ideas establishes a barrier to further learning in measurement.

Transitivity

Transitivity is a comparison idea. If three line segments are of different lengths, and a > b and b > c, then you can conclude a > c. Children initially do not have the capability to make this conclusion. Bailey (1971) was convinced transitivity developed reasonably early in children, as young as age four. Smedslund (1963), who reported several studies of transitivity, was of the opinion that transitivity was not a feature of children's thinking until about age eight. The studies have controlled a variety of factors thought to affect whether children attain transitivity. Considerable effort has been invested in trying to accelerate the attainment of the concept by training and in examining whether the concept is acquired at the same time for different measurement systems. This evidence is not clear for many of the questions. Generally there is agreement that children must be old enough to have had considerable experience with the concept if they are to exhibit it.

One type of experiment separates the objects being compared so they cannot be in the same visual field of the subjects. For example, rods A and C are to be compared, but A and C are separated by a wall and tied down so they cannot be moved (see Fig. 4–14). A movable rod B is in the room with A. Will the child pick up B, compare it to A, transport it to C, and reach a conclusion about the comparative lengths of A and C? Children do not naturally use B to make a comparison.

FIGURE 4–14
Transitivity
experiment

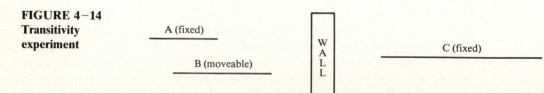

Assignment

Design and administer an interview for kindergarten or first-grade children similar to that described above but encompassing both length and area. Do you think your subject(s) understand transitivity?

Conservation

Conservation is related to the additivity property. If a region is partitioned in two parts, is the area of the parts taken together the same, less than, or greater than the original? If the child conserves, the answer will be "the same." Analogous questions can be asked relative to length, volume, and weight. Does a child view line segment AB in Fig. 4−15 as having the same total length as it does in its split version?

Researchers have been concerned about whether children acquire conservation before, after, or simultaneously with transitivity. The results are not clear. Beilin (1971) reports that within rough age limits, training accelerates attainment of conservation.

Unit

The concept of unit of measure depends on children recognizing the attribute to be measured and that the unit influences number assignment. The studies have been primarily concerned with measurement attributes directly available to perception. Some of the more salient research concerning readiness to learn and units of measure have studied whether children can respond to both visual cues concerning attributes and to numerical cues about unit measures. Carpenter (1976) found that virtually all first- and second-grade children respond as well to numerical cues as to perceptual cues. Most children centered on a single dominant cue, either numerical or perceptual, rather than considering them together. Children exhibit difficulty in coordinating numerical information with perceptual information when one type of cue is dominant or confusing.

The critical feature of the studies of attainment of the unit concept is whether children are able to coordinate what they know or observe about the attribute in question with what they know or observe about number assignment. Young children are unable to coordinate the two sets of information; older children can.

FIGURE 4−15
Conservation task

A _____ B

A _____   _____ B

Implications

Readiness to learn is a difficult psychological concept for the teacher to accommodate in planning activities for children. On the one hand, it appears to waste the teacher's and the child's time to teach concepts and skills if the child cannot learn. There is the risk of alienating the child to mathematics because of repeated failures.

On the other hand, if there is one emphatic conclusion about learning in Piagetian psychology, it is that children must have experience in order to learn. Children use experience to construct their own version of reality. If that experience is limited to the self-selection of the child, will learning migrate to the point of being close to useful adult conceptions?

Teachers must repeatedly provide experiences to challenge and stimulate children. Part of the art of teaching the young child is to select activities not too far beyond the capabilities of the child but at the same time to maintain a tension for growth and development of new ideas. Teachers get into trouble when they design activities that are too far separated from the capability of the child *and at the same time* are unforgiving in their expectations of performance by the child. The key attribute the teacher must have is the ability to listen and watch children at work and to adjust their expectations accordingly.

For attaining measurement concepts, activities focusing on the foundational ideas are essential in a well-conceived instructional program. Readiness studies show that most children in early elementary school are at a stage in development in which if the ideas have not yet been attained, then this is about to happen. Providing well-designed activities and supporting discourse with children assures that growth is in preferred directions.

LEARNING ACTIVITIES SUGGESTED BY RESEARCH

Constructing activities to teach measuring skills and measurement systems is a challenge. Three major goals of measurement instruction are to provide students with (1) measurement skills that are used every day, (2) an understanding of measurement to enhance scientific learning, and (3) concepts to expand a student's knowledge of mathematics.

This section is devoted to instructional activities suggested by the performance of children in research or evaluation studies concerned with measurement.

INTERPRETATIONS OF LENGTH

The NAEP studies (Carpenter, Coburn, Reys, & Wilson, 1978) help to understand children's misconceptions about length. Most of the 9- and 13-year-old children could measure distances shorter than a ruler but had difficulty with longer measures. Students used whole number units but had difficulty with fractional units. Some students have difficulty positioning the ruler to measure. They are not careful to begin measurement at zero or to compensate for starting at a position other than zero.

Students confuse area and perimeter. A possible explanation is that this is a result of not focusing on length being a one-dimensional attribute.

Length Objectives

1. Students will understand length is a one-dimensional attribute.
2. Students will be able to compare lengths of two objects without placing them side by side. Using the transitive property they will be able to compare objects A and B to a third object and indirectly compare A and B.
3. Students will be able to use both standard and non-standard units of measure to help compare lengths of objects.
4. Students will learn the inverse relationship between the size of a unit and the number of units needed to measure a distance.
5. Students will learn to use a ruler to measure a segment and construct a segment of a specified length.

Comparing Activities

1. Give each student three straws or rods about eight inches, six inches, and two inches long. Ask them to arrange the straws from shortest to longest. Then ask them to find something in the room longer than the longest straw and shorter than the shortest.
2. List three stationary objects in the room that are about the same length (for example, width of the window, width of the floor, and the width of the teacher's desk from front to back). Ask the students to rank the objects from shortest to longest. Urge students to solve the problem without using a ruler or yardstick. Students may choose any standard of comparison (including themselves!) to compare items they cannot place side by side.

Arbitrary Unit Activities

1. Stretch about six feet of masking tape across the floor to create a straight line segment. Ask students to measure the line segment using at least two different units. As a class discuss units appropriate for measuring the length of the segment (for example, footsteps, textbook length, piece of string, cardboard tube, a two-foot board). List on the chalkboard or the

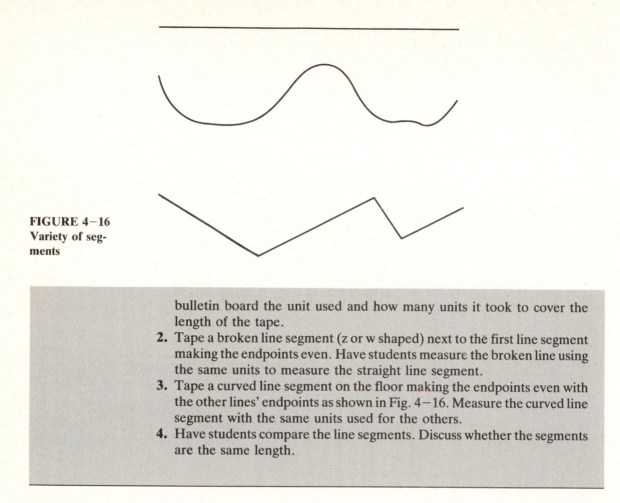

FIGURE 4–16
Variety of segments

bulletin board the unit used and how many units it took to cover the length of the tape.
2. Tape a broken line segment (z or w shaped) next to the first line segment making the endpoints even. Have students measure the broken line using the same units to measure the straight line segment.
3. Tape a curved line segment on the floor making the endpoints even with the other lines' endpoints as shown in Fig. 4–16. Measure the curved line segment with the same units used for the others.
4. Have students compare the line segments. Discuss whether the segments are the same length.

Foundational Idea Activities

1. Draw a line segment on the chalkboard and discuss what units would be appropriate to measure the segment. Focus on the distance attribute and linear units used to cover the segment without overlap or leaving space between. Discuss problems that would occur if any of these fundamentals were ignored.
2. Have students consider measuring a straight line segment using a long rod and a short rod. Discuss which measuring device (unit) would produce a larger number and why. Verify the ideas by measuring the line segment.

Standard Unit and Instrument Activities

1. Discuss the use of a ruler and the advantages and disadvantages of starting at the zero point. Decide how to measure around the corners of a broken line segment. Will every one get the same answer? Why?
2. Measure the lines taped on the floor using a ruler marked with centimeters, a yardstick marked in inches, and a tape measure marked in inches. Discuss the advantages of each unit and instrument.
3. Convert the measurement in inches to feet. Measure the lines with a foot ruler to check the conversion.
4. Using a ruler marked in inches draw a line segment 6 inches long; draw a line segment 14½ inches long.

INTERPRETATIONS OF AREA

Students need to learn about area in a variety of settings and ways. Unit counting and formula learning are not sufficient (Beilin, 1964; Hirstein, Lamb, and Osborne, 1978). Students need to estimate the area before using any particular strategy to figure out the area (Hiebert, 1981b). Students need activities in which they physically move units and rearrange figures. Formulas should not be taught independent of a conceptual basis (Osborne, 1976). If students understand area, they are able to use a variety of approaches including estimation, unit counting, formulas, and partitioning and recombination of areas.

Students should understand an area can be divided or partitioned in parts and that the parts can be recombined, preserving the area. Hirstein (1981) suggests the measurement process should include additivity of areas and the subtracting of complementary areas.

Area Objectives

1. Students will understand area is a measure of a two-dimensional region.
2. Students will understand area is preserved when it is partitioned and recombined.
3. Students will develop a rule of multiplication to relieve the tedium of counting units in rectangular regions.
4. Students will feel confident finding the area of irregular regions.
5. Students will realize different figures may have the same area but congruent figures must have the same area.

Comparing Activities

1. Using a sheet of construction paper for a standard, have students find a region in the room with more area than the sheet of paper and a region with a smaller area. Ask students to explain how they knew the regions were larger or smaller.

2. If region A fits within region B, then it is clear the area of A is less than the area of B, and the area of B is larger than A. How is the comparison to be made if one region does not fit nicely in the other region? Demonstrate comparison of an 8 by 8 square with a rectangle that is 4 by 16. Before announcing the dimensions, ask students which rectangle is larger. Cut the 4 by 16 rectangle in two pieces to reassemble into the 8 by 8 square.

   Have students compare the areas of the surface of objects found in the room using construction paper. The construction paper can be cut in parts when it is useful for the comparison. Encourage students to estimate which area is greater before making the comparison.

Arbitrary Unit Activities

1. Ask students to use a textbook to measure the surface of their tables or desks. Discuss what it means for units to cover a region.

2. Prepare square units (two inches by two inches) cut from colorful construction paper. Provide 12 units for each student. Each student should arrange the squares in a variety of patterns using all 12 squares. Explain that the squares should not overlap and must fit together. Encourage students to create irregularly shaped figures as well as rectangles.

   Students should choose their favorite designs and draw around the perimeter of each figure or paste the squares on a piece of paper. Display the shapes around the room and note that all have an area of 12 square units.

3. Use nonsquare units to cover an area. Stress that units should be congruent for convenience. Discuss the disadvantages of using different sizes and shapes of units to cover a region. Why would a triangle be a better unit than a pentagon?

4. Create a masking tape rectangle 28 inches by 20 inches on the floor. Have students cover the area with large units (four inches by four inches) and small units (two inches by two inches). Before beginning the measurement task of counting, ask students whether more large units or small units will be required to cover the figure. After measuring, discuss the results and the relationship between the small and large unit. Demonstrate that four small units are contained in the large unit.

Foundational Ideas Activities

1. Using paper with a small grid, centimeter-square graph paper, ask students to trace around objects such as a small book, a crayon box, a greeting card. Have the students count the congruent units on the grid paper to assign a number for area. Note that it is much easier to compare the areas of different regions when they have a number assigned to the area and you are not required to cut up regions in order to make a direct comparison.

2. Prepare a rectangular piece of paper six units by eight units with a rectangular unit grid as in Fig. 4−17. Ask students to find the area of the paper by counting the square units. Have the students draw around the outside of the rectangle on a piece of paper and record the number of square units in the region. Then, have the students slice the grid paper in two pieces by cutting along one grid line and recombine them to form a new figure such as shown in Fig. 4−18.

   What is the area of the new figure? Compare the outline of the new figure with the outline of the prior figure. Repeat the activity several times, continuing to find the area of each new figure and comparing the outlines to the original figure's outline. Stress the preservation of the same number for the area whatever the shape of the new figure.

FIGURE 4−17
Rectangle with unit grid

FIGURE 4−18
Recombined figure

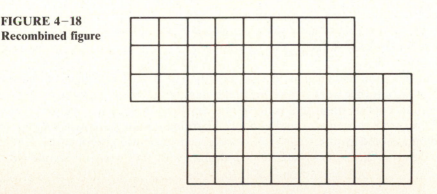

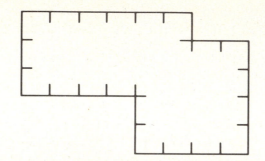

FIGURE 4–19
Indicated grid

Suggest to some students cutting along the diagonal to create figures that are not rectangles. Counting the units may be difficult for some students when they are counting fractional parts of a unit.
3. Ask students to draw irregular shapes on graph paper but to keep their pencils on the grid lines in drawing. Then find the areas by counting the squares. Move to figures in which the grid is only indicated as shown in Fig. 4–19.

Standard Unit Activities

1. Give students a rectangle that is four inches by six inches. Have students use a ruler to mark inches along all four sides. By connecting the points on the opposite sides, the students create a one-inch grid. Have students count the units created.
2. Let students measure the dimensions of the classroom and discuss as a class what the area should be. Encourage students to look for methods of finding the area that avoid counting every square. For example, they might suggest counting rows knowing that each would contain a common number of square feet, say 18. Help students understand why the number of rows times the number of units per row is the area.

INTERPRETATIONS OF VOLUME

Many children find volume difficult initially. Hirstein (1981) points out a need for more intuitive work to be done in the classroom. He notes students confuse the concepts of area and volume and suggests activities to help students distinguish between area and volume. Learning the measurement system for volume should involve transfer of knowledge from learning about area. Just as students worked with square units in dealing with area, students should work with unit cubes to explore volume. Rather than covering, now the premium is on filling the space. Have students work directly with three-dimensional objects; many misconceptions arise because students have worked with representations of three-dimensional figures on a two-dimensional textbook page.

Students often only count the cubes they can see in a rectangular solid (Driscoll, 1981). Hart (1984) noticed children could count layers of cubes in a rectangular solid but did not know how to handle fractional layers.

The first and second NAEP studies confirmed student difficulties in finding volumes. The 1978 study noted only one-third of the 13-year-old children could find the volume of a rectangular solid with small one-digit dimensions and only 16% were successful with larger rectangular solids with two-digit dimensions. Examination of the errors revealed some students counted only the units of the visible faces. Other students doubled the number to include the units contained in the nonvisible faces but failed to include units in the interior. Involving students in activities that allow the physical construction of three-dimensional solids from unit cubes helps destroy some misconceptions about volume.

Volume Objectives

1. Students will understand volume is a measure of three-dimensional space.
2. Students will be able to compare the volumes of two different solids.
3. Students will be able to use both standard and non-standard units of measure to compare the volumes of objects.
4. Students will be able to find and describe differences and similarities between volume and area measure.

Comparing Activity

Provide a variety of containers to be filled with rice. Pour rice back and forth between the containers in order to arrange them from largest to smallest volume. Use containers with different shapes and discuss the deceptive nature of perception.

Arbitrary Unit Activity

Estimate how many jellybeans will fill a quart jar. Discuss strategies for finding the volume of the jar using the jellybean unit. What are the advantages and disadvantages associated with the jellybean unit?

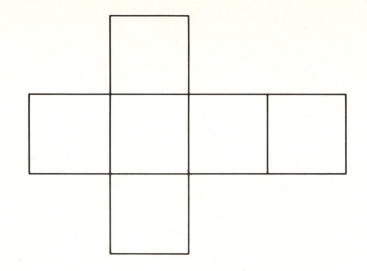

FIGURE 4—20
Pattern for cube
construction

Foundational Ideas Activities

1. Use a two-dimensional pattern (see Fig. 4—20) to have students create a three-dimensional cube for measuring a rectangular solid. Note that both the cube and the rectangular solid have six faces. Discuss why a cube is a good unit of measure for volume.
2. Using 64 cubes, build a large cube. Change two dimensions of the cube (height, width) and form a rectangular solid (that is, four by four by eight). Note that it still has a volume of 64 cubic units. Make as many different rectangular solids as you can from the 64 cubes. How many different rectangular solids can be formed with a volume of 64 cubes?

STANDARD UNITS AND INSTRUMENTS

1. Compare measure units of volume like cup, quart, and liter to volume measures such as cubic inches and cubic centimeters. Discuss strategies for getting started. Construct rectangular solids comparable to a measuring cup and a quart. (Milk cartons might be a good place to start.)
2. Compare surface area and volume by covering a rectangular solid with square inch units of construction paper and filling it with cubic inches. Make a table recording the dimensions of the figure, the surface area, and the volume.

WHAT IS A UNIT?

Children's ability to measure depends on their understanding of a unit of measure, but many students have major misconceptions (Osborne, 1974; Hiebert, 1981a, NAEP, 1979; Hart, 1984). Some students will not consider a unit to be anything other than a single entity. For example, they do not think of a unit being one-half meter or of a unit being 2 feet. When students were asked to find the area of an irregular figure drawn on a grid, they did not attempt to count or compensate for partial units. They did not recognize fractional parts of a unit. Students incorrectly read a thermometer because they failed to recognize that each mark on the scale represented two degrees. Such common misconceptions interfere with a child's ability to measure.

Students should use non-standard units of measure to help them understand measurement (Hirstein, Lamb, & Osborne, 1978; Hiebert, 1981a; Hart, 1984). Students will compare two lengths by counting units but will fail to be concerned that the units are the same. They are too involved in associating a number with the length and do not understand what the number represents.

Students need to know they can choose units arbitrarily but that a single measurement is made by placing *congruent* units side by side to make a covering. If students are measuring the length of a room and the unit of measure is "book," they must choose *one* book to be the standard unit of measure. They cannot use a variety of books differing in length. The books must be placed without overlaps or vacant spaces. These ideas are not known or practiced by some students.

Using a variety of units in different measurement systems helps establish the idea of unit (Osborne, 1974). Students need to see different units measure the same item and the same unit measure different objects.

Unit Objectives

1. Students will use both ratio and ordinal scales to measure items.
2. Students will measure items using different units. They will understand that using different units results in different numbers representing the measurement of the same object.
3. Students will work with fractional units.
4. Students will work with multiple units.

Comparison Activities

List objects you wish to compare in length on separate posterboard cards.
1. Discuss the importance of making an agreement to work in a particular dimension. It is not possible to compare the length of a table to the area of a desktop.

2. Discuss estimating the length of items and supply some strategies for estimation (see Osborne, 1981).
3. As a class, arrange the cards in order corresponding to the longest object through the shortest object.
4. Be sure to discuss the strategies children are using. If the class cannot agree on the order of some pairs of objects, place the cards side by side to indicate the disagreement. Examine strategies for removing the disagreement.
5. With a new set of cards, make a second listing for ranking the objects by area of major surface (for example, desktop, largest face of a cupboard).
6. Compare the lists. Are the orders the same? Highlight these ideas.
   You did not use measuring instruments.
   You do not know the length or area of any object.
   Measurement of area is different from measurement of length.
7. When is this kind of ranking useful?

Arbitrary Units Activities

1. Discuss what kind of unit would be appropriate to measure the length or area of different objects. Encourage the students to consider a variety of objects such as shoes, hands, notebook paper, inches, meters. Be sure students choose units that can be placed end-to-end to measure length and units that will cover the surface area.
2. Measure objects on the list. Have different teams of students measure different items but each student should have a chance to use a variety of units. For example, team A will measure the table length using a shoe, a spoon, and a 12-inch ruler. Team B may measure the length of the teacher's desk using a shoe, a pencil, and a ruler.
3. Have the teams report their findings by taping their measurements to the list of items. Be sure the measurement includes the number of units *and* the unit (for example, shoe). Discuss why both pieces of information are important.
4. Repeat the activity but find measures of area rather than length.
5. Choose one unit and make a ratio scale (number line in terms of a selected unit) and illustrate where the items will fall on the scale.
6. The follow-up discussion should note if the use of the scale resolves the disagreements in ranking from Activity 1. Note that the first list only ranked the items. The second list with the scale gave an idea of how much bigger one object is than another. Discuss when you would want a ranking (ordinal) scale and when a ratio scale would be preferred.

Arbitrary and Standard Units Activity

Use the previous activities as a basis but now include the following ideas:

1. Discuss which units are appropriate for measuring a certain object and which are inappropriate. Have students defend their suggestions.
2. Have students use both standard and non-standard units.
3. Have students measure using fractional parts of a unit. If the length of a bookshelf is between eight and nine shoes, encourage students to choose eight and one-half or eight and one-quarter or whatever fractional part they think appropriate.
4. Construct and use a ratio scale in which marks represent and are labeled by two or more units.

Assignment

Devise a timetable, plan the physical arrangements, and collect the materials necessary to conduct these activities at a second-grade level and at a sixth-grade level. Compare the two grade levels. Highlight the changes you made and explain why.

FOUNDATIONAL IDEAS :

1. Units are arbitrary.
2. Standard units represent an agreement for purposes of communication.
3. Ranking items by size only shows a *comparison* of items.
4. Making a *number assignment* and placing items on a scale show a relative size comparison as well as a ranking.
5. A measurement is made by using congruent units to cover the dimension being measured.

AREA AND PERIMETER

The 1978 NAEP study confirmed that many student difficulties come from misconceptions rather than computational errors (Hirstein, 1981). A common misconception at all age levels is the confusion between area and perimeter (Anderson & Cuneo, 1976; Hirstein, Lamb, & Osborne, 1978; Hart, 1984). Twenty-three percent of the 13- and 17-year-old students tested gave the perimeter instead of the requested area on an item from the second NAEP study. Anderson and Cuneo report that primary students used a height plus a width strategy to estimate the area of rectangles. Hart reported children had difficulty believing the perimeter could change if the area stayed the same.

Some children do not understand perimeter is a linear measure of one dimension and area is a surface measure of two dimensions. Children need experiences covering linear distances and covering regions with units to focus attention on the attributes. A common error in measuring both length and area is to count points rather than to think in terms of covering. Students may think length is the only dimension necessary for estimating area. For both length and area, students may allow units to overlap and may not cover the entire figure. The teacher should look for these errors as the children work. Use and placement of physical units to cover help children who exhibit these misconceptions.

Area and Perimeter Objectives

1. Help students distinguish the attributes of distance covering (length) and surface covering (area).
2. Help students learn that perimeter is a measure of length.
3. Help students realize area is a measure of a covering by two-dimensional units.
4. Encourage students to explore the relationship between area and perimeter.

BEGINNING ACTIVITY (PRIMARY GRADES)

1. Create one-dimensional units called "sticks" by cutting a toothpick in two congruent pieces. Create two-dimensional units by cutting construction paper squares one stick wide. Give each student a set of 12 sticks and 10 squares and a paper with both one- and two-dimensional figures. Discuss with the class which unit is appropriate for measuring each figure. If you are working with a two-dimensional figure, you must specify whether you are measuring area or perimeter. (You can measure both in two-dimensional figures.) Figure 4–21 offers some suggestions.
2. Draw rectangles with various orientations on poster board or on worksheets. Include the following sizes (in sticks): one by five, two by four, three by three, two by three, two by two, and one by three. Ask students to measure the perimeter by placing and counting sticks around the outside of the figures.
3. Use the same figures and ask students to measure the areas by placing square units so that the interiors are covered without overlap or gaps.
4. Help students keep a record of the perimeter and area for each rectangle by creating a table of all the information. Display the rectangles with the table.

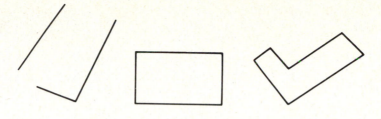

FIGURE 4–21
One- and two-
dimensional figures

Assignment

Complete Activities 1 through 3 above. Make a list of questions you would use in class discussion to focus on the attributes of length and area. What points would you emphasize to help students realize length must be measured by a one-dimensional unit and area by a two-dimensional unit?

Extension 1 (Upper Elementary)

Increase the number of sticks and squares to 20 for each student.

1. Have students design their own figures and then find the area and perimeter of each. Require students to build a table to keep the information orderly and encourage them to look for patterns. Suggest figures like those shown in Fig. 4–22.
2. Challenge students to make a rectangle with the number of sticks in the perimeter equal to the number of squares in the area.
3. Ask students to make two rectangles each having an area of 16 square units. One rectangle should have as many sticks as possible in the perimeter; the other as few as possible.

FIGURE 4–22
Area and peri-
meter for different
figures

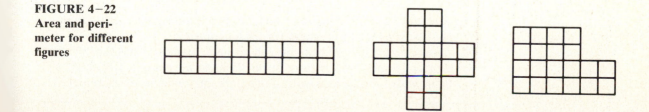

Assignment

Complete Activities 2 and 3. List the length and width of each rectangle you tried. What did you gain by the trial and error process that might have been lost if a teacher had demonstrated the solutions and asked the students to imitate the solutions?

Extension 2 (Middle School)

Using graph paper (centimeter square) and a ruler, design some figures that are rectangles or are built by joining rectangles. Find both perimeter and area of each figure. Present challenges similar to the following:

1. Make a figure with a perimeter of 20 units but the smallest possible area.
2. Make the number of units in the perimeter twice the number of square units in the area.
3. Make the number of units in the area twice the number of units in the perimeter.
4. Draw two figures that have the same area but do not look alike (are not congruent).
5. You have 36 feet of fence and want to fence a garden in the shape of a rectangle against a wall. Draw a picture of the shape of the fenced garden with the largest area.

Assignment

Plan a set of activities using geoboards that would teach the same objectives as the graph paper activities.

FOUNDATIONAL IDEAS:

1. By counting either one-dimensional or two-dimensional units, a *number assignment* can be made for each measure.
2. A *comparison* of line segments can be made to see which is shorter. A shorter segment will require fewer sticks to measure it. Similarly, a figure with a greater area will require more squares in the measurement.

FORMULAS FOR MEASURE

Formulas for measurement are typical goals for the upper elementary school and middle school students. Formula learning is important because it makes measurement significantly easier if you are successful in learning the formulas *and* in recognizing when to apply them. Interviews of numerous children (see, for example, Hart, 1980; Hirstein, Lamb, & Osborne, 1978) indicate that many children who have difficulty in remembering formulas have an inadequate understanding of the basis of the measurement systems. Whether they remember the formula matters little because they have little sense of what measure is. Thus, teaching measurement formulas is a waste of a teacher's effort if the majority of students in the classroom do not have the foundational ideas under control.

Establishing the Formula

Before teaching measurement formulas, the teacher should use diagnostic procedures to see whether students understand the fundamentals of the measure.

The purpose of teaching a formula for measurement is to save children a considerable amount of work and time. Formulas are for dealing with frequently encountered measurement situations. Formulas help the learner by structuring the memory to focus on relevant features in the measurement situation. In the case of the formula for the area of a parallelogram, the A triggers the notion of area, the b that of the length of a base, and h that of the height of the parallelogram, and then provides the relation among them. Instruction must provide a rich set of examples.

Establishing a formula with children should be approached from the standpoint of making a generalization across many different cases. The generalization process should incorporate the relevant geometric characteristics of the situation. In the case of a rectangle, initial encounters with the area formula should reach back to counting area units and puzzling through the relation to the lengths of the sides (see Fig. 4–23). The child should encounter numerous situations that allow counting before withdrawal of perceptual supports. Using Fig. 4–23 as an example, children should count the number of area units, 28,

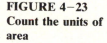

FIGURE 4–23
Count the units of area

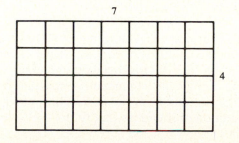

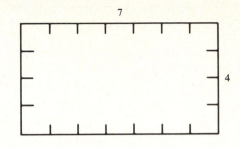

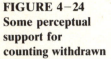

**FIGURE 4—24
Some perceptual
support for
counting withdrawn**

and the number of length units in the base, 7, and in the height, 4. This helps to relate the ideas of the two-dimensional measure of area and the one-dimensional measure of length for the base and height.

It still is too early to introduce the area formula. First, withdraw some of the perceptual support for the counting (see Fig. 4—24). Consider the previous sample of the rectangle with base 7 and a height of 4. Again, the stress should be on the relation in the triple of 28 area units, 7 length units, and 4 length units. You are trying to help the children move to thinking in terms of the relationship between measurements and labels that will be the foundations for the formula. Ask students to describe or state orally a computation rule for area of rectangles.

Vary the situation by giving the children the problem of finding either the base or the height when they are given the area measure and either the height or base measure, respectively. Look for other ways to vary the situation. Examine rectangles that are not oriented vertically and horizontally. Move children from looking only at dimensions that are whole numbers. Insofar as possible, maintain a problem-solving orientation.

The sequence of steps leading to the generalization were designed to:

1. Focus on the attributes represented by the variables in the formula
2. Provide ample opportunity to count and compute before starting a rule
3. Allow children to talk about the rule before capturing it with variables
4. Pose problems based on different critical elements in the formula
5. Provide experience with numerous examples before formalization of the formula.

Learning When to Use the Formula

The next step is to help students with retrieval of the formulas. Recognizing when to use a formula is a skill separate and distinct from remembering the formula. Many teachers take children to task for failure to remember a formula when the problem is not a matter of memory but rather that nothing cues the child to retrieve the formula from memory. Thus, children need tasks that focus on the recognition of situations that fit the use of the formula. Provide ample opportunities.

CHAPTER 4 SUMMARY

This chapter used research results to suggest teaching approaches for measure and measurement. Most of the research about how children measure and think about measurement does not indicate specifically and directly how the teacher should behave or plan for instruction. Rather research has focused on what children cannot do and do not understand. The principles of instruction advocated are inferred from this research evidence, from the mathematics of measure, and from considerable experience in teaching young children about measurement.

By way of summary, the following principles in teaching are offered:

1. Children must measure frequently and often, preferably on real problem tasks rather than textbook exercises.
2. Children should encounter activity-oriented measurement situations with them doing and experimenting rather than passively observing. The activities should encourage discussion to stimulate the refinement and testing of ideas and concepts through oral interactions.
3. The best sequence for introducing children to a measure system is
   a. Focus on the attributes that characterize the measure of making comparisons.
   b. Use arbitrary units for measurement tasks.
   c. Design activities for foundational ideas.
   d. Use a standard unit for measurement tasks.
   e. Provide children with opportunities to use the measurement ideas and skills they have learned.
4. The emphasis in instructional planning should be on the important foundational ideas of measurement which transfer or work across measurement systems.
5. Do not rush the teaching of formulas for measurement: rather wait until the children have an adequate understanding to make the generalization—the formula.

REFERENCES

Anderson, N. H., & Cuneo, D. O. 1978. The height and width rule in children's judgments of quantity. *Journal of Experimental Psychology,* 107:335–378.

Bailey, J. H. 1971. The concept of transitivity in children. *Dissertation Abstracts International,* 31B:7618.

Beilin, H. 1964. Perceptual-cognitive conflict in the development of an invariant area concept. *Journal of Experimental Child Psychology,* 1:208–226.

Beilin, H. 1971. The training and acquisition of logical operations. *Piagetian-cognitive development research and mathematical education.* In M. F. Rosskopf, L. P. Steffe, & S. Taback (Eds.), Washington, DC: National Council of Teachers of Mathematics.

Carpenter, T. P. 1976. Analysis and synthesis of existing research on measurement. In

R. A. Lesh (Ed.), *Number and measurement: Papers from a research workshop.* Columbus, OH: ERIC Clearinghouse for Science, Math and Environmental Education.

Carpenter, T., Coburn, T., Reys, R., & Wilson, J. 1978. *Results from the First Mathematics Assessment of the National Assessment of Educational Progress.* Reston, VA: National Council of Teachers of Mathematics.

Driscoll, M. J. 1981. Measurement in elementary school mathematics. In *Research within reach,* CEMREL, Inc. Reston, VA: National Council of Teachers of Mathematics, pp. 29–36.

Hart, K. M. 1980. *Secondary school children's understanding of mathematics* (research monograph). In D. C. Johnson (Ed). Mathematics Education Centre for Science Education, Chelsea College, University of London.

Hart, K. 1984. Which comes first—length, area, or volume? *Arithmetic Teacher,* 31(9):16–18, 26–27.

Hiebert, J. 1981. Cognitive development and learning linear measurement. *Journal for Research in Mathematics Education,* 12(3):197–211.

Hiebert, J. 1981b. Units of measure: Results and implications from National Assessment. *Arithmetic Teacher,* 28(6):38–43.

Higgins, J. L. 1974. *A metric handbook for teachers.* Reston, VA: National Council of Teachers of Mathematics.

Hirstein, J. 1981. The second National Assessment in Mathematics: Area and volume. *The Mathematics Teacher,* 74(9):704–708.

Hirstein, J., Lamb, C., & Osborne, A. 1978. Student misconceptions about area measure. *Arithmetic Teacher,* 25(6):10–16.

Kieren, T. E. 1976. On the mathematical cognitive and instructional foundations of rational numbers. In R. A. Lesh (Ed.), *Number and measurement: papers from a research workshop.* Columbus, OH: ERIC Clearinghouse for Science, Math and Environmental Education.

National Assessment of Educational Progress (NAEP). 1979. *Changes in mathematical achievement, 1973–1978,* Report No. 09-MA-01. Denver, CO: Education Commission of the States.

Mathematical Knowledge and Skills, Report No. 09-MA-02.

Mathematical Applications, Report No. 09-MA-04.

Nelson, D., & Reys, R. E. 1976. *Measurement in school mathematics.* National Council of Teachers of Mathematics Yearbook. Reston, VA: National Council of Teachers of Mathematics.

Osborne, A. R. 1974. Metrification, measure and mathematics. In Jon Higgins (Ed.), *A metric handbook for teachers* (pp. 107–137). Reston, VA: National Council of Teachers of Mathematics.

Osborne, A. R. 1976. The mathematical and psychological foundations of measure. In R. A. Lesh (Ed.), *Number and measurement: Papers from a research workshop.* Columbus, OH: ERIC Clearinghouse for Science, Math and Environmental Education.

Osborne, Alan. 1981. Measurement: How much? In Mary Lindquist (Ed.), *Selected issues in mathematics education* (pp. 54–68). Chicago, IL: National Society for Study of Education.

Piaget, J., Inhelder, B., & Szeminska, A. 1960. *The child's conception of geometry* (E. A. Leenzer, Trans.) New York: Basic Books.

Smedslund, J. 1963. Development of concrete transitivity of length in children. *Child Development* 34:389–405.

Wilson, P. S. 1986. Feature frequency and the use of negative instances in a geometric task. *Journal for Research in Mathematics Education.* 17(2):130–139.

5 Arithmetic Operations on Whole Numbers: Addition and Subtraction

JAMES M. MOSER

Wisconsin Department of Public Instruction

INTRODUCTION

There is a maxim that says, "There is nothing quite so practical as a good theory." While it was originally coined in reference to educational research, the saying has relevance for classroom practice. Classroom learning activities must be based on what a teacher believes to be true about mathematics and about pedagogical practice. If a teacher does not have a sound underlying rationale for what goes on in the classroom, then chances are the learning activities will not be as effective as they might be. On the other hand, the teacher also needs some guidance on what to do on a daily basis—the "nuts and bolts" so to speak. To some degree the basic textbook and teacher's guide provide that help. But other sources of ideas must be identified.

The goal of this chapter is to seek some balance between helpful hints on classroom practice and a presentation of selected research findings to assist the teacher in developing a sound rationale for mathematics instruction in the area of whole number addition and subtraction.

THE ROLE OF WHOLE NUMBER ADDITION AND SUBTRACTION IN THE SCHOOL MATHEMATICS CURRICULUM

Advances in electronic technology have catapulted the world at the end of the twentieth century into the Information Age. We now realize that well-educated persons must be quantitatively literate regardless of their field of endeavor. Despite the fact that computers and calculators can perform difficult and tedious calculations with amazing speed and accuracy, the understanding of and the facility with arithmetic computation are still important objectives of school mathematics instruction.

In 1980 the National Council of Teachers of Mathematics (NCTM) published *An Agenda for Action: Recommendations for School Mathematics of the 1980s* (NCTM, 1980). Although the title speaks of the 1980s, the recommendations have and will influence instruction in the 1990s and beyond also. The primary recommendation is that problem solving be the focus of mathematics instruction. Within such a context, computation becomes a means toward the end of problem solving and not an end in itself. Assuming the need for computation arises out of a real-world problem, then what constitutes computational efficiency? Characteristics are

- Realize computation of some sort is required
- Know what arithmetic operation(s) are needed
- Decide which method of computation to use—mental computation, paper-and-pencil, mental estimation, or calculator or computer
- Use the decided-upon method with a minimum chance of error.

Thus, there is more to consider as computational efficiency than simply proficiency with paper-and-pencil algorithms.

The reader should not draw the conclusion that the ability to use mental or paper-and-pencil algorithms and to know basic number facts are not important. Quite the contrary. But, arithmetic and mathematics should not be equated with computation only. As *An Agenda for Action* (NCTM, 1980), other influential reports issued during the 1980s,[1] and other chapters of this book readily attest, the contemporary view of mathematics is that it must encompass a broad view with problem solving as a major unifying goal. Nonetheless, number sense and an ability to "work" with numbers must be addressed.

Within the general area of mathematics instruction, addition and subtraction hold a special place. These two operations are the child's first exposure to formal mathematics and occupy much of the mathematics curriculum during

---

[1]See, for example, Conference Board of Mathematical Sciences 1982. *The Mathematical Sciences Curriculum K-12: What is Still Fundamental and What is Not.* Washington, D.C.: National Science Foundation; National Commission on Excellence in Education 1983. *A Nation at Risk: The Imperative for Educational Reform.* Washington, D.C.: U.S. Department of Education.

the first several years of schooling. Thus, it is frequently the case that permanent attitudes and ways of thinking mathematically are formed during this period. Addition and subtraction are basically abstract operations whose meanings are rooted in physical, pictorial, verbal, and mental manipulations of real-world problem situations. The building of the bridges between the concrete and the abstract takes place during the early years of formal mathematics instruction.

One of the basic strengths of mathematics is that it allows a modeling of real-world entities and problems by mathematical symbols. Then the symbols themselves may be manipulated, processed, and operated on to produce a solution. The solution can then be related back to the real-world situation. The initial stages of learning the skill of mathematical modeling and problem solving occur as the child is dealing with addition and subtraction in the primary grades. Thus, proper teaching and learning of these two operations are of fundamental importance to mathematics instruction.

RESEARCH RELATED TO THE LEARNING OF ADDITION AND SUBTRACTION

Addition and subtraction have proven to be very popular subjects for researchers for many years. The content domain is fairly tightly defined, which allows for carefully controlled experimentation and observation. On the other hand, pupil response has been sufficiently varied and rich to make the results interesting. The age of the subjects has turned out to be a positive factor because in many cases the children have not been overly affected by formal school instruction, thereby permitting naturalistic studies of behavior. And finally, the results of the research have had a great deal of direct classroom applicability because the content is such a major part of the early school curriculum.

Conceptual Fields

The contemporary French psychologist, Gerard Vergnaud, describes a conceptual field as an "informal and heterogeneous set of problems, situations, concepts, relationships, structures, contents, and operations of thought, connected to one another and likely to be interwoven during the process of acquisition" (Vergnaud, 1982, p. 40). In a sense Vergnaud is suggesting there is a "big picture" such as in a jigsaw puzzle, having lots of parts that fit together. As some parts are assembled, one can get a partial picture, but to get the whole thing, all the parts have to fit. Putting all of them together takes a long time. In the conceptual field of additive structures, the acquisition of total understanding can begin at age 3 or 4 and last until at least age 15 or 16.

Figure 5–1 shows a stylized diagram of a portion of the conceptual field for addition and subtraction. For example, the large nodes could represent such big ideas as numeration, place value, algorithms, number sentences, inverse

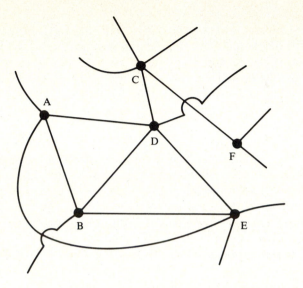

FIGURE 5–1
Schematic representation of part of a conceptual field

relationship between addition and subtraction, order relations such as greater than or less than, counting-on, and so forth. No big idea stands alone, but is connected in one or more ways with others. From a learning point of view, the more connections there are between major ideas, the better the learning and the greater the likelihood of recalling information and skills. A key implication for teachers is the importance of helping students to make the connections between ideas. While these connections are often made automatically as the learner organizes and structures knowledge internally, research on metacognition has shown that explicit mention by a teacher can facilitate this structuring of knowledge.

Early Number Concepts

Much of the focus on preschool research is on the acquisition of the concept of number (Carpenter, Moser, & Romberg, 1982; Ginsburg, 1977; Rea & Reys, 1970). There is not complete agreement among researchers and psychologists on just how the concept is developed although all would agree it does so over a period of years. But it is clear the following elements are involved:

- Classification—The ability to group a collection of objects together on the basis of a common quality or attribute
- Seriation—The ability to put a collection of entities in order from smaller to larger
- Conservation—The ability to recognize that the numerosity ("how-many-ness") of a set is unaffected by the position or conformation of the elements of that set or by a change in position of the elements

- Subitizing—The ability to immediately perceive the numerosity of a set (usually no more than four or five elements) without counting the individual elements
- Counting—The ability to determine the numerosity of a set through an association of counting words with elements of that set.

A major finding is that children do not come to school completely ignorant of arithmetic. They have some very strong fixed ideas (not always correct), which Ginsburg (1977) calls informal arithmetic in the sense that ideas and notions of what constitutes "arithmetic" have been constructed by the young child independent of formal school instruction. Much of this knowledge depends on social transmission, often coming from parents or older siblings. Ginsburg believes that counting plays such an important role in children's concept of number that even after formal instruction, "the great majority of young children interpret arithmetic as counting" (Ginsburg, 1977, p. 13).

Counting

American researcher Rochel Gelman (Gelman & Gallistel, 1978) has theorized five counting principles that define a successful counting experience.

1. *The one–one principle.*   Each item in a set to be counted must be assigned one and only one label. This involves partitioning the objects of the set at each count into two sets—those that have been counted and those that are yet to be counted.
2. *The stable order principle.*   The number words that are uttered must come from the same list of words, ordered in exactly the same way, for each repetition of the counting act.
3. *The cardinal principle.*   The final word assigned to a set identifies the numerosity of that set.
4. *The abstraction principle.*   Any collection of objects whatsoever may constitute a set to be counted.
5. *The order irrelevance principle.*   The order in which the objects of the set are tagged with a number name has no effect on the counting process nor on the numerosity of the set.

For efficient counting it is necessary that the child eventually memorize the so-called standard number word sequence (SNWS), "one, two, three, four, five, six, and so forth." Yet, the recitation of some correct portion of the SNWS should not be taken as evidence of a complete understanding of "number" or of the counting process. Leslie Steffe and his colleagues at the University of Georgia (Steffe, Thompson, & Richards, 1982) argue that what is being counted is an indication of the degree of understanding and abstraction of number. Steffe identifies three major types of "items" that children count.

- *Perceptual unit items*—Things that can be seen and touched as they are being counted
- *Motor unit items*—The touching or pointing movement itself is the thing being counted. Actual objects need not be present
- *Abstract unit items*—Counting words themselves are being counted.

The abstract unit items includes the sophisticated Counting-On and Counting-Back procedures children frequently use to solve various addition and subtraction problems. These are actually double-counting techniques and may be completely subvocal, existing only at a mental level.

Numeration and Place Value

Although it is relevant to all areas of mathematical conceptual and skill development, the role of manipulative materials has been found to be particularly strong with regard to numeration. It is useful to remember a Piagetian finding that children's learning is a process of manipulating and mentally transforming the real world. Manipulation leads to understanding and abstraction, and it is only then that a child can fully accept the symbols attached to abstractions (Suydam & Weaver, 1975).

Place-value work is one area in which the question of multiembodiment comes up (Dienes, 1971). For example, hundreds, tens, and ones can be shown with multibase blocks (see Fig. 5–2), with two-dimensional graph paper models, with counting sticks bundled into tens and ten tens, or with an abacus. The notion of multiembodiment argues that symbols take on more meaning when the child is ready to think in terms of multiple events rather than in terms of a single event. Research suggests that multiembodiment may not affect immediate learning but there may be long-term benefit if the teacher is willing to teach children to generalize from one representation to the other.

Symbolic Problems

Basic Facts

In the first half of this century when the emphasis of arithmetic instruction was on repetition and drill, research concentrated on the basic fact combinations in an effort to determine which were the easiest to learn and which presented more difficulty (Brownell, 1941). Not unexpectedly, the smaller combinations with sums less than ten were found to be easier. Contemporary research has, in general, confirmed those earlier results but has extended them to suggest that number size alone is not the only predictor of ease of learning (Baroody, 1984; Beattie & Deichmann, 1972). It has been found that the doubles facts and their related subtraction facts (for example, $4 + 4, 5 + 5, 12 - 6$) are the easiest to learn. Also very easy to learn are the "zero" facts (for example, $3 + 0, 9 - 0$)

and the successor/predecessor facts (for example, $6 + 1$, $8 - 1$). Combinations of 10 (for example, $7 + 3$, $6 + 4$, $10 - 2$) and doubles-plus-one facts (for example, $5 + 6$, $4 + 5$) have also been found to be relatively easy for children to learn.

Closely related research has investigated pupil performance on open sentences (Weaver, 1971). Table 5–1 shows the various kinds of sentences, where the letters *a, b,* and *c* stand for whole numbers. In most studies the number size was limited to the basic fact domain of sums being 18 or less. The results suggest

- Open subtraction sentences are harder to solve than addition ones.
- Right-hand sentences are harder to solve than left-hand ones.
- Canonical sentences (*c* position) are the easiest to solve.
- Subtraction *a* position sentences are clearly the most difficult.
- Sentences with numbers between 20 and 100 are more difficult than those within the context of basic facts, even for older students.

Research on student solution procedures has shown a progression in sophistication of technique as students get older (Carpenter, Blume, Hiebert, Anick, & Pimm, 1982). Less sophisticated responses are counting based. Simpler versions use Counting-All or Counting-Back in which all counting sequences begin with the number "one" and are often executed with the assistance of manipulatives or fingers. The next level of sophistication involves more efficient counting such as Counting-On in which, for example, to find the sum of $3 + 6$, a child might say "six, . . ., seven, eight, NINE." Of course, many responses involve direct recall of basic facts in which acquisition of addition facts tends to precede subtraction.

Also observed in a number of studies was the use of so-called thinking strategies (Rathmell, 1978; Thornton, 1978), which means the use of certain memorized facts to derive the solution to other problems. Some of the more frequently observed strategies were

- *Doubles plus one (or two)*—$6 + 8 = ?$ "Six and six are twelve, so the answer must be two more, or fourteen."
- *Bridging through ten*—$8 + 5 = ?$ "Eight and two are ten, so three more makes thirteen."

TABLE 5–1
Types of Open Sentences

	Left-hand		Right-hand	
"a" Position	$\Box + b = c$	$\Box - b = c$	$c = \Box + b$	$c = \Box - b$
"b" Position	$a + \Box = c$	$a - \Box = c$	$c = a + \Box$	$c = a - \Box$
"c" Position	$a + b = \Box$	$a - b = \Box$	$\Box = a + b$	$\Box = a - b$

- *Compensation*—9 + 7 = ? "If I take one away from nine, that's eight. Then I give that one to seven and that also makes eight. Eight and eight are sixteen."
- *Subtracting through ten*—13 − 5 = ? "Thirteen take away three is ten. Then I take away two more from ten and that's eight."
- *Nine is one less than ten*—9 + 6 = ? "Ten and six are sixteen, the answer is one less than sixteen, and that's fifteen."

While some research has shown that many children will come up with one or more of these thinking strategies on their own (Thornton, 1978), other research has shown that children will not necessarily invent all of them and thus explicit teaching of a strategy is necessary if a teacher wants all children to be exposed to it. Even after explicit teaching, there is no guarantee a child will use the strategy (Steinberg, 1983).

Algorithms

Much of the current research on algorithms deals with the kinds of errors children make when computing. Some of the more useful results are

- Addition and subtraction without regrouping (carrying and borrowing) are relatively easy to master.
- Addition with regrouping is easier to learn than subtraction with regrouping.
- Subtraction problems that involve borrowing across zeroes (for example,

$$\begin{array}{r} 4003 \\ -1247 \\ \hline \end{array}$$

are the most difficult.
- Computational errors in algorithms are usually systematic. This means a child will consistently make the same kind of procedural error, following a routinized algorithm that may be quite correct except for a single "bug" somewhere in the procedure (Brown & VanLehn, 1980).

Another major line of research on algorithms concerns the use of manipulative materials when teaching the algorithms. Studies have found that using materials, such as the multibased blocks shown in Fig. 5−2 or bundled counting sticks, can lead to better understanding and to higher skill levels (Ekman, 1967; Gibb, 1956). When teaching regrouping, it has been found that each step of the algorithm must be seen as a representation of an action performed on the manipulatives. But the work must alternate between the operation on the objects and the symbolic recording of that operation within the algorithm. In other words, the child should not do all the work with the objects first and then turn to the symbolism (Resnick, 1982).

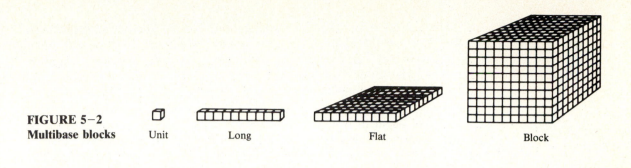

FIGURE 5–2
Multibase blocks   Unit   Long   Flat   Block

Verbal Problems

A number of contemporary researchers have been studying children's performance on verbal addition and subtraction problems as a way of determining what kind of meanings children assign to the operations of addition and subtraction as well as simply to measure their ability to solve certain classes of problems (Carpenter & Moser, 1983; Riley, Greeno, & Heller, 1983).

Table 5–2 lists four different kinds of verbal subtraction problems. Because all could be solved by using the symbolic sentence 14 − 9 = □, they are called subtraction problems. Yet each has a different semantic structure to describe how the entities of the problem are related one to another.

Some of the more important results can be summarized as follows:

- Young children, even kindergartners, are able to solve a variety of verbal problems. Certain problems, such as Separating problem in which the initial set is unknown, are very difficult, however, and are accessible only to older children.
- Action-oriented problems, such as Joining and Separating, in which the final resulting set is the unknown, tend to be the easiest for children to solve.
- Children do pay attention to the semantic structure of verbal problems and use differing strategies that correspond to those structures.

TABLE 5–2
Four Semantically Different Verbal Subtraction Problems

1. *Separating*. Wally had 14 marbles. He lost 9 of them in a game. How many marbles did Wally have left?

2. *Joining, missing addend*. Gloria had 9 candies. A friend gave her some more candies and then she had 14 of them. How many candies did Gloria's friend give her?

3. *Part-part-whole*. There are 14 dogs in the park. Nine of them are big dogs and the rest of them are small. How many small dogs are in the park?

4. *Comparison*. Joe won 9 prizes at the fair. His sister Connie won 14 prizes. How many more prizes did Connie win than Joe?

The last point merits some amplification. For the Separating problem in Table 5–2 a child might model it by constructing a set of 14 objects, then taking away 9 objects from that set, and determining the answer by counting the remainder set of 5 objects. At a more sophisticated level, the same child might use a Counting-Back procedure, "Fourteen, . . ., thirteen, twelve, eleven, ten, nine, eight, seven, six, FIVE." By contrast, the Joining, missing addend problem in Table 5–2 is solved using additive procedures. With objects, the child starts by constructing a set of 9 objects, then adds objects to that set one at a time until a set of 14 is accumulated. The answer is determined by counting the number of objects added on—in this example, five. The higher level counting analogue of this procedure is called Counting-Up, "nine, . . . , ten, eleven, twelve, thirteen, fourteen." By keeping track of the number of counting words uttered—in this example, five—the answer is determined. The implication of this protracted example is that a child does not have a unified notion of what constitutes subtraction (the addition situation is somewhat better advanced), but is bound by the context of the verbal problem being presented.

Several teams of psychologists have theorized what type of mental knowledge or mental presentation is necessary for children to have a unified understanding of addition/subtraction and the inverse relationship between these two operations, and thereby be able to solve all of the various classes of simple one-step verbal problems (Briars & Larkin, 1984; Riley et al., 1983). The consensus is that a complete understanding of the part-part-whole relationship is required. This entails recognizing that an entity (a whole) may be decomposed into component parts and that those parts may be reconstituted to produce the whole. It has been suggested that most children by the age of eight or nine years have developed a fairly complete understanding of the part-part-whole relationship.

PROVISIONS FOR INDIVIDUAL DIFFERENCES

Individual children vary on many attributes—gender, age, height, weight, hair color, ethnicity—and so when the question of individual differences comes up, the immediate response should be, "Differences on what attribute?" Teachers should not just focus on difference in intelligence or achievement but on other things such as learning styles, need for praise, ability to work with others, attention span, or presence of some handicapping condition.

Knowledge of an individual child's characteristics comes from a systematic program of evaluation. Evaluation does not mean administration of tests, but rather a process of gathering desired information. Two major sources of information are structured individual interviews and regular classroom observation. Though time-consuming, a one-on-one interview during which a child is asked to work one or two problems while the teacher-interviewer observes behavior and asks probing or leading questions can be an invaluable source of information. Classroom observations and interviews should be planned and scheduled just as much as instruction should be planned.

Children learn at different rates, but they also learn in different ways. This is particularly true for special education students. Thus, it is important to provide alternative approaches to the learning of a concept or the practicing of a skill. Sometimes a large group presentation works; at other times small groups of two or three can work together. The small group or pairing can be particularly effective if children are working on verbal problems and one child may be a poor reader or visually handicapped and the other is a good reader. There are some children (though not all!) who do like to work alone on printed worksheets; the sense of satisfaction on completing one or more such sheets provides a feeling of accomplishment. Many games can be used to good advantage, especially if the games have some element of chance to them and do not always favor the brighter students.

As an example, imagine a problem has been posed to find three numbers whose sum is 9. To a child who is having difficulty, ask what would happen if one of the numbers were 2. To another who has found that 2, 3, and 4 add up to 9, ask if another triple of numbers can be found. To a brighter child, ask if one of the three numbers can be 8; if not, what is the largest possible number that can be included. Such questions or variations on a single problem do not come by accident; they are planned by the resourceful teacher.

An orientation toward problem solving can accommodate individual differences, especially if the philosophy is adopted that there is more than one way to solve most problems. Consider, for example, a verbal Comparison problem involving the numbers six and nine, where the difference must be found. One child may construct a set of six cubes and a set of nine cubes, put the sets into one-to-one correspondence by a matching procedure, and then count the difference of three. Another child might use the Counting-Up procedure, "six, . . ., seven, eight, nine. The difference is three." Still another might employ the Counting-Back procedure, "nine, . . ., eight, seven, six. The difference is three." And yet another might use knowledge of basic facts, saying, "Nine take away six is three." None of the children are wrong, even though the problem-solving procedure was different for each. The accepting teacher who is concerned about individual differences will acknowledge all four responses and try to see that the various methods are understood by all students.

TEACHING ABOUT WHOLE NUMBER OPERATIONS OF ADDITION AND SUBTRACTION

Of necessity the following sections on number, numeration and place value, symbolic problems with its subsections on basic facts, open sentences, thinking strategies, algorithms, and verbal problems must be presented independently. However, the reader is reminded that the conceptual field of additive structures contains all these notions (and more) in a highly interconnected fashion. Thus the learning and teaching of the various aspects of whole number addition and subtraction cannot be carried out in an independent fashion. The teacher must be aware of the interrelationships and use them effectively to facilitate learning on the part of his or her pupils.

Number

Numerosity ("how-manyness") is a particular property of a set of discrete objects. Counting a set in order to assign a number to that set on the basis of the property of numerosity is actually a measurement process that is very fundamental to the acquisition of much of the informal arithmetic children bring to initial school experiences. Meaningful counting is not simply the recitation of a string of counting words; rather it is the association of a sequence of counting words with a collection of objects. There can be two distinct acts connected with meaningful counting. The first is the determination of the numerosity of a preexisting set and the other is the production of a set having a predetermined numerosity. In both cases, counting with its varying stages of sophistication and abstraction provides a basis for the understanding of number and number properties and for the understanding of the operations of addition and subtraction. The wise teacher takes this fact into account, and rather than try to discourage counting at too early a stage of development, helps the child become an efficient and accurate counter, recognizes how counting can be used to develop deeper understanding of number and addition/subtraction, and builds on these strengths in the conduct of lessons.

Nevertheless, counting is not the sole contributor to the development of number concepts. There are certain prenumerical activities in which children can engage. Young children should have many experiences with describing, classifying, and sorting sets. Describing is basic to language development and can be carried out in almost any context, many of which are not strictly numerical or mathematical in nature. Classmates, objects, events, homes, neighborhoods, pets, TV programs, and cars are some examples. Classifying is the process of sorting objects into sets on the basis of one or more attributes. Again, a variety of different objects and attributes can be used.

A nice way of sorting is to use graphic displays. Children can participate in a group activity in which objects to be sorted are drawn or displayed on cards that then become part of a bar graph. Figure 5−3 shows how commercial or teacher-prepared pictures can be used. All the children must do is cut out pictures and paste them on a graph. As an alternative the children draw their own pictures on three-by-five cards, or simply write their names above a picture drawn by the teacher.

Graphic displays permit other prenumerical activities such as comparing and ordering. Good problem-solving opportunities abound within the context of comparing and ordering, especially when the objects or sets to be compared cannot be placed side by side for direct comparison, or when the attribute is not readily observable. As examples, have children order two or more objects on weight when the only tool available is a simple balance, or order two or more irregularly shaped containers on the basis of their liquid capacity.

The variety of practical activities that deal directly with counting is almost limitless. Although the focus should be on meaningful counting, there are times when simple practice at recitation of the standard number word sequence (SNWS) is useful. Variations on recitation can include Counting-On and

FIGURE 5–3

Counting-Back, beginning with a number other than one, or skip counting by twos, fives, or tens. There is some safety and anonymity with reciting together in a large group, so there need not be concern if several students cannot keep up with others. A key to memorization is lots of repetition. However, there are many opportunities for meaningful learning even in repetitious activities. Aspects of order—greater than and less than—can be introduced by asking children whether a particular number comes before or after some other given number, or to name one or more numbers that come between two other given numbers.

Exercises

1. Explain why classification, seriation, and conservation are so important to the development of the concept of number.
2. Suppose you hear a child saying, "one, two, three, four, five" while she is pointing to five cubes on a desk, one at a time. Can you assume from this that the child is capable of counting with complete understanding? What other tasks or questions might you present to this child to get more information to decide?

3. Devise some counting tasks so you could assess whether a child is counting perceptual unit items, motor unit items, or abstract unit items, and is able to use the Counting-Up and Counting-Back procedures. Then use these tasks with several young children, preferably of differing ages.

4. A primary school—age child might look at two sets and state that one set is larger than the other when, in fact, the opposite is true. What might account for such an error? Devise two sets of objects to illustrate your reason(s). Then test several young children to see if the phenomenon described above might actually happen. Be sure to have children count the sets in question as part of the testing procedure.

Numeration and Place Value

The term "numeration" is taken to mean the association of some symbolic representation with a real or imagined set of objects or with a single object or event of a particular measure. Ordinarily, the symbolic representation will be the familiar numerals such as 2, 13, or 986. Yet other types of symbols such as tally marks, domino patterns, or Roman numerals could be used. The association of a symbol with an entity includes both recognition and reproduction of symbols as well as the ability to read the symbol.

The process of symbolic representation is of fundamental importance. Adults take for granted the ability to visually process symbolic information, whether it be numerical or literal. The very fact that you can read this page or make sense of the equation $45 + 27 = 72$ is testimony to your ability to function at an abstract level. Yet this is a learned skill that young children may not yet have attained.

The association of symbols with sets or with a single object goes both ways. Given a symbol, a child should be able to produce a set having the numerosity corresponding to that symbol, and given a set a child should be able to produce or recognize the symbol that describes the set. The symbol can be produced by actually writing the appropriate numeral or by selecting a numeral from a collection of already written numerals.

Often there is concern about beginners who write numerals backwards. While this might seem to be a cause for concern, it need not be. It is a phase some children go through, but with sufficient practice and gentle reminders from the teacher, they grow out of it. Usually when a child writes a numeral backwards, that child can still tell you what the numeral is supposed to be and does recognize that it is written backwards.

In many commercial textbook series the so-called name for a number often appears (for example, $5 + 1$, $2 + 4$, or $9 - 3$ as "names" for the number 6). These are quite a bit more complex than a simple numeral. What makes things more complex from the child's point of view is that a typical interpretation for the $+$ or $-$ symbol is not some neutral representation of an abstract operation but rather as standing for some action of joining or separating.

Several research studies have found that children reject as meaningless the symbolism of 5 + 1 and insist that it be written as $5 + 1 = \square$ or $5 + 1 = 6$. Also, exercises such as $5 + 1 = 9 - \square$ may have little or no meaning and children will cross out the right side of the equation and replace it with a 6. This means the = symbol is not read as "another name for" but is interpreted as "Complete the action on the left" or "Give the answer." Caution is advised with premature use of these "names for a number."

Simple numeration activities can be carried out by displaying pictured sets on an overhead or flannelboard. Children can select a numeral from a set of numeral cards at their seats or they can come to the flannelboard and place a proper felt numeral on the board. With such an activity they may also write appropriate numerals on a worksheet at their seats. Writing on the chalkboard is not recommended for very young children because their motor skills may not be properly developed.

Another activity is to give children printed worksheets on which numerals are printed. Their task would be to find in magazines or newspapers pictured sets to match each numeral. This activity serves to bring mathematics out of the classroom and to inject some measure of reality into the children's work.

Graphing and some preliminary statistical ideas may also be brought into activities. Using graph paper (see Fig. 5–4), the child colors in the appropriate number of squares above the numerals. The advantage of the geometric patterns is that there may be some incidental learning of other subjects taking place—geometry, pattern recognition, order of numbers. This particular example gets at an important general principle teachers should try to follow—if an activity can have several desirable learning outcomes, it should be chosen over one with a single focus.

As an example of an exercise that deals with numeration but also with some preliminary notions of addition, subtraction, and the part-part-whole relationship, consider the worksheet shown in Fig. 5–5. Give a child a small piece of string or yarn and a set of washers, counting chips, or other nonrolling objects. Have the child spread out the objects on the desk or floor and then partition the set into two parts by placing the string through the set (see Fig. 5–5a). Then the child records the results on the sheet shown in Fig. 5–5b. Repositioning the string can provide some variations. Changing the size of the set also allows for meaningful repetition of this activity. The same general effect can be achieved by using Hainstock blocks.

Activities dealing with the writing and recognition of numerals should involve seeing the numerals in their proper order. Bulletin board or individual desk copies of the number line are appropriate. Interesting activities for the classroom, gymnasium, or playground center around large copies of a number line on which children can actually pace out the intervals between numbers. Both backward and forward movements accompanied by oral recitation of the numbers are advised. Written records of movements should involve a starting point, an ending point, and the number of steps to go from one to the other.

Figural patterns for numbers are symbolic but not nearly as abstract as numerals. Domino configurations and the ones on playing cards have appeal because many children may have become familiar with them through play at

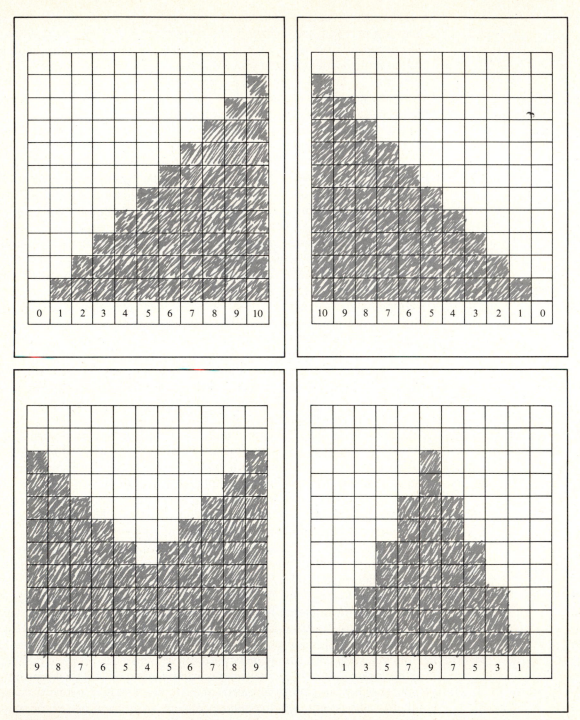

FIGURE 5-4

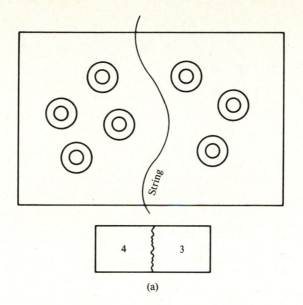

(a)

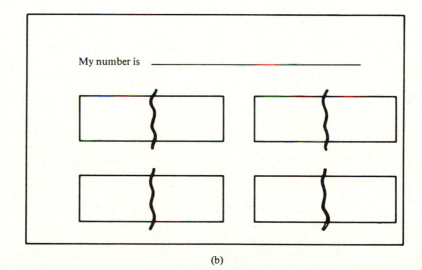

FIGURE 5-5   (b)

home. Some incidental learning also can come from figural patterns. Take, for example, some of the patterns for the number six shown in Fig. 5–6. Six can be seen to be equal to $1 + 2 + 3$, three 2s and two 3s. The geometric patterns—triangular, rectangular, and hexagonal—serve to break down any artificial barriers between geometry and arithmetic.

As quantities become larger, the necessity of considering place value notation naturally arises. There are several key aspects children must learn.

FIGURE 5–6
Some figural
patterns for the
number six

- It is a base ten system with only ten symbols being used. Though apparently chosen because humans have ten fingers, the use of ten as a base is completely arbitrary. Systems with other bases are possible, and some such as binary (base two) and octal (base eight) are used.
- It is a positional system. The position or location of any of the ten symbols within a numeral determines the value that symbol represents. For example, in 27,302 the initial 2 represents 20,000 (or 2 ten-thousands) whereas the final 2 represents simply 2 (or 2 ones).
- Explicit grouping rules and procedures exist. Ten is thought of as 10 ones, hundred as 10 tens, thousands as 10 hundreds, and so on.
- Reading or writing the oral names for numbers involves a double positional scheme in which every block of three digits—hundreds, tens, ones—has its own particular name, except for the first (see Fig. 5–7).

It is important to keep in mind that the numbers being represented by place value notation are or can be associated with some real object or set. In actual practice it is sometimes difficult to assemble and have each child work with large sets. But, to the degree possible, children should have opportunities to actually count large sets, keeping in mind that the amount of experience in counting such large sets will never approach the amount of similar practice they have had with smaller sets.

Most children will be able to recite correctly a sizeable portion of the standard number word sequence (SNWS) before formal instruction on place value begins. This ability should not be taken as evidence of understanding place value, although knowing the repetitive patterns for each decade (twenty, twenty-one, twenty-two, . . ., thirty, thirty-one, thirty-two, . . ., and so forth) does indicate a solid base on which to build such understanding. Using knowledge of the SNWS and counting skills, children should be required to count large sets. Confusion that may arise from keeping track of such large sets and

FIGURE 5–7
Block system of
naming numbers

Quadrillions	Trillions	Billions	Millions	Thousands	Ones
Hundreds Tens Ones	Hundreds Tens Ones	Hundreds Tens Ones	Hundreds Tens Ones	Hundreds Tens Ones	Hundreds Tens Ones
3 5 6 ,	2 6 1 ,	5 9 0 ,	0 4 7 ,	2 2 8 ,	1 9 5

the requirement of restarting at "one" if a count is lost can give motivation for the need for grouping by tens. At the start objects that lend themselves nicely to physical grouping should be chosen. Counting sticks and rubber bands, attachable cubes such as Unifix, or chips that can be stacked are good possibilities. Written records of grouping should be made on charts such as the one shown in Fig. 5–8.

Having large sets of physical materials to be grouped together begins to get impractical as the size of the sets increases into the hundreds and thousands. Structured materials such as the multibase blocks shown in Fig. 5–2 are available for teacher demonstration or individual pupil use. Graph paper squares can be duplicated for student use. Figure 5–9 shows arrangements up to 100, but if a very small unit square such as one millimeter is used as the unit, it is possible to get up to 1000 squares in one piece. A particular feature of these types of materials is that the objects are already grouped in tens, hundreds, or thousands and cannot be ungrouped into smaller groups. Thus, the need for trading ten of one group for one of the next larger group, or vice versa, arises. Trading, as opposed to actual physical grouping and ungrouping, should not pose any difficulty for children.

All of the materials discussed thus far are one-for-one in nature. At a higher level of abstraction are the one-for-ten materials in which one single object stands for ten of another type of object. Thus, objects take on differing values by reason of shape, color, or position. With money one dime equals ten cents and one dollar equals ten dimes or one hundred cents. Colored chips are often used in place value activities; for example, a white chip represents the unit value of one, a blue chip represents ten white chips (a ten), a red chip represents ten blue chips (a hundred or 10 tens), and so on. The best known instance of the one-for-ten manipulative that uses position to indicate a particular value is the abacus. Figure 5–10 shows two versions of the abacus, one with ten beads and one with an intermediate grouping of five. When using physical materials,

FIGURE 5–8

Place Value

ten thousands	thousands	hundreds	tens	ones
		6	7	2

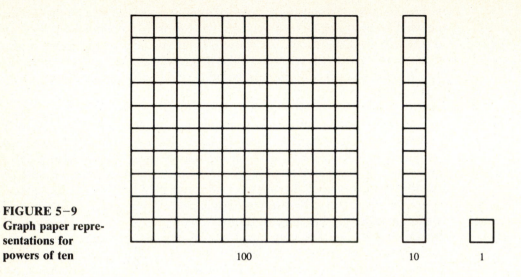

FIGURE 5–9
Graph paper representations for powers of ten

100   10   1

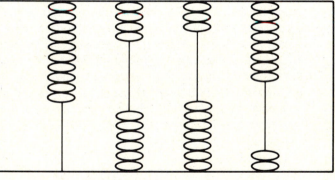

FIGURE 5–10
a, **Ten-bead abacus showing the number 672;** *b,* **five-bead abacus showing the number 672**

a   Ten-bead Abacus Showing the Number 672

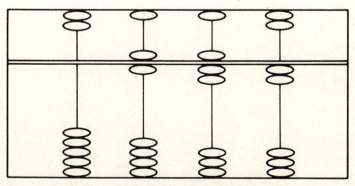

b   Five-bead Abacus Showing the Number 672

the one-for-one materials should precede the one-for-ten materials because they are less abstract.

When building the bridge to strictly symbolic notation, the use of expanded notation is recommended, for example, 356 = 300 + 50 + 6 or 356 = 3 hundreds + 5 tens + 6 ones. In actual practice the particular textbook series in a school determines the choice of what form of expanded notation is used.

A way of becoming familiar with both compact and expanded notation is suggested by the cards shown in Fig. 5–11. Three different ways of writing the same number are illustrated. Make sets of three for as many different numbers as desired, and with as many digits as desired, on plain white cards or card stock. The cards can then be used to play some familiar card games such as Concentration, Fish, or War.

During early stages of learning place value numeration, the ten-by-ten numeral chart shown in Fig. 5–12 is useful. The recurring pattern of the ones digits in each decade is shown by the columns, and the rows show how the tens digits increase. A completed chart can be displayed in the front of the room while each child can have a copy at his seat. This chart is also helpful when addition and subtraction are introduced.

FIGURE 5–11

FIGURE 5–12

0	1	2	3	4	5	6	7	8	9
10	11	12	13	14	15	16	17	18	19
20	21	22	23	24	25	26	27	28	29
30	31	32	33	34	35	36	37	38	39
40	41	42	43	44	45	46	47	48	49
50	51	52	53	54	55	56	57	58	59
60	61	62	63	64	65	66	67	68	69
70	71	72	73	74	75	76	77	78	79
80	81	82	83	84	85	86	87	88	89
90	91	92	93	94	95	96	97	98	99

The use of a calculator is strongly recommended as an adjunct to counting activities in which the entities are being counted are the physical depressions of the ⌐=⌐ key. Many calculators can be made to count by ones, by tens, by hundreds, and so on. Once set up, the calculator display will count as high and as fast as the child likes, simply by repeatedly depressing the ⌐=⌐ key. It is important to have the child look at the display and observe how the ones and/or tens digits change, particularly at every tenth depression.

Another calculator activity pairs children with a single calculator and has them combine what they know about place value with some simple addition and subtraction. One child can enter a multidigit number, say 493. The object is to have the other child change one of the digits by a single addition or subtraction. For example, "change the 9 to a 5" requires the subtraction of 40; "change the 4 to a 7" requires the addition of 300.

Exercises

1. Survey two or three current textbook series to identify what kinds of pictorial models they use to develop place value ideas—blocks, bundled sticks, abacus, or others. If any use more than one model at the same grade level, evaluate the instructional suggestions to determine if the multiple usage is helpful or possibly confusing to the student.
2. Enumerate the advantages and disadvantages that could have resulted if the inventors of our place value system had decided to use the number of fingers on one hand as the base. In other words, what would things be like if the world used a base five system?
3. The American Dozenal Society meets each year, presumably to extol the virtues of the number 12. Enumerate the various aspects of our daily lives that involve 12 or multiples of 12. What might be the advantages of using a base 12 numeration system?
4. Differentiate between a number system and a numeration system.
5. What properties of the base ten numeration system are also present in the Roman numeral system?

SYMBOLIC PROBLEMS

Basic Facts

It has been pointed out that children can assign different real-world interpretations to addition and subtraction and that they can also use a variety of sophisticated counting procedures to determine answers to problems. The concern here is with the internalization of the basic facts. Even though computing machines are available it is still absolutely necessary to be able to rapidly and correctly respond to basic computational fact situations.

The possibility exists that for basic facts a child may be executing a retrieval procedure to find and then recite a fact stored in long-term memory. On the other hand, that child may be using some very rapid production system that generates an answer to a particular number combination. The truth may be that the child is capable of both and is employing some idiosyncratic choice procedure that at one time uses a retrieval procedure and at other times the production system. In actual practice it really doesn't matter which method is used so long as the child can perform rapidly and correctly. The criterion for what constitutes a rapid response should be left to the individual teacher and how that teacher wants to deal with individual students Despite the folklore associated with the practice, there is nothing special about doing 100 facts in three minutes or less with a maximum of n errors allowed.

It is worthwhile to consider what some of the proposed principles of fact generation are. The first is the $N + 0$ and $0 + N$ principle, which is recognized as the identity element for addition. The suggestion is that children learn this principle fairly easily and rather than store all the zero addition facts separately in memory, they simply invoke the principle when appropriate. A second principle is the $N + 1$ and $1 + N$ relationship, which can be described as the "successor function." When presented with a basic addition fact of this type the child uses the familiar counting process and recites the number that comes just after N. A third principle is commutativity, which states that if a child knows a fact such as $4 + 3$, then the fact $3 + 4$ is also known if commutativity is accessible. And finally, for the entire range of subtraction facts there is the position that children do not memorize many of those facts at all but rather try to relate a subtraction combination to its related addition fact. For example, for $13 - 8 = \square$, the child thinks "What is the number I add to get 8 to get 13?" The children who do use this way of thinking most likely have the add-on interpretation of subtraction. These principles can also help to attain internalization if the child is made aware of them and has some measure of understanding of the principles. A second major category of helpful ideas centers around so-called thinking strategies (Rathmell, 1978; Thornton, 1978). The discussion of these is delayed until a later section.

One thing seems fairly clear from research on activities that help and motivate students to learn and practice basic facts. An instructional program that concentrates and progresses from easier sets of facts—for example the "six" facts, $0 + 6, 1 + 5, 2 + 4, 3 + 3, 4 + 2, 5 + 1, 6 + 0$, which are mastered first and then followed by the "seven" facts, $0 + 7, 1 + 6$, and so forth—to the harder ones is *not* the way to proceed. Rather, natural clusterings like the doubles, the zero facts, the $1 + N$ and $N + 1$ facts, and combinations of ten should be stressed. In order to stress the important part-part-whole relationship, it is also useful to talk in terms of number triples, such as 3, 4, 7, and addition and subtraction instead of presenting simple stimuli such as $7 - 4 = \square$.

Certain features of an acquisition and drill-and-practice program should be emphasized.

- Children must be aware of the goals of the program and be constantly informed of and rewarded for the progress made toward that goal. Often, the reward need be nothing more than satisfaction of knowing that progress is being made.
- Most activities should be self-checking in nature. Children need immediate reinforcement and knowledge of whether they are right or wrong. (And teachers don't need a lot of papers to correct!)
- Such programs must take into account individual differences of learners. Some progress faster than others; some have a tolerance for long periods of practice while others do not; some like paper-and-pencil activities while others prefer group games or working with a friend.
- Activities should be kept short instead of being long, hard, and boring.
- Don't always include just facts the children don't know; mix up the practice so that at least half are facts children already know. This breeds a feeling of success.
- Remember that learning basic facts does not equal an entire mathematics program. Content such as geometry, statistics, measurement, and above all, problem solving, merit attention as well.

Flash cards are always helpful. A good electronic flash card is the hand-held calculator or the specially designed electronic devices such as the "Little Professor." These should be used as a self-verification device where the child keys in a particular combination, gives the desired response, and then uses the calculator to check for correctness. Interestingly enough, one of the major outcomes of using a calculator in the context of learning basic facts should be the realization that the calculator is not the best tool for figuring basic facts. Rather, the human mind is much, much faster.

Decks of cards with basic fact combinations (answers not written on either front or back) can be generated by teacher and/or student for use with a variety of games such as Concentration, Fish, or War. The cards can also be used in playing number fact Bingo. Children can generate three by three, four by four, or five by five "Bingo" cards according to rules established by the teacher. Another type of game involves dominoes. Rather than match ends on the basis of having the same number of spots, rules can be made to match ends that differ by 1, by 2, or by any other possible number, or by having a predetermined sum.

A paper-and-pencil activity with a lot of appeal is the number-square puzzle shown in Fig. 5-13. Only certain numbers are given and the child must work both horizontally and vertically to find the missing numbers. Although shown here as a vehicle for practicing basic facts, the puzzle is adaptable to larger numbers, multiplication, fractions, decimals, mixed numbers, and even signed numbers. With larger numbers children can use the puzzle in connection with a calculator and guess-and-test ways of thinking. Another variation is to have children make up their own puzzles from blank forms and then give them to classmates.

There are other activities with multiple outcomes, particularly in statistics, problem solving, and simply developing a keener "number sense." In small

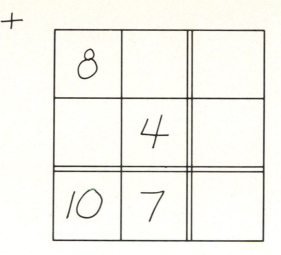

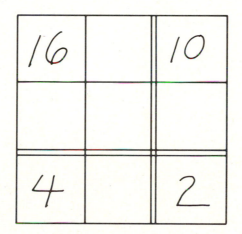

FIGURE 5–13

groups have children generate data by tossing a pair of regular dice and determining either the sum or difference. Collect information and display it on a bar graph. Certain patterns will result, and it is very important that the results be discussed in a large group. As a variation, a set of cards with a single number on each can be produced. Children draw two cards at random and then determine the sum or difference or both. As before, the intent is to graph the results and discuss them. Depending on the initial numbers chosen for the cards, the pattern of results can vary.

Exercises

1. Two articles in the March 1985 issue of the *Journal for Research in Mathematics Education* debate whether young children store basic fact information in a long-term memory retrieval system or use an efficient production system to generate the answer to a basic fact question. Read and summarize these two articles and then decide if you favor one position over the other.

2. No mention was made in the text of the use of an addition table. What advantages does the use of such a table have in classroom practice? Are there any dangers in its use?

3. As a follow-up to Exercise 3, consider a subtraction facts table. How would you construct such a table? Would it be better to simply use the addition facts table for subtraction as well? Is so, how would you make the connection between addition and subtraction clear to the students?

4. In the number-square puzzles shown in Fig. 5−13, the four numbers entered into the puzzle were placed in such a way that it is possible to determine the numbers to be entered in the vacant cells. However, it is possible to put the four numbers in certain positions so that the complete puzzle cannot be solved. What are those positions?

Writing and Solving Number Sentences

The various forms of open number sentences were displayed in Table 5−1. Canonical sentences such as $3 + 9 = \square$ or $11 - 4 = \square$ are essentially basic fact combinations and need not be discussed further here except within the general context of mathematical models. When solving problems it is frequently useful to represent that problem with a mathematical model that uses language and/or symbolism. For the problems of interest here, that mathematical model will be an open sentence or, later on, numerals written in algorithmic form.

During initial instruction with addition and subtraction symbolism and with open sentence writing and solving, it is crucial that the symbolism and sentences be viewed as the response to a basic question, "How can we use numbers and other kinds of symbols and pictures to represent the problem we are trying to solve?" Early on, young children can apply natural counting strategies to solve familiar problem situations. Teachers cannot expect them to apply basic fact knowledge or computational algorithms during initial stages because those skills will not yet have been learned. Later on, when these symbolic skills are being learned, it is appropriate to present open sentences as a symbolic problem stimulus and ask children to solve them. What many children will do at first is to apply the representational process in reverse and try to think of a familiar verbal problem that could be associated with the open sentence. The teacher should know what particular type of problem situation an individual child might associate with an open sentence or to offer several logical possibilities to those children who are having difficulty with this association process. Research has shown that children do best with action type problems such as simple Joining or Simple separating, and that the tendency is to write literal translations that sequentially show the action of the problem regardless of whether it may be noncanonical in nature (for example, $3 + \square = 12$ or $\square - 5 = 2$ (Carpenter, Bebout, & Moser, 1985).

Instruction in the writing and solving of number sentences should begin with representing complete problem situations performed on visible sets of objects which can be quickly counted. Thus, a set of three might be joined with a set of four to produce a total set of seven. The number sentence representation would be $3 + 4 = 7$. Once the basic representational process and the meaning of the $+$, $-$, and $=$ symbols have been learned, then attention can be turned to open sentences in which the unknown can be represented by a box ($\square$). To avoid one type of sentence being considered harder than another, both canonical (for example, $4 + 9 = \square$) and noncanonical (for example, $17 - \square = 11$) situations/sentences should be used. If simple situations with relatively small numbers are used and physical manipulatives are present so that any situation can be solved by direct counting, then one type of sentence or situation should not be much harder than another. When practical, each child or pair of children should have a collection of objects to use as problem situations are presented. The part-part-whole relationship must usually be considered at some time during the course of the solution of the problem. Figure 5–14 shows a sequence of steps occurring during the solving of a Separating problem in which the initial set is unknown. Similar situations can be constructed by masking the unknown set with a hand, by putting objects in a bag or sack, or by covering with a card. During early stages of instruction, any handwriting difficulties can be overcome by "writing" sentences with symbol and numeral cards.

Once number sentences have been introduced and children have become familiar with their form and are able to associate some meaning to them, the sentences can be presented symbolically with the goal of learning ways to solve them. Such solution methods should include appeal back to verbal problems, to basic fact knowledge, to the part-part-whole relationships and the inverse relationship between addition and subtraction, and to the use of guess-and-test procedures with a calculator.

Thinking Strategies

Some of the more common "thinking strategies" that children use are listed on pages 117–118. Research has demonstrated that many children invent one or more of these strategies on their own but that it is unlikely that all children will come up with all of them. If a teacher wants to ensure that students have exposure to the strategies, then explicit teaching is necessary. And research has shown it is possible to teach them (Steinberg, 1983). Some suggestions for teaching these thinking strategies are as follows:

• The best time for teaching thinking strategies is when they come up naturally as part of a discussion regarding solution of a verbal problem or when finding basic fact combinations.

FIGURE 5–14
A sequence of steps in writing and solving a number sentence

- When possible, let a student who has "discovered" and verbalized a thinking strategy explain it to the rest of the class.
- Don't expect mastery of any strategy by all students.
- There is tremendous variability in children's ability to learn and use these strategies. Teaching is probably best done on an individual or small group basis.
- Any attempt at symbolically representing a strategy should be accompanied by a concurrent demonstration with physical objects.

The final point deserves some amplification. An examination of the more common strategies reveals a common theme of decomposition of one or more of the given numbers into parts, one of which is then combined with one of the other numbers. For example, the doubles-plus-one strategy for 7 + 8 might be represented by $7 + 8 = 7 + (7 + 1) = (7 + 7) + 1 = 14 + 1 = 15$. Mathematically, this symbolism involves the associative property for addition. There is no suggestion whatsoever that this property should be taught formally or that the word be even used at the primary level. But, if the above symbolism were to be used, and there is probably no reason why it should not be, it should be explained in terms of its representing actions on objects, where decomposition, grouping, associating, and re-associating are done with string or yarn on sets of objects.

Computational Algorithms

Facility with paper-and-pencil computational algorithms is still an important part of mathematical competency. However, it is not an end in itself and it must be considered within the context of problem solving and also within a larger framework of computing in which mental computation, estimation, and use of electronic calculating devices play equal roles. There is no real need to demand computational proficiency with addition and subtraction algorithms for numbers having more than three digits or with sums involving more than four addends. Algorithms, by their repetitive nature, are easily generalized to larger digit numbers and many children transfer what they know about two- and three-digit algorithms and become proficient with larger numbers with little or no instruction. Excessive drill and practice with large number algorithms are simply not necessary.

What is necessary is that algorithmic procedures be taught with understanding. At some point in time it is desirable that an algorithm becomes routine and automatic and can be used to produce a correct answer in an efficient way. But there does exist the danger that initial teaching is carried out to promote a rote acceptance of routinized procedures. Children should know basic facts and be comfortable with place value ideas to perform well with algorithms. Yet, instruction should not be delayed until basic fact mastery is attained. Often, the slow progress through an algorithm because basic facts are not immediately recalled serves as a strong motivational factor to memorize facts.

In order to provide the understanding of algorithms, instruction should involve the use of structured manipulative materials. Figure 5−15 shows a step-by-step progression through a subtraction problem that requires regrouping. Note that the work alternates back and forth between actual manipulation of objects and the symbolic recording of that action. Although multibase blocks are shown, other structured place value materials such as Cuisenaire materials, bundled sticks, graph paper squares, or colored chips could be used. The other feature to notice is the use of the place value chart for recording. To emphasize the important role of the base ten numeration system in algorithms, some form of expanded notation is recommended. The chart shown in Fig. 5−15 is preferred because it is less cumbersome than others that have some notation for the powers of ten connected directly to the numerals. During initial instruction, each child should have a set of manipulatives to work with rather than sit and watch demonstrations by a teacher.

Problem: 562 − 147 = ☐

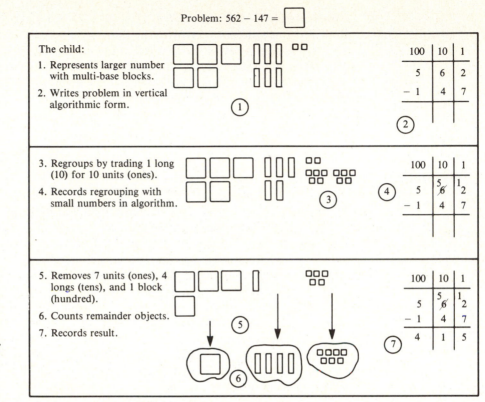

FIGURE 5-15
Solution of a sub-traction problem using multibase blocks as a way of providing under-standing of an algorithm

---

Exercises

1. Outline a lesson to second or third graders in which the objective is to learn the regrouping algorithm for addition, using the problem

   $$\begin{array}{r} 48 \\ +27 \\ \hline \end{array}$$

   Describe how you would use concrete materials and how you would try to make the transition from the concrete materials to the abstract symbolism.

2. One of the most frequent "bugs" in the subtraction algorithm is the Smaller-From-Larger bug (Brown & VanLehn, 1980) (for example,

   $$\begin{array}{r} 72 \\ -26 \\ \hline 54 \end{array}$$

   in which students reason "I can't take 6 from 2, so I will do what subtraction always says to do—take the smaller from the larger. Two from 6 is 4 and 2 from 7 is 5. The answer is 54." What remedial instruction would you give to a child who exhibits this behavior? What might you do during the initial instruction of the algorithm to try to avoid this bug?

3. On a series of addition problems, a child performs as follows:

45	16	8	32	75	26
+ 2	+40	+23	+55	+ 6	+ 4
11	56	13	87	18	12

Describe the "bug" this child has. What would be this child's response to the following problems:

47	25	13
+ 5	+31	+ 9

What might you do to try to correct this bug?

4. Figure 5−10 showed how an abacus can be used to demonstrate place value. In actual practice in many countries around the world, the abacus is used to compute. Describe how the abacus can be used to add and subtract. Pay special attention to regrouping.

VERBAL PROBLEMS

Much has already been said about attaching meaning to the abstract operations of addition and subtraction and how, for younger students, the meaning comes from solving a variety of verbal problems. The position is taken that work with verbal problems in addition and subtraction must begin at the very early stages and not be delayed until children "know their facts." The research cited earlier in this chapter strongly indicates children are able to solve verbal problems, at first with the counting strategies and thinking strategies they invent by themselves but later by applying basic facts and computational algorithms. This is not to suggest younger students are able to read the verbal problems; in most of the research the problems were read to the subjects. But ability to read should not be a deciding factor in the decision to include verbal problems as part of instruction. Large group work, pairing good readers with weaker ones, parent volunteers, or audio recordings are some suggestions for overcoming the problem of poor readers.

The previous section on Writing and Solving Number Sentences gave ideas for early instruction on solving verbal problems which essentially rely on children's natural ability with counting-based strategies. At a later point it is necessary to make the gradual transition to a somewhat logical analysis of problems which permits representation of the problem by the mathematical model of the direct computational forms for addition and subtraction. Put another way, children need to be able to analyze a one-step verbal problem and decide whether to add the two numbers of the problem or to subtract them. The recommended analysis is based on the part-part-whole relationship.

- If the two parts are known, then add the numbers representing those parts to find the size of the whole.
- If the whole and one of the parts are known, subtract the number representing the known part from the number representing the whole to find the size of the missing part.

The important aspect, then, is to be able to identify whether entities described in a problem are the parts or the whole. Familiarity and practice are components needed to gain this ability. Representation of the problem by physical materials is another. Careful explanation and explicit use of the words "part" and "whole" by the teacher are also important. A visual device that can be used to help students remember the part-part-whole relationship is shown in Fig. 5–16. The diagram shows that the whole is equal to the sum of the parts and that the whole is bigger than either of the parts. In actual practice the diagram is left blank and the child fills in the appropriate spaces with numbers as the analysis is made. In the example of Fig. 5–16, the child reasons that the whole and one of the parts are known and that subtraction is the required operation.

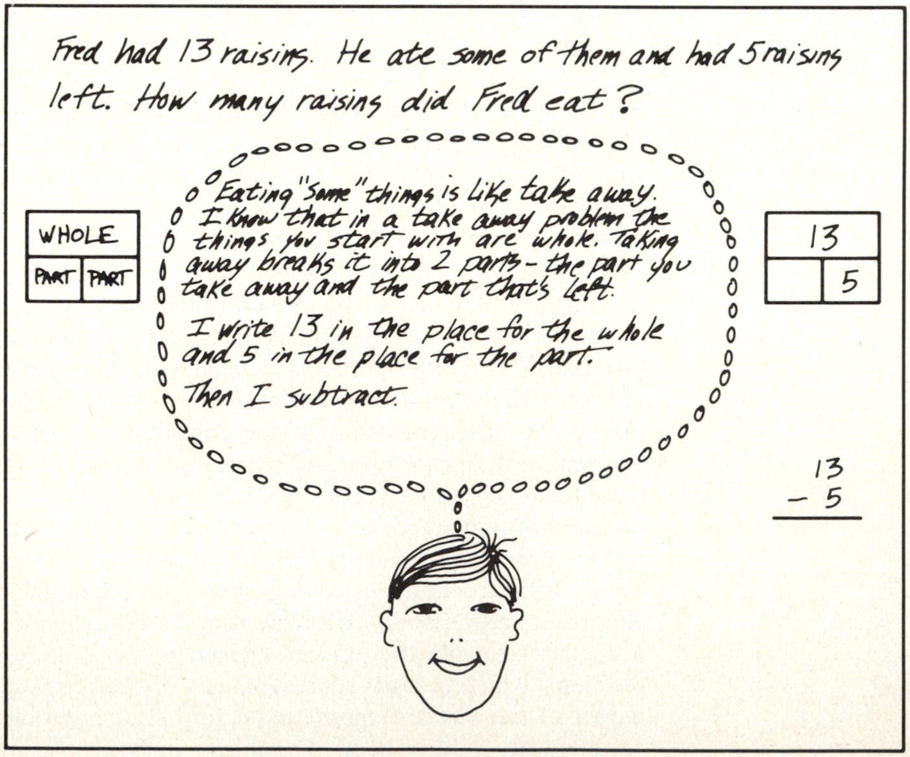

**FIGURE 5–16
Using the part-part-whole analysis to solve a verbal problem**

Fred had 13 raisins. He ate some of them and had 5 raisins left. How many raisins did Fred eat?

Eating "some" things is like take away. I know that in a take away problem the things you start with are whole. Taking away breaks it into 2 parts - the part you take away and the part that's left.

I write 13 in the place for the whole and 5 in the place for the part.

Then I subtract.

WHOLE
PART | PART

13
5

$$\begin{array}{r} 13 \\ -\ 5 \\ \hline \end{array}$$

In helping children to analyze problems it is useful to be aware of semantic analyses that have been made of the typical verbal problems primary students encounter. A major class involves Change problems in which there is an initial state followed by a change that either makes the initial state larger or smaller, and then the final state. If the change makes the initial state larger, then it is a Join problem; if the change makes the initial state smaller, then it is a Separate problem. In Join problems, the final state is always the whole; in Separate problems, the initial state is always the whole. As an example, consider the Join missing addend problem listed earlier in Table 5−2:

> *Joining, missing addend.* Gloria had 9 candies. A friend gave her some more candies and then she had 14 of them. How many candies did Gloria's friend give her?

The final state of 14 candies is the whole, and the initial state of 9 candies is the known part. The mathematical solution is the subtraction of 9 from 14. This example also serves to demonstrate that so-called key word analysis of word problems can have some serious pitfalls. In the key word approach the words "gave more" are supposed to indicate addition, which would be the wrong operation for this problem.

As with many of the aspects of addition and subtraction mentioned in this chapter, the analysis of verbal problems is not easy to teach and requires a great deal of practice. But the pay-off in later years is worth the effort.

CHAPTER 5 SUMMARY

The conceptual field of additive structures is really a big idea in mathematics. We have considered selected research findings and teaching suggestions dealing with the major aspects of addition and subtraction—the concepts of number, counting, numeration and place value, symbolic problems such as basic facts, thinking strategies, number sentences, computational algorithms, and verbal problems. These various aspects are highly interrelated. It is usually the case that teaching and learning of one of these aspects are dependent on at least one of the others. Much of the early instruction in addition and subtraction must be devoted to giving meaning and understanding to these operations and the algorithms of addition and subtraction. This meaning can come from the solution of realistic and interesting problems, the solution coming at first from children's natural problem-solving procedures, which are usually based on counting, and then leading into the analysis of problems and the application of basic fact knowledge and algorithmic skills. The teaching and learning of all these things requires patience and a long period of time.

Exercises

1. Change problems were characterized as having an initial state, a described change, and then a final state. Depending on whether the un-

known is the initial state, the size of the change, or the final state, and on whether the change is incremental or decremental, there can be six Change problems. Write an example of each of the six.

2. Comparison problems can be characterized as having a referent set, a compared set, and the difference between the two. (See Example 4 of Table 5–2. Joe's prizes are the referent set and Connie's prizes are the compared set.) Depending on whether the unknown is the referent set, the compared set, or the difference, and whether the compared set is larger or smaller than the referent set, there can be six Comparison problems. Write an example of each of the six.

3. For each of the problems written for Exercise 1 and 2, identify which problem entities are the whole and which are the two parts.

4. Compare a pre-1980 textbook with a post-1985 one at either second-grade or third-grade level for the amount of calculator-based lessons contained in each. For those lessons you do find, decide whether the calculator usage is aimed at conceptual learning, drill and practice, or problem solving.

REFERENCES

Baroody, A. J. 1984. Children's difficulties in subtraction: Some causes and questions. *Journal for Research in Mathematics Education,* 15:203–213.

Beattie, I. D., & Deichmann, J. W. 1972. *Error trends in solving number sentences in relation to workbook format across 1st and 2nd grades.* Paper presentd at the annual meeting of the American Educational Research Association. (ERIC No. ED 064 170)

Briars, D. J., & Larkin, J. G. 1984. An integrated model of skills in solving elementary word problems. *Cognition and Instruction,* 1:245–296.

Brown, J. S., & Van Lehn, K. 1980. Repair theory: A generative theory of bugs in procedural skills. *Cognitive Science,* 4:379–426.

Brownell, W. A. 1941. *Arithmetic in grades I and II: A critical summary of new and previously reported research.* Duke University Research Studies in Education, No. 6. Durham, NC: Duke University Press.

Carpenter, T. P., Bebout, H. C., & Moser, J. M. 1985. *The representation of basic addition and subtraction word problems.* Paper presented at the annual meeting of the American Educational Research Association.

Carpenter, T. P., Blume, G., Hiebert, J., Anick, C. M., & Pimm, D. 1982. *A review of research on addition and subtraction.* Working Paper No. 330. Madison, WI: Wisconsin Center for Education Research.

Carpenter, T. P., & Moser, J. M. 1983. The acquisition of addition and subtraction concepts. In R. Lesh and M. Landau (Eds.), *Acquisition of mathematics concepts and processes.* New York: Academic Press.

Carpenter, T. P., Moser, J. M., & Romberg, T. A. (Eds.) 1982. *Addition and subtraction: A cognitive perspective.* Hillsdale, NJ: Lawrence Erlbaum Associates.

Dienes, Z. P. 1971. An example of the passage from the concrete to the manipulation of formal systems. *Educational Studies in Mathematics,* 3:337–352.

Ekman, L. G. 1967. A comparison of the effectiveness of different approaches to the teaching of addition and subtraction algorithms in the third grade. (Doctoral dissertatation, University of Minnesota, 1966) *Dissertation Abstracts International,* 27A:2275–2276.

Gelman, R., & Gallistel, C. R. 1978. *The child's understanding of number.* Cambridge, MA: Harvard University Press

Gibb, E. G. 1956. Children's thinking in the process of subtraction. *Journal of Experimental Education,* 25:71–80.

Ginsburg, H. P. 1977. The psychology of arithmetic thinking. *The Journal of Children's Mathematical Behavior,* 1:1–89.

National Council of Teachers of Mathematics. 1980. *An agenda for action: Recommendations for school mathematics of the 1980s.* Reston, VA: National Council of Teachers of Mathematics.

Rathmell, E. C. 1978. Using thinking strategies to teach the basic facts. In M. N. Suydam (Ed.), *Developing computational skills.* Reston, VA: National Council of Teachers of Mathematics.

Rea, R. E., & Reys, R. E. 1970. Mathematical competencies of entering kindergartners. *Arithmetic Teacher,* 17:65–74.

Resnick, L. B. 1982. Syntax and semantics in learning to subtract. In T. P. Carpenter, J. M. Moser, & T. A. Romberg (Eds.), *Addition and subtraction: A cognitive perspective.* Hillsdale, NJ: Lawrence Erlbaum Associates.

Riley, M. S., Greeno, J. G., & Heller, J. I. 1983. Development of children's problem-solving ability in arithmetic. In H. P. Ginsburg (Ed.), *The development of mathematical thinking.* New York: Academic Press.

Steffe, L. P., Thompson, P. W., & Richards, J. 1982. Children's counting in arithmetical problem solving. In T. P. Carpenter, J. M. Moser, & T. A Romberg (Eds.), *Addition and subtraction: A cognitive perspective.* Hillsdale, NJ: Lawrence Erlbaum Associates.

Steinberg, R. 1983. *A teaching experiment of the learning of addition and subtraction facts.* Unpublished doctoral dissertation, University of Wisconsin-Madison.

Suydam, M. N., & Weaver, J. F. 1975. Research on mathematics learning. In J. N. Payne (Ed.), *Mathematics learning in early childhood.* Reston, VA: National Council of Teachers of Mathematics.

Thornton, C. A. 1978. Emphasizing thinking strategies in basic fact instruction. *Journal for Research in Mathematics Education,* 9:214–227.

Vergnaud, G. 1982. A classification of cognitive tasks and operations of thought involved in addition and subtraction problems. In T. P. Carpenter, J. M. Moser, & T. A. Romberg (Eds.), *Addition and subtraction: A cognitive perspective.* Hillsdale, NJ: Lawrence Erlbaum Associates.

Weaver, J. F. 1971. Some factors associated with pupils' performance levels on simple open addition and subtraction sentences. *Arithmetic Teacher,* 18:513–519.

Arithmetic Operations on Whole Numbers: Multiplication and Divison

6

JULIE ANGHILERI

Froebel Institute College
Roehampton Institute of
   Higher Education
London, England

DAVID C. JOHNSON

King's (London) College
London, England

INTRODUCTION

While notions of counting, place value of arithmetic, and subtraction are usually considered the basic building blocks of mathematics, multiplication and division are equally important. Multiplication and division are essential concepts for many topics throughout school mathematics. Research has demonstrated that failure to recognize the appropriateness of multiplication or division in particular contexts can lead to considerable difficulty in dealing with more advanced topics, such as area (particularly when measurements are fractions or decimals), proportion, and early ideas of algebra.

This chapter will help you decide how best to teach the foundations underlying multiplication and division and to cope effectively with children's difficulties and misconceptions. Research indicates that children should be given the opportunity to observe the operations in a variety of situations or contexts with far less emphasis on the computational algorithms than has been traditionally provided. It is our belief that calculators should always be available and used as an important part of the learning activity. This belief is shared by other authors of this book.

HISTORICAL PERSPECTIVE

This century has witnessed many changes in school mathematics and most people are aware that "modern mathematics" differs fundamentally from that taught to our parents.

In the early twentieth century the idea of a prescribed rule of procedure was still in the forefront of many teachers' minds and the most common models of multiplication and division to be found were the "equal grouping" aspect of multiplication and the "sharing" aspect of division (see Fig. 6–1). Widespread use was made of counters for illustrating these procedures.

It is now accepted that these models are very limited. Information on other models is given later in this chapter and in *Developing Computational Skills* (NCTM 1978).

FIGURE 6–1

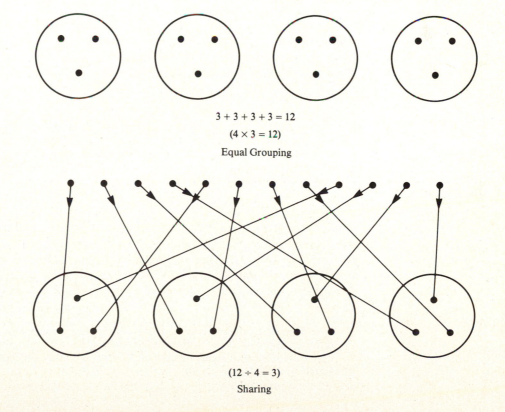

3 + 3 + 3 + 3 = 12

(4 × 3 = 12)

Equal Grouping

(12 ÷ 4 = 3)

Sharing

Modern Mathematics

Consideration of the needs of children in the learning process changed the nature of arithmetic teaching, but a more fundamental change has been required in the last quarter century as the more widespread use of calculating devices and aids has considerably reduced the premium placed on calculational skill and placed it instead on applications and interpretive ability, and an appreciation of the nature of the operations.

Structure

Two National Council of Teachers of Mathematics (NCTM) yearbooks, *The Growth of Mathematical Ideas K-12* (1959) and *Instruction in Arithmetic* (1960), note the importance of structure in providing for "maximum meaning and understanding." This study of structure attaches particular importance to the properties of the arithmetic operations, the commutative, associative and distributive properties, with special consideration given to the last of these for multiplication over addition.

The Array

The publication in 1962 of two years of research by the School Mathematics Study Group (SMSG) gave impetus to pervasive and profound changes in elementary school arithmetic (SMSG, 1962). These changed the nature of arithmetic teaching. Some implications for the operation of multiplication are clearly expressed in the following quote:

> Multiplication is usually taught in elementary arithmetic as repeated addition. It is not taught so in the SMSG program. The reason again is because of the great importance of the operation concept. Of course the statement $2 \times 3 = 6$ can be viewed as a short way of stating the result of counting by twos and threes to six. But how about the statements
>
> $$\frac{1}{2} \times \frac{1}{3} = \frac{1}{6}$$
>
> or
>
> $$\sqrt{2} \times \sqrt{3} = \sqrt{6}$$
>
> It is difficult to regard either of these multiplications as repeated additions. A different approach is therefore needed which will set it (multiplication) forth as an operation in its own right, this is exactly what the array concept gives us (SMSG, 1962).

The big idea here is that of the array as an illustration for multiplication and division. An array is a rectangular arrangement of objects in equal rows (horizontal) and columns (vertical). A three by four array of dots is shown in Fig. 6−2.

When such an array consists of adjacent squares, its applications to multiplication may extend beyond whole numbers and an example for multiplication of fractions is illustrated in Fig. 6−3b. (Fig. 6−3a illustrates use of the squares for multiplication of whole numbers.)

Cartesian Product

As noted in the introduction, when multiplication is to be considered as an operation in its own right, the dependence on addition is unsatisfactory, and more recently mathematicians have sought a definition of multiplication that does not directly involve the operation of addition. This definition is based on the idea of sets and may be illustrated by the following example:

> John has two pairs of different colored jeans and three different colored shirts. How many different outfits could John choose to wear by combining different colored jeans and shirts?

The outfits can be found by matching each pair of jeans with each shirt in turn (an organized approach is necessary to identify all possible outfits) (see Fig. 6−4).

FIGURE 6−2

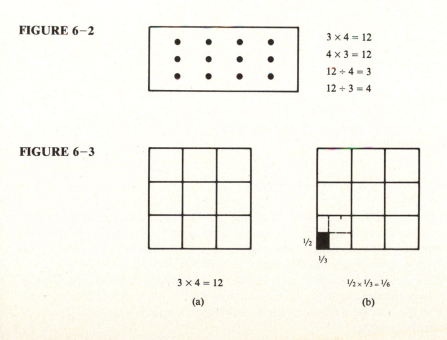

$3 \times 4 = 12$
$4 \times 3 = 12$
$12 \div 4 = 3$
$12 \div 3 = 4$

FIGURE 6−3

$3 \times 4 = 12$

(a)

$1/2 \times 1/3 = 1/6$

(b)

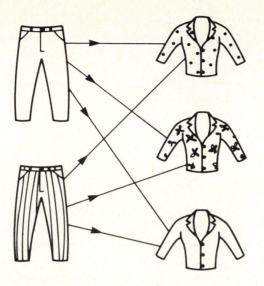

FIGURE 6−4

From the two *sets,* containing two and three *elements* respectively, a set of *ordered pairs* called the *Cartesian product* set has been formed, which has precisely six elements. When multiplication is defined in terms of the Cartesian product of two sets, the number of elements in each set is a *factor* of the number of elements in the Cartesian product set, the *product.*

$$2 \times 3 = 6$$

factor   factor   product

Inverse Operations

Multiplication and division are related in much the same sense that addition and subtraction are related. The operation of division is the *inverse* to the operation of multiplication in that the division process will "undo" the process of multiplication.

$$3 \xrightarrow{\times 4} 12 \xrightarrow{\div 4} 3$$

But their relation is even more than just "division will undo" multiplication. Inherent in every multiplication fact is a number triple that embodies the corresponding division facts (see Fig. 6−5), and the division process can be considered as finding a missing factor in a multiplication (see Fig. 6−6).

More detailed discussion of structure and alternative models, or illustrations, in particular the array and Cartesian product, and their role in teaching is given in the section "Teaching the Concepts of Multiplication and Division" later in this chapter.

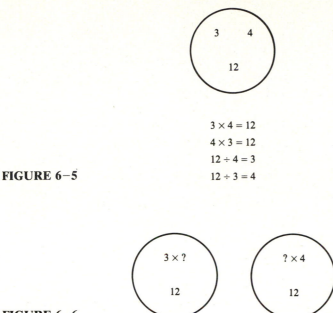

$$3 \times 4 = 12$$
$$4 \times 3 = 12$$
$$12 \div 4 = 3$$
$$12 \div 3 = 4$$

FIGURE 6-5

FIGURE 6-6

THE RESEARCH: AN OVERVIEW

Research on the learning of multiplication and division, while somewhat diverse, has generally focused on four main areas—teaching methods, structure and properties, children's understanding of the operations, and children's use of the algorithms. Research by Fullerton (1955), Norman (1955), and Gunderson (1955) provide some useful results in the area of teaching methods (and these are reflected in the recommendations noted in later sections in this chapter).

Useful work in the area of structure and properties has been carried out by Schell (1964), Gray (1965), and Willington (1967). Of particular interest in this area are those studies that have shown that different models of the operations of multiplication and division vary in their relative difficulty. Zweng (1964) found that children can understand the "measurement" (repeated subtraction) concept of division more readily than the "partition" (sharing) concept. Hervey (1966) considered the responses made by second-grade children to multiplication problems based on the "equal addends" concept and on the "Cartesian product" concept and found that the equal addends problems were significantly less difficult. Hervey noted that it was less difficult for the children to choose the way to think about the problem for this type. This result was corroborated by Brown (1981) whose work in the United Kingdom with older children (10 to 14 years of age) showed that "repeated addition" and "rate" models for multiplication were easier than "Cartesian product" models.

Understanding

Since its publication in 1952, Piaget's *The Child's Conception of Number* has had a major influence on research, and much subsequent work has reflected an increasing concern for the learning process as contrasted with the product of learning (Piaget, 1952). When assessing children's knowledge of multiplication facts, a pencil-and-paper test may suffice but the majority of such tests do not reveal what understanding a child has of the processes involved. Different techniques have been adopted to assess children's thinking patterns when solving problems. Weaver (1955) describes the method used by one teacher who was anxious to become aware of the thinking patterns of her class as they responded to a group of multiplication problems.

The children were presented with six multiplication combinations on separate cards (see Fig. 6–7). Four of these involved previously taught facts and may have been solved by immediate recall while the remaining two involved untaught facts which would have to be solved in some way by the children. Children who failed to give an immediate response to any of the combinations were encouraged to think aloud (an activity regularly practiced by this particular teacher). Through this process of interviewing, it was found that children who ultimately gave the same correct response to these combinations differed significantly in their understanding of the process of multiplication. They differed in their mastery of the facts, their ability to use other mathematical concepts and relations, and their general understanding. Had they been assessed by working the problems on a sheet of paper, the observable results may have been the same for children who differed fundamentally in their level of understanding. This points to the importance of talking with (interviewing) students and to the role of discussion in the mathematics classroom.

It is not easy to assess children's understanding through means other than interviewing but the Concepts in Secondary Mathematics and Science (CSMS) project (1974–1979) used a pencil-and-paper test in combination with some interviewing. As part of this U.K. research program, Brown (1981) examined children's (11 to 13 years of age) understanding of the four basic number operations (addition, subtraction, multiplication, division) by finding to what extent children could both recognize which operation to apply in order to solve

FIGURE 6–7

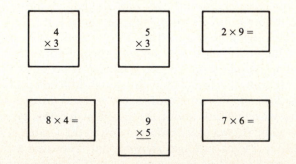

a word problem set in the real world and supply an appropriate context for a formal computational sum (for example, write a story for a given numerical expression such as 9×3). Children were not required to do the computations. Two examples of the word problems are given below (Brown, 1981):

A gardener has 391 daffodils. These are to be planted in 23 flower beds. Each flower bed is to have the same number of daffodils. How do you work out how many daffodils will be planted in each flower bed?

$391 - 23$	$23 \div 391$	$32 - 319$	391×23
$319 + 23$	$23 + 23$	23×17	$391 \div 23$

A shop makes sandwiches. You can choose from three sorts of bread and six sorts of filling. How do you work out how many different sandwiches you could choose?

3×6	$6 - 6$	$6 + 3$	$3 - 6$
$18 \div 3$	$6 \div 3$	6×3	$3 + 3$

CSMS results showed that many secondary children in England did not have a good understanding of the operations of multiplication and division. In fact 10% of children at the age of 12 years had little appreciation at all of multiplication and division and another 40% had considerable difficulty with these concepts.

It was found that many children did not distinguish between expressions like $391 \div 23$ and $23 \div 391$ and when children were subsequently interviewed it was evident there was confusion between "divided by" and "divided into" and children tended to use both of these expressions quite interchangeably, along with "shared between."

The "make up a story" items were found to be useful in establishing both whether children could produce a concrete situation to embody a symbolic expression and which models of certain operations were most widely used. Multiplication proved to be the most difficult operation for the children to illustrate—only 53% of the 12-year-old children could provide a multiplication story when the numbers involved were small, and this dropped to 41% when the numbers were large. For divisions, a correct story was given by 69% for small numbers and by 56% for large numbers. Brown (1981) notes that the major difficulty seemed to be that of choosing the units for each number. Children who failed to produce a satisfactory story often ran into trouble through failure to select two quantities that could be combined. Brown quotes an example by one 12-year-old child.

Lee has 9 and Jim had 3 chocolates. If you mulity ply them how much do they have? [Original spelling has been retained.] (Brown, 1981).

Vergnaud (1983) in his research involving multiplicative structures suggests that one reason why children experience difficulty is that even in its simplest format, a multiplication problem consists of a four-term relationship from

FIGURE 6–8

M_1	M_2
1	15
4	?

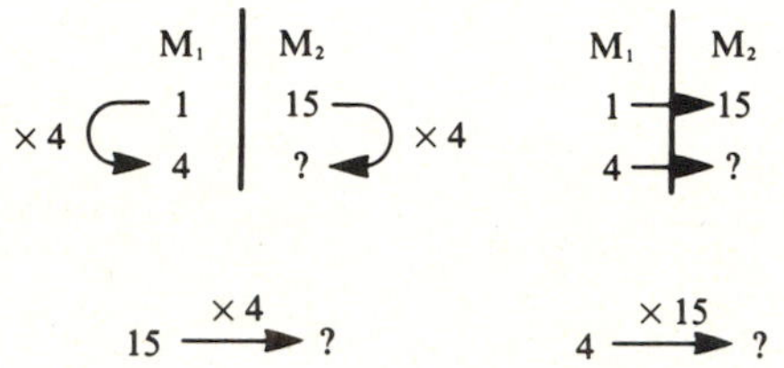

FIGURE 6–9

which one must extract a three-term relationship. Consider the following example:

David buys four cakes priced at 15 cents each. How much does he have to pay?

According to Vergnaud there are two measures involved: M_1 = (cakes) and M_2 = (costs). The four items in the relationship are shown in Fig. 6–8.

A child who recognizes the situation to be multiplicative multiplies 4 × 15 or 15 × 4 to find the answer (see Fig. 6–9). Vergnaud notes that this is correct if the 4 and 15 are viewed as numbers but a further difficulty arises if they are viewed as magnitudes because it is not clear why 4 cakes × 15 cents yields cents and not cakes.

Vergnaud's work provides important information on the complexity of the multiplicative structures and points to the need for a careful analysis of the problem situations used for teaching and practice.

ALGORITHMS[1]

Studies investigating the use of the algorithms for multiplication/division have typically examined children's processes and/or errors. Cox (1975) reports on several such studies and notes that the analysis of errors was/is profitable as a means of gathering data and planning individual instruction. Analysis of the strategies used by children (4 years to 11 years) to solve multiplication tasks and

[1]The word algorithm, which we use to refer to the standard pencil-and-paper procedures of arithmetic, comes from the name of a ninth century mathematician Al-Khowarizmi. He developed step-by-step procedures, algorithms, for solving certain kinds of equations.

the difficulties they encounter (Anghileri, 1986) reveals the complexity of the operation and will assist the development of appropriate teaching.

Cox identified a total of 233 different systematic errors found in the four operations, the largest number occurring in multiplication. It was noted that since the multiplication algorithm is so complex, a large number of the errors were such that each error was unique to a particular child.

An important study involving Italian children in fifth, seventh, and ninth grades (Fischbein, Deri, Sainati Nello, and Sciolis Marino, 1985) showed children's methods for solving verbal problems in multiplication and division were not consistent but were strongly influenced by the types of numbers used. The children were asked to choose the operation needed to solve a number of verbal problems which included pairs of similar or identical problems involving different numbers. Some examples are

1 kilo of oranges costs 1500 lire. What is the cost of 3 kilos?

The price of 1 m of suit fabric costs 15000 lire. How much does 0.75 m cost? (Fischbein et al., 1985)

In the first problem the majority (over 90%) of the 623 pupils tested correctly identified the operation as multiplication by choosing the expression 1500×3. In the second problem about half the pupils selected the correct multiplicative expression 15000×0.75 and about a third chose instead the division expression $15000 \div 0.75$.

In explanation, the authors suggest that children relate multiplication to the repeated addition interpretation in which the factor must be a whole number and the product must be bigger than either factor. This interpretation reflects the way in which the operation was initially taught, and first learned, in school and the researchers note that "the initial didactical models seem to be so deeply rooted in the learner's mind that they continue to exert an unconscious control over mental behavior even after the learner has acquired formal mathematical notions that are solid and correct" (Fischbein et al., 1985).

It would appear that children not only need experience of the variety of different models of multiplication and division but also need assistance in developing mental strategies for problem solving that would enable them to control the forceful impact of the early primitive models.

SPECIAL PROBLEMS

Several researchers (Brown, 1981; Groen & Parkman, 1972; Vergnaud, 1983) have noted that multiplication and division are more difficult operations than addition and subtraction. Much of the difficulty appears to relate to the structure of the operations and language and notation.

Structure of the Operations

The operations of addition and subtraction are usually associated with a situation in which two sets of similar objects are combined or disassociated, for example, a set of three fish together with a set of two fish make a set of five fish.

As noted in the previous section, in multiplication and division not only can the objects in the two sets be of different types, but each element in one set must be associated with every element of a subset of the other, for example if three cats have two fish each there is a resulting set of six fish.

The difficulties related to the identification of suitable units are illustrated in a report by McIntosh (1979) in which he describes some attempts by 9- to 11-year old children to produce a number story to match the multiplication expression 6 × 3:

1. Tim had 6 books Marg had 3 books = 6 × 3
2. In the farmyard there were 6 chickens and 3 pigs.
   My father said six times three is 18.

Even when considered in the absence of any concrete model the expressions 6 × 3 and 6 ÷ 3 involve two numbers with different roles to play in the execution of the operation. In 6 × 3, the number 3 is the multiplier and 6 is the multiplicand (number to be multiplied).

In 6 ÷ 3, the number 3 is the divisor and the number 6 is the dividend (number to be divided).

For children these operations can only make sense when related to concrete situations or in their application to real-life problems, usually in the format of verbal problems. Take for example, the two following division problems: (1) 12 pieces of candy are to be shared among 3 children. How many pieces would each child receive? (2) 12 pieces of candy are distributed equally among some children and each child receives 3 pieces. How many children are there?

If one considers the strategies that could be employed to solve each problem, the first problem relates to a sharing action. A diagrammatic representation could be that given in Fig. 6−10. In symbolic form this would be represented as 12 ÷ 3.

FIGURE 6−10

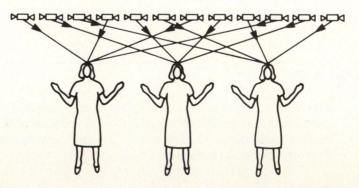

The second problem may not be solved by sharing because the number of children is not known. The solution may be found by successively removing 3 candies from the set of 12 until one is unable to remove another set of 3. This problem is again represented in symbolic form as $12 \div 3$ but relates to a completely different action and a completely different situation (no child would deny that three candies each is different from four candies each).

Difficulties with Language and Notation

Multiplication

When considering how the symbolic expression 3×4 is interpreted by adults and children, we find the most common expressions are "3 multiplied by 4," "3 times 4," and "3 fours." Some people will use the expressions quite interchangeably on the understanding that all three are equivalent; in the domain of mathematics this may be acceptable but in real life there is an important distinction between these different interpretations. On one hand "3 times 4" and "3 fours" usually relate to three sets of four objects and are consistent with "3 lots of 4."

For children, three lots of four and four lots of three are fundamentally different. They think in concrete terms—three children each having four candies are luckier than four children each having three candies although the total number of candies is the same.

Division

There are three common symbolic representations for simple division: (1) $6 \div 3$; (2) $3\sqrt{6}$; (3) $\frac{6}{3}$ or 6/3.

The first two of these are generally introduced early on, and the third is delayed until children encounter rational numbers or fractions. The first representation is normally interpreted as "6 divided by 3" and the second as "3 divided into 6." These two expressions are strictly not interchangeable. Brown (1981) found children interchange these expressions with the expression "shared between" and do not distinguish between the expressions $6 \div 3$ and $3 \div 6$. This is likely to be due to the fact that in early work with whole numbers the smaller number is always divided into the larger. Children may be under the mistaken impression that given any two numbers and an operation, the resulting solution is unique, that there is only one answer. For example, given the numbers 8 and 2 and the operation of division, children will only consider the answer 4 and not consider the possibility of dividing 2 by 8 to obtain ¼.

This is likely to cause difficulties at a later stage when the fraction expression, the third representation for division, is introduced (for example, $6 \div 3$ is $\frac{6}{3}$ and $3 \div 6$ is $\frac{3}{6}$.

The subtle changes in phraseology in such expressions as "divided into," "divided by," "shared by," "shared out," "how many will each get," and "how many parts may a set be divided into" often cause difficulties for children.

One further difficulty arises when remainders occur in division. Even the word "remainder" is not normally used by children, who will talk about "left overs" that may or may not be subdivided. Further, the left overs may not be the item being "shared out" but rather refers to those not getting an additional item. For example, "one remainder two" as an answer for eight candies shared among five children can mean each child gets one, then three children each get one more so there are two children remaining who did not get their second piece of candy (a not unreasonable explanation and one actually given by a child for his answer of "one remainder two" for the problem).

Exercises

1. Give some real-life examples of situations in which a multiplication product $a \times b$ (for example, 5×6) is not the same as $b \times a$ (6×5).
2. Make up a set of problems for division with the same three numbers (for example, 15, 3, and 5) in each, but using different verbal expressions so that answers may be different. Show the symbolic representation for each problem.

TEACHING THE CONCEPTS OF MULTIPLICATION AND DIVISION

Multiplication and division are often postponed until after the formal introduction of addition and subtraction with their symbolic representation. The seeds of these (new) operations, however, exist in many situations within the grasp of very young children, but the symbolic representation should not arise until much later. By actively working with materials the language for discussion is acquired and an understanding of the mathematical concept will grow. As there are many different aspects of multiplication and division, children will need to become familiar with the different situations that embody these aspects and the different language they involve.

A Variety of Contexts

Equal Groupings—Multiplication

This aspect of multiplication arises when there are a number of equivalent disjoint sets. An example of this is three pairs of boots (see Fig. 6–11). A less obvious example would be three nests each containing two eggs.

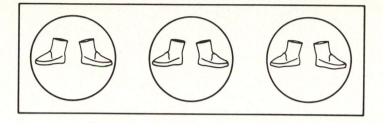

FIGURE 6–11

If the child is unable to see that there are the same number of objects in each set then the number of objects may be referred to as "three sets of two" or "three lots of two." The multiplicative idea occurs when the child is able to identify the number of equivalent sets as distinct from the total number of objects involved. The child must distinguish the question: "How many pairs of boots?" from the question: "How many boots?"

At a later stage the children may record the total number of boots

$$2 + 2 + 2 \longrightarrow 3(2)$$

In the notion 3(2) the numeral inside the brackets denotes the number of members in each set; the numeral in front of the brackets tells how many sets there are. While not commonly used in the United States, the notation is useful in that it does not involve the multiplication symbol. It is not wise to introduce the multiplication symbol, ×, at this stage.

Equal Groupings—Division

This aspect of division is sometimes called the measurement concept of division and relates to the rearrangement of members of a set into equal subsets in which the number of elements in each subset is known. An example of this is seen if there are six apples that must be arranged into sets of two.

It is clear this aspect of division relates to the equal groupings aspect of multiplication, and here division may be seen as the inverse operation to multiplication.

In multiplying, it is noted that three sets of two objects make a total of six objects. In dividing, it is noted that six objects may be rearranged to make three sets each with two objects. The language involved in this aspect of multiplication and division relies heavily on the children understanding the phrase "in each."

Allocation/Rate—Multiplication

This arises when there is a many-to-one matching in which equal sets (portions) are matched using a tally of objects (owners). The example in Fig. 6–12 shows three cats each with two fish.

FIGURE 6–12

At first, this may appear to be identical with the previous equal groupings. Note however the presence of a tally set, the cats, which in fact makes it easier. Young children find it easier to "give two candies to each doll" (three dolls) than to "make three equal portions of two candies." The language of matching is more familiar to them, and the presence of a tally set means that only one of the two numbers involved needs to be internalized and acted on.

Allocation/Sharing—Division

This aspect of division is also called the partition or partitive aspect. Again a set of objects is to be rearranged, but this time the number of subsets or partitions is known and the problem is how many objects should go into each subset.

If six apples were to be shared equally among three children, the apples would be shared by allocating them one at a time to the appropriate child (see Fig. 6–13).

The language involved in this aspect of multiplication and division again involves the word "each," but this time the phrase is "for each," which arises through the action of sharing.

FIGURE 6–13

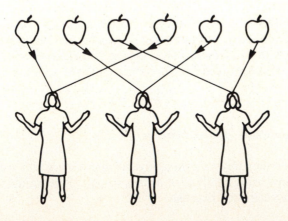

Number Line—Multiplication

This aspect concerns the movement to the right along a number line so that each displacement has the same magnitude or equal steps (see Fig. 6–14). This does not occur as readily in real life as the previous two contexts, but can be linked to climbing steps three at a time or stepping across stepping stones two at a time.

It must be noted that movement always starts at zero and a multiplication pattern will emerge by recording the landings. Confusion may arise over the fact that each time a hop of magnitude three is taken, there are two intermediate numbers that are passed over. Remind children that the unit distances are of concern and not the number of points crossed. Structural apparatus, such as cuisenaire rods and a number line made to match the unit-size of the material, can be used to illustrate the hops and help overcome the problem of the intermediate numbers.

Recording may involve the idea of equal addition

$$
\begin{aligned}
3 &= 3 \\
3 + 3 &= 6 \\
3 + 3 + 3 &= 9 \\
3 + 3 + 3 + 3 &= 12
\end{aligned}
$$

and recording the landings gives rise to a multiplication pattern of numbers: 3, 6, 9, 12, ... Research in the United Kingdom (Anghileri, 1985) shows that children find this counting pattern most useful in their later years for solving multiplication problems.

Number Line—Division

This aspect of division is repeated subtraction and may also be illustrated by hops on the number line, but this time all movements are to the left, toward zero, and starting at the number to be divided.

Starting at eight and hopping in twos, it will take four hops to reach zero. This will show the number of times two may be taken from eight is four. Notice however that looking at division, such as questions as "how many threes in eight" can lead to problems. Do you see why? Try it. Is your answer two?

The language involved in number line work for multiplication and division is complex, and an understanding develops gradually. The idea of moving four at a time or in fours will develop when children have an understanding of one at a time and in ones and two at a time or in twos, and these require careful consideration of their meaning early on.

FIGURE 6–14

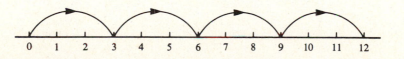

The Array

As noted earlier, an array is arranged as a regular rectangular pattern of rows and columns. The horizontal rows each have the same number of elements and the vertical columns have the same number of elements (and this may or may not be the same as the number of elements in a row). A cupcake pan and an egg carton are real-life examples of an array.

The array gives a visual pattern to both multiplication and division when the child is able to see this pattern is made up of discrete rows or discrete columns.

Each array illustrates several related multiplication and division facts. Figure 6–15 shows the facts for an array of three rows with fives stars in each row.

Scale/Multiplying Factor

This aspect does not concern repeated sets but an enlargement that may apply to either discrete objects or to a continuous medium. For example, one box may contain two candies, and a second box may contain three times as many, or one beaker may contain a quantity of liquid and another may contain three times as much (see Fig. 6–16). This factor approach will be useful later when dealing with standard proportional reasoning problems.

Experiences of constructing three times as many or three times as much usually involve the actions of adding two subsequent parts equal in size to that in existence initially; rarely do children meet a direct enlargement.

Dienes (1959) notes that a child comparing two blocks will consider the

FIGURE 6–15

5 lots of 3 make 15
3 lots of 5 make 15
The number of threes that make 15 is 5
The number of fives that make 15 is 3

FIGURE 6–16

3 times
as many

3 times
as much

single block first and then mentally build two more to make the longer one. The child is unlikely to see the longer one as three times as long until after considerable experience of such comparisons. The understanding that this involves multiplication is essential because an adding on strategy can lead to difficulties in solving problems later on (see Hart, 1981, for a discussion of the difficulties associated with ratio).

Scale/Reduction Factor

This aspect of division is precisely the same as the scale factor aspect of multiplication, but the transformation involved is a reduction rather than an enlargement. One can view the representations in Fig. 6−16 as starting with the greater amount and taking a third as many or a third as much. This may be regarded as division or as multiplication with a scale factor whose magnitude is less than one. The latter is an interpretation involving rational numbers (see Chap. 7).

Cartesian Product

As noted earlier in this chapter, the Cartesian product involves the construction of a set of ordered pairs from two sets (see Fig. 6−4).

In Fig. 6−4 each element in the first set is matched with *every* element in the second set, and a many-to-many matching is constructed. A systematic arrangement to include all the possible ordered pairs of a Cartesian product set will usually involve a sequencing pattern. The sets can be denoted (formally) as

(Pants) $A = \{a_1, a_2\}$
(Blouse) $B = \{b_1, b_2, b_3\}$

The Cartesian product set is denoted as $A \times B$ (and this is read as "A cross B" *not* "A times B") and is a set whose elements are ordered pairs:

$$A \times B = \{(a_1, b_1), (a_1, b_2), (a_1, b_3), (a_2, b_1), (a_2, b_2), (a_2, b_3)\}$$

Notice that (1) each ordered pair has as its first entry an element of the set A and its second entry an element of the set B, and (2) the number of elements, ordered pairs, in $A \times B$ is the product of the number of elements in each of the two sets A and B, that is 2×3 or 6. In this example 2 and 3 are called factors and 6 is the number of elements in the cross product of the two sets.

Because the Cartesian product model involves the construction of a set of ordered pairs from two given sets, a Cartesian product model of division could only be related to a procedure that "undoes" this construction. It is not usually meaningful to attempt this reverse process.

Review

The different aspects of multiplication and division have been considered alongside each other because there are close relationships between the two operations in each of the situations discussed.

Take for example, the allocation aspects of multiplication and division. One example given involves a concrete example in which three children have two apples each.

Related multiplication and division problems may be illustrated by this same concrete example:

1. Three children are given two apples each. How many apples do they have altogether?
2. If six apples are shared among three children, how many apples will each child receive?
3. If six apples are shared equally among a group of children so that each child received two apples, how many children are in the group?

Teachers may capitalize on the relations between these two operations by using the same situation to illustrate multiplication and division problems and by discussing the relations among the problems that arise. It may be possible for some children to formulate for themselves division problems that relate to a multiplication situation or multiplication problems that relate to a division situation. All children should ultimately become aware that the same number triple will be involved in each situation. In the examples above the number triple involves the three numbers 3, 2, and 6. A diagrammatic representation of this is shown in Fig. 6−17.

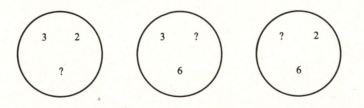

FIGURE 6−17

The listing below illustrates further the types of verbal problems that relate to different aspects of multiplication and division:

Multiplication	Division
1. *Equal Grouping* A tower block is made using three different different colors with four blocks of each color. How many blocks are used?	*Equal Grouping* If a tower made of 12 blocks consists of three different colors, how many blocks of each color would there be? (If there is an equal equal number of each.)

Multiplication	Division
2. *Allocation/Rate* If three children have two apples each, how many apples are there altogether?	*Allocation/Sharing* If six apples are to be shared among three children, how many would each child get?
3. *Number line* Jumping up steps three at a time, where would you be after four jumps?	*Number line* Starting on the twelfth step and jumping down three at a time, how many jumps would you need to reach the bottom?
4. *Array* If eggs are arranged in boxes with four rows and three in each row, how many eggs would there be in each box?	*Array* Twelve eggs fit in a box. If there are four equal rows, how many eggs would be in each row?
5. *Scale factor* John has three pieces of candy, Mary has four times as many. How many pieces does Mary have?	*Scale factor* John as twelve cookies. This is the same as four times Mary's portion. How many cookies does Mary have?
6. *Cartesian product* Ice creams come in three different sizes and four different flavors. How many different combinations are there?	No meaningful counterpart.

Exercises

1. Illustrate each of the verbal problems given above with concrete materials and discuss the "actions" needed to reach a solution.
2. Draw pictures and number sentences to illustrate.
   a. equal grouping for 4×3 or 4 multiplied by 3
   b. sharing for $15 \div 3$
3a. Use a picture to illustrate all the outfits that can be obtained from three different colored jeans (set A) and three different colored shirts (set B).
   b. Write down all the elements in the Cartesian product set $A \times B$.
   c. Write the numerical expression needed to find the number of elements in the Cartesian product $A \times B$.
   d. Make up colors for the jeans and shirts and indicate which outfits might be appropriate and which may not in terms of color combinations (there is no single correct answer). How many outfits are OK? not OK? (Is their sum = 9?)

4a. Illustrate with a number line the multiplication product 4 × 5.
   b. Show with the number line how it is not possible to reach zero when dividing nine by four (9 ÷ 4).

LANGUAGE

From the preceding examples it may be seen that different types of situations involve different words and an understanding of these words is vital for an understanding of multiplication and division. Among those words encountered most frequently are the following: each, every, equal, lots of, sets of, share, between, row, column, times, portion.

It is important that this language is understood before any attempt is made to introduce the symbols for the operations. If children understand the language then they may successfully tackle word problems.

Introducing the Symbols

It has been noted earlier in this chapter that an interim representation involving brackets may be used to record multiplication situations (for example, "three sets of two" may be represented as 3(2). This notation is, however, only suitable in situations in which equal groups occur and is not suitable for other contexts (for example, scale factor).

In division, an interim diagrammatical form for a sharing situation for a problem such as: Twelve sweets are shared between two children. How many sweets each? This form relates to the action of sharing that is involved in the concrete model.

In other types of division (for example, partitioning) in which the number ot subsets is not specified this would not be appropriate. One needs to consider the form of representation that relates to the strategy for solution. Consider, for example, the problem: Twelve sweets are distributed so that children get three sweets each. How many children are there?

The strategy for solving this problem involves successive subtractions of three to find how many portions would result. A diagrammatic representation should relate to these actions, hence the strategy could be recorded as

$$12 \xrightarrow{\text{take 3}} 9 \xrightarrow{\text{take 3}} 6 \xrightarrow{\text{take 3}} 3 \xrightarrow{\text{take 3}} 0.$$

The formal mathematical symbols × and ÷ relate to a variety of different situations and must be interpreted accordingly. For this reason it is essential that children have experienced a variety of different contexts for these operations and successfully solved word problems before the symbols are introduced.

LEARNING THE MULTIPLICATION FACTS

The knowledge of basic multiplication facts is essential for success in later school mathematics. For children who have difficulty in memorizing the facts, a variety of other resources should be readily available, including a calculator, which is probably the most useful aid for developing and reinforcing multiplication facts and concepts.

Little research has been undertaken on the methods young children use to solve multiplication problems, but work in the United Kingdom (Anghileri, 1985) reveals that the majority of primary school children do not use the facts they have learned in their multiplication tables but prefer to use addition or to recite a number pattern such as 3, 6, 9, 12, 15, 18 . . . while tallying on their fingers or mentally. This can have long term negative consequences. Children do not find it difficult to recite the number patterns of two and three in this manner, provided the children have some understanding of the meaning of the patterns and they are able to use them to rapidly produce the required number facts.

The following ideas will provide children with the concrete models they need to gain understanding of the number patterns:

2s—feet, boots, gloves, Noah's animals, eye, ears, wings on birds.
3s—edges of triangles
4s—wheels on cars, legs on animals, legs on chairs, edges of squares
5s—fingers on hands and gloves, toes on feet
6s—legs on insects, eggs in boxes
7s—days in week
8s—tentacles of an octopus, legs of a spider.

It may be useful to record these patterns in a table (see Fig. 6–18).

At all times the teacher should try to provide a variety of experiences in number work so that patterns and relationships are seen in many situations.

At this stage children may be checked for immediate recall: "What are four twos?" or for their understanding: "How many twos make six?" This latter question will form the basis of a division fact.

FIGURE 6–18

Hands	0	1	2	3	4	5	6	— — —
Fingers	0	5	10	15	20	25	30	— — —

Because of the difficulties associated with the interpretation of the multiplication symbol it is suggested that multiplication tables are learned in their verbal forms: One two is two, two twos are four, three twos are six, and so on. Be careful not to perseverate with this activity.

Number Patterns

The 100 Square

The 100 square (in which numbers between 1 and 100 or numbers between 0 and 99 are arranged in order) is a most useful aid to children for creating visual patterns by coloring or otherwise marking certain numbers. The pattern of twos may be obtained by coloring 0 and 2 and then every other number in the square. The very action of coloring may help to focus children's attention on the pattern obtained. Figure 6−19 shows two 100 squares and the inclusion of zero in the second square reinforces the fact that 0 is a multiple of 2 because $0 \times 2 = 0$.

Different visual patterns will be obtained for each of the tables. Color the multiples of nine and note the striking patterns.

Exercises

1. On separate 100 squares or 0 to 99 squares investigate the patterns of the three, four, five, six, seven, eight, and ten times tables. Can you account for similarities in some of these patterns?
2. On the same 100 or 0 to 99 square color the multiples of two in blue and the multiples of three in yellow. Make comments about the numbers that are colored twice.
3. An interesting situation arises when the 100 square is used as follows:

FIGURE 6−19

Put a ring around the number two; this is the first prime number. Now cross out every second number after two; this will mean that all multiples of 2 are crossed out. Put a ring around the number three; this is the second prime number. Now cross out all the other multiples of three. Put a ring around five, and cross out all the other multiples of five. Put a ring around seven, and cross out all the other multiples of seven.

All the numbers remaining in the table should now have a ring put around them. These numbers are all the prime numbers between 1 and 100. A prime number is a number whose only factors are 1 and itself. (This process is called the Sieve and Eratosthenes after the mathematician Eratosthenes, 276−196 BC.)

4a. On square paper or on a geoboard make as many different rectangles as you can whose area is 12 square units. You should be able to make three different rectangles.

b. How many different rectangles can you make whose areas are 17 square units?

c. Discuss how these activities are related to the number of factors of 12 and 17. What other numerical area would give rise to unique rectangular constructions?

Patterns with a Calculator

Working with a calculator can be great fun for children, and a better appreciation of the multiplication number patterns may be obtained from the rapid response.

Patterns of 2s	Patterns of 3s
$2 \times 1 = 2 (+ 2 = ?)$	$3 \times 1 = 3 (+ 3 = ?)$
$2 \times 2 = 4 (+ 2 = ?)$	$3 \times 2 = 6 (+ 3 = ?)$
$2 \times 3 = \quad \cdot$	$3 \times 3 = \cdot$
$2 \times 4 = \quad \cdot$	$3 \times 4 = \cdot$
$\cdot$	$\cdot$
$\cdot$	$\cdot$
$\cdot$	$\cdot$
$2 \times 10 =$	$3 \times 10 =$

With a calculator it is not necessary to stop at ten or even twenty! Calculators may be used to investigate multiples of large numbers, for example, the multiples of 27.

Exercises

1. With a calculator make a table of multiples of 27. Add the digits that result (for example, 2 + 7 = 9, 5 + 4 = 9). Can you account for this pattern?

2. At this stage there are many observations that may be made about the different number patterns. Look at the pattern in the multiples of five:

$$0, 5, 10, 15, 20, 25, 30, 35, 40, 45, 50 \ldots$$

Children are quite likely to put forward the hypothesis that all multiples of five end with the digit 0 or 5 (and this result holds for even very large numbers and may be checked with a calculator). When such a pattern is readily apparent the next question is "why do you suppose this is so?"
   a. Which of the following numbers are multiples of five?

$$145, 269, 1375, 2900$$

   b. Do all multiples of five end in 0 or 5? Explain why or why not.

3. Adding the digits of each of the following numbers, which are the multiples of 9?

$$271, 342, 801, 1233$$

4. Determine which of the following numbers are multiples of 45 without actually dividing. How did you do this?

$$225, 1735, 4320$$

5. Investigate this pattern:

$$142857 \times 2 =$$
$$142857 \times 3 =$$
$$142857 \times 4 =$$
$$142857 \times 5 =$$
$$142857 \times 6 =$$
stop

Guess what the next product will be, then continue the pattern to 142857×10. Could you continue the table without your calculator? Describe the pattern(s) you have found.

Some Special Numbers

Children love to learn the zero times table and the one times table.

$$0 \times 1 = 0 \qquad 1 \times 1 = 1$$
$$0 \times 2 = 0 \qquad 1 \times 2 = 2$$
$$0 \times 3 = 0 \qquad 1 \times 3 = 3$$
$$0 \times 4 = 0 \qquad 1 \times 4 = 4$$
$$\cdot \qquad\qquad\quad \cdot$$
$$\cdot \qquad\qquad\quad \cdot$$
$$\cdot \qquad\qquad\quad \cdot$$
$$0 \times 10 = 0 \qquad 1 \times 10 = 10$$

These special multiplication patterns are simple to learn, but they represent very important number facts. The significance of zero is most apparent in multiplication of two-digit numbers.

Another special pattern is obtained when multiplying by powers of ten. A calculator provides a powerful tool for children to investigate the multiplication patterns of 10s, 100s, and 1000s.

COMPUTER PROGRAMMING—MULTIPLES

The power and role of the computer in school mathematics is described in Chapter 12. With a computer children can write their own programs for investigating mathematics relationships and solving problems. There is considerable support, research findings, and personal opinion that computer programming is best learned by following a sequence of activities using short programs and modifying or extending these and finally designing or preparing new programs for solving problems. Multiplication provides a particularly appropriate context for the first of these activities, using and modifying/extending short programs. This, of course, is only after the children have developed an appreciation for the symbolism.

Children can begin with a working block of code to do a task and can modify this to do other related tasks and finally extend the program to be more general and use it to investigate a wide range of mathematical ideas. As a starting point children might be given the following program (or if the children have already learned a little about a programming language, they may design their own program):

A Program for multiples of 5

BASIC

```
10 FOR N=1 TO 10
20 LET M=N*5
30 PRINT N,M

40 NEXT N
```

Logo

```
TO MULTIPLES5
MAKE "N 0
  REPEAT 10 [MAKE "N :N+1 MAKE "M :N*5
  PRINT SENTENCE :N :M]
END
```

Note: The examples above have been given both in the form of a generic BASIC program, which will run on any microcomputer that has BASIC, and a Logo program—the version of Logo is LSCI. In the case of Logo the spacing is critical. One must use a space before and after the operation symbols of +, −, and * (times). Each new word also must be separated by a space.

Children should type the program in, run it, and then observe the output and discuss their observations with one another (this could also involve some of the questions indicated with the calculator activity previously described).

They might also consider some questions specific to the program, such as "Which multiples of five end with 0? What can you say about *N* when *M* ends with a 0? What is the difference between any two *consecutive* multiples (consecutive means they come one after the other)? Why is this so?"

Finally the children can be encouraged to change parts of the program so that it prints, for example, the first 20 multiples of five or even the first 20 multiples of some number other than five. And different groups of children can investigate patterns for different numbers.

After some time using the program the children should work on the challenge of producing a more general procedure, for example, one that allows the user to enter a value for the base number and the number of multiples (size of the set). The result will probably look something like the following:

A Program for Multiples of Any Number

BASIC

```
5 INPUT V
6 INPUT S
10 FOR N=1 TO S

20 LET M = N*V
30 PRINT N,M
40 NEXT N
```

Logo

```
TO MULTIPLES :VALUE :SETSIZE
MAKE "N 0
REPEAT :SETSIZE [MAKE "N :N+1 MAKE "M
:N*: VALUE PRINT SE :N :M]
END
```

An Alternative Using Recursion

```
TO MULT :V :S
IF :S = 0 [STOP]
MULT :V :S-1
PRINT SE :S :V*:S
END
```

Notes: 1. Most versions of BASIC also allow words as variables, hence V could be VALUE or value. 2. For purpose of space the Logo programs use the short for SE for SENTENCE.

Notice that the computer programs given in this section are somewhat transparent, that is, the words suggest what is happening and the computer output confirms or helps alter the child's expectations and thinking. The result of this is that the child is learning about the programming words or statements in the context of a working program.

Exercises

1a. Type in and run the BASIC and Logo program for the multiples of five. Change (that is, edit) the program so it prints the first 20 multiples of nine.

b. In your output for multiples of nine is there a pattern in the *units* place? the *tens* place? Look at the sum of the digits for each multiple—is there a pattern? Do you see any other patterns?

2. Extend your program to produce a more general program for multiples, using different variable names than those given in the Program for Multiples of Any Number (that is, use different letters and/or words for value and set size). Use your program to look for patterns in a set of multiples you choose (for example, 9 or 11 or 13 or 25).

3. Use your new program to produce the first 20 multiples of any two base numbers and look at the two sets and write down your observations. (You might try 8 and 12, 7 and 13, 8 and 9). This could be a first look at common multiples and the idea of least common multiple, LCM. For those of you who know a little bit about programming: you might like to try to extend your program for multiples to actually print the number of the multiple and of the two sets in a three-column format.

4. Describe the mathematics involved in your multiples of five program and the more general multiples program. What mathematical ideas are used?

THE DIVISION FACTS

As noted earlier, the language of multiplication and division may arise from the same concrete situation. The relationship between these two operations is again evident when the division facts are encountered. A multiplication fact expresses a relationship among three numbers (for example, 3, 4, and 12), and the same number triple will give rise to a division fact—every multiplication fact has an associated division fact.

Until children are able to recall the division facts, they will need to represent the division process with concrete materials. They should be able to use a variety of actions including sharing, partitioning, and successive jumps on a number line.

When the relationships between multiplication and division are understood it will be appreciated that one does not need to learn any new triples for division.

Division with Remainders

If children are tackling real-life problems of division, they will inevitably encounter some problems that are not solved exactly. Such an example would be the problem of sharing seven apples among three people (see Fig. 6−20).

The difficulty arises when each person has two apples and there are not enough left for another apple each. There are two possible actions that may be taken:

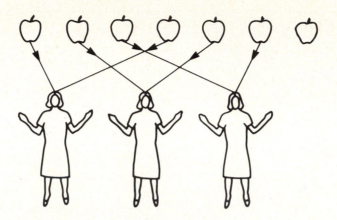

FIGURE 6-20

1. Leave the apple as a remainder.
2. Cut the remaining apple into three equal pieces. Each person will then get an extra third of an apple.

This type of problem is an excellent introduction to (1) division problems in which the solution is not an exact whole number and (2) the need for a new type of number.

It is important that children gain experience in dividing the remainder and gaining an exact answer that may be either a whole number or a fraction depending on the situation (for example, dividing apples might involve fractions; dividing marbles would involve remainders).

When simple divisions are done on a calculator the remainders will not appear as whole numbers. Consider the result of performing the following calculations:

$10 \div 5 = 2$
$10 \div 4 = 2.5$
$10 \div 3 = 3.3333333$
$10 \div 2 = 5$

Children who are given an opportunity to investigate and relate such problems to concrete situations will learn about decimal notation. A full understanding will develop slowly probably over a period of years, but the distinctive feature that *factors* always appear as whole numbers is soon apparent.

Exercise

Use a calculator to divide the number 12 by each of the numbers from 1 to 12 in turn. Record all your calculations and answers and then discuss what these results mean.

COMPUTER PROGRAMMING—FACTORS

As with multiples, the computer can be a great help in investigating divisors or factors of a number.

An initial experience here might involve giving children a program something like the following:

A Program for Factors of 18

BASIC

```
10 FOR D=1 TO 18
20 LET Q=18/D
30 PRINT D,Q

40 NEXT D
```

Logo

```
TO FACTORS18
MAKE "D 0
REPEAT 18 [MAKE "D :D+1 MAKE "Q 18/:D
 PRINT SE :D :Q]
END
```

The program for factors of 18 can be used to generate discussion. As all divisions are output in this program the children can discuss what there is about each result to help them decide whether or not a particular number is a factor (as in the calculator exercise at the end of the previous section).

While there are some decimal results it is not necessary that the children be familiar with decimals to make sense of the activity (see earlier remarks about division using a calculator). Children are quick to appreciate the concept of the "whole number and a bit" and the "bit" may be a big bit or a small bit.

The work on factors is just an introduction to the fascinating world of number theory. A variety of mathematical programming examples including work on multiples and factors as well as other elementary and junior high school topics (for example, square numbers) can be found in Johnson (1983).

A TABLE OF MULTIPLICATION AND DIVISION FACTS

Figure 6–21 shows a tabulation of the multiplication and division facts for all numbers between zero and ten in the form of a square. This square, known as a multiplication-square, is constructed by placing the product $3 \times 4 = 12$ in the *row* corresponding to the 3 and the *column* corresponding to the 4 as indicated by the arrows. The multiples of two will appear in the row with two at its head; the multiples of three will appear in the row with three at its head; and so on.

Exercises

1. Complete the table shown in Fig. 6–21 by filling in the remaining entries. What do you notice about the fourth row and the fourth column?

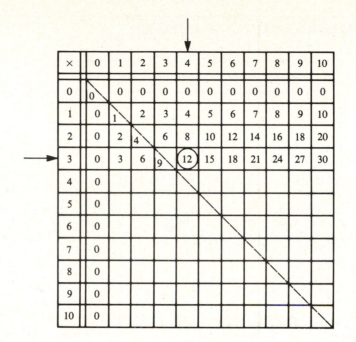

FIGURE 6–21

2. Use the table shown in Fig. 6–21 to solve the following problems: 49 ÷ 7, 35 ÷ 5, 72 ÷ 9. Write a rule for using the table to solve a division problem.
3. What is special about the numbers on the diagonal in Fig. 6–21?
4. Why does the number 24 occur so frequently in the table shown in Fig. 6–21? Predict how frequently the number 36 will occur and then check. What numbers will occur only once in the table (why?)?

The multiplication square constitutes an easy reference for children to use. Children who have difficulty remembering the multiplication facts may need to refer to it frequently and a pocket version may be useful. Such children given an opportunity to check facts readily will in turn gain confidence, and reference to the table will quite likely decrease.

Frequent use of this table with reference to both multiplication and division problems will also help children to understand the relationship between these two operations.

THE PROPERTIES

The Commutative Property

Inspection of the multiplication table completed in the last section will reveal that the table is symmetrical—the numbers appear to balance on either side of the diagonal.

This is because the product of two numbers will appear in the row corresponding to each factor (for example, 12 is the product of 3 and 4 and will appear in the rows for multiples of 3 and multiples of 4.

Exercise

1. On a multiplication square, color in red the number 35 wherever it occurs. Color in blue the number 36 wherever it occurs. Color in yellow the number 18 wherever it occurs. Note that the pattern of colors is reflected on both sides of the diagonal.

The balance or symmetry in the multiplication square relates to a very important property called the commutative property of multiplication, which states that for any two numbers a and b, $a \times b = b \times a$ (for example, $3 \times 4 = 4 \times 3$). Note that this is a property of numbers. While it is true that 3×4 *is equal to* 4×3, 3×4 may not be *the same as* 4×3 in a real-life situation.

When the commutative property is understood it may be noted that the number of multiplication facts to be learned is almost halved.

Exercises

1. Discuss why the number of multiplication facts to be learned is "almost" halved and not exactly halved.
2a. Give two concrete examples you would use to demonstrate that there is not a commutative property for division.
   b. Can you find some numbers for which $a \div b = b \div a$ is true?

The Distributive Property

Possibly the most important and useful property of multiplication is the rule known as the distributive property (its full name is the distributive property for

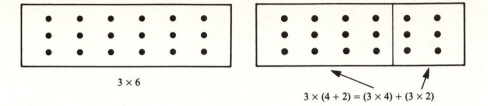

3×6

FIGURE 6–22

$3 \times (4 + 2) = (3 \times 4) + (3 \times 2)$

multiplication over addition). The distributive property enables new multiplication facts to be derived from facts already known. When calculating, for example, the number of objects that will constitute three groups of six, it is possible to consider the total of three groups of four and three groups of two (see Fig. 6–22). This may be expressed in symbolic terms as

$$3 \times 6 = 3 \times (4 + 2) = (3 \times 4) + (3 \times 2)$$

The distributive property of multiplication over addition states that for any three numbers, a, b, and c, $a \times (b \times c) = (a \times b) + (a \times c)$.

In multiplication of whole numbers this rule is particularly useful when two-digit numbers are to be used. Consider, for example, the product of 7 times 12:

$$7 \times 12 = 7 \times (10 + 2) = (7 \times 10) + (7 \times 2) = \ldots$$

Again, as in the case of the commutative property, it will be useful to consider other pairs of operations to see if they also have a distributive property. For example, is addition distributive over multiplication—is $a + (b \times c)$ equal to $(a + b) \times (a + c)$? Try $4 + (3 \times 2)$—is this equal to $(4 + 3) \times (4 + 2)$? What about multiplication over subtraction? Yes, the property holds for subtraction, and this is particularly useful for finding certain products with mental arithmetic. For example,

$$7 \times 19 = 7 \times (20 - 1) = (7 \times 20) - (7 \times 1) = \ldots$$
$$8 \times 99 = 7 \times (100 - 1) = (7 \times 100) - (7 \times 1) = \ldots$$

Two further points warrant mention here. First, it is necessary for children to gain some understanding of the distributive property if they are to progress to multiplication involving two- and three-digit numbers though it is not necessary for them to know the property by name. Second, children do not appear to develop an understanding of the distributive property unless it is specifically taught.

Exercise

Use the distributive property, multiplication over addition or subtraction, to solve the problems below. Write down each step in your solution. (*Note:*

You will also need to use the commutative property in d.)
   a. 8 × 15
   b. 7 × 98
   c. 6 × 49
   d. 199 × 5

The Associative Property

The associative property of multiplication establishes how three numbers may be multiplied and states that if *a, b,* and *c* are the three numbers then $(a \times b) \times c = a \times (b \times c)$. Because multiplication is a binary operation, the numbers must be multiplied in pairs. For example, 3 × 4 × 2 can be calculated by first obtaining the product 3 × 4 and then multiplying by 2 *or* first obtaining the product 4 × 2 and then multiplying by 3. As multiplication is associative, both processes will result in the same number and this means one can choose which to do first.

The associative property may be illustrated by building a cuboid of bricks whose length, width, and height are three, four, and two units long, respectively, and then finding the total number of bricks used. The total number of bricks used may be calculated by finding how many bricks are in the bottom layer and then multiplying by the number of layers, or alternatively by finding the number of bricks that form a side layer and then multiplying by the number of vertical layers (Fig. 6−23 illustrates both approaches). Because the total

FIGURE 6−23

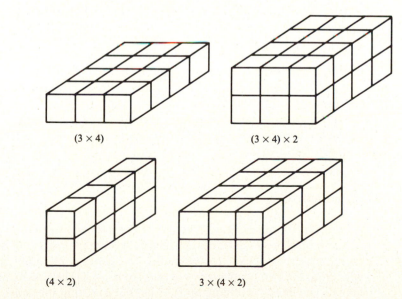

(3 × 4)   (3 × 4) × 2

(4 × 2)   3 × (4 × 2)

(3 × 4) × 2 = 3 × (4 × 2)

number of bricks is constant, each method will give the same result. This example also illustrates the usefulness of the associative property in calculating volumes of rectangular prisms.

Once again, it is important to consider whether there is an associative property for division. An example or two will be sufficient to answer the question.

Exercises

1. Explain how the associative property may help to simplify the following calculations.
   a. $11 \times 25 \times 4$
   b. $5 \times 17 \times 2$ (*Hint:* use the commutative property as well.)

2a. Give two numerical examples to show that

$$(a \div b) \div c \neq a \div (b \div c)$$

b. Is this statement true for any particular values of a and/or b and/or c? Can you explain your result?

COMPUTATION

When children have a sound knowledge of basic multiplication and division facts and an understanding of the properties, methods such as pencil-and-paper procedures may be developed for working with larger numbers.

Because few present-day real-world problems rely on people for complex computation, children should no longer be required to conform to the standard format of traditional algorithms. There will be more opportunity to encourage them to develop their own approaches. The development of mathematical strategies for solving more complex arithmetic problems will focus children's attention on the processes required and will encourage children's development in mathematical thinking and their ability to *produce* rather than merely *reproduce* solutions.

Algorithms for Multiplication

Algorithms for multiplication become necessary when the processes applied to small number products becomes tedious in their application to double-digit (or more) numbers. Take, for example, the process of equal additions when applied to the two products 6×4 and 16×14. In the first example a solution may be obtained by adding up four 6s, but applying the same method to the second gives fourteen 16s, a formidable prospect. Despite this some children still cling to an addition approach because they feel confident in its use and prefer it to the methods they do not understand. The development of more economical processes will take a considerable time if children are to be as confident with their application as with the application of more basic processes.

Before moving on to algorithms for multiplying double-digit numbers, children should have knowledge of the basic multiplication facts, including zero, properties, place value, and the number patterns associated with multiplying by 10 and 100.

Multiples of Ten

Multiplication patterns are very apparent when multiplying by 10, 100, and 1000. Before progressing to multiplication of numbers with two digits it is useful to consider the effect of multiplication by 20, 30, 40, . . ., 90 and also multiplication by 200, 300, 400, . . ., 900.

A calculator may be used to investigate such multiplication patterns, and a tabular display such as that given in Fig. 6−24 will help children to formulate rules for the patterns.

Two- and Three-Digit Numbers

Consider the product 23 × 4. Using the process of equal additions, this may be interpreted as "4 lots of 23" and rearranged in a vertical format. At this stage it is possible to note that the addition may be accomplished by adding 4 lots of 3 and then adding 4 lots of 20. This links to the distributive property—23 × 4 = (20 × 4) + (3 × 4). Considering the problem as multiplication the calculation may now be accomplished by finding the partial products (20 × 4) and (3 × 4) and adding them. The method may be easily extended to larger numbers, for example, 137 × 6 = (100 × 6) + (30 × 6) + (7 × 6).

The algorithm for multiplication may cause problems and most children will need considerable time to develop an understanding of the process. Hence the use of concrete materials to illustrate the process is essential, and base ten

FIGURE 6−24

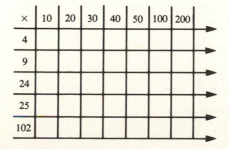

×	10	20	30	40	50	100	200
4							
9							
24							
25							
102							

cuboid blocks or squared paper cut into units, longs (one square by ten squares), and blocks (ten squares by ten squares) are particularly helpful. The problem of 137 × 6 is illustrated with blocks in Fig. 6–25. In all examples, children should be encouraged to estimate what the resulting product will be before attempting to compute the precise result. Such a result may require the recording of several stages. For example, consider the problem 217 × 7.

Estimate: 200 × 7 = 2 × 7 × 100 = 14 × 100 = 1400
Computation: 200 × 7 ⟶ 1400
        10 × 7 ⟶   70
        7 × 7 ⟶   49
      217 × 7   1519

Premature introduction of any more economical format may inhibit children's understanding of all the processes involved.

When multiplication with single-digit multipliers is well understood, children may consider how to develop strategies for double-digit multipliers. A problem such as 285 × 17 may be broken down into partial products by application of the distributive property.

285 × 17 = 285 × (10 + 7) = (285 × 10) + (285 × 7)

FIGURE 6–25

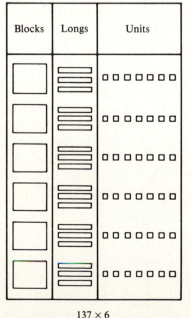

137 × 6

This expression may be evaluated in several stages.

$285 \times 10 = 2850$

$$
\begin{array}{lll}
285 \times 7 \longrightarrow & 200 \times 7 \longrightarrow & 1400 \\
& 80 \times 7 \longrightarrow & 560 \\
& \underline{5 \times 7} \longrightarrow & \underline{35} \\
& 285 \times 7 & 1995
\end{array}
$$

$285 \times 17 = 2850 + 1995 = 4845$

Exercise

After estimating the values of the following products, decide what partial products are required to suggest different formats in which complete solutions may be presented:

a. 197×7

b. 208×63

c. 268×49

Some examples may be more economically computed by using subtraction facts. In Exercise a above notice that $197 = 200 - 3$ and the partial products (200×7) and (3×7) may be used to formulate a solution. This will require only two partial products while any additive format will require three partial products.

Algorithms for Division

There are two main strategies for solving simple division problems and these involve the processes of sharing and partitioning. In many practical situations the former process will form the basis for an active solution, but the latter process is most useful for the development of algorithms for division with larger numbers. The process of partitioning will involve the successive subtraction of equal quantities until no more subtractions are possible. For example, to find $24 \div 3$

$$
24 \xrightarrow{-3} 21 \xrightarrow{-3} 18 \xrightarrow{-3} 15 \xrightarrow{-3} 12 \xrightarrow{-3} 9 \xrightarrow{-3} 6 \xrightarrow{-3} 3 \xrightarrow{-3} 0
$$

Eight 3s have been subtracted from 24, so $24 \div 3 = 8$.

This process may be speeded up when some multiplication facts are incorporated. If it is known that $3 \times 2 = 6$ a quicker procedure for this example may be implemented, that of subtracting 6 each time:

```
  24
-  6   3 × 2
  18
-  6   3 × 2
  12
-  6   3 × 2
   6
-  6   3 × 2
   0       8
```

When larger numbers are to be divided by a single-digit divisor further multiplication facts may be used. The division problem $464 \div 8$ would take a considerable time to compute if the nubmer 8 were subtracted at each stage, but subtracting 80 will provide a solution more quickly. Or, first estimating the final result will provide a useful approximation for the subtraction. For example, an estimation of 50 leads to

```
  464
- 400   8 × 50
   64
-  64   8 × 8
    0      58
```

It is important to note that concrete materials should still be used and activities using both the sharing and partitioning methods should be investigated.

Exercises

1. Using base ten cuboid blocks or squared paper cut into units and longs (one square by ten) demonstrate the processes of sharing and partitioning for each of the following:
   a. $69 \div 3$ (no grouping required)
   b. $72 \div 3$ (regrouping required)
   c. $49 \div 3$ (regrouping and a remainder)
2. Show in a vertical format what $464 \div 8$ would look like if ten 8s or 80 were subtracted at each stage.

Division with two-digit divisors produces some of the most difficult algorithms for children to master. Computation not only involves the processes of subtraction and multiplication but also requires the use of estimation for trial products. Many children are reluctant to guess because they know there is very little likelihood of arriving at the precise answer and hence the process must relate to considerable experience of number patterns using rounded or leading digit (for example, 778 is 700) approximations (see also Chapter 9).

When considering the division problem $288 \div 18$, it will be useful to first consider the related estimates $200 \div 10$ or $300 \div 20$. Either of these will give an approximation of the solution and will determine the size of the solution in terms of units, tens, or hundreds. This in turn can be used to check a calculator-produced result. One might wish to consider calculating some trial quotients and subtracting these from the dividend as follows:

$$
\begin{array}{r r}
288 & \\
- \underline{180} & 18 \times 10 \\
108 & \\
- \underline{90} & 18 \times 5 \\
18 & \\
- \underline{18} & \underline{18 \times 1} \\
0 & 16
\end{array}
$$

The original approximations, $200 \div 10 = 20$ and $300 \div 20 = 15$ gave close approximations of the solution. The use of approximations is an important skill in today's society in which exact calculations will be performed by calculator or machine.

EXPLORING AND PROBLEM-SOLVING WITH A CALCULATOR

Johnson (1981) describes a particular type of calculator activity with implications for all levels of school mathematics; however, the examples given (see Fig. 6–26) are specific to the four basic operations on whole numbers, $+$, $-$, $\times$, $\div$. These examples illustrate "exploration for concept reinforcement"—the feature of such an activity is that the concept has already been introduced or taught and the calculator activity is planned to provide an opportunity to practice or apply the concepts and/or relationships that have been studied. In the event that the concepts or relationships have not yet been studied or understood, the activity can still be used, but its role is then one of "concept demonstration."

The activity shown in Fig. 6–26 has particular appeal for a number of reasons:

1. The activity provides for individual differences (that is, even lower ability children can try the problems on a trial and error basis while others will soon see the problems are more readily solved by making use of key relationships).
2. Correct answers are apparent (that is, once a solution has been found the calculator, not the answer book or teacher, provides the verification or check).

FIGURE 6−26

NUMBER RELATIONSHIPS
Each box represents a
missing digit

*(One in this set is not possible.
Which one and why?)*

1. $93 \times 8\square = 8\square\square 1$
2. $83\square \times \square 6 = 46816$
3. $\square\square 6 \times 84\square = 232668$
4. $3\square\square \times \square 7 = 18001$
5. $4\square\square 6 \div 8\square = 48$
6. $9805 \div 8\square = \square 2$
7. $23 \times 3\square \times \square 7 = 13294$
8. $91\square 7 - \square 7\square = 8271$
9. $5418 \div \square\square = 8\square$
10. $7 \times (\square 8 - 2\square) = 112$

ESTIMATION
Each circle represents a
missing operation

$+, -, \times, \div.$

1. $(37 \bigcirc 21) \bigcirc 223 = 1000$
2. $(756 \bigcirc 18) \bigcirc 29 = 1218$
3. $27 \bigcirc (36 \bigcirc 18) = 675$
4. $31 \bigcirc (87 \bigcirc 19) = 2108$
5. $476 \bigcirc (2040 \bigcirc 24) = 391$
6. $(3461 \bigcirc 276) \bigcirc 101 = 37$
7. $(967 \bigcirc 34) \bigcirc (1023 \bigcirc 654) = 369369$
8. $(2^9 \bigcirc 8^2) \bigcirc 9 = 64$
9. $619 \bigcirc 316 \bigcirc 425 \bigcirc 196 = 924$
10. $6975 \bigcirc (36 \bigcirc 39) = 93$

3. Children are freed from tedious calculations and can concentrate on concepts or relationships.
4. The model is flexible (that is, a teacher can create exercises of this type at any level).

Exercises

1. Complete the exercises given in Fig. 6−26.
2. Use the idea of "missing digit" or "missing operation" and create your own worksheet for use at an early stage in the teaching of multiplication or division. Make note of your objectives. (Did you include an item that did not work?)
3. Another calculator problem with some interesting potential is the "Six-Digit Problem."

1 2 3 4 5 6

Using all the digits from 1 to 6 each only once, make two numbers and multiply them such that you get the largest possible product. Here are two possibilities. Can you do better?

$12345 \times 6 = 74070 \qquad 4321 \times 56 = 241976$

(*Note:* The two numbers are whole numbers and you are not to use exponents or other special notation—although this restriction may be removed for pupils studying at a higher level of mathematics.) When you think you have come up with a strategy for solving the problem, explain your reasoning to a student. In particular try to justify your answer as being the best. (*Note:* This is a good problem for reinforcing ideas of place value and multiplication by tens, hundreds, thousands, and so forth.)

4. The six-digits problem in Exercise 3 can be extended to make two numbers that form the
   a. smallest product
   b. smallest sum, largest sum
   c. smallest (positive) difference, largest difference
   d. smallest quotient, largest quotient (but this may include a consideration of decimals, or does it?)

Some of these are quite easy and others are not. Try them.

Hopefully the exercises have helped convince you of the exciting potential of the calculator as an aid in demonstrating and reinforcing concepts and relationships and in problem solving. The calculator is not merely a device for doing sums. Evidence suggests the calculator has an integral role in promoting number sense or what Brownell in 1935 (as quoted by Bidwell and Clason, 1970) called "quantitative thinking." As noted earlier in this section, the child is freed from the burden of computational algorithms and can concentrate on mathematics involved.

In closing, think about the message Lewis Carroll was trying to communicate when he included the following exchange in his book *Through the Looking Glass:*

"Can you do addition?" the White Queen asked.
"What's one and one and one and one and one and one and one and one and one and one?"
"I don't know." said Alice. "I lost count."
"She can't do addition," the Red Queen interrupted.

CHAPTER 6 SUMMARY

To gain a full understanding of the operations of multiplication and division children need a variety of experiences with different interpretations and contexts. These experiences should begin in the earlier years of school when children meet situations that embody the concepts. These should be discussed in the language of the operations well before any use of the symbols. This is an idea you have heard before!! The discussion of the relationships will form the basis of an operational understanding, which will enable the child to handle confidently the more formal aspects in later school mathematics.

Experience and familiarity with the commutative, distributive, and associative properties of multiplication in later years of elementary school are also essential both in terms of understanding the operations of multiplication and division and in terms of future learning of other mathematical topics such as algebra.

Finally, this chapter has noted the important contribution calculators and computers have to make to the learning of multiplication and division. You will learn more about this in Chapter 12. Multiplication and division form an important foundation for the learning of rational number concepts. This idea is considered more fully in Chapter 7.

REFERENCES

Anghileri, J. 1986. *An analysis of young children's difficulties with multiplication and the strategies used by successful children.* Paper presented to the British Psychological Society Conference, Exeter, U.K.

Anghileri, J. 1985. *Young children's understanding of multiplication.* Paper presented at Annual B.E.R.A. Conference, Sheffield, U.K.

Bidwell J. & Clason R. 1970. *Readings in the history of mathematics education.* Reston, VA: National Council of Teachers of Mathematics.

Brown, M. 1981. Number operations. In K. Hart (Ed.), *Children's understanding of mathematics: 11–16.* London: John Murray.

Cox, L. S. 1975. Systematic errors in the four vertical algorithms in normal and handicapped populations. *Journal for Research in Mathematics Education,* 6(4): 202–220.

Dienes, Z. P. 1959. The growth of mathematical concepts in children through experience. *Educational Research,* 2:9–28.

Fischbein, E., Deri, M., Sainati Nello, M., & Sciolis, M. 1985. The role of implicit models in solving verbal problems in multiplication and division. *Journal for Research in Mathematics Education,* 16(1):3–17.

Fullerton, C. 1955. *A comparison of the effectiveness of two prescribed methods of teaching multiplication of whole numbers.* Unpublished doctoral dissertation, College of Education, State University of Iowa.

Gray, R. 1965, March. An experiment in the teaching of introductory multiplication. *The Arithmetic Teacher.*

Groen, G., & Parkman, J. 1972. A chronometric analysis of simple addition. *Psychological Review,* 79:329–343.

Gunderson, A. 1955. Thought patterns of young children in learning multiplication and division. *Elementary School Journal,* 55:453–461.

Hart, K. 1981. Ratio and proportion, in K. Hart (Ed.), *Children's understanding of mathematics: 11–16.* London: John Murray.

Hervey, M. 1966, April. Children's responses to two types of multiplication problems. *The Arithmetic Teacher,* pp. 288–291.

Johnson, D. C. 1981, June. Calculators: Exploration for concept reinforcement. *Mathematics Teaching,* pp. 28–29. No. 95

Johnson, D. C. 1983. *Explore maths with your micro: A book for kids aged 9–90.* London: Heinemann Educational.

McIntosh, A. 1979. Some children and some multiplication. *Mathematics Teaching,* 87:14–15.

National Council of Teachers of Mathematics. 1959. *Twenty-fourth yearbook, the growth of mathematical ideas K–12.* Reston, VA: National Council of Teachers of Mathematics.

National Council of Teachers of Mathematics. 1978. *Yearbook, developing computational skills.* Reston, VA: National Council of Teachers of Mathematics.

National Council of Teachers of Mathematics. 1960. *Twenty-fifth yearbook, instruction in arithmetic.* Reston, VA: National Council of Teachers of Mathematics.

Norman, M. 1955. Three methods of teaching basic division facts. *Dissertation Abstracts International,* 15, 2134.

Piaget, J. 1952. *The child's conception of number.* London: Routledge & Kegan Paul.

Schell, L. 1964. *Two aspects of introductory multiplication: The array and the distributive property.* Unpublished doctoral dissertation, College of Education, State University of Iowa.

School Mathematics Study Group. 1962. *Mathematics for the elementary school, grades 4−6.* New Haven, CN: Yale University Press.

Vergnaud, G. 1983. Multiplicative structures. In R. Lesh & M. Landall (Eds.), *Acquisition of mathematics concepts and processes.* New York: Academic Press.

Weaver, J. 1955. Big dividends from little interviews. *The Arithmetic Teacher,* 11(2): 40−47.

Willington, G. 1967. *The development of the mathematical understanding of primary school children.* Unpublished master's dissertation. University of Manchester, England U.K.

Zweng, M. 1964. Division problems and the concept of rate. *The Arithmetic Teacher,* 11:547−556.

7

Teaching Rational Number and Decimal Concepts

MERLYN J. BEHR

Northern Illinois University

THOMAS R. POST

University of Minnesota

INTRODUCTION

By this time you should be getting the impression that mathematical topics exist as part of an intricate web of interrelationships. Rational numbers are no exception. To understand rational numbers (fractions, ratios, decimals, number lines, parts of wholes) one must have a solid foundation in the four operations with whole numbers and an understanding of measurement concepts. Rational numbers are the first set of numbers children experience that are not based on a counting algorithm of some type. To this point, counting in one form or another (forward, backward, skip, combination) could be used to solve all of the problems encountered. Now with the introduction of rational numbers the counting algorithm falters (that is, there is no next rational number, fractions are added differently, and so forth). This shift in thinking causes difficulty for many students.

This chapter will develop a wide variety of ideas relating to rational numbers and will discuss how student misunderstandings might be effectively corrected. As with previous chapters, and in concert with the cognitive perspective of human learning, emphasis will be placed on student understanding of the ideas involved.

WHAT DO CHILDREN KNOW?

Rational number concepts are among the most important concepts children will experience during their presecondary school years. There is cause to be concerned about children's apparent lack of ability in this area. The National Assessment of Educational Progress (NAEP), conducted in 1972–73 and again in 1977–78 (Carpenter, Corbitt, Kepner, Lindquist, & Reys, 1980), suggests that children seem to be learning many mathematical skills at the level of rote memorization and do not understand underlying concepts.

Other reported findings of NAEP studies (Carpenter, Coburn, Reys, & Wilson, 1976; Carpenter et al., 1980) indicate many children have difficulty with elementary rational number concepts. For example, both assessments found that most 13- and 17-year-old children successfully add fractions with like denominators, but only one-third of 13-year-old children and two-thirds of 17-year-old children could correctly add 1/3 + 1/2. Reporting on other NAEP findings, Post (1981) raised questions about children's ability to estimate rational numbers. Only 24% of the nation's 13-year-old children were able to estimate the sum of 12/13 and 7/8 by selecting the correct answer among 1, 2, 19, and 21. The fact that two popular choices were 19 (28%) and 21 (27%) hints at some misconceptions these students had.

Looking at children's performance on estimating 12/13 + 7/8 one can begin to make some conjectures about their lack of understanding: (1) These children apparently did not realize that both 12/13 and 7/8 are close to one, because this understanding would have made the answer 2 an easy choice; this raises a more general question about whether or not children understand that a rational number has size, and whether or not they are able to determine its size. (2) The popular choices of 19 and 21 suggest: the application of memorized (and incorrect) rote procedures, in this case simply adding numerators and denominators; children did not have a sense of the reasonableness of answers; children do not clearly distinguish between whole number operations and operations with rational numbers; children do not understand a fraction such as 12/13 to be one number with a single value, but rather understand it to be two numbers each with a distinct value and meaning.

AN OVERVIEW OF RESEARCH

Analysis of Rational Numbers

Rational numbers can be interpreted in at least six ways: a part to whole comparison, a decimal, a ratio, an indicated division (quotient), an operator, and as a measure relatable to a number line.

The Part-Whole and Measure Subconstructs

The part-whole interpretation of rational numbers depends directly on the ability to partition either a continuous quantity or a set of discrete objects into equal sized subparts or sets.

The notion of continuous quantity usually refers to length, area, or volume. In this case, the whole, of which a fraction is a part, is made up of one single object such as a sheet of paper, one apple, one pie, or one rectangle. When the whole consists of more than one object—a dozen eggs, 8 cookies, 15 counting chips, 25 cents—then this whole is referred to as being discrete; it is made up of several discrete (separate) objects. The part-whole notion of rational numbers is fundamental to the other interpretations.

The part-whole interpretation is usually introduced very early in the school curriculum. Children in first and second grades have primitive understanding of the meaning of 1/2 and the basic partitioning process (Kieren, 1976). It is not until fourth grade, however, that the fraction concept is treated in a substantial and systematic fashion. Students normally explore and extend their rational number ideas through the eighth grade, then these understandings are applied in elementary algebra. Many student difficulties in algebra can be traced back to an incomplete understanding of earlier fraction ideas.

Geometric regions, sets of discrete objects, and the number line are the models most commonly used to represent fractions in the elementary and junior high school.

For example, 1/2 could be represented with a geometric region as:

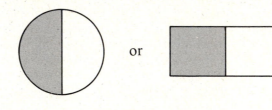

or

with a discrete set as

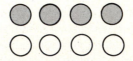

and on the number line as

FIGURE 7-1

$$\begin{array}{c|c|c|c}
\vdash & \dashv & \dashv & \dashv \\
0 & \frac{1}{2} & 1 & 2
\end{array}$$

Interpretation of geometric regions apparently involves an understanding of the notion of area.

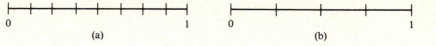

FIGURE 7–2

              (a)   (b)

The number line model adds an attribute not present in region or set models, particularly when a number line of more than one unit long is used. Novillis-Larson (1980) presented seventh-grade children with tasks involving the location of fractions on number lines that were one or two units long and for which the number of segments in each unit segment equaled or was twice the denominator of the fraction. Results of the study indicated that among seventh-graders, associating proper fractions with points was significantly easier on number lines of length one and when the number of segments equaled the denominator. For example, it was easier for students to locate 7/8 on the number line in Fig. 7–2a than the number line in Fig. 7–2b.

Novillis-Larson's findings suggest children's apparent difficulty in perceiving the unit of reference: when a number line of length two units was involved, almost 25% of the children tested used the whole line segment as the unit. Novillis-Larson's data also indicate that children are unable to associate the rational number 1/3 with a point when the partitioning suggests 2/12 (Fig. 7–3).

More recent work (Behr & Bright, 1984) confirms the findings of Novillis-Larson. Behr and Bright found children especially have difficulty coordinating symbolic fraction symbols with points on the number line. They found that children had difficulty associating a fraction such as 3/8 with a point on the number line if the number line was partitioned to show anything but eighths (for example, fourths, halves, or sixteenths). Such results suggest an imprecise and inflexible notion of fraction among seventh-graders.

Hiebert and Tonnessen (1978) investigated whether or not the type of embodiment (continuous quantity versus discrete quantity) demands different student skills. In this study children were required to divide a quantity equally among a number of stuffed animals. Hiebert and Tonnessen found that children performed considerably better on tasks involving the discrete case (set/subset) than the continuous case. The part-whole interpretation is an important foundation for other rational number interpretations. It is especially useful in developing the language and naming of rational numbers, and can be used to show the relationship between unit fractions, such as 1/3, 1/4, 1/20, and nonunit fractions. For example, looking at the rational number 3/4 (a nonunit fraction) from a part-whole perspective, one easily sees that 3/4 is equal to 1/4 and 1/4 and 1/4 (Fig. 7–4).

FIGURE 7–3

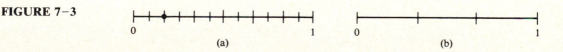

              (a)   (b)

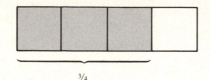

FIGURE 7−4

The association between unit and nonunit fractions also seems to make the transition particularly easy from fractions of a size less than or equal to one to those of a size greater than one. For example, 5/4 becomes 1/4 + 1/4 + 1/4 + 1/4 + 1/4, or one whole and 1/4.

The part-whole interpretation seems to be important in providing "pre-concept" activity for equivalence and order relations and for operations on rational numbers. The demonstration of the equivalence (or nonequivalence) of fractions based on manipulative materials requires the ability to "reparti-tion" a continuous object or a set of discrete objects. That is, 3/4 = 6/8 because the diagram in Fig. 7−4 can also be viewed as the diagram in Fig. 7−5.

The multiplication of rational numbers can be introduced as an extension of the multiplication of whole numbers—as the problem of finding a part of a part, or a fraction of a fraction. We will illustrate these ideas in a later section of this chapter.

Rational Numbers as Ratios

The ratio interpretation of rational numbers conveys the notion of relative magnitude. When two ratios are equal they are said to be in proportion to one another. A proportion is simply a statement equating two ratios. The use of proportions is a very powerful problem-solving tool in a variety of physical situations and problem settings that require comparisons of magnitudes.

Rational Numbers as Indicated Division

According to the part-whole interpretation of rational numbers, the symbol *a/b* usually refers to a part of a single quantity. In the ratio interpretation of rational numbers, the symbol *a/b* refers to a relationship between two quanti-ties. They symbol *a/b* may also be used to refer to the operation of division. That is, *a/b* is sometimes used as a short way to writing $a \div b$. This is the *indicated division* (or *indicated quotient*) interpretation of rational numbers.

The major component of understanding involved in the quotient interpre-tation is that of partitioning. Thus, the problem of dividing three pizzas equally among four persons can be solved by cutting (partitioning) each of the three pizzas into four equivalent parts (Fig. 7−6) and then distributing one part from each pizza to each individual (Fig. 7−7). Thus, each person will receive 1/4 + 1/4 + 1/4, or 3/4.

FIGURE 7–5

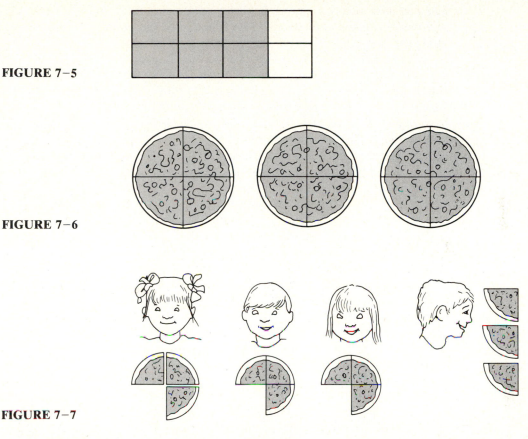

FIGURE 7–6

FIGURE 7–7

Exercises

1. If five pizzas are shared equally among four people, how much pizza does each person get? Solve this problem with partitioning.
2. Discuss how your solution to Exercise 1 suggests the answer 5 ÷ 4.

LEARNING ABOUT RATIONAL NUMBERS: SPECIAL PROBLEMS

Whatever interpretation one takes for the concept of rational numbers, other than decimal, the standard symbol for it is *a/b*, where *a* and *b* are whole numbers and *b*≠0. For example, the symbol for three-fifths is 3/5. This symbol, 3/5, is both simple and complex. In one sense its interpretation is simple; the 5 tells how many parts a whole is partitioned into while 3 tells how many of these are considered. In this consideration the 3 and the 5 each are separate and distinct numbers. On the other hand, the symbol 3/5 represents a single rational number with a unique value.

When children add 2/3 + 3/4 and incorrectly state 5/7 is the answer, do you believe they understand each of 2/3 and 3/4 as one or two numbers? When children estimate 12/13 + 7/8 to be 19 or 21, they are not treating 12/13 and 7/8 each as a single number. In order to arrive at either 19 or 21 they had to have detached 12 from 12/13 and 7 from 7/8. How does a child achieve the understanding that 3/5, for example, represents one single conceptual entity as well as three and five equal parts? What instructional experiences will help the child to develop this notion? What tasks can be used to assess whether the child has this notion?

Let's think carefully about what might be involved for a child to understand that 3/5 represents a single entity, and in addition understand what that entity is, and that it has a size and what that size is. When the child begins to study rational numbers he or she already has a good understanding of whole numbers. In 3/5, both the 3 and 5 have meaning. The child initially understands them in terms of size, both in a relative and absolute sense. The child has a sense of how big 3 and 5 are, that 5 is two greater than 3. When a child sees 3/5 and 6/8, how does he or she begin to see these same things? In a symbol such as 3/5 there are at least three important things expressed: (a) The size of the numerator (3), (b) the size of the denominator (5), and (c) a relationship between 3 and 5. There are at least two important relationships between 3 and 5; one is additive, the other is multiplicative. The additive relationship between 5 and 3 is what the child already knows; it is expressed by the difference between 5 and 3—2. The multiplicative relationship is something the child doesn't know, and this relationship is essential to understanding that 3/5 is a single number, that it has a size, and what that size actually is.

The Rational Number Project (RNP)—a research project sponsored by the National Science Foundation since 1979—has investigated children's learning of rational numbers and has given special consideration to the question of children's development of the size concept of rational numbers. This project has also investigated which learning experiences facilitate or impede children's progress toward understanding rational number size, as well as other rational number related concepts. (Behr, Lesh, Post, & Silver, 1983; Post, Behr, Lesh, & Wachsmuth, 1985).

The Effect of Perceptual Distractors

RNP investigators gave fourth-grade children the following task:
In each diagram (see Fig. 7–8), shade 2/3.
While the first part of this task was easy, the investigators were surprised to find the amount of difficulty the second diagram posed for many children. The extra horizontal line represented a significant perceptual distractor for them. One child explained after much frustration and effort, "If I pretend the line isn't there, it's easy." Another child observed, "I know I should pretend the line

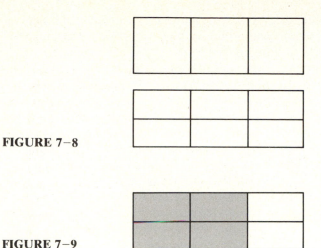

FIGURE 7–8

FIGURE 7–9

isn't there, but I can't." Keep this observation in mind in the section on methods for teaching children the concept of equivalent fractions later in this chapter. To understand that 2/3 is equivalent to 4/6 (that is, 2/3 = 4/6), it is important for a child to see that the diagram in Fig. 7–9 represents both 2/3 and 4/6. In order to do so, the child must deal with the perceptual distraction caused by the horizontal line when seeing the diagram as 2/3. Children will mentally "put in" and "take out" the line. (A chapter by Behr, Lesh, Post, and Silver (1983) provides more information about children's ability to deal with perceptual distractors and hypothesize causes for these difficulties.)

Order and Equivalence

RNP investigators gave considerable attention to teaching and assessing children's ability to order rational numbers and their ability to generate equivalent fractions. The information presented here about children's strategies in dealing with questions of the order or equivalence of rational numbers emanates from experimental work of the Rational Number Project (see Behr, Wachsmuth, Post, & Lesh, 1984; and Post, Wachsmuth, Lesh, & Behr, 1985). During 18 weeks of project teaching experiments with fourth-grade children in two locations, the RNP emphasized the use of manipulative aids and considered five topics: naming fractions, identifying and generating fractions, comparing fractions, adding fractions with the same denominators, and multiplying fractions. The children modeled these ideas using materials, pictures, symbols, and verbal descriptions. Each child was given individual assessment interviews on 11 separate occasions. The interviews were conducted approximately every 3 weeks during the 18-week instructional period. Each interview was audiotaped or videotaped and later transcribed.

During these RNP interviews children were asked to order (decide which is greater) fractions of three basic types: same numerator fractions, same denominator fractions and fractions with different numerators and denominators. Analysis suggested five or six different strategies were used by children for each of the three types of conditions. The majority of these were valid strategies and in some way recognized the relative contributions of both numerator and denominator to the overall size of the fraction. In some cases, however, children focused only on the numerator or only on the denominator and as a result made incorrect conclusions. In other instances they compared each to a common third number (usually 1/2 or 1) and were successful in ordering the given fractions. For example, 1/3 is less than 5/8, because 1/3 is less than 1/2 and 5/8 is greater than 1/2. This is called the transitive strategy.

Even after extensive instruction some children were at times negatively influenced by their knowledge of whole number arithmetic and as a result made errors such as 1/3 < 1/5, explaining that this is true because 3 < 5.

Exercises

1. Discuss the phenomenon of children's whole number knowledge influencing their learning of fractions. In what ways is this a positive thing and in what ways is it a negative?
2. Design some tasks about fractions. Include a perceptual distractor in some but not in the others. Give the tasks to children and observe and discuss their performance.

Going back to the children's performance on the NAEP item of estimating the sum of 12/13 + 7/8, one can begin to see the understanding of the relative size of rational numbers is important. It seems essential that children be able to answer questions about the order or equivalence of two rational numbers to have an understanding of the meaning of operations with addition, subtraction, multiplication, and division of fractions. Teaching suggestions for developing this important concept are in a later section of this chapter.

Another task, which proves to be a challenge to children, called Construct-the-Unit, requires the child to construct the unit-whole from a given fractional part. It is the reversal of the problem of finding a fractional part of a unit-whole, and although important, it is almost never included in the elementary school fraction related curricula. We consider this reversal task important from a point of view consistent with Piagetian psychology. Piaget suggests the understanding of a process is greater when a child is able to see that the process can be reversed to return to the starting point. In this case the process of finding a fraction of a whole can be reversed to find the whole of which a fraction is part. A typical task was given as: If this ⬜ is 3/5, find the unit-whole. Or in a discrete context: If 8 8 8 is 3/5, find the unit.

Children's responses were of various types. Some explanations indicated that they first decomposed the given fractional part into unit fractions (in this cases three 1/5s), and then the unit-whole was developed by repeating this unit fraction, that is, ☐ becomes ☐☐☐ , each part identified as 1/5. The whole is 5/5 so the correct answer becomes ☐☐☐☐☐ . Some explanations indicated the child was not aware that the fractional part is composed of, or decomposable to, unit-parts or unit-fractions equal in number to the numerator. Another explanation suggested that the child used the given fractional part as the unit-whole or used the fractional part as a unit fraction.

Partitioning Behavior

The concept of partitioning or dividing a region into equal parts or of separating a set of discrete objects into equivalent subsets is fundamental to an understanding of rational number. Pothier and Sawada (1983) investigated the development of this skill from kindergarten to third grade. The basic finding of this interesting study is that partitioning ability develops gradually through a succession of five stages.

A child first learns to partition in two. This is followed by the ability to perform successive halvings so that partitioning in 4, 8, 16, and so forth can be accomplished. This is followed by the ability to make other even numbered partitions such as six and ten. Partitioning the whole into an odd number of parts follows when a child first observes that a cut other than that which divides in two equal parts is possible. After this discovery is made, the ability to partition into three, five, seven, or an odd prime number of parts is possible for the child. Finally, the ability to partition into a number of parts that is a product of two odd numbers such as 9 and 15 follows.

Exercises

1. Read and discuss the article by Pothier and Sawada (see references).
2. Discuss ways to help children learn to partition into thirds and fifths.
3. Fold a paper in half. What do you do to it to get it folded into four parts, eight parts? Do you think it is easy for children to do this? Try it with children. Discuss your observations.

TEACHING SUGGESTIONS

Developing the Basic Fraction Concept

Partitioning—A Basic Skill

It is easy to see that partitioning or subdividing is a fundamental concept underlying children's understanding of fractions. In the learning of the fraction concept it is important that a child has actual physical experience with partitioning; later just imagining partitioning will suffice and may ultimately be desirable.

In this section we will demonstrate manipulative aids the teacher will find useful in helping children learn about fractions. Two of these aids, paper folding and centimeter rods, are called continuous models; the other, counting chips (for example, game chips such as poker chips), is called a discrete (countable) model.

The concept of a whole underlies the concept of a fraction. We will refer to a whole also as unit, or unit-whole. When we refer to 2/3 of an apple, then the apple is the whole, or unit, to which 2/3 refers. If we speak of 2/3 of a dozen apples, then the set of 12 apples serves as the unit to which 2/3 refers. In both cases one can imagine that 2/3 is arrived through a partitioning process. When the unit-whole is one apple, 2/3 is obtained by partitioning the unit-whole (one apple) into three (equal-sized) parts and designating two of the parts. Similarly, when the whole is 12 apples, 2/3 can be obtained by partitioning this whole (12 apples) in three equal-sized parts (equivalent subsets) and choosing two parts.

At this point, you should think carefully about the different kinds of knowledge the child needs to partition discrete and continuous units. For a continuous unit, one object is made into three parts, and each part is a single continuous connected entity. This singleness, continuity, and connectedness are evident to the child perceptually and therefore are likely to be conceptually evident as well. On the other hand, for the discrete set of 12 apples, each equal-sized part (equivalent subset) consists of four separate, nonconnected objects. Nevertheless, in the process of partitioning and conceptualizing 2/3 of 12 apples, the child must conceptually think of the twelve apples as one whole unit. That is, the 12 objects must become a conceptual entity. Similarly, it is difficult for the child because each of the three parts has four objects, so now the child must mentally think of four objects as one part. Can you guess what error children might make early on in their learning about fractions when asked to find 2/3 of a set of twelve? You guessed it! Some children will pick out two of the twelve, thinking that that's what the numerator means, two parts. It is difficult for some children to understand initially that each part has four subparts in it. While the research does not provide clear-cut suggestions about this matter, we recommend the fraction concept first be developed on the basis of continuous models and then a transfer can be made to discrete models.

We also recommend children be given the opportunity to partition various types of objects. For example, partition a sheet of paper into two equal parts, later into four equal parts, then eight. Young children will need some special guidance in partitioning a sheet of paper into an odd number of parts. Where to make the first cut, other than in the middle, needs to be given special attention. Similarly, children can be given sets of 4, 8, or 12 counting chips and asked to partition these sets into four parts. After a child has made the partitioning into four parts, an important activity is for the child to designate (that is, show the teacher and other children) what is one part, two parts, three parts, and four parts. Notice that one doesn't have to bring in the language of fraction for a child to have a meaningful experience with partitioning. These early experiences with partitioning may be as important to a child's development of fraction concepts as counting is to their development of whole number concepts. By the way, these early experiences should also include more involved challenges. For example

(1) Partition three circular cookies into 4 parts; that is, share the cookies equally among 4 children.

(2) Partition three rectangular cookies into 4 parts.

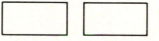

(3) Partition the rectangle below into 4 parts.

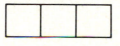

(4) Partition the set of chips into 3 parts.

(5) Partition the rectangle below into 6 parts.

(6) Partition the rectangle below into 3 parts.

FIGURE 7−10

Paper folding is an excellent partitioning activity for children. Take a standard size sheet of paper. Ask the children to fold the sheet in either of the two ways suggested by a dotted line as shown in Fig. 7−11. When the paper is folded, it looks like the picture in Fig. 7−12.

Now have the children fold the paper again. The second fold can be accomplished in more than one way, as shown in Fig. 7−13. After the second fold is made in accordance with one of the patterns shown in Fig. 7−13, the child sees one of the shapes shown in Fig. 7−14.

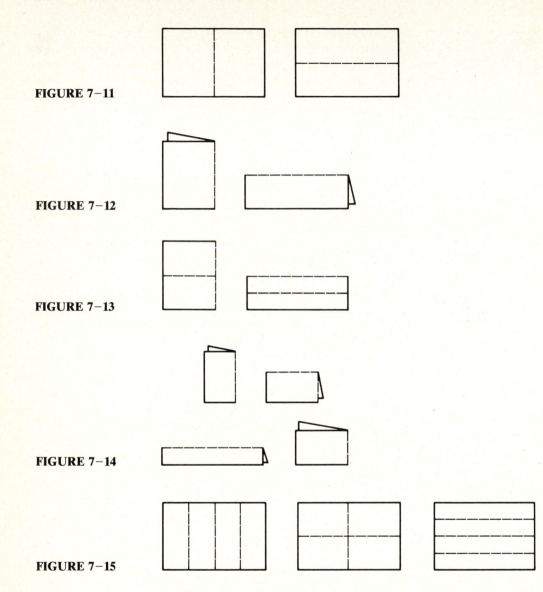

FIGURE 7–11

FIGURE 7–12

FIGURE 7–13

FIGURE 7–14

FIGURE 7–15

Next, the child should be asked to unfold the paper; the result will look like one of the three designs shown in Fig. 7–15. Then the child should be asked to show one, two, three, and four parts.

A challenge activity would be to continue folding any one of the results shown in Fig. 7–15 to show eight parts and then to imagine removing fold lines to see four parts again.

Exercise

Discuss difficulties children might have with these paper-folding activities. Try them with children and discuss your observations.

Using Partitioning to Show Fractions

In this section we will show how partitioning is used in showing fractions in the part-whole interpretation of rational numbers.

Using the rectangles partitioned into four parts as shown in Fig. 7−15, any one of the diagrams in Fig. 7−16 is satisfactory for showing 1/4; each of the diagrams in Fig. 7−17 illustrates 3/4.

Also observe that each demonstration of 3/4 can be interpreted as 1/4 + 1/4 + 1/4, or as 2/4 + 1/4, or 1/4 + 2/4. Thus, even as the basic concept of fraction is being developed, the concept of adding fractions with like denominators can be foreshadowed.

Chips can be used as a discrete model. For example a child might proceed, with a teacher's help, to show 2/3 using a set of six chips as a unit-whole (see Fig. 7−18).

Not all children will necessarily know that to partition a set of six chips into three equal subsets two chips go into each group. To help you might suggest that the child start three sets by moving three chips, each to a separate spot (see Fig. 7−19). Then a child can put more chips into each subset, one at a time, until all chips are used up (Fig. 7−20). Finally, two parts (two subsets each with two chips) are covered with different colored chips (Fig. 7−21).

Note: Throughout these activities, whenever we use the chip model for fractions, we will assume that the chips representing the unit are white and chips used to cover or show the actual fractional part are a darker color.

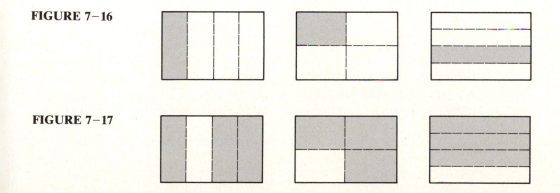

FIGURE 7−16

FIGURE 7−17

FIGURE 7–18

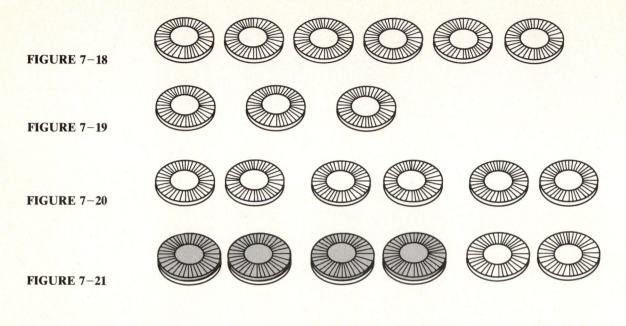

FIGURE 7–19

FIGURE 7–20

FIGURE 7–21

Exercise

1. Use a set of six white chips to show 2/3. Use the same set of six white chips as a unit and show 1/6, 2/6, . . ., 6/6.
2. Use a set of 12 white chips as a unit to show 3/6. Also, you should reinterpret the chip display, regroup if necessary, to show 6/12, 3/6, and 1/2.

Cuisenaire Rods

Another manipulative aid to use in teaching the concept of fraction is the centimeter rod. We will illustrate by constructing a representation of 3/4. The first question to consider is what rod to use for a unit (the whole). It should be a rod that can be partitioned by another rod (evenly) into four parts. Let's choose an eight-rod (Fig. 7–22).

Having chosen a unit, a child may have to experiment to find a rod to accomplish the partition shown in Fig. 7–23.

Some children may experiment with a three-rod or a one-rod before discovering a two-rod will work. Others will use division to immediately determine that the two-rod will work. Finally, the fraction 3/4 is represented as in Fig. 7–24.

Figs. 7–22, 7–23, and 7–24 show that the unit rod (eight-rod) was partitioned into four parts and three of them were singled out. They also show that the six-rod is 3/4 of the eight-rod. After more experience with the rods,

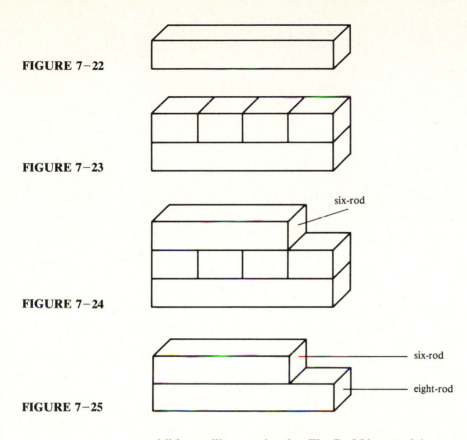

FIGURE 7–22

FIGURE 7–23

six-rod

FIGURE 7–24

six-rod

eight-rod

FIGURE 7–25

children will recognize that Fig. 7–25 is a model or representation of 3/4 and of 6/8 as well.

Fractions Greater than One

The realization that a single shaded part in Fig. 7–26 represents 1/4 is especially important when the idea of fractions greater than one whole (5/4, for example) is considered. The model in Fig. 7–27 must first be understood to illustrate that 4/4 equals 1, or one whole-unit. This will help the child realize that 5 one-fourth parts will cover more than one whole unit and will require the use of a second unit region.

Figure 7–28 suggests a method for showing 5/4 with paper folding.

FIGURE 7–26

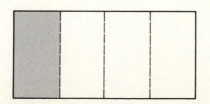

FIGURE 7—27

Step 1.   Fold one region into 4 parts.

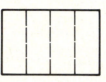

Step 2.   Point to a region that is 1/4 of the whole. Can you shade 5 one-fourth parts? No! We need to fold another region in order to show 5 one-fourth parts.

Step 3.   Fold another region.

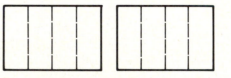

Step 4.   Now shade 5 one-fourth parts.

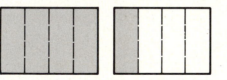

Step 5.   How many wholes would you need to shade thirteen one-fourth parts?

FIGURE 7—28

Exercise

Use Cuisenaire rods to show 2/5, 3/7, 5/13, and 9/7. Show each fraction in at least two ways.

Comparing Fractions—Order and Equivalence

A child's understanding of the ordering of two fractions (that is, deciding which of the relations is equal to, is less than, or is greater than holds for two fractions) needs to be based on an understanding of the ordering of unit fractions (that is, fractions with a numerator of one: 1/2, 1/3, 1/4, 1/5, . . .). Let's look at what is involved in the ordering of 1/5 and 1/8. Early in the learning of fractions children understand 1/5 to be less than 1/8 because 5 is less than 8. Through work with manipulatives, children will begin to understand why 1/8 is less than 1/5. It has to do with an important relationship between the size of each part and the number of parts when two unit-wholes of the same size are partitioned into 8 and 5 parts respectively. By paper folding or drawing partition lines, children can achieve a reasonable approximation (drawings will be less precise) to Fig. 7–29.

The first observation children can make is that the part shaded to represent 1/8 is smaller than the part shaded for 1/5. From this observation the children must learn to make the symbolic statement 1/5 is less than 1/8.

We are going to repeat part of the previous sentence here for emphasis: *From this observation* children must learn to *make the symbolic statement* . . . . More accurately, it is from *many* similar observations that the child learns to make the symbolic statements.

After considerable experience with ordering unit fractions, children should be asked to compare fractions such as 4/8 and 7/8. Here we can again observe how important it is for a child to understand (1) that 1/8 is an entity with a specific size and (2) that 4/8 is four 1/8s (that is, 4/8 is four iterates of size 1/8, and similarly that 7/8 is seven iterates of the same size). From this the notion that 4/8 is less than 7/8 has a strong conceptual foundation, both by the logic of comparing four of something (1/8s) with seven of the same something. These concepts are nicely derived from the physical model. In explaining why 4/8 is less than 7/8 some children exhibit this logic while others exhibit thinking directed to their memory of physical displays: 4/8 is less than 7/8 because the size of the parts is the same but there are fewer parts (four) in 4/8 than in 7/8.

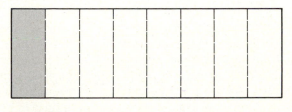

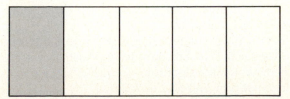

FIGURE 7–29

Always a word of caution! Would you be surprised to hear a child say, "7/8 is less than 4/8 because seven is more parts and as the parts become more in number, they become smaller in size?" Several of our students did just that!

Understanding of the important relationship between the size and number of parts into which a whole is partitioned is very important in determining the order of fractions such as 4/8 and 4/13 (that is, fractions with the same numerator). Children who correctly order these as 4/13 is less than 4/8 is often explain that each has the same number of pieces (four) but the pieces in 4/13 are smaller because there are more pieces.

Finally, the question of ordering two "general fractions" (that is, neither their numerators nor denominators are equal) comes into instruction. For some fractions in this category children invent (and can be taught) interesting strategies. One that we found in our work in the RNP is as follows. To decide which of 7/8 or 12/13 is less, some children reason 7/8 is one (part) away from one whole or 8/8s (meaning 1/8) and 12/13 is one (part) away (meaning 1/13). Because 1/13 is less than 1/8, 12/13 is closer to 1, so 7/8 is less than 12/13. Observe the sophistication in the thinking just described. Not bad for a fourth-grade student.

Exercise

Apply this thinking to 5/8 versus 10/13.

Some general fractions, for example 5/8 and 7/12, have neither equal numerators nor equal denominators. They lend themselves to a small modification of the above strategy in which one was used as a reference point. In this case, 5/8 is 1/8 more than 1/2, while 7/12 is 1/12 more than 1/2. Because 1/12 is less than 1/8, 7/12 is closer to 1/2, so 7/12 is less than 5/8. Some children we worked with in the RNP also invented this strategy. We refer to these strategies as "reference point strategies."

In the two preceding examples observe how important concepts such as "close to one" or "close to 1/2" were applied. And also observe how important was the ability to order (determine which was larger) unit fractions appeared to be. In the second example (comparing 7/12 and 5/8 to 1/2), the children must have realized both 6/12 and 4/8 are equal to 1/2. It appears that the reference point strategy is a powerful strategy. The range of its applicability is subject to having well understood reference points. One and 1/2 were the two used most often. If children had equally good understandings of other fractions such as 3/4 or 2/5, there might also be cases when these could serve as appropriate reference points.

Ultimately the problem of ordering two general fractions rests on considerable knowledge of fraction equivalence. A general algorithm—usually called a common denominator algorithm—could be applied to determine the order or equivalence of 6/15 and 5/12 as follows:

1. Find the lowest common denominator (that is, find the lowest common multiple (LCM) of 15 and 12—3 · 5 · 4 = 60).
2. Change 6/15 and 5/12 to equivalent fractions with denominator of 60.

$$\frac{6}{15} = \frac{6 \times 4}{15 \times 4} = \frac{24}{60}$$

$$\frac{5}{12} = \frac{5 \times 5}{12 \times 5} = \frac{25}{60}$$

3. Use the fact that 24/60 is less than 25/60 to decide that 6/15 is less than 5/12.

The notion of equivalence of fractions must be understood before other rational number tasks can be performed.

Before children learn an algorithm based on a common denominator, they must have had much experience with fraction equivalence. Children must develop a meaningful algorithm or procedure for determining which fractions are equivalent fractions. We suggest that it be developed through experience with physical and diagrammatic models.

The usual algorithm for generating equivalent fractions is

$$\frac{a}{b} = \frac{a}{b} \times \frac{n}{n} = \frac{a \times n}{b \times n}$$

where n is any number except zero. Note that $n/n = 1$, so a/b is simply being multiplied by 1. This does not change its value. With children we usually limit n to whole numbers although there are long-term advantages to allowing n to be a fraction or mixed number as well. For example, 4/6 = 6/9 because $4 \times 1\frac{1}{2} = 6$ and $6 \times 1\frac{1}{2} = 9$.

Children can determine several fractions equivalent to 1/2 (or another fraction) by using paper folding. Figure 7−30 suggests the folds to be made in establishing that 1/2, 2/4, 3/6, and 4/8 are equivalent. It can also be observed that

$$\frac{4}{8} = \frac{1 \times 4}{2 \times 4} \qquad \frac{3}{6} = \frac{1 \times 3}{2 \times 3} \qquad \frac{2}{4} = \frac{1 \times 2}{2 \times 2}$$

Generalizing from the manipulative displays and the patterns with the symbols, whenever the numerator and denominator of a fraction are multiplied by the same nonzero whole number, then an equivalent fraction results. Symbolically this generalization can be written as

$$\frac{a}{b} = \frac{a \times n}{b \times n}$$

for all fractions a/b and for all whole numbers n, $n \neq 0$.

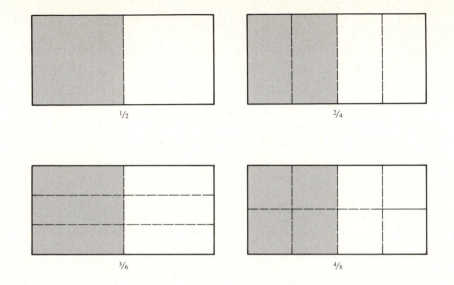

FIGURE 7–30

Exercises

1. Use Cuisenaire rods to compare: 3/4 and 5/4, 5/6 and 5/8, 2/5 and 3/7.
2. Use symbolic procedures to compare the fractions in Exercise 1.

OPERATIONS ON RATIONAL NUMBERS

As we consider procedures for teaching children to add and subtract rational numbers the reader should be alert to the fundamental nature of previously learned concepts to a meaningful understanding of addition and subtraction. Especially keep in mind:

1. The concept of a unit fraction (for example, 1/2, 1/3, 1/4)
2. The notion that any fraction m/n is m iterates (repetitions) of the associated unit fraction $1/n$. For example, 5/4 is 1/4 and 1/4 and 1/4 and 1/4 and 1/4, or 1/4 + 1/4 + 1/4 + 1/4 + 1/4
3. That rational numbers of the form a/b are complex entities consisting of at least three separate but yet related concepts—the numerator a, the denominator b, and the multiplicative relationship between a and b, which defines the entity a/b
4. That every rational number a/b has size
5. That the notions of order and equivalence play a central role in understanding addition and subtraction.

Addition and Subtraction—Developing Understanding with Manipulative Aids

Manipulative aids can be used to help children develop concepts for addition and subtraction of rational numbers with like denominators.

We will use paper folding to illustrate 1/4 + 3/4. We begin by partitioning a piece of paper into four parts (Fig. 7−31). Then we will shade 1/4 (Fig. 7−32).

The next step is to show 3/4 more, as indicated by the shading in Fig. 7−33. Because the entire region is shaded, the child can see that 1/4 + 3/4 = 1. Also from the pictures, it can be seen that

$$\frac{1}{4} + \frac{3}{4} = \frac{1 + 3}{4}$$

$$= \frac{4}{4}$$

After the child has seen and done several such examples with manipulative objects, the common pattern should be observed: to add fractions with the

FIGURE 7−31

FIGURE 7−32

FIGURE 7−33

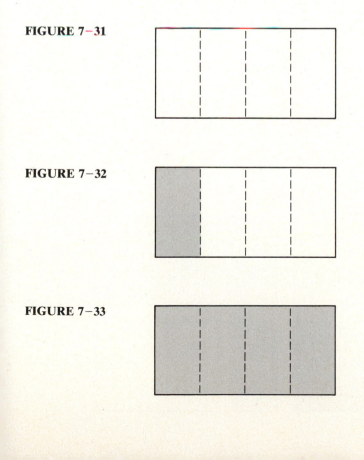

same denominator, add the numerators and keep the same denominator. For upper-grade children, this generalization is usually stated as

$$\frac{a}{b} + \frac{c}{b} = \frac{a + c}{b}$$

The cases in which the sum is greater than one are somewhat more difficult for children. Figure 7−34 shows how the following problem would look when carried out with paper folding.

$$\frac{2}{4} + \frac{3}{4} = \frac{2 + 3}{4}$$

$$= \frac{5}{4}$$

Exercise

Interpret each of the pictures in Fig. 7−34 in terms of the problem.

Understanding addition of fractions with the same denominator helps in understanding subtraction. The generalization for subtraction of fractions is similar to that of addition:

$$\frac{a}{b} - \frac{c}{b} = \frac{a - c}{b}$$

for $a > c$.

FIGURE 7−34

Paper folding

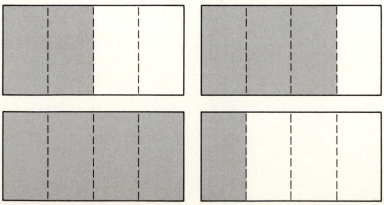

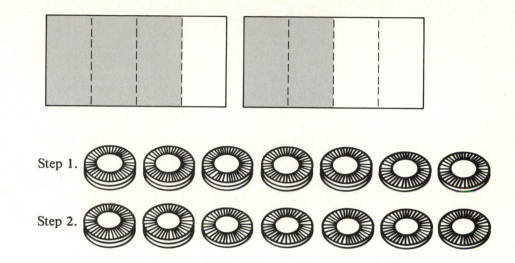

FIGURE 7−35

Step 1.

Step 2.

FIGURE 7−36

We demonstrate next how to solve 3/4 − 1/4 using paper folding.

Fold the paper into fourths, Identify three of the fourths, and mentally remove or physically erase one of the fourths (Fig. 7−35).

Exercise

Interpret the chip demonstration shown in Fig. 7−36.

Typically, the school curriculum separates the teaching of addition and subtraction of fractions with like denominators from the teaching of addition and subtraction with unlike denominators, as we have done in our discussion. Children should consider addition problems such as 1/2 + 3/4 in a teacher−group discussion before they learn the lowest common denominator algorithm. A child with a good understanding of 3/4 will see 3/4 as 2/4 + 1/4, and will see 2/4 as equal to 1/2. Thus, 1/2 + 3/4 is two halves and 1/4 more, or 1 and 1/4, illustrating the associative property as it relates to addition. Similarly, many children will be able to "reason out" an answer to 1/2 + 5/8 without knowledge of the formal common denominator algorithm. This is highly desirable.

Paper folding is useful for developing concepts that underlie addition and subtraction of fractions with unlike denominators. A long narrow slip of paper (for example, adding machine tape) works well for this activity. The relative error due to folding inaccuracies will be small and frequently not noticeable. We illustrate the use of such a strip of paper with an addition example, 1/2 + 2/3. Take a strip of paper (perhaps 1 meter in length) like that shown in Fig. 7−37. Fold it and shade one-half as shown in Figure 7−38. Fold the same strip into thirds and shade one third as shown in Fig. 7−39.

To tell the sum, we need to know what fraction of the whole strip is shaded. By folding the paper into lengths corresponding to the shortest section in Fig.

FIGURE 7–37

FIGURE 7–38

FIGURE 7–39

FIGURE 7–40

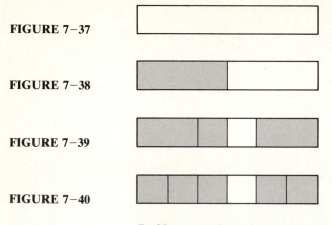

7–39, we get the strip to look as it appears in Fig. 7–40. It can be seen from this figure that 1/2 + 1/3 = 5/6.

From Fig. 7–40 it can also be seen that 1/2 was changed to the equivalent fraction 3/6 and 1/3 was changed to the equivalent fraction 2/6, so that

$$\frac{1}{2} + \frac{1}{3} = \frac{3}{6} + \frac{2}{6}$$

$$= \frac{3 + 2}{6}$$

$$= \frac{5}{6}$$

Centimeter rods can also serve as a useful aid when unlike denominators are involved. The following sequence of diagrams illustrates the problem 1/2 + 2/5. The reader should have centimeter rods at hand and follow the steps while reading.

Step 1. Find a rod (or rods) that can be partitioned into both two and five parts. Build rod trains of two-rods and five-rods side by side until both trains are the same length (Fig. 7–41), to find the least common multiple of two and five, which is ten. Then find the one rod that matches the two trains in length (Fig. 7–42).

Step 2. Show 1/2 as 5/10 (Fig. 7–43).

Step 3. Add 2/5 shown as 4/10 (Fig. 7–44).

Careful observation of the steps above suggests each of the following:

1. $\frac{1}{2} = \frac{1 \times 5}{2 \times 5}$ Observe that the five-rod on top of the ten-rod could cover one five-rod.

$= \frac{5}{10}$ Observe that the ten-rod serving as the unit is the same length as 2 five-rods.

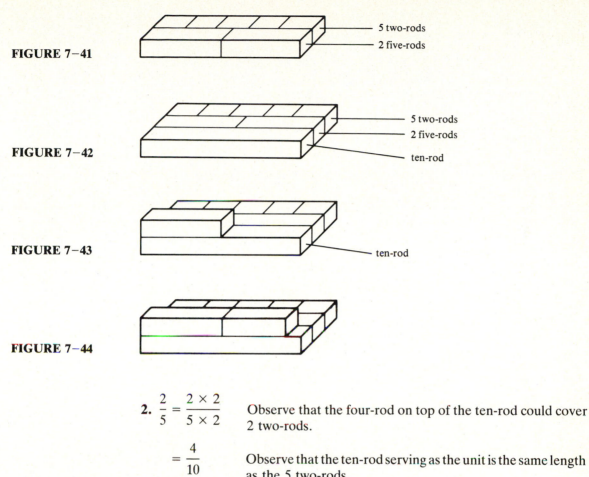

FIGURE 7–41

5 two-rods
2 five-rods

FIGURE 7–42

5 two-rods
2 five-rods
ten-rod

FIGURE 7–43

ten-rod

FIGURE 7–44

2. $\dfrac{2}{5} = \dfrac{2 \times 2}{5 \times 2}$ Observe that the four-rod on top of the ten-rod could cover 2 two-rods.

$= \dfrac{4}{10}$ Observe that the ten-rod serving as the unit is the same length as the 5 two-rods.

Thus

$$\frac{1}{2} + \frac{2}{5} = \frac{1 \times 5}{2 \times 5} + \frac{2 \times 2}{5 \times 2}$$

$$= \frac{5}{10} + \frac{4}{10}$$

$$= \frac{5 + 4}{10}$$

$$= \frac{9}{10}$$

The exact parallel between these demonstrations and the symbolic method for adding fractions needs to be carefully observed by the teacher with the children. The time taken to carefully build such concepts, however, will pay large dividends in students' understanding.

Exercises

1. Use manipulative aids to subtract fractions with unlike denominators. (These procedures are analogous to those for addition of such fractions.)
2. Find 2/3 + 1/4 with paper folding as described above.

Multiplication of Fractions—Developing Understanding with Manipulative Aids

The symbolic algorithm for multiplication of rational numbers is mechanically simpler than the symbolic algorithm for addition or subtraction. Some writers and teachers argue that multiplication should be taught to children before addition and subtraction because of this fact. We disagree. While the algorithm for multiplication is simpler, the question of whether multiplication is conceptually simpler is not so easily resolved. It is well known from research that children are able to perform additive operations before they can perform multiplicative operations. For whole numbers this is probably true because one of several interpretations for multiplication is that of repeated addition. However, one cannot really think of 2/3 × 4/5 in this way. From a manipulative perspective, it appears the operation of multiplication has the more complex manipulative base. For this reason we suggest multiplication be introduced after addition and subtraction. To illustrate the conceptual complexity mentioned above, ask yourself why the product of two rational numbers less than one is always less than either of the original numbers. In the example above, the product is less than 2/3 and less than 4/5. Try it!

Using a continuous region model we proceed to find 2/3 × 4/5 as follows:

1. Exhibit the unit-whole (that is, exhibt the model for one) (see Fig. 7−46).
2. Find 4/5 of the unit-whole; find 4/5 of one (Fig. 7−47).
3. Find 2/3 of (4/5 of one); note, we find 2/3 of 4/5 not 2/3 of one (Fig. 7−48).
4. Now we want to know (2/3 of 4/5) of 1. The region marked as ⨯⨯⨯⨯⨯ (with the double cross-hatch) in Fig. 7−48 is it. We need to find what fraction this is of one (the original unit-whole). To do this, we complete the partition of the unit-whole (see dotted lines in Fig. 7−49).
5. Now observe that the region marked ⨯⨯⨯⨯⨯ is 8 of 15 parts. We have determined that 2/3 of 4/5 is 8/15, or 2/3 × 4/5 = 8/15.

FIGURE 7−45

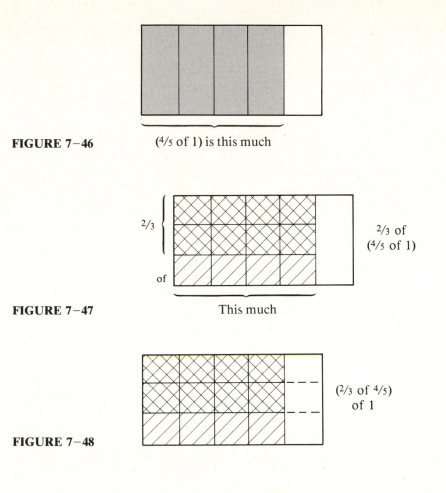

FIGURE 7–46

($^4/_5$ of 1) is this much

FIGURE 7–47

$^2/_3$ of 1)

of

This much

$^2/_3$ of
($^4/_5$ of 1)

FIGURE 7–48

($^2/_3$ of $^4/_5$)
of 1

6. Now look carefully at Fig. 7–48 and observe that the eight parts appear as two rows of four; that is, 2 × 4. Also observe that the 15 parts appear as three rows of five; that is, 3 × 5. Thus, we can observe that the numerator for 2/3 × 4/5 is 2 × 4 and the denominator is 3 × 5 or

$$\frac{2}{3} \times \frac{4}{5} = \frac{2 \times 4}{3 \times 5}$$

$$= \frac{8}{15}$$

In addition to using manipulatives, teachers can also use number patterns and previously developed concepts to help children remember how to perform operations. Notice the pattern in each of the following divisions.

$$\frac{3}{4} \div \frac{5}{4} = \frac{3}{5}$$

$$\frac{5}{8} \div \frac{2}{8} = \frac{5}{2}$$

$$\frac{9}{12} \div \frac{13}{12} = \frac{9}{13}$$

This pattern suggests a common denominator algorithm for division. It is a satisfactory division algorithm which avoids the troublesome rule of "invert and multiply." This common denominator algorithm can also be used to divide fractions with unlike denominators by changing the original fractions to ones having a common denominator.

$$\frac{7}{12} \div \frac{6}{15} = \frac{7 \times 5}{12 \times 5} \div \frac{6 \times 4}{15 \times 4}$$

$$= \frac{35}{60} \div \frac{24}{60}$$

$$= \frac{35}{24}$$

The usual invert and multiply algorithm can be developed from number patterns and previous concepts as follows.

By the time children do division they will have already seen that multiplying both the numerator and denominator of a fraction by the same number results in another name for the original fraction (that is, an equivalent fraction). They also know that any number divided by one is that number. These facts can be used to develop a pattern for dividing fractions. First, we show the steps in a specific case.

$$\frac{3}{4} \div \frac{5}{7} = \frac{\dfrac{3}{4}}{\dfrac{5}{7}} = \frac{\dfrac{3}{4} \times \dfrac{7}{5}}{\dfrac{5}{7} \times \dfrac{7}{5}} = \frac{\dfrac{21}{20}}{1} = \frac{21}{20}$$

Note that 7/5 was chosen as the multiplier because 5/7 × 7/5 results in 1 in the denominator. Let us generalize this pattern to obtain a general procedure for changing a problem of dividing two fractions to a multiplication problem.

$$\frac{a}{b} \div \frac{c}{d} = \frac{\dfrac{a}{b}}{\dfrac{c}{d}} = \frac{\dfrac{a}{b} \times \dfrac{d}{c}}{\dfrac{c}{d} \times \dfrac{d}{c}} = \frac{\dfrac{a}{b} \times \dfrac{d}{c}}{1} = \frac{a}{b} \times \frac{d}{c}$$

Thus, dividing one fraction by another is the same as multiplying the first fraction by the reciprocal of the second: $a/b \div c/d = a/b \times d/c$.

Exercises

1. Use paper folding to find 2/3 × 3/4.
2. Parallel the steps shown in the text above to find 2/3 × 4/5 with chips.
3. Find 2/3 × 3/4 with chips.
4. Carefully observe how the manipulatives suggest the algorithm.

Division of fractions is one of the more difficult concepts for children. It will help children if the teacher knows and observes with the children basic ideas associated with division. Children will know from whole number work that an answer to a division problem such as $a \div b$ is equal to, greater than, or less than one according as whether $b = a$, $b < a$, or $b > a$, respectively. This knowledge will help the child see that the same relationship holds for $a/b \div c/d$. The answer to this division is less than one when $c/d > a/b$, is equal to one when $c/d = a/b$, and is greater than one when $c/d < a/b$. Note again how the notions of fraction order and equivalence underlie other concepts of rational numbers, in this case division.

OTHER INTERPRETATIONS OF RATIONAL NUMBERS

We next turn to other interpretations of rational numbers—measurement, quotient, operator, ratio, and decimal. Some of these will be brief because the most extensive interpretation given to rational numbers in U.S. schools is that of part-whole.

The Measurement Interpretation

The measurement interpretation is usually reflected in the use of the number line as a physical model. As was indicated earlier in the review of research, it is known that children have difficulty with the number line. This does not necessarily suggest that the number line not be used, but rather that it be used appropriately, and with knowledge on the part of the teacher of what difficulties a child might have. The reason for the term *measurement* interpretation is that rational numbers are defined as a measure. When one thinks of measure, the notion of a unit of measure and of subunits of that unit of measure come to mind. On a number line the unit of measure is the distance on the line from zero to one (Fig. 7–49).

Obviously in some cases this distance is a centimeter, in others an inch, and in still others a kilometer or a light year, but the basic notion of the distance

FIGURE 7–49

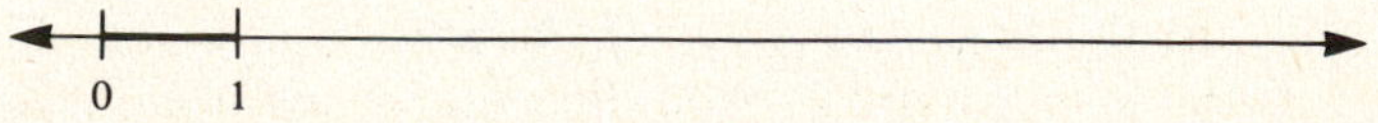

between zero and one defining the unit remains intact. Multiples of this unit distance are generated on the number line by iterating the distance from zero to one along the line (Fig. 7–50).

Now, what is the meaning of a fraction such as 5/8 on the number line? To show 5/8 we establish the sub-unit of 1/8 (Fig. 7–51); 5/8 is now simply the distance on the number line equal to five iterations of 1/8 (Fig. 7–52). The point 5/8 on the number line is usually understood to mean a point whose distance from zero on the line is five 1/8-units.

Similarly, to show 5/13, 7/12, and so forth on the number line, we think of partitioning units on a number line into subunits of 1/13, or 1/12, and then traveling a distance on the number line from zero until we have traversed five or seven of these subunits.

Frequently teachers suggest to children that each rational number represents a point on the number line. More accurately, it represents a distance on the number line. We can think of 5/8 as being associated with a point on the number line, provided we take the distance starting at zero and iterate five subunits of 1/8 in the direction of one.

In Fig. 7–53 5/8 is associated with a point that is 5/8 of the distance from zero to one. On the other hand, consider the number line in Fig. 7–54. The distance from A to B also is five iterates of 1/8, so this distance is also 5/8. It is important for children to be able to represent fractions such as 5/8 in various places on the number line. Why? One reason is because a

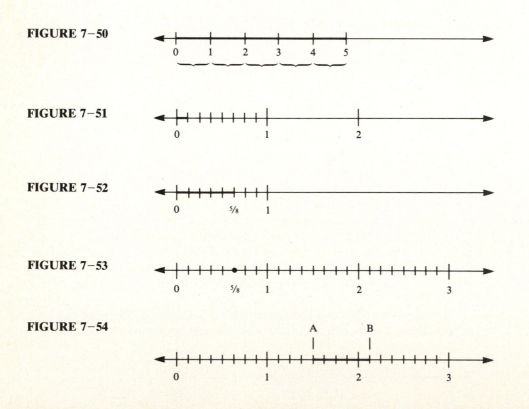

FIGURE 7–50

FIGURE 7–51

FIGURE 7–52

FIGURE 7–53

FIGURE 7–54

number line is frequently used to model addition. Consider 3/8 + 7/8. The interpretation of this addition on the number line is one of finding the sum of two measures, that is, two distances. First 3/8 is represented (Fig. 7−55).

Next a distance of 7/8 is extended beyond the point corresponding to 3/8. Do you see now why a child needs to be able to represent a fraction as a distance anywhere on the number line?

From Fig. 7−56 a child can observe that 3/8 + 7/8 = 10/8 and also that 3/8 + 7/8 = 1-2/8.

A number line can be used to model rational numbers greater than one (mixed numbers) provided the child already understands certain basic concepts about fractions before starting number line work. These notions include the concept of a unit fraction, and the idea that all other fractions are simply iterates of the appropriate unit fraction.

For example, to show 13/3 on the number line, the child must be aware that 1/3 is the appropriate subunit and that 13/3 is found by traveling from the zero point a distance of 13 iterates of 1/3 (Fig. 7−57).

Once a child finds 13/3 as a point 13 1/3s away from zero, then the child can also observe that

$$\frac{13}{3} = 4 \frac{1}{3}.$$

The number line concept can fortify children's understanding of fraction order and equivalence concepts. Several number lines are used for this (Fig. 7−58).

FIGURE 7−55

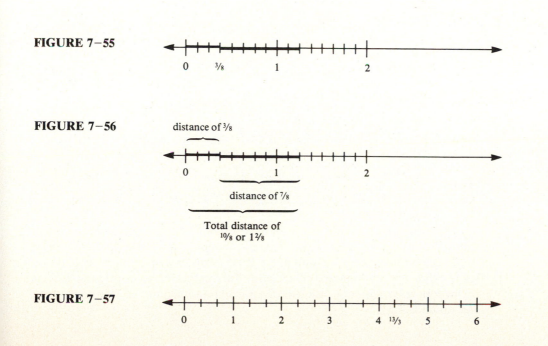

FIGURE 7−56

distance of ³/₈

Total distance of
¹⁰/₈ or 1²/₈

FIGURE 7−57

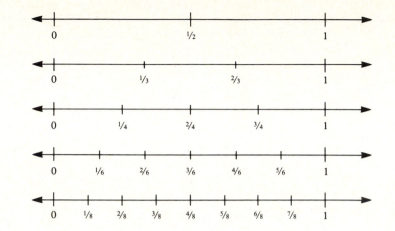

FIGURE 7−58

With the teacher emphasizing that it is the distance from zero that is important children can:

Observe	and	*conclude*
1. The distance from zero to 2/3 is less than the distance from zero to 3/4.		2/3 < 3/4
2. The distance from zero to 2/4 is equal to to the distance from zero to 3/6 and to the distance from zero to 4/8.		2/4 = 3/6 2/4 = 4/8

Exercise

These questions are challenging for most children. Do them and discuss difficulties children might have.

1. Show 2/3 on the number line in Fig. 7−59.
2. Show 4/6 on the number line in Fig. 7−60.
3. An even more challenging activity is to show 2/3 on the number line in Fig. 7−61.

The number line seems to be a useful model for helping children learn rational number concepts. It is not recommended that it be the first model used. The number line is helpful in concepts of order and equivalence, and to some extent for addition and subtraction. Interestingly, it has little applicability for concepts of multiplication or division of rational numbers. No one model can do all things.

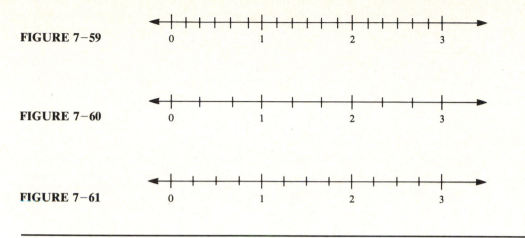

FIGURE 7–59

FIGURE 7–60

FIGURE 7–61

DECIMALS

Decimals are yet another important interpretation of rational number and are very useful in a wide variety of settings. Measurement using the metric system, percent, and money are three of the more important ones.

Carpenter and co-workers (1981) report a lack of conceptual understanding about decimals in 9-year-old and 13-year-old students surveyed by the National Assessment of Educational Progress (NAEP). Carpenter advocates building a strong understanding of decimal concepts before proceeding to computation and application. Carpenter and co-workers suggest two approaches: capitalizing on students' knowledge and skill with whole numbers, and tying their understanding of common fractions to that of decimals. To accomplish this, students need a firm understanding of the place value system and how it relates to decimals, and a good background with common fractions, which can aid in the development of tenths and hundredths.

O'Brien (1968, as cited by Suydam & Osborne) investigated the effects of three treatments on students' learning of decimal computation. O'Brien found that students who were taught decimals with an emphasis on the principles of numeration, with no mention of fractions, scored lower on tests of computation with decimals than those taught the relation between decimals and fractions.

Decimals can pose special problems for children. They have characteristics similar to both whole numbers and fractions. Decimals, however, are different from each of these in the way they are conceptualized and in the way they are manipulated. For example, a student in our teaching experiment, when asked which was less, 0.37 or 0.73, suggested that 0.37 was greater because 0.37 was three tens and seven hundreds (not three ten*ths* and seven hundred*ths*) and 0.73 was seven tens and three hundreds (not seven ten*ths* and three hundred*ths*). The student then concluded that 0.37 (three tens and seven hundreds) was certainly greater than 0.73 (seven tens and three hundreds). Although such a comment implies an impressive string of logical thought, the problem occurred when the student attempted to apply whole number reasoning strategies to the newly evolving decimal understandings. This phenomenon is common and was alluded to earlier in this chapter when other students made similar errors when attempting to deal with other emerging rational number concepts.

Decimals are in their own right an important extension of both the base ten place value system and of rational number. Decimals can be correctly interpreted from either perspective. The first highlights the place value aspect of decimals and considers decimals as a logical extension of the base ten numeration system to include tenths (one-tenth of one whole); hundredths (one-tenth of one-tenth) and so forth. The second considers the decimal concept to be a special case of the area based part-whole interpretation of fractions in which whole is divided into a number of parts equal to some multiple of ten, the most common being 10, 100, or 1000. These two interpretations are not entirely separate. We shall see that both understandings interact and are important to understanding the decimal concept and operations with them. Consequently the student embarking on the study of decimal fractions for the first time should have a firm understanding of the base ten numeration system, including the ability to add and subtract whole numbers, and a grasp of a variety of fraction concepts including the ability to order two fractions, to generate equivalent fractions, and to perform simple calculations with fractions.

Operations with Decimals

Let us consider a simple operation with two decimals and note the interplay between previously learned place value and fraction concepts. The assumption here is that children have already used graph paper (one by ten and ten by ten grids), multibase arithmetic blocks, and place value charts extended to the right past tens and ones to one-tenths and one-hundredths. In other words, previously used materials and ideas can be exploited to develop meaning for the new concept. Incidentally the prefix "deci" means "tenth part."

A Fraction Interpretation of Addition

Consider the task of adding 0.6 and 0.73. Fraction understandings imply that 0.6 is simply six of ten strips on a ten by ten grid as indicated in Fig. 7−62a. Now 0.6 can be written as 6/10. Repartitioning each of the strips into ten parts allows us to reinterpret the six shaded strips (6/10) as 60/100, an equivalent fraction. Similarly 0.73 can be interpreted 7/10 + 3/100 or as more commonly written 73/100 (see Fig. 7−63b). Now 0.6 can be interpreted

$$\frac{60}{100} + \frac{73}{100} = \frac{133}{100} = 1\frac{33}{100}$$

When adding decimals we generally do not interpret each decimal as a fraction. It is important to do this initially however to communicate to children that decimals are not an entirely new concept but rather an extension of ideas already encountered.

FIGURE 7−62a
The meaning of 0.6 using a 10 × 10 grid.

FIGURE 7−62b
Fraction interpretation of 0.73 as 73 of 100 parts. Denoted as 7 tenths and 3 hundredths.

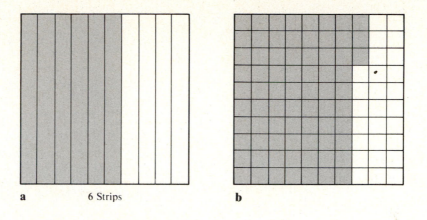

a   6 Strips   b

Place Value Interpretations

Multibase arithmetic blocks can be used to depict decimals in a place value setting. If the flat were defined as the unit, longs would be tenths, and units would be hundredths. If the block were defined as the unit, flats would be tenths, longs would be hundredths, and units would be thousandths. The ease with which children are able to redefine the unit is an important rational number-related skill and was discussed earlier in this chapter.

Children can use the physical pieces and make the regroupings in a manner similar to that discussed in Chapter 5. Figure 7−63 illustrates a place value chart using multibase arithmetic blocks.

Student's initial calculations should involve the actual manipulation of these materials or a reasonable facsimile such as graph paper cut into units (one by one), longs (one by ten), and flats (ten by ten). Materials should be used in conjunction with place value charts similar to Figs. 7−63 and 7−64. After some experience with these concrete embodiments, calculations with symbols can be undertaken. Place value charts emphasize the place value nature of the decimal calculations.

To add 0.6 and 0.73 in the conventional manner we could also adapt understandings from whole number addition, particularly the ideas that each column is ten times the column to its immediate right and that all addends must be correctly aligned. To add 0.6 and 0.73 we could use the place value charts as follows: Using previously learned strategies the sum of 0.6 and 0.73 in the enactive mode (Fig. 7−65) would be one flat, three longs, and three units after exchanging ten longs for one flat. Adding 0.6 and 0.73 symbolically (Fig. 7−65b), the sum would be 133, disregarding the placement of the decimal point for a moment. Where should it be placed? The interpretation of this result can again rely on fraction understandings. That is, $60/100 + 73/100 = 133/100$, which is a "bit more than" one whole, so 133 must become 1.33. Using regrouping procedures similar to those used with whole numbers, the answer becomes 1.33 rather than 0.133, 13.3 or 133.

What is important in this discussion is the subtle interplay between the place value concept derived from previous work with whole numbers and various

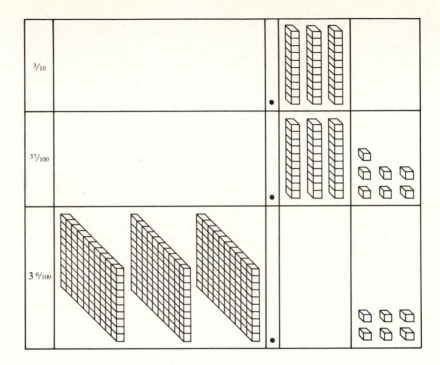

FIGURE 7–63
Place value charts
using multibase
arithmetic blocks
(flat defined as unit)

Fraction	100's (Hundreds)	10's (Tens)	1's (Ones)	Decimal Point	$1/10$ (Tenths)	$1/100$ (Hundredths)
$3/10$				•	3	
$73/100$				•	7	3
$8/10$				•	8	
$80/100$				•	8	0
$3\ 6/10$			3	•	6	
$15\ 6/100$		1	5	•	0	6

FIGURE 7–64
Place value chart
showing fraction/
decimal equivalents

fraction understandings. If done effectively this interplay supports the development of a new idea and its associated symbolic system. Other operations with decimals can be developed and validated in a similar manner.

Multiplication and Division of Decimals

Multiplication and division of decimals can be taught by using either the common fraction or the place value approach. When using the common fraction approach, students should use their existing knowledge of fractions, performing the fraction multiplication, writing the answer as a decimal. For example,

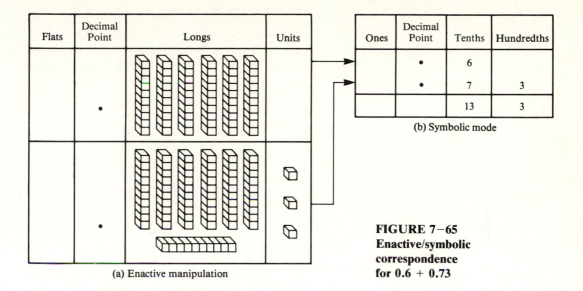

Flats	Decimal Point	Longs	Units

(a) Enactive manipulation

Ones	Decimal Point	Tenths	Hundredths
	•	6	
	•	7	3
		13	3

(b) Symbolic mode

FIGURE 7−65
Enactive/symbolic correspondence for 0.6 + 0.73

$$0.6 \times 0.2 \text{ becomes} \quad 6/10 \times 2/10$$
$$\text{which is equal to} \quad 12/100$$
$$\text{which is equivalent to} \quad 0.12$$
$$\text{so } 0.6 \times 0.2 = 0.12$$

After completing several exercises of this type, students will generalize the rule for multiplying decimals: the number of decimal places in the product is equal to the total number of decimal places in each factor. In this way the students develop the multiplication algorithm for themselves, rather than merely memorizing a procedure they do not understand.

Division by decimals has long been an area of difficulty for students. It is important that an understanding of the meanings of division and division by a decimal is developed before any algorithm is introduced.

There are two basic interpretations of division (Fischbein et al., 1985). The first is called partitive division, the second is called measurement or quotative division. In partitive or sharing division, the divisor specifies how many groups the dividend should be separated into, while in measurement division, the divisor specifies the size of the groups to be made. The following example highlights this difference:

Example: 6/2
Partitive Interpretation: Make 2 groups: 000   000
    Answer is the size of the groups (i.e. 3 per group). (Answer is 3.)
Measurement or Quotative Interpretation:
    Make groups of size 2 until initial quotient is exhausted: 00   00   00
    Answer is the number of groups. (Answer is 3.)

When dividing the number by a decimal, the partitive interpretation tends to be a bit more cumbersome. Using the example 3/0.5, the partitive interpretation would ask us to make 0.5 of a group or to suggest that 3 is 0.5 of a group. This is a rather difficult concept to learn especially if the divisor were a number more complicated than 0.5.

The measurement or quotative interpretation is more helpful because in the example 3/0.5 it asks us to make groups of size 0.5. This can be done using a variety of manipulatives, including base ten blocks and fraction pieces or Cuisenaire rods.

Completing this example

3/0.5 = dividing 3 into groups of 0.5 we get
0.5 0.5   0.5 0.5   0.5 0.5

Result = (the number of groups, in this case 6).

Thus 3 ÷ 0.5 = 6.

Activities of this sort are crucial to the development of the concept of division by decimals. Of course, more complex divisions will ultimately be handled with a calculator.

Children should have a variety of experiences with each of the models. Teachers should continually emphasize the order and equivalence within and between the two different symbolic systems.

For example, 0.4 is less than 0.41; 0.4 is equal to 0.40
0.37 is less than 0.38; 0.37 is equal to 37/100
0.8 = 8/10 = 80/100
0.62 × 0.3 = 62/100 × 3/10 = 186/1000 = 0.186, and so forth.

When children are comfortable with the underlying concepts, operations with decimals can begin to be developed. Of course there is no reason to spend valuable time developing speed and accuracy with these decimal operations because calculators will ultimately replace complicated work with pencil and paper.

CHAPTER 7 SUMMARY

Chapter 7 presented a variety of ways to think about rational numbers and suggested that a variety of mathematical interpretations and a variety of physical materials are necessary if children are to fully understand these complex concepts. Ideas about rational numbers evolve over several years in the school curriculum. Like measurement, rational numbers permeate the school curriculum and are a very important area of investigation. Without them, much of what is to be taught later cannot be comprehended. Rational numbers are difficult in and of themselves because they are such a broad and reaching topic. To add to the problem, they are generally poorly developed by textbooks.

The section on decimals in Chapter 7 suggested two important approaches to the understanding of decimals and provided a variety of activities for teaching them.

An omnipresent theme has been the development of understanding of concepts before algorithms are introduced. Because fractions and whole number operations will already be familiar to students, it seems reasonable to exploit these previous understandings in developing decimal and other rational number concepts. After students understand these concepts they should be free to use calculators as needed, thus freeing valuable instructional time for other important activities including real-world applications and the development of other mathematical concepts.

REFERENCES

Behr, M. 1977. *The effects of manipulatives in second graders' learning of mathematics,* Vol. I. PMDC Technical Report No. 11. Tallahassee, FL: Project for the Mathematical Development of Children.

Behr, M., & Bright, G. 1984, April. *Identifying fractions on number lines.* Paper presented at the meeting of the American Educational Association, New Orleans, LA.

Behr, M. J., Lesh, R., Post, T. R., & Silver, E. A. 1983. Rational-number concepts. In R. Lesh & M. Landau (Eds.), *Acquisition of mathematics concepts and processes* (pp. 92–126). New York: Academic Press.

Behr, M., Wachsmuth, I., Post, T., & Lesh, R. 1984. Order and equivalence of rational numbers. *Journal for Research in Mathematics Education,* 15:323–341.

Bell, M., Fuson, K. D., & Lesh, R. 1976. *Algebraic & arithmetic structures.* New York: The Free Press.

Bruner, J. 1966. *Toward a theory of instruction.* New York: W. W. Norton & Co.

Carpenter, T. P., Coburn, T. G., Reys, R. E., & Wilson, J. W. 1976. Notes from national assessment: Addition and multiplication with fractions. *Arithmetic Teacher,* 23(2):137–141.

Carpenter, T. P., Corbitt, M. K., Kepner, H. S., Jr., Lindquist, M., & Reys, R. E. 1980. National assessment: Prospective of students' mastery of basic skills. In M. Lindquist (Ed.), *Selected issues in mathematics education.* Berkeley, CA: McCutchan.

Carpenter, T. P., Corbitt, M. K., Kepner, H. S., Jr., Lindquist, M., & Reys, R. E. 1981. Decimals: Results & implications from national assessment. *Arithmetic Teacher,* 28(8):34–37.

Dienes, Z. 1960. *Building up mathematics.* London: Hutchinson Educational Ltd.

Ellerbruch, L. W., & Payne, J. N. 1978. A teaching sequence for initial fraction concepts through the addition of unlike fractions. In M. Suydam (Ed.), *Developing computational skills.* Reston, VA: National Council of Teachers of Mathematics.

Faires, D. 1963. Computation with decimal fractions in the sequence of number development (Doctoral dissertation, Wayne State University). *Dissertation Abstracts International,* 23:4183.

Fischbein, E., Deri, M., Sainati, N. M., Sciolis, M. M. 1985. The role of implicit models in solving verbal problems in multiplication and division. *Journal for Research in Mathematics Education,* 16(1):3–17.

Gagne, R. M., & White, R. T. 1978. Memory structures and learning outcomes. *Review of Educational Research,* 48:187–222.

Grossman, A. S. 1983. Decimal notation: An important research finding. *Arithmetic Teacher,* 30(9):32–33.

Hiebert, J., & Tonnessen, L. H. 1978. Development of the fraction concept in two physical contexts: An exploratory investigation. *Journal for Research in Mathematics Education,* 9(5):374–378.

Hiebert, J. & Wearne, D. 1984, April. A model of students' decimal computation procedures. Paper presented at the Annual Meeting of the National Council of Teachers of Mathematics, San Francisco, CA.

Hoffer, A. 1978. *Number sense and arithmetic skills. A resource for teachers.* Palo Alto, CA: Creative Publication.

Karplus, R., Karplus, E., Formisano, M., & Paulsen, A. C. 1979. Proportional reasoning and control of variables in seven countries. In J. Lochhead & J. Clements (Eds.), *Cognitive process instruction.* Philadelphia, PA: Franklin Institute Press.

Karplus, R., Karplus, E. F., & Wollman, W. 1974. Intellectual development beyond elementary school: Ratio, the influence of cognitive style (Vol. 4). *School Science and Mathematics,* 76(6):476–482.

Kidder, R. F. 1980. Ditton's dilemma, or what to do about decimals. *Arithmetic Teacher,* 28(2):44–46.

Kieren, T. E. 1976. On the mathematical cognitive and instructional foundations of rational numbers. In R. A. Lesh & D. A. Bradbard (Eds.), *Number and measurement: Papers from a research workshop* (pp. 101–144). ERIC/SMEAC.

Kieren, T. E., & Southwell, B. 1979. Rational numbers as operators: The development of this construct in children and adolescents. *Alberta Journal of Educational Research,* 25(4):234–247.

Kurtz, B., & Karplus, R. 1979. Intellectual development beyond elementary school: Teaching for proportional reasoning (Vol. 7). *School Science and Mathematics,* 79(5):387–398.

Lesh, R., Landau, M., & Hamilton, E. 1980. Rational number ideas and the role of representational systems. In R. Karplus (Ed.), *Proceedings of the Fourth International Conference for the Psychology of Mathematics Education.* Berkeley, CA: University of California.

Noelting, G. 1980. The development of proportional reasoning and the ratio concept: Part I—The differentiation of stages. *Educational Studies in Mathematics,* 11: 217–253.

Novillis, C. 1976. An analysis of the fraction concept into a hierarchy of selected subconcepts and the testing of the hierarchy dependences. *Journal for Research in Mathematics Education,* 7:131–144.

Novillis-Larson, C. 1980. Locating proper fractions. *School Science and Mathematics,* 53(5):423–428.

O'Brien, T. C. 1968. An experimental investigation of a new approach to the teaching of decimals. (Doctoral dissertation, New York University, 1967). *Dissertation Abstracts International,* 28A:4541–4542.

Post, T. R. 1974. A model for the construction and sequencing of laboratory activities. *Arithmetic Teacher,* 21(7):616–622.

Post, T. R. 1981. The role of manipulative materials in the learning of mathematical concepts. In M. Lindquist (Ed.), *Selected issues in mathematics education.* Berkeley, CA: McCutchan.

Post, T. R., & Reys, R. E. 1979. Abstraction generalization and design of mathematical experiences for children. In K. Fuson & W. Geeslin (Eds.), *Models for mathematics learning.* Columbus, OH: ERIC/SMEAC.

Post, T., Wachsmuth, I., Lesh, R., & Behr, M. 1985. Order and equivalence of rational numbers: A cognitive analysis. *Journal for Research in Mathematics Education,* 16:18−36.

Post, T., Behr, M., Lesh, R., Wachsmuth, I. 1985. Selected results from the rational number project. *Proceedings of the Ninth Psychology of Mathematics Education Conference.* The Netherlands: International Group for the Psychology of Mathematics Education, pp. 342−351.

Pothier, Y., & Sawada, O. 1983. Partitioning: The emergence of rational number ideas in young children. *Journal for Research in Mathematics Education,* 14:307−317.

Schmalz, R. S. P. 1978. A visual approach to decimals. *Arithmetic Teacher,* 25(8): 22−25.

Suydam, M., & Higgins, J. 1976. *Review and synthesis of studies of activity-based approaches to mathematics teaching.* (Final Report, NIE Contract No. 400-75-0063). Columbus: ERIC Center, Ohio State University.

Suydam, M. N., & Osborne, A. R. (Eds.). Algorithmic learning. *Mathematics Education Information Report.* Columbus, OH: The ERIC Science, Mathematics, & Environmental Education Clearinghouse (no date given).

Willson, G. H. 1969. A comparison of decimal-common fraction sequence with conventional sequence for fifth grade arithmetic (Doctoral dissertation, University of Arizona, 1969). *Dissertation Abstracts International,* 30A:1762.

Zawojewski, J. 1983. Initial decimal concepts: Are they really so easy? *Arithmetic Teacher,* 30(7):52−56.

8 Geometry and Visual Thinking

ALAN R. HOFFER

Boston University

INTRODUCTION

Geometry has been identified as a basic skill by the National Council of Teachers of Mathematics. As such, it should be a central topic throughout school mathematics curricula. Unfortunately such is not the case. In many schools the geometry chapter is delayed until the end of the school year to allow children more time to develop and perfect computational skills, many times at a rote level.

A recent study comparing student achievement in two dozen countries found that many geometry topics taught internationally are not considered in many U.S. eighth grade classrooms. It is no wonder that the same study found that geometry achievement in U.S. schools ranks in the bottom 25% of all countries. Perhaps this is because many students have never had the opportunity to learn these important ideas.

This chapter will develop a case for the importance of geometry, address a wide variety of circumstances in which it is appropriate, and provide examples of how geometric concepts can be effectively taught.

WHY GEOMETRY IS A BASIC SKILL

It is sad that so many children do not have the opportunity to learn geometry and to have visual thinking experiences because their teachers or school systems do not consider geometry a basic skill. Geometry is really a basic skill in several ways.

We use visual representations of arithmetic concepts quite often. The intent is to convey an idea about arithmetic by using a picture. The saying, "A picture is worth a thousand words," is appropriate here because it is often much easier to communicate a concept or skill by creating a visual image of it. The idea represented in the picture is often understood quickly by students and retained for a longer period of time than is a sequence of words. Also, it is of utmost importance that a picture or graph image not be used to explain a concept until the children have studied the intrinsic geometry of the picture. Here are some examples of how geometry relates to the arithmetic program.

Multiplication and Rectangular Areas

When teaching children about multiplying two whole numbers we often display the situation in a rectangular grid. Figure 8−1 shows an arrangement of three rows that each contain four objects. The picture conveys the idea of 3 times 4; the students count the total number of objects to obtain 12 and thus learn that $3 \times 4 = 12$. Other multiplication facts are displayed as a rectangular areas in Fig. 8−2. Indeed, we might more closely interrelate the children's experiences

FIGURE 8−1

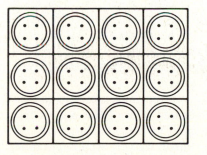

FIGURE 8−2

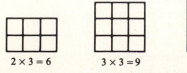 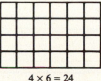 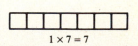

$2 \times 3 = 6$ $3 \times 3 = 9$ $4 \times 6 = 24$ $1 \times 7 = 7$

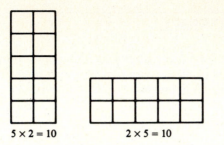

FIGURE 8-3 $5 \times 2 = 10$ $2 \times 5 = 10$

in learning multiplication with that of learning about the area of rectangles. This implies that they have sufficient knowledge of geometry to be able to identify rectangles in various shapes and positions and that they have some understanding of the concepts of interior (inside), in a line (lined up), and area.

The rectangles in Fig. 8–3 show how to visualize the commutative property of multiplication and how it relates to conservation of areas of rectangles in different positions.

Fractions and Rectangular Areas

An experienced teacher once told how perplexed she was with the textbook the district had selected. She said things were going smoothly until she got to Chapter Four, which covered some geometry. She was very unhappy with the authors of the book for putting geometry between chapters that covered basic skills, so she skipped the geometry chapter "because it isn't a basic skill." When the teacher was asked what topic followed the geometry chapter, the teacher said, "Fractions come next. But, you know children have a very difficult time with fractions." Many teachers think of fractions as one of the most difficult ideas to teach, and they are. However, it is essential for students to understand a good deal of geometry before they can progress very far in the study of fractions. Often fractional parts are displayed for students in terms of parts of geometric shapes.

Figure 8–4 shows how a rectangle is used to convey the idea of 6/8 as well as the much more complicated idea of the equivalence between 6/8 and 3/4. Many ideas about fractions involve geometric concepts. By skipping over the geometry part of the course, we very well might make some arithmetic ideas inaccessible to students.

FIGURE 8-4

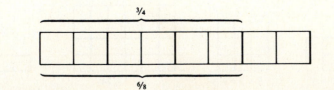

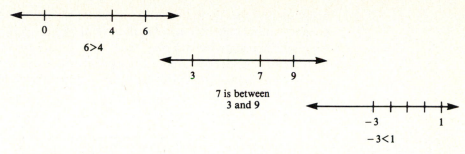

FIGURE 8–5

Geometry of the Number Line

For some other examples of how geometric ideas relate to arithmetic, consider the geometry of number lines and how children can use number lines to visualize the concepts of greater than, less than, betweenness, and even negative numbers (Fig. 8–5). Addition and subtraction of whole numbers as well as various rules of arithmetic can be displayed on number lines (Fig. 8–6).

In addition to recognizing ways geometry can help in the teaching and learning of arithmetic, we should realize there are students who are more visually oriented than other students. For students who are "right brain dominant," visual tasks are more readily received and are easier to work on. We should present mathematical experiences to children to provide them with outlets for or to at least enable them to exercise the visual or holistic functions in their brains, and this often means geometry experiences. You will find several examples of such experiences in the "Instructional Activities" section later in this chapter.

Areas of rectangles relate closely to whole number multiplication and to fraction concepts. Distances also relate to number line geometry. Areas and distances are measurements that are quite useful in daily physical situations. Many practical problems a person encounters in science or society involve representing the situation of the problem in some visual format. It seems silly to devote so much of the school day to teaching arithmetic if students are unable to visualize the problem situations well enough to apply the arithmetic facts (see Hoffer, 1983a).

Furthermore, we can justify providing experiences in geometry and visualization in the elementary school simply because students find so many of these

FIGURE 8–6

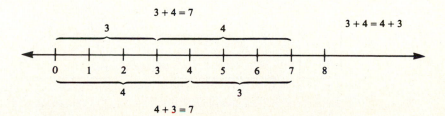

activities interesting and exciting. Many of these experiences, especially for primary school children, involve the use of objects they can hold, move, and work with in somewhat of a play mode as they learn the mathematical ideas; in other words, this is their laboratory where they can explore with their hands as well as with their minds. See the "Instructional Activities" section for some examples.

GEOMETRY IN THE SCHOOL CURRICULUM

It is worthwhile to look at mathematics textbooks that are one hundred or more years old. For example, you will find that a typical mathematics textbook for elementary schools of that vintage, which includes kindergarten through eighth grade, is less than two centimeters thick. Compare that with typical K−8 textbook series today which, when stacked up with the ancillary materials, can be taller than some children. But bigger doesn't necessarily mean better, so while today's texts have lots of so-called motivational pictures and colored photographs, and formats that may appeal to textbook purchasing committees, we should not assume they are better organized for student learning (see "Overcoming Obstacles to Learning" later in this chapter). In fact in the early textbooks, in addition to the emphasis on arithmetic and ratios, you will find numerous measurement activities of a geometric nature and suggestions to the teacher for other explorations dealing with geometric shapes.

Gradually the geometry content of the textbooks took on a new complexion. While there was still a heavy emphasis on measurement as a way to view or at least justify geometry in the books, vocabulary and symbols started to

FIGURE 8−7

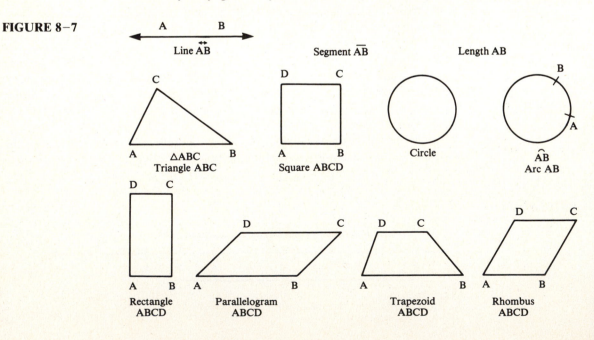

become major issues. Students were required to learn words for different types of polygons as well as symbols for designating various types of objects (see Fig. 8–7). Children were drilled on the words for the various shapes and even tested on whether or not they could recognize when to use certain symbols to label the various objects. Most of the shapes were those that lie in a plane. Rarely can one find in these books any questions that ask the students to think about and analyze the various geometric shapes.

There is now a new role for geometry in the school curriculum. There is now a realization that there is more to learning geometry than memorizing vocabulary and measuring lengths. This increased importance of geometry at the elementary school level is the result of research studies conducted over the past fifty years in several countries and the availability of reasonably inexpensive computers and powerful computer programs. We discuss these factors in the following chapters.

WHAT WE CAN LEARN FROM RESEARCH

In several locations around the world researchers have made serious investigations about why students seem to have difficulty learning geometry. Initially, the efforts were often motivated by the search for answers to why so many older students did poorly in the proof aspects of geometry. That question forced the investigators to look at younger and younger students. These investigations began 50 years ago with the work of Russian and Swiss psychologists and more recently have involved American researchers. Possibly it is the result of this early work in Europe that European schools include more geometry experiences for their students and effectively begin those experiences at an earlier age.

Our discussion of the research into the learning of geometry will focus on two school teachers from the Netherlands, Pierre van Hiele and Dina van Hiele-Geldof. The van Hieles (1959) were interested in finding ways to help their students think and to analyze problems, or in their words, in developing insight in their students. Troubled by the way their students performed in geometry, the van Hieles eventually formulated explanations for why students had such difficulty. The van Hieles proposed that there are levels of thought in which to discuss, learn, and work with geometry. These levels include obstacles for communication between students and teachers as well as between students and textbooks. If a teacher or textbook presents an idea at a level above that of the students, it is not likely that the students will understand the question or assignment, and so they will be unable to do the requested work or answer the question. The van Hieles published their work in Dutch in 1957 and then later in English (Freudenthal, 1958). Below we summarize the thought levels in geometry that were proposed by the van Hieles.

Level 0: This is a holistic level. The students perceive figures by their appearances as a whole. When students call a figure a square, they react to the total figure and not to specific properties of the square such as right angles and

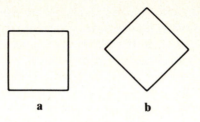

FIGURE 8–8   a   b

equal side lengths. The students may not even be explicitly aware of the properties of and relationships among the parts of the figures. They may call a shape a square "because it looks like a square" (Fig. 8–8a) and for no other reason. Also, they do not call the shape in Fig. 8–8b a square "because it doesn't look like a square."

Level 1: Students at Level 1 are able to analyze figures. They are alert to various properties of the figures. What was only implicitly recognized by the students at Level 0 is made explicit now. Their analysis, for example, may assert that all sides of a square are congruent and all of its angles are right angles. They can also identify figures by knowing their properties. For example, if a figure is described as one with each pair of sides parallel, the students will relate it to the word parallelogram if they have heard the word before, irrespective of the position of the object (Fig. 8–9). Even though the students now are able to acknowledge various relationships among the parts of figures, they, at most, implicitly realize there are relationships among figures. At this level, for example, the students do not perceive any relationship between squares and rectangles.

Level 2: Students at Level 2 begin to see relationships among figures and even among the properties of the figures. They acknowledge that a square is also a rectangle and that a rectangle is also a special type of parallelogram. These relationships, which may have been implicit at Level 1, are now very explicit with the students. Students are formulating a detailed classification of the figures as well as of the properties of the figures. If they are asked what type of quadrilateral has both the properties that all of its angles are right angles and all of its sides are congruent, the students acknowledge that the figure is a square. While the students are now able to recognize properties of figures and relationships among different types of figures (Fig. 8–10) and they even may

FIGURE 8–9

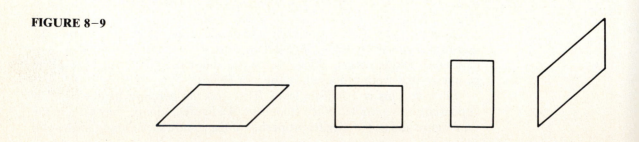

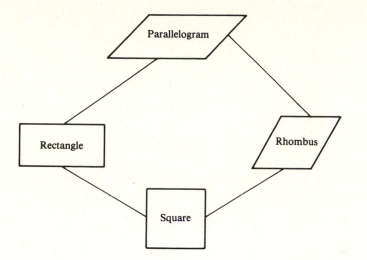

FIGURE 8-10

be able to observe various such relationships themselves, they only have an implicit understanding of how these relationships link to justify their observations. In other words, the students have not yet developed the ability to prove theorems.

Level 3: Students at Level 3 begin to understand deductive reasoning. They can follow the line of argument in proofs of statements presented to them, and they can develop sequences of statements to deduce one statement from another. What may have been an implicit understanding at Level 2 of why certain statements were true (the level at which students might say, "I think I understand it, but I can't explain it") now develops into reasoning patterns that enable the students to create sequences of statements to formally explain, that is, prove why the statement is true (Fig. 8-11).

Level 4: This is the most rigorous level of thought—the depth of which is similar to that of a mathematician. At this level the person has deep understanding of mathematical structures and is able to justify to a very high degree statements made about the structures.

In the United States most of the geometry experience of students is concentrated in the high school years when students are expected to think at Level 2, and yet, as we note below, recent studies have confirmed that even at the high school level a large percentage of students are still at Level 0. It is no wonder then that students have difficulty in what is called "high school geometry" when they have not been adequately prepared in elementary school.

For nearly 50 years Soviet psychologists have researched how students learn and how to improve students' understanding of geometry (see Kilpatrick & Wirszup, 1969–1977). The Soviets immediately were attracted to the van Hiele ideas, and around 1960 they began to research the authenticity of the van Hiele model. By 1964 the Soviets had conducted several studies based largely on the van Hiele model, and they organized and experimented with a new

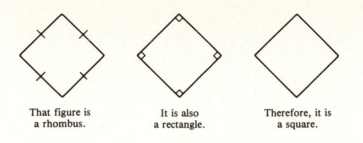

FIGURE 8-11

That figure is
a rhombus.

It is also
a rectangle.

Therefore, it is
a square.

curriculum. Many of the assertions made by the van Hieles were also made by the Soviet educators (Kilpatrick & Wirszup, 1969–1977) namely that

- There are levels of thinking, especially in relation to understanding geometry, and the levels occur as obstacles to the students. We must be aware of these obstacles and try to find ways to help the students overcome them.
- Concepts that may be only implicitly understood by students at a lower level become explicit at higher levels so we need to give students adequate experiences to familiarize them with new ideas.
- Two people who are reasoning on two different levels do not understand each other so teachers and textbooks need to recognize at what level the students are and to address them at that level.
- In order for students to be able to reason at a higher level, they must first have had sufficient and effective learning experiences at the lower levels. If one tries to skip levels by learning things in a rote manner, for example, as is usually done with fractions, we can expect that the students will not retain much of what was studied.

Recently three major concurrent studies, based on the work of the van Hieles and the Russian psychologists, were conducted in the United States. The studies were centered in Oregon (University of Oregon and Oregon State University), (Burger, 1981; Hoffer 1979, 1981), Brooklyn (Brooklyn College), (Fuys, Geddes, & Tischler, 1984) and Chicago (The University of Chicago). The studies dealt with students from the second grade level through high school. Here is a summary of some of the findings of these studies (see Hoffer, 1983b):

- Children are familiar with some geometric vocabulary, but they often have gross misconceptions or totally incorrect ideas about what many of the words mean. For example, many students thought the only way a figure can be a triangle is if it is equilateral.
- Children often are unduly influenced by the orientation of figures. For example, a large proportion of the students did not recognize a figure to be a triangle if it did not have a side parallel to the bottom of the page on which they were working.
- Students at all ages use converse reasoning in the sense that they would change necessary conditions about a figure into sufficient conditions. For

example, in a guessing game to identify a figure, students were given some clues. If the students were asked to pick a square and were given the clue "It has four sides," they would identify any figure with four sides as a square. They reasoned as follows: "A square has four sides. I am looking for a figure with four sides. It must be a square."

- Textbook series analyzed were found to be deficient, even confusing in the way topics in geometry were organized and presented. For example, the work largely consisted of naming shapes and some relations like parallelism. Students were seldom asked to reason with the figures.
- Children tend to idealize figures and, in a sense, restrict their thinking about the figures. Children would tend to pick out one type of figure from a collection and use it as reference no matter how vastly different the figures in the collection may be.
- Children tend to believe that various changes to figures do not affect changes in other aspects of the figure. For example, many children at all ages were convinced that the area of a quadrilateral can be obtained by transforming it into a rectangle with the same perimeter.

The various studies about the way children reason with geometric figures indicate that geometry in the schools should involve much more than just vocabulary and measurement. Solid figures, for example, often receive little attention in U.S. school curricula. Yet, solid figures offer opportunities to relate mathematics to everyday living, to develop aspects of space perception, and to practice problem-solving techniques through discovery lessons. In general, European school children do more work with geometry and do it earlier. What can their experiences teach us about instruction in geometry? Most younger students and unfortunately many adults in the United States think at Level 0 or Level 1.

Teachers must address the student at the student's level. Try to imagine what it is like for a student who is reasoning at Level n when the instructor is teaching at Level $n + 2$. For example, a textbook may begin a treatment of geometry by bringing in definitions very early in the course. According to the van Hiele model this is a Level 2 activity. However, usually many students are still operating at Level 0 where they are reacting to geometric figures as wholes. Hence there is a considerable gap between what is expected in the course by the textbook and the teacher and what the student is prepared to study. The outcome is quite predictable: the students become confused by the topic and the teachers are frustrated with the students' poor performances. The van Hieles (Fuys et al., 1984) feel it is possible to skip levels by learning things rotely, but only at the risk of subsequent rapid forgetting. In other words, at best the students only partially learn the concepts and very rapidly forget much of what they learned.

Instructional activity for students should be based on their level of thinking. Besides enriching their thinking at that level, the lessons should move the students toward the next level. Because even an occasional college student may not know rudimentary geometry vocabulary, we should check our younger students for knowledge of the basic shapes: square, rectangle, triangle, circle.

The concepts of parallelogram, trapezoid, rhombus, and more specialized ideas will need development or at least some reminders. Geoboard work—showing a figure given its name, or naming and copying a given figure—would strengthen vocabulary and give the students chances to notice some of the interrelationships among parts (for example, that the opposite sides of a parallelogram have the same length).

Our aim is to give Level 0 students experiences oriented toward Level 1, the awareness of the relationships among the parts of a figure. In saying, ". . . it is the manipulation of figures which causes a structure to be born. This nourishes the thinking at Level 1 . . ." (1958, p. 205) van Hiele agrees with Piaget. Inhelder, a Piaget co-worker, believes that ". . . children with richer possibilities of manipulative and visual tactile explorations have better spatial reasoning" (Sherman, 1967, p. 296). Hands-on activities usually help Level 0 students move toward Level 1.

These activities are used to encourage children to study the parts of a figure and how figures are related to each other, and hence they pave the way to Level 1 thinking. Once the proper Level 1 background is set up, occasional efforts toward Level 2 type thinking can be tried (see the "Instructional Activities" section later in this chapter).

In teaching middle school geometry, it is not necessary either logically or psychologically to start with points, segments, and so forth and end with solids. You could, for example, organize your students' work in geometry by beginning with cubes, rectangular solids, pyramids, and cones, and developing the terminology associated with these solid figures. The students at Level 0 could collect solids, empty boxes, cans, pieces of scrap from the shop, and so forth, to become familiar with vocabulary and develop an alertness to solid figures. Students could use sticks, rods, and the like to make shell and skeletal models. Making models of the figures is an unthreatening activity and provides opportunities, while the students are making the objects, to introduce vocabulary dealing with lower dimensional figures, such as segment, point, angle, parallelogram, and rectangle. Exploration of the figures could naturally lead to some Level 1 thinking as could some practice in drawing two- and three-dimensional figures. The reading of drawings can be enhanced by making drawings. By branching off from the basework with solid figures, one could certainly intermingle activities that focus on polygons, angles, segments, or measurement.

Teachers in other countries favor starting geometry work with three-dimensional objects not only because of their emphasis on physical experiences with (three-dimensional) concrete materials, but also because of the belief that too much work with only plane figures can "deaden" one's spatial perception (Freudenthal, 1973, pp. 408−409). We do live in a three-dimensional world. Symmetries and motions with their dynamic nature are also favored by many European teachers and can serve as the focal point for geometry work.

Individual Differences

You will notice unusual differences in children and many adults during the work in geometry, particularly during the work presented by drawings. Students' visual perceptions vary so greatly that "top" students may not do as well as they do on other topics and some of the so-called weaker students may do very well on visualization topics. One interesting aspect of these individual differences is that girls in general do not seem to do as well as boys in tasks involving judging or manipulating spatial figures (Tyler, 1965, p. 245). There are, of course, many girls who excel at such tasks just as there are many boys who do not do well (Fennema & Tartre, 1985). However, this on-the-average difference is apparent by the middle grades (Davis, 1973; Karnovsky, 1974), is more pronounced with complicated tasks, and seems to increase through the teens (Sherman, 1967). Plausible explanations lie in the different amounts of practice in spatial processing involved in the activities usually associated with culturally imposed sex roles in which (1) boys are expected to be more physically active with mechanical things such as model building, blocks, and sports and (2) the greater verbal facility usually noted in girls, which enables them to do many things without the physical action required by the less-verbal boys (for additional explanations see Maccoby and Jacklin, 1974). Whatever the reason for the differences, there is some evidence that the spatial-visualization ability of junior high boys and girls can be improved by instruction (Wolfe, 1970).

Some geometry tasks may best serve as diagnostics to determine which students need preliminary or supplementary work with hands-on experiences. For example, Boe (1968) found that American youngsters in eighth, tenth, and twelfth grades were not proficient at predicting shapes cut from a solid. Davis (1973) repeated the experiment with students in sixth, eighth, and tenth grades but provided a practice session during which the students actually cut some irregular styrofoam solids. Sections from oblique cuts were the hardest ones for students to predict.

In planning instruction in geometry, there may be benefits in considering the van Hieles' first levels of thinking: Level 0, in which a figure is regarded as a whole without considering its parts; Level 1, in which interrelationships among parts are used; and Level 2, in which some degree of logical organization is used. It is more important that we work at the student's level, giving instruction that leads to the next level. Recognizing the models available in real-world objects, you can build your geometry work on three-dimensional figures. You can include experiences with spatial perception, keeping in mind that some students may not give their usual performance. Finally, work with Piaget-type interview tasks where thought processes are probed by the investigator will give data on students' cognitive development (Piaget et al., 1956, 1964).

OVERCOMING OBSTACLES TO LEARNING

To help students raise their thought level, several plans have been suggested that are quite similar in that they all seem to move the students from very direct instruction to a degree of independent study. The van Hieles specified such a sequence, which they referred to as phases of learning. Here are the phases of learning in their plan.

Phase 1: Inquiry—The teacher engages the students in conversations about the topics to be studied. The teacher evaluates the students' responses and learns how the students interpret the words used and provides the students with some awareness of why they are studying the topic. Students and teacher ask questions and make observations about the vocabulary and objects of the topic, and these discussions set the stage for further study.

Phase 2: Directed orientation—Next, the teacher carefully sequences activities for the students to explore. The students begin to realize what direction the study is taking, and they become familiar with the structures involved in the topic such as the vocabulary, symbols, figures, properties, and relations. The teacher usually organizes the activities in this phase as one-step tasks which call for very specific responses or very specific actions on the part of the students. Essentially the students are following the teacher's instruction step-by-step.

Phase 3: Expliciting—The students now have had experience in working with the structures of the topic so during Phase 3 they learn to verbally describe what they have observed or at least they learn to express their opinions about the structures of the study. The teacher learns also, by the way, what perceptions the students have about the topic and can help the students develop their observations toward the goals of the lesson. During this phase the students explicitly form a system of relationships as they make their own observations.

Phase 4: Free orientation—Now the students are becoming somewhat experienced in the topic. They encounter multistep tasks as well as tasks that can be completed in different ways (as opposed to the one-step tasks of the directed orientation phase). The students have experience in solving problems and resolving tasks. By orienting themselves in the topic, they start to perceive the most important relations in the topic and recognize how to apply these relations.

Phase 5: Integration—The students form an overview of the topic for themselves. They are no longer bound by small details of the topic; they are able to see the larger picture. The objects and the relations are unified and internalized into a new domain of thought. The teacher aids this process by providing summaries of some of the major ideas of the topic that the students already know. These summaries reaffirm the concepts for the students.

According to the van Hieles, when the students arrive at the fifth phase, they have increased their thought level with regard to the topic.

Text Analysis

In a thorough analysis of the geometry content of elementary school textbooks conducted in the United States (see Fuys, Geddes, and Tischler, 1984), The following questions were posed:

1. What geometry topics are taught by grade level? Does the inclusion of topics indicate continuity of instruction and richness of geometry experience?
2. At what van Hiele level are the geometry materials at each grade level?
3. Is the van Hiele level of material sequenced by grade level?
4. Are there jumps across van Hiele levels, within a grade or from grade to grade?

5. Is the text presentation of geometry topics consistent with the van Hiele model?

Three popular text series were used for the analysis. Features that differed among the series as well as common features of the series were noted. The study described how lessons were presented in the texts; how geometric vocabulary was used; the number of pages devoted to geometry; how the text materials fit into the van Hiele levels; how the test questions distributed among the levels; the characteristics of the diagrams in the student editions; how properties and relations are formulated; and how three content strands (polygons, angle measurements, and area measurements) are viewed in terms of the van Hiele model. Here is a summary of the findings.

With reference to Question 1, there were 152 topics identified in the reviewed texts but there were differences in where the topics were introduced. There does seem to be continuity of instruction but not much richness of geometry experience.

In response to Question 2 the study concluded, "There is very little level 2 thinking exhibited in the texts, starting only in grades 7−8. There is some level 1 thinking from grade 3 on. However, average students do not need to think above level 0 for almost all of their geometry experience through grade 8."

Concerning Question 3 about the sequencing of material, the study observed that there was not much to sequence because the texts did not move very deeply through the levels. The report noted, "[M]aterial in the exposition of the texts is in general sequenced by level. But this question is not in general relevant to consideration of exercises and tests as there is so little progression here beyond level 0." (Fuys et al., 1984; Burger, 1981).

With reference to Question 4 concerning the jumps across levels, the study observed, "The most significant jumps found were within a text page. Frequently exposition is at a higher level than exercises. . . . *Students will presumably encounter difficulty with a secondary school geometry* course at level 2 if they can successfully complete grade 8 with level 0 thinking."

With regard to Question 5: Is the text presentation of geometry topics consistent with didactic principles of the van Hieles?, the study noted that the characteristics of the diagrams and the formation of properties and relationships were not in general consistent with the didactic principles of the van Hieles.

Properties and relationships among polygons were not always taught clearly and sometimes taught incorrectly (for example, squares as nonrectangles).

Development of angle measurement and angle sum relations for polygons is also unsatisfactory and does not follow the recommended development of the van Hieles.

Development of measurement of area is taught with counting squares and then by learning a formula. The area measurement of a rectangle, for example, is not related to a model of multiplication. Thus, reduction of level occurs. Students can often correctly answer a question without understanding why the answer is correct, merely by resorting to clues and thinking at a lower level.

In conclusion, the report by Fuys, Geddes & Tischler (1984) discusses the mediocrity of American students in mathematics, especially in "more sophisticated questions." It suggests examination of foreign series, especially van Hiele's texts and Soviet texts, which use van Hiele principles, for development of better American texts and curriculum. Included are some suggestions for improved texts, curriculum, and teacher training.

INSTRUCTIONAL ACTIVITIES

Children use words differently than adults do. For example, the word triangle to many children means a certain equilateral triangle while teachers and textbooks use the word to include a much more general concept. Certainly, we want students to understand the meaning of the words used in the problems they work; on the other hand, learning vocabulary is not the main reason for studying geometry. Geometric ideas and relationships are much more important than the memorization of vocabulary. Here is a horror story for you; it is a true story: There is at least one elementary textbook series that has a fifth grade book with twelve chapters. The first ten chapters completely ignore geometry even when there are splendid opportunities to enrich the arithmetic with geometric or visual representations. Then in Chapter 11 the text unloads every possible geometry vocabulary word on the students all at once! It is likely that most teachers who use that text series (or others just like it) skip that chapter entirely and thereby further inhibit their students' visual learning.

In this section we offer some suggestions for instructional activities you could organize for students at various grade levels and levels of thinking. We choose to start with solid objects and then work toward shapes in a plane because children encounter solid objects early in their daily experiences.

Polyhedra

Young children like to build with blocks. Let the children investigate blocks in various shapes and, by holding the objects in their hands, become familiar with the differences and similarities of the shapes. Invite the students to talk about the objects to each other and to the class.

Older children can make skeletal polyhedra with straws, rods, and commercial fasteners. Show pictures of the shapes to the students, as in Fig. 8–12, and ask them to try to build models like them out of the sticks.

Children of all ages need to express themselves, and one manner of expression is graphic. Even nonartists may need to draw diagrams of objects sometime in their lives. Try a drawing technique like that shown in Fig. 8–13. More advanced students could try to draw other polyhedra with which they have worked.

Have the students try to visualize how solids would look if they were cut apart and flattened out. For example, you could ask, "What does a tetrahedron look like when it is unfolded?" The students would then be designing nets (cardboard patterns) for the solids (see Fig. 8–14). A supply of cardboard

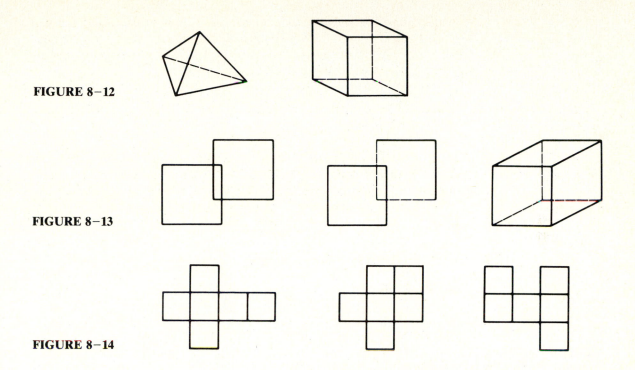

FIGURE 8–12

FIGURE 8–13

FIGURE 8–14

figures that could be cut up certainly helps. While the students are working with the solid objects, ask them to look at the object more carefully (analyze it) and ask how many faces it has, how many edges, and so forth.

Have the students compare the various nets they have designed for a specific figure. Ask them to find all the different possible nets that could be used to form that type of figure, such as a cube. For example, which of the nets in Fig. 8–14 folds up to form a cube? Are there others?

Polygons

Students can begin to work on and even review polygons by sorting and classifying. Give each student a collection of shapes cut out of cardboard or tagboard. (Students can help to cut out the shapes.) Ask the students to sort the shapes in some way. At first they might choose their own way to sort and later you could ask for specific sorting methods. Listen to the children talk about the figures and learn how they are using the words as well as what ideas they use to classify figures into various categories. If students do not ask for the names of various shapes, you could prompt such interest by asking questions like: Who has a rhombus? Does anyone have an isosceles triangle? Who has two trapezoids?

An effective and painless way to familiarize students with vocabulary as well as to become aware of geometric properties is to use the example-counter-example method or the so-called is-isn't method as illustrated in Fig. 8–15.

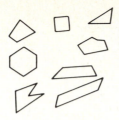

FIGURE 8—15   These are polygons.   These are not polygons.   Which are polygons?

The structure of this method is:

* These are blablas.
* These are not blablas.
* Which of these are blablas?

Ask the student to provide their own descriptions of the objects with which they work. It is instructive for you as the teacher to hear how your students use words and try to explain concepts out loud. The class learns to critique, clarify, and improve the definitions offered by other students. As an example, using Fig. 8—16, ask the students to verbally describe a convex polygon.

Ask the students to use the straightedge of their rulers to draw various figures. At first the students can play and draw whatever geometric shapes they want. Again, it will be instructive for you to walk around the class and notice what figures the students draw and how they draw them (for example, look for triangles with curved sides and so forth). After the exploration you or the students can request that members of the class draw certain types of figures, such as obtuse triangles, trapezoids, rectangles, and so forth. Look to see if the students draw all their figures in the "textbook position," that is, with a side parallel to the bottom of the page. If so, ask the students to draw figures that look turned or rotated, such as a square that looks like a diamond. This gives the students experience with figures in various positions.

Polygons and polyhedra do not occur only in a geometry setting. There are wonderful examples of these shapes in the environment of the children. Here are some activities you could use to help the students realize that geometry appears outside of the classroom.

Use a slide projector to show pictures of polygons and polyhedra that appear in the school or in familiar places in the city. Take some 35-mm slides of these places yourself or encourage students or their parents to take the pictures and bring them into the class. Often many old buildings have decorations in the shape of plane geometric figures. With the slides it is possible to project real occurrences of solid objects on the screen. Encourage the students to discuss what they see in the pictures; to see if they can identify the picture; and to check if they have seen other familiar shapes in their environment.

Ask the students to bring to class newspaper and magazine clippings that

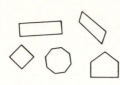   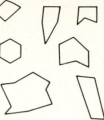

FIGURE 8–16   These are convex.   These are not convex.   Which are convex?

illustrate some geometric figures. You can put these together to make a bulletin board. The students could make a separate bulletin board out of trademarks they find in advertisements.

Students could design furniture, kites, and other types of objects with some functional purpose and be aware not only of the shapes involved in the objects but might ask questions about why triangles occur so often in the objects.

Lines and Planes

The students have seen numerous examples of lines and planes before they began school. Encourage them now to explicitly notice how and where lines and planes appear in their environment. As you let the children discuss in class what they have seen outside of class, you can learn more about how they perceive things and what they think about the things they do observe. Again, these are fine opportunities to let the children critique each other and refine the way they describe, define, or explain what they have in their minds' eye.

Have students examine the lines, planes, and angles that occur on the polyhedra they have investigated. Polyhedra and polygons form an excellent basis to introduce students to lines and planes. For example, ask the students to count the number of faces of a cube. These faces, when extended, form planes. Either let the children use a model of a cube or let them refer to a drawing of a cube (as in Fig. 8–17) and let them respond to and discuss questions like the following. You can use questions like these to introduce the children to the figures and relations called for in the questions.

How many plane faces are there?
How many line segments are there?
How many vertices are there?
How many angles are there?
How many edges are parallel to a given edge?
How many edges are perpendicular to a given edge?
How many edges intersect a given edge?
How many right angles are there?

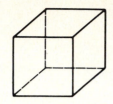

FIGURE 8–17

Numerous books have excellent pictures of optical illusions. Let the students examine the pictures, possibly in small groups, and try to explain what the illusion is, why it is an illusion, and how they would correct the picture. Students who are artistically talented could try to draw the illusion themselves and even enlarge the figure to put on the bulletin board.

Either read to the students or let the more capable students read a book that deals with lines and planes. Some examples of such books are *Flatland, Sphereland; The Dot and the Line; An Adventure in Geometry;* and *Points, Lines, and Planes.*

For students who have difficulty drawing pictures, especially solid objects, you could make up some questions that enable the students to make decisions based on the comparisons. A familiar example is the one used on intelligence tests in which the students are asked to identify the object on the right that is in some way most like the object on the left. Figure 8–18 shows an example of this type of question. Students with artistic ability could design some questions like these for other students.

Geoboards (Fig. 8–19) offer a wealth of examples of geometric figures and relationships. Teachers of vocational courses, parents, and even some students could help make a geoboard for each student. Several excellent books and journals (see Mathematics Resource Project, 1978 a and b) offer activities for young children built around geoboard investigations. In addition to the opportunities for conceptual development on the geoboard, the students are freed from the fear of making errors. If they place a rubberband on the board incorrectly, they need only to move the rubberband to the correct position—there is no record of their error.

Use dot paper in conjunction with or even as a somewhat inadequate replacement for geoboards. Unfortunately, with dot paper there is a record of the students' errors, unless you cover the paper with a transparency. The dot paper, however, provides a basis to enable the students to represent their ideas.

FIGURE 8–18

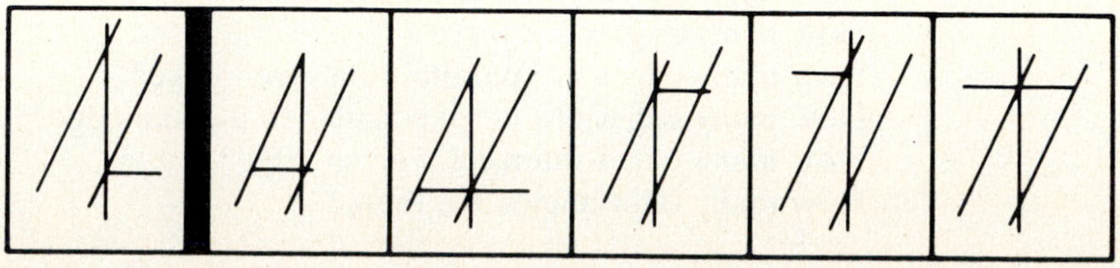

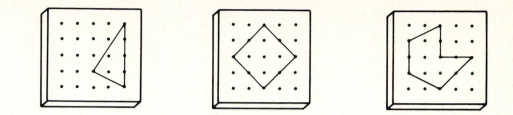

FIGURE 8–19

Provide the students with graph paper and show them how to use the structure of the grids to represent lines, planes, angles, and even polyhedra (as in Fig. 8–20). Grids provide a very rich source for a variety of activities, not only for geometry but also for fractions, ratios, areas, and other measurements.

It seems students have as much difficulty with angles as they have with any other geometric concept. There are in fact three main aspects to angles

- Turns or rotations are natural for young children, and the early experiences children have with turns or rotations can carry over to the study of angles (as in Fig. 8–21). This dynamic way of working with angles should be started early and carried throughout the students' work.
- Stationary figures relate to the children's experiences as corners of buildings, furniture, inclines of hills, stairs, and even ski slopes (Fig. 8–22). This static

FIGURE 8–20

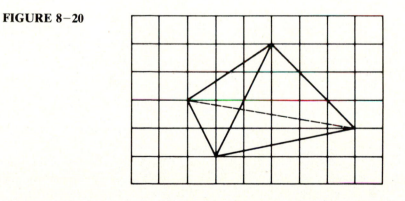

FIGURE 8–21

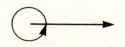 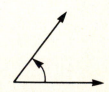

A full turn: (360°)   A ¼ turn: Right   Less than ¼ turn:
                             angle (90°)   Acute angle

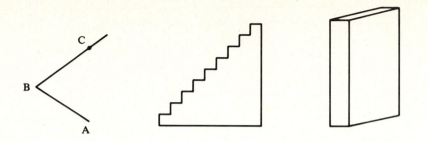

FIGURE 8-22

way of considering angles is, unfortunately, the main approach taken in most school textbooks.

- Measurement is probably the most unnatural way for children to consider angles and the one that causes the most difficulty. Usually a protractor is used and often used incorrectly to measure angles as static objects (Fig. 8-23). Children are expected to learn to classify the angles according to their measurements as acute, obtuse, right, and sometimes as straight angles.

Give the students experiences with turns and rotations and have them draw the figures they rotate. Finally have the students use their protractors to measure the angles and rotations they generate. In this way the students bring together all three aspects of angles and the dynamic view, as motions, is not lost.

You can use the example-counterexample method to help the students understand the classification of angles and be able to rapidly recognize the various types of angles (Fig. 8-24).

FIGURE 8-23

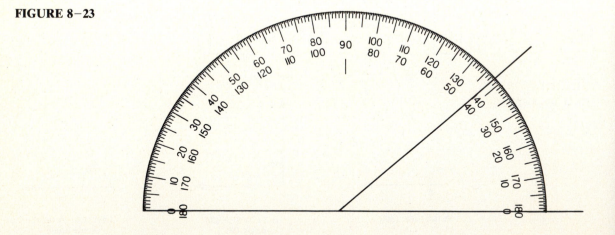

FIGURE 8—24

These are
acute angles.

These are not
acute angles.

Which of these
are acute angles?

Curves and Surfaces

The children are familiar with several types of figures with curved surfaces, such as spheres, cylinders, and cones (Fig. 8—25). These words, on the other hand, are likely not in the student's vocabulary. You can use this deficiency as a means to help the students recognize differences and similarities in shapes as well as to gain facility in classifying objects. For example, ask the children to help list as many objects as possible with the same shape as a baseball. Eventually the children learn that the word sphere is used to name objects, like the earth, that have that shape. Likewise, the word cylinder arises out of the student's list for objects like a pipe, tube, or drinking glass. The classification activity can be extended to other words as well. Some students might want to try to place all the objects they can think of in one of their lists and, if there are no technical words to describe the figures, they might suggest or insist on making up words of their own.

Students enjoy making designs even if just for doodling. You can build on this interest as you help the students to improve their drawing skills and to learn to analyze properties of objects. Figure 8—26 demonstrates how a circle can be used to form an attractive design. The students can color the designs in various ways and use them for decorations or pinwheels. See *Geometry and Visualization* (Mathematics Resource Project, 1978a) for many more of these activities.

FIGURE 8—25

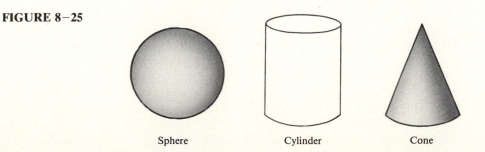

Sphere   Cylinder   Cone

FIGURE 8–26

Logo

The computer language, or utility, called Logo has many uses in the school program. Actually, Logo is much more than a children's drawing tool. It is a structured programming language that allows for extensive list processing capabilities. For our purposes, Logo is easy to use and enjoyable for children. (See Billstein, Libeskind, & Lott, 1985, for a thorough elementary treatment of Logo.) An essential feature of Logo is that very young students easily learn to program a microcomputer to solve problems and to discover geometric relations. Here is just one example. Suppose the students want to tell the computer to draw an equilateral triangle. They can use Logo to draw the figure just as they might draw it with a pencil. Logo permits the students to draw on the screen by telling the cursor (called the "turtle") where to move. For example, in Fig. 8–27 the turtle starts at point S and moves 100 picture units (or pixels) up to point N; next the turtle turns 120 degrees and faces toward point R; then the turtle moves 100 units to point R; again, it turns 120 degrees; and finally, it moves 100 units back to the original point S; thereby completing the triangle. A sequence of Logo commands to do this might look like this:

```
TO EQUI-TRIANGLE      (begins the progam and gives it a name)
FORWARD 100           (draws the first side)
RIGHT TURN 120        (turns the turtle 120°)
FORWARD 100           (draws the second side)
RIGHT TURN 120        (the second 120° turn)
FORWARD 100           (draws the third side)
RIGHT TURN 120        (turns to face toward N)
END                   (tells the computer to finish the program)
```

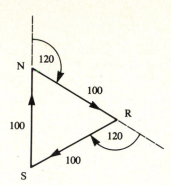

FIGURE 8—27

The same program can be written more concisely by using the repeat feature and abbreviations for the forward and right turn commands, as follows:

```
TO EQUI-TRIANGLE            (begins the program)
REPEAT 3[FD 100 RT 120]     (does the bracket commands three times)
END                         (completes the program)
```

Once a program is written in Logo it can be used in another program (in fact it can even be used in itself). Here is an example of how children can use the EQUI-TRIANGLE program to create a design (Fig. 8—28):

```
TO DESIGN
REPEAT 3[EQUI-TRIANGLE LT 60]
END
```

By experimenting with Logo commands in the graphic mode children can learn a great deal about the properties of geometric figures. This is especially so because there is immediate reinforcement and verification of the correctness of the childrens' ideas—correct programs run as we want them to while students can correct incorrect programs and try them again.

FIGURE 8—28

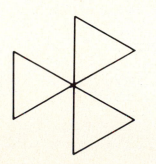

Visualization

In most of the activities described above there are, of course, requirements to perceive concepts and relationships visually. Many of the activities involve more visualizing and drawing demands on the part of the students than others. We indicated in some of the previous activities how drawing and visualizing skills can be improved. There are numerous other examples and an extensive bibliography in *Geometry and Visualization* (Mathematics Resource Project, 1978a). Last, but certainly not least, in this brief survey of geometric topics we consider motions or, more technically, geometric transformations. Some of these ideas were approached in various other places above. Transformations are dynamic actions that ask the students to imagine a figure, a rule, or a procedure for moving the figure, and a final resting place for the figure after the move. The visual skills developed in the study of transformations are quite different from those called for in stationary space figures, cross-sections, optical illusions, plane figures and designs, and so forth.

Transformations

Of the four transformations that do not change the shape and area of figures, there are three accessible for student investigations. These are reflections (flips), rotations (turns), and translations (slides) (Fig. 8−29). The fourth transformation is a glide-reflection—a combination of a reflection and a translation.

Students can look for objects in nature that are symmetric in one of these senses, or at least nearly symmetric. For example, frieze patterns on buildings and many wallpapers consist of designs that can be reflected, rotated, and translated onto themselves. The students can use such aids as tracing paper and cardboard cutouts to draw figures and then flip, turn, and slide them to find transformation images. Once again, grids provide a useful structure to help students draw images of motions. For example students could be asked to draw the reflection of the design given in Fig. 8−30. You can help the students realize various properties of transformations such as the way reflections reverse orientation (Fig. 8−30). Logo also offers an exciting way to use computers to draw transformations of figures.

FIGURE 8−29

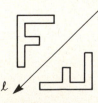

Reflection (flip)
across line ℓ.

Rotation (turn)
about point P.

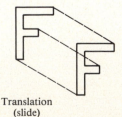

Translation
(slide)

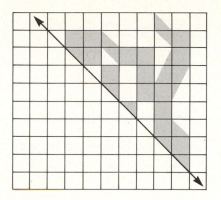

FIGURE 8–30

ACTIVITIES

1. Examine elementary school textbooks to see at what van Hiele level the geometric topics are introduced. Compare your observations to our discussions of the van Hiele levels.
2. Choose some geometric figure, such as a parallelogram, rhombus, or cube, and outline the Level 0 and Level 1 work you would use to help students learn the concept.
3. Investigate what you can do with Logo. Have fun and experiment and then prepare lesson plans for your students.
4. The following are some aspects of visual perception identified by McKim (1972). Write some lessons that emphasize one or more of these aspects for your students.
   a. Finding figures that are part of a complicated drawing
   b. Recognizing figures that are congruent (identical) to a given figure
   c. Completing a partially drawn figure or pattern
   d. Reproducing a design from memory
   e. Visualizing a figure after it has been rotated or reflected
   f. Visualizing cross-sections of solid figures
   g. Visualizing an object from different viewpoints
   h. Imagining a solid that can be formed from an unfolded pattern
   i. Imagining how to put pieces together to form a given figure
5. Using the aspects in Activity 4, consider how students might work on the following activities:
   a. The students are to draw a picture of a geoboard that has been turned 90° clockwise from the horizontal.
   b. Show the students a drawing of a cube. The students are to hold their cube so that the drawing shows how their cube would look to them. Then show the students a new drawing and ask them to hold the cube so that the drawing shows how the cube would look to the student seated next to them.

6. Davis (1973) noted sex differences with his sectioning-of-solids tasks in which the boys performed better than the girls. Ask your students to draw the cross-sections as you suggest cuts of different sorts (perpendicular to an axis of symmetry, along an axis of symmetry, oblique to an axis of symmetry) through a rectangular prism, a cube, a circular cylinder, and a circular cone. If your results show a girl-boy difference, try to account for this difference by thinking of specific everyday experiences that might give one sex better background for such tasks.

FIGURE 8–31
Geowords

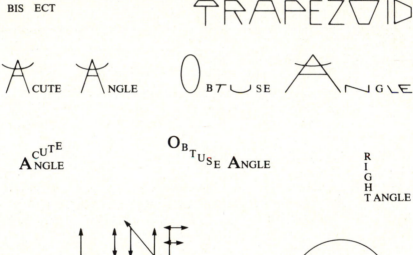

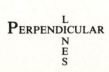

BIS ECT

TRAPEZOID

Acute Angle   Obtuse Angle

A CUTE ANGLE   O B T U S E ANGLE   R I G H T ANGLE

LINE

ARC

RAY

PARALLELINES   PERPENDICULAR   PERPENDICULAR LINES

SYMMETRY   ROTATION

HALFTURNNRUTFLAH

AESSELLATETESSEL.....
AESSELLATETESSEL.....
ATESSELLATETESSE.....
AETESSELLATETESS.....   FRIESEPATTERNFRIESEPATTERNFRIESEPATTERNF
ATETESSELLATETES.....

7. Plan a unit in geometry, possibly using manipulatives, in which you start with solid figures and try to lead the students from Level 0 to Level 1.
8. Experiment with transformations of figures, possible using grids to display the figures. Draw a uncomplicated figure at first; reflect it across a line; rotate it around a point; translate it in some direction. Investigate various figures for their symmetry properties across a line or around a point. Look in nature for objects with some degree of symmetry.
9. Make a bulletin board of geometric words. See Fig. 8−31 for examples.

CHAPTER 8 SUMMARY

Geometry and visual thinking should be included in children's school work starting in kindergarten and continuing in every grade thereafter. Geometry should be much more than memorizing names of figures and rote learning of simple relationships. There are geometric relationships inherent in many of the arithmetic topics children study in the elementary school. These range from addition and multiplication to work with fractions. By interconnecting visual experiences with other aspects of the children's mathematical experiences students get a more effective and much more enjoyable learning situation.

In addition to relating geometry to other school topics there is the need to offer students opportunities to exercise the holistic brain functions. For those students who tend to think globally, the geometric experiences provide enjoyable activities in which they can excel. This is in marked contrast to the ordinary arithmetic curriculum, which heavily emphasizes the analytical computation strand. Also, for those students who do not, a priori, have fully developed visual imagery and imagination, the geometric experiences provide opportunities to develop those mental facilities. In short, geometry and visual experiences are good for everybody!

Research has shown that obstacles are placed in the curriculum which severely hinder children's learning of geometric concepts. These obstacles take on several forms and occur in various topics. The van Hieles attempted to described thought levels which can be used to form a sequence of increasingly more difficult mental processes. Concepts that students are only aware of at one level become explicit to them at higher levels as the students increase their understanding and insight into the subject. It is essential that children experience carefully developed sequences of lessons which enable them to increase their thought level in a systematic fashion or they will not be prepared for later work. The results of its lack of systematic development are especially evident during high school when students are not prepared to study geometry. Such failure often prevents students from taking mathematical courses that are prerequisites for college or advanced technical studies.

This chapter described a teaching-learning plan which can be used to organize sequences of lessons for students to supplement the deficient manner in which many textbook series cover geometry. The plan was proposed by the van Hieles and is in some ways similar in structure to other proposals for organizing curriculum materials. In this plan, very direct instruction occurs right after motivational discussions introduce the topic.

The direct instruction on the part of the teacher gradually leads to student verbalization, followed by exploratory activities in which the students learn to solve problems for themselves. In the final phase of the plan students internalize ideas and develop a firm understanding of the concepts.

REFERENCES

Billstein, R., Libeskind, S., & Lott, J. 1985. *Logo*. Menlo Park, CA: Benjamin/Cummings Publishing Co.

Boe, B. 1968. A study of the ability of secondary school pupils to perceive the plane sections of selected solid figures. *The Mathematics Teacher*, 61:415−421.

Brown, S. I., & Walter, M. 1983. *The art of problem posing*. Philadelphia: Franklin Institute Press.

Burger, W. 1981. Thought levels in geometry, interim report. "Guessing Childrens' Development in Geometry." NSF SED 79-20568. Oregon State University, Corvallis.

Davis, E. 1973. A study of the ability of school pupils to perceive and identify the plane sections of selected solid figures. *Journal for Research in Mathematics Education*, 4:132−140.

Flavell, J. 1963. *The developmental psychology of Jean Piaget*. Princeton, NJ: Van Nostrand.

Fennema, E., & Tartre, L. 1985. The use of spatial visualization in mathematics in boys and girls. *Journal for Research in Mathematics Education*.

Freudenthal, H. (ed.) 1958. *Report on methods of unit iteration into geometry*. Groningen: Walters.

Freudenthal, H. 1973. *Mathematics as an educational task*. Dordrecht, Holland: D. Reidel Publishing Co.

Fuys, D., Geddes, D., & Tischler, R. 1984. *English translation of selected writings of Dina Van Hield-Geldof and Pierre M. Van Hiele*. Brooklyn, NY: Brooklyn College.

Hoffer, A. 1979. Geometry, a model of the universe. Menlo Park: Addison-Wesley.

Hoffer, A. 1981. Geometry is more than proof. *The Mathematics Teacher*, 74:11−18.

Hoffer, A. 1983a. A child is more than a machine. In *Basic Skills Conference*. Washington, DC: National Institute of Education.

Hoffer, A. 1983b. Van Hiele-based research. In R. Lesh & M. Landau (Eds.), *Acquisition of Mathematics Concepts and Processes* (pp. 205−227).

Karnovsky, A. 1974. Sex differences in spatial ability: A developmental study. (Doctoral dissertation, Harvard University, 1973). *Dissertation Abstracts International*, 34A: 7586.

Kilpatrick, J., & Wirszup, I. 1969−1977. Soviet studies in the psychology of learning and teaching mathematics. *School of Mathematics Study Group*. (20+ vols.). University of Chicago.

Maccoby, E., & Jacklin, C. 1974. *The psycohology of sex differences*. Stanford, CA: Stanford University Press.

Mathematics Resource Project. 1978a. In A. Hoffer (Dir.), *Geometry and visualization*. Palo Alto, CA: Creative Publications.

Mathematics Resource Project. 1978b. Planning instruction in geometry. In A. Hoffer (Dir.), *Didactics and mathematics*. Palo Alto, CA: Creative Publications.

McKim, R. 1972. *Experiences in visual thinking*. Monterey, CA: Brooks/Cole.

Piaget, J., & Inhelder, B. 1956. *The child's conception of space* (F. J. Langdon & J. L. Lunzer, Trans.). London: Routledge and Kegan Paul.

Piaget, J., Inhelder, B., & Szeminska, A. 1964. *The child's conception of geometry* (E. A. Lunzer, Trans.). New York: Harper and Row.

Sherman, J. 1967. Sex differences in space perception. *Psychological Review,* 74: 290–299.

Tyler, L. 1965. *The psychology of human differences* (3rd ed.). New York: Appleton-Century-Crofts.

Van Hiele, P. and M. 1959. La Pensee de l'enfant et la geometrie. *Bulletin de l'Association des Professeurs de Mathematiques de l'Enseignement Public,* 38:199–205.

Wolfe, L. 1970. The effects of space visualization training on spatial ability and arithmetic achievement of junior high school students. (Doctoral dissertation, State University of New York at Albany, 1970). *Dissertation Abstracts International,* 31A: 2801.

9 Estimation

BARBARA REYS

University of Missouri

INTRODUCTION

Estimation is an important topic that has not received a great deal of emphasis in the mathematics curriculum. In fact you may not have been taught to estimate as an elementary school student. The topic is receiving more attention, in part due to the increasingly technological world in which in our students will live. Estimation has been listed as one of ten basic skills by the National Council of Supervisors of Mathematics (NCSM) (1978) and as an area of emphasis in the National Council of Teachers of Mathematics (NCTM) *Agenda for Action* (NCTM, 1980).

In this chapter you will learn about recent research findings on the process of estimation. Five specific estimation strategies will be outlined and methods of teaching these strategies will be presented. This chapter also deals with the characteristics of good estimators, presents guidelines for developing a complete estimation program, and suggests techniques for evaluating estimation skill.

THE ROLE OF ESTIMATION IN THE SCHOOL MATHEMATICS PROGRAM

Computational estimation refers to the process of obtaining an approximate answer to a problem without using traditional paper-and-pencil algorithms or recording devices. It is an important and practical skill because of its utility and convenience.

The problems presented in Fig. 9–1 illustrate only a few ways computational estimation is used in our daily lives. Estimation skills can also be part of a successful school mathematics program. For example, errors can be detected and eliminated if a student has the estimation skill necessary to answer the question, "Does my answer seem reasonable?"

FIGURE 9–1
Selected estimation problems. From *Developing Skills in Estimation, Book B,* **by Dale Seymour. Copyright 1981 by Dale Seymour Publications. Reprinted by permission of the publisher.**

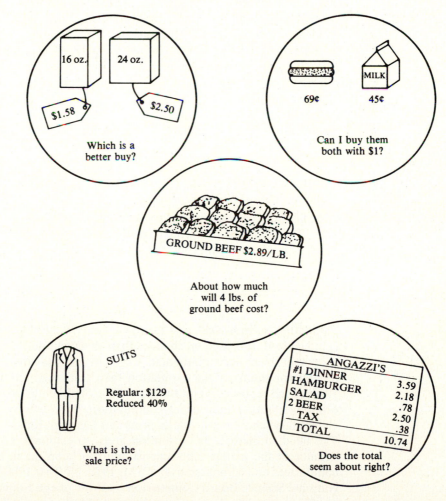

Research suggests that being able to produce a "ballpark" answer quickly is one characteristic of people who are good at doing computational estimation. Other characteristics of good estimators include:

- They generally make their estimates without writing their computations, instead relying heavily on mental computation.
- They produce answers that are not exact but adequate for making the necessary decision.
- They are tolerant of error and feel comfortable with an estimate.
- They have developed a variety of different estimation strategies, and their selection of a particular strategy depends on the problem.

In the examples in Fig. 9−1, how did you decide which box of detergent was the "better buy?" Perhaps you concluded that the price of the 24-ounce size was more then ten cents per ounce whereas the 16-ounce size cost less than ten cents per ounce. These two mental calculations produced estimates that enabled you to decide that the smaller size is really the "better buy."

Reflecting back on how you solved each of the problems will provide greater insight into this discussion of estimation. For example, each of the problems was probably solved using some mental computation. Also, each question could be answered without computing an exact answer. Finally, you likely used different estimation techniques on each problem, catering to the particular numbers and operation of the problem.

RESEARCH RELATED TO THE LEARNING OF ESTIMATION

Computational estimation has been the target of a new wave of research since 1980. This effort has produced a rapidly growing research base which provides some valuable guidelines for curriculum, instruction, and evaluation.

Curriculum

Estimation is a basic skill, and its growing importance in a technological society is recognized. It is used much more than exact computation. Surveys of adults show that most of the mathematics used in everyday living relies far more on mental computation and estimation than traditional computation (Carlton, 1980). Such reports suggest that over 80% of all mathematics applications use estimation rather than exact computation. Ironically the major portion of elementary school mathematics programs has centered on exact computation. The need to increase the attention given to estimation and reach a proper balance in the mathematics curriculum has been made by several national committees and commissions (NCSM, 1978; NCTM, 1980). In a report by the National Science Board Commission on Pre-College Education in Mathematics, Science and Technology entitled "The Mathematical Sciences Curriculum

K−12: What is Still Fundamental and What is Not," the recommendation was made that ". . . substantially more emphasis be placed on the development of skills in mental arithmetic, estimation and approximation and that substantially less be placed on paper and pencil execution of the arithmetic operations" (National Science Board, 1982). Strong and convincing cases for teaching computational estimation are encouraging careful examination of mathematics programs to ensure that estimation receives the attention it deserves.

In the past, elementary mathematics textbooks have devoted very little attention to teaching computational estimation. A survey of several of the most widely used fourth grade textbooks showed that only about 4% of the lessons contained in them were on estimation, and that total included both measurement and computational estimation (Driscoll, 1981). Significant changes in textbooks are being made to give estimation and traditional written computation the attention each merits.

Where estimation has been included, instruction generally centers on the strategy of rounding. However, the connection between rounding and its use as part of the estimation process is not always clearly established. This is supported by a recent survey in which good estimators said they were taught to round numbers as an isolated skill and never actually applied rounding to estimating (Reys, Bestgen, Rybolt, & Wyatt, 1980). Most people interviewed suggested that their estimation skills were learned on their own, not as a part of their mathematics program. This research documents that many other effective strategies not only exist but are essential tools in the estimation process. Although major curriculum changes occur slowly, there is evidence that estimation is not only receiving more attention but that fresh approaches to estimation are appearing in mathematics materials.

Instruction

Recent research by Reys and co-workers has established that good estimators draw upon a variety of computational techniques to form estimates (Reys, Bestgen, Rybolt, & Wyatt, 1982). These researchers claim that if students are to learn to estimate, they must be taught a variety of estimation strategies beginning in the early grades and systematically carried through to the higher grades.

Research data from the National Assessment of Educational Progress (NAEP) reveal that most students do not develop good estimation skills on their own. Measures of computation estimation skills have consistently shown low levels of performance. Significant differences were evident between ability to compute exact answers through paper-and-pencil techniques and ability to estimate. In every case, performance was higher on exact computation.

Computational estimation skills do improve with instruction. Research has documented that teaching estimation strategies and related skills on a systematic basis over a year-long period can produce dramatic improvements in estimation performance (Schoen, Friesen, Jarret, & Urbatsch, 1981; Reys,

Reys, Tafton, & Zawajewski, 1984). The content of a systematic sequence of instruction on estimation should include attention to different strategies. Today, we know that good estimators use a variety of strategies and that these strategies can be taught. Some strategies are more appropriate to teach young students while others are more sophisticated and require a higher level of reasoning. No single estimation strategy is appropriate for every problem so a number of different strategies must be available to the user.

Evaluation

Reliable measures of a student's estimation skills are difficult to obtain. When students are asked to estimate, they often try to work the problem quickly with paper and pencil, obtain an exact answer, and then round their answer to reflect an estimate (Reys & Bestgen, 1981). The amount of time allowed in an assessment setting must be controlled carefully. If too much time is allowed, the test may only be a measure of paper-and-pencil computation. Research related to timing confirms that adding only five seconds to the time allowed per question produces dramatic difference in performance as well as the processes used to estimate. To control the time, it is recommended that estimation questions be administered one at a time. An overhead or slide projector is an effective means of showing questions one at a time and allows the presenter to pace the questions. Microcomputers also provide an effective means of delivering the questions individually as well as controlling time for each question. If test booklets are used, it is essential to control the amount of time available to do each page. The testing directions must make it clear that written algorithms are not to be used. Even then it is difficult to monitor the group administration of such a test to ensure that the directions are followed. Some students may plod through the test doing traditional paper-and-pencil computation and their resulting scores are not an indication of their computational estimation skill.

The test questions themselves should be complex enough to encourage and reward estimation. It should be clear to respondents that there will not be enough time to compute an exact answer, and even if there were, it would be a lengthy, laborious exercise. Some problems lend themselves particularly well to estimation and others don't. For example, 68×10 is a mental computation problem, whereas 68×12 more clearly encourages estimation. A problem such as $78 + 83$ could easily be mentally computed; but $83,427 + 83,334$ promotes estimation. The more students encounter problems that can take a long time to compute but can be estimated quickly, the more their appreciation for the power of estimation will grow.

Research has helped us better understand some of the difficulties associated with learning and teaching estimation. Practical findings that have direct implications for the classroom have been highlighted. Ideas from both research and practice are blended in the following discussion of special problems and the teaching of estimation.

ACTIVITIES

1. Examine a current textbook series to determine how much emphasis is given to estimation. When is it introduced? How is it taught?
2. Read "Evaluating Computational Estimation Skills" by Reys in the 1986 NCTM Yearbook (Reys, 1986). According to the author, how much emphasis is given to estimation on standardized tests? Make a list of testing suggestions the author offers.
3. Read the NCSM list of Basic Skills in the February 1978 issue of the *Mathematics Teacher*. What emphasis does NCSM place on estimation?
4. Form an estimate for each problem in Fig. 9–1. Briefly outline your estimation method for each problem.

PROVISIONS FOR INDIVIDUAL DIFFERENCES

By its very nature, estimation is a different process than exact computation. Whereas exact computation produces an exact answer, estimation might produce a variety of acceptable answers depending on the technique used, the numbers involved and the context of the estimation situation. The variety of possible approaches to an estimation problem creates an open-ended, problem-solving-oriented atmosphere in the classroom. Because of this openness, teaching computational estimation can introduce unique instructional problems. Following are some actual comments from students that illustrate several difficulties in teaching estimation. Hopefully these discussions will not only make you more sensitive to the challenges of teaching estimation but will better prepare you to anticipate difficulties.

"How can it be wrong, I got the 'right' answer."

Suppose you asked your fifth-grade class to use estimation to solve the following problem:

If one box weighs 59 pounds, about how much do 48 of these boxes weigh?

59 lbs.
net weight

Is an estimate of 2800 pounds a "good" estimate? Consider the following estimation techniques used by three different students:

Rex computed 48 × 59 on his paper and found the product to be 2832. He then rounded 2832 to 2800 and reported his "estimate" to be 2800.

Pat rounded 48 × 59 to 50 × 60 and mentally found the product to be 3000. She reported her "estimate" to be 3000.

Tim rounded 48 × 59 to 50 × 60 and mentally found the product to be 3000. He thought this would be too high so he adjusted his answer and reported his "estimate" to be 2800.

Each of these answers would be acceptable "estimates." Pat and Tim used the same technique of rounding, but Tim's adjustment process went beyond the initial estimate of 3000 to produce an adjusted estimate of 2800. Although Rex and Tim produced the same estimate, their processes were very different. Whereas Tim used several important estimation techniques, Rex never estimated. Rex applied a written computation algorithm and then "rounded" his exact answer to satisfy the directions. Although this procedure is clearly not computational estimation, there is a strong tendency by many students to do it, because the procedure produces a "right" answer. We must not only consider the answers students provide, but examine the processes behind their answers.

"If estimation is important, how come it's not on the test?"

One way to determine the importance of a topic is to examine the emphasis the topic is given on tests. If computational estimation skills are valued and taught in a mathematics program, then it is essential that they be tested. Do standardized tests include estimation? A review of standardized achievement tests show that computational estimation is omitted in some and given only token representation in others (Reys, 1986). Are estimation skills tested in class? Plans can and should be made to include the systematic testing of computational estimation. Unless estimation is a visible part of our testing program, its omission suggests that computation estimation is not considered as important as the things that are tested. Students, indeed all of us, use this approach in determining what is important.

"You mean we don't always have to start on the right?"

Traditional computation with written algorithm begins with the digits on the right. This is in contrast to the process of estimation. Experiences with place value help students appreciate the significance of the position of the digit. This knowledge helps students realize that the digit "1" in 1234 represents thousands and has far more relative importance than the "4" in the ones place. Despite the attention given to place value, the hours and years of practicing written algorithms have conditioned many students to always start on the right. Consequently students may become very mechanical in applying the written algorithms. This habit of starting on the right needs to be broken and a fresh approach taken for estimation.

"Here's my estimate, how close is it to the correct answer?"

One of the comforts of working with exact computation is that there is no gray area. Either an answer is right or wrong. If you ask "What is 5 × 3?" an answer of 15 is correct and 16, even though it is close, is incorrect. This experience leads many students to expect "one right answer" and in fact demand "What is *the* right answer?"

In estimation, gray areas not only exist but abound. Students must eventually realize that many good estimates may exist for a particular problem. This does mean that correcting a set of estimation exercises is more difficult. You may have to allow several different answers because all are reasonable estimates. For example, if you ask "About how much will 3.5 pounds of apples at $0.23 per pound cost?" estimates might range from $0.60 (3 × $0.20), $0.69 (3 × $0.23), $0.75 (3 × $0.25), to $1.00 (4 × $0.25). Any of these would provide an acceptable estimate. If you want to make sure you have enough money to buy the apples then an overestimate, such as $1.00, would be a safe estimate. Often the conditions of the problem help us determine a good estimate and students should be encouraged to use the context of the problem to guide their estimation process.

Unfortunately an expectation for a "best estimate" is reinforced by some exercises in textbooks that suggest that students make an estimate then calculate an exact answer and determine how far their estimate is from "the correct answer." Such an exercise is counterproductive. It indirectly suggests to students that the only correct answer is the exact answer. One logical approach to this dilemma is to form an estimate very close to the correct answer, thereby eliminating any error. Such an approach reinforces the "one right answer syndrome" and destroys enthusiasm for developing estimation skills.

"You mean we can estimate in a mathematics class?"

The search for exact answers has falsely suggested to many students that estimation has no place in mathematics classes. Their experience with computation has always produced exact answers that were either right or wrong. They realize estimation produces ballpark answers, so they do not view it as useful. Thus one key focus for early instruction on estimation is to help students realize its value.

"When do I estimate?"

A comprehensive treatment of estimation should include discussion of when its use is appropriate. For example, we would not estimate the sum of 23 and 41. This is a mental computation problem and cries out for an exact answer. Suppose you are in the checkout lane of a grocery store. You have $10 and wonder if you have enough to pay for all the items in your cart. This is an excellent time to estimate.

These comments remind us of a few of the unique problems associated with computational estimation. It is a challenge to teach, but the time spent teaching estimation also helps in other important areas of mathematics, including problem solving and mathematical thinking.

ACTIVITIES

1. Give the following problem to a fifth-, sixth-, or seventh-grade student: There are 48 candy bars in a box. Fifty-seven boxes are ordered for the school sale. About how many candy bars are ordered? Observe how the student attacks and solves the problem. Does the student estimate? What technique is used to form the estimate?
2. Write a brief summary stating where you learned to estimate.
3. List several different situations you've encountered recently in which estimation was required.
4. Describe two real-life situations in which you might want to overestimate. Describe two situations in which you might want to underestimate.
5. From the two-book series *Developing Skills in Estimation* by Dale Seymour choose two activities you feel are exceptionally good and be ready to demonstrate them to the class.

TEACHING ESTIMATION

The difference between knowing something should be taught and actually teaching it is immense. While the importance and benefits of teaching estimation are generally recognized, the specific content and sequence of study are less clear. Classroom instruction on estimation should begin in the primary grades and extend into secondary school.

Young children are generally encouraged to begin the estimation process in a measurement context by guessing linear measurements then verifying their estimates by measuring. Numerosity estimation is also appropriate at the primary level. Such questions as How many beans in the jar? or How many books on the shelf? help students gain experience guessing and checking. Computational estimation strategies are generally introduced in third grade.

Computational estimation, much like problem solving, calls on a variety of skills and is developed and improved over a long period of time. A comprehensive estimation curriculum includes several aspects:

1. Development of an awareness for and an appreciation of estimation
2. Development of number sense
3. Development of number concepts
4. Development of estimation strategies

Each of these concepts along with example activities will be illustrated.

Developing an Awareness of Estimation

For most students estimation is a new skill, one they have not been encouraged to develop in their school program. To them mathematics is restricted to finding exact answers. Yet, as adults, we know that the real world of mathematics calls for approximate as well as exact computations. The narrow view of mathematics which many students have developed makes it essential that specific classroom discussion center around the important uses and nature of estimation. Activities 9−1 and 9−2 will help students see and appreciate the practical nature of estimation. Each is designed as a teacher-led discussion activity.

Activity 9−1 illustrates that many numbers we encounter in such daily activities as reading the newspaper are actually estimates. Students quickly sort

ACTIVITY 9−1 Numbers are sometimes estimates and sometimes exact values. From *Developing Skills in Estimation, Book B*, by Dale Seymour. Copyright 1981 by Dale Seymour Publications. Reprinted by permission of the publisher.

NEWSPAPER HEADLINES

Numbers in newspaper headlines are sometimes approximations and sometimes exact figures. Circle each number below that you think is approximate.

1. WE SELL 100 CARS FROM OUR LOT EACH WEEK TO SATISFIED BUYERS
2. Bowl Game nets $12,500,000 for
3. Census figure at 227,000,000
4. Unemployment figures at 7.5% says White House
5. Senate cuts budget by $5.9 million
6. 84 DIE IN RESCUE ATTEMPT
7. New jet liner design to hold 456 passengers
8. YEAR-END CLEARANCE ALL STOCK 20% OFF
9. $25,000 PRIZE OFFERED TO WINNER
10. Horse pays $235.70
11. 'Musick' publishes 100th hit song
12. Market drops 7.32 points
13. 57,500 watch Reds
14. 2500 killed in massive quake

Look at real newspapers to find 10 headlines that include numbers. Find 5 that are approximations and 5 that are exact.

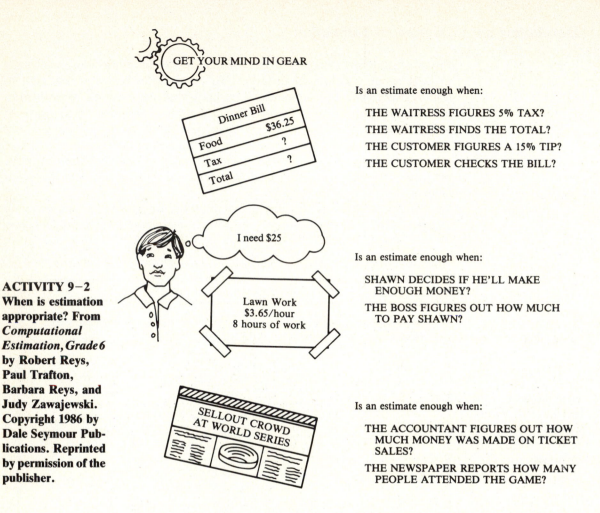

GET YOUR MIND IN GEAR

Dinner Bill	
	$36.25
Food	?
Tax	?
Total	

Is an estimate enough when:

THE WAITRESS FIGURES 5% TAX?

THE WAITRESS FINDS THE TOTAL?

THE CUSTOMER FIGURES A 15% TIP?

THE CUSTOMER CHECKS THE BILL?

I need $25

Lawn Work
$3.65/hour
8 hours of work

Is an estimate enough when:

SHAWN DECIDES IF HE'LL MAKE ENOUGH MONEY?

THE BOSS FIGURES OUT HOW MUCH TO PAY SHAWN?

SELLOUT CROWD AT WORLD SERIES

Is an estimate enough when:

THE ACCOUNTANT FIGURES OUT HOW MUCH MONEY WAS MADE ON TICKET SALES?

THE NEWSPAPER REPORTS HOW MANY PEOPLE ATTENDED THE GAME?

ACTIVITY 9−2
When is estimation appropriate? From *Computational Estimation, Grade 6* **by Robert Reys, Paul Trafton, Barbara Reys, and Judy Zawajewski. Copyright 1986 by Dale Seymour Publications. Reprinted by permission of the publisher.**

out these approximate numbers and can explain why the writer chose to use them rather than exact values.

Activity 9−2 illustrates situations in which the context helps us decide whether an estimate or exact value is necessary. Discussing these situations is valuable to students and will help them appreciate the value of estimation.

Developing Number Sense

Teachers quickly recognize the students who have good number sense. This feel for numbers is an important skill for both recognizing unreasonable answers and for estimating. How do we get our students to think about their mathematical solutions and judge whether the answers are sensible? This skill develops slowly but can be nurtured. Several activities that emphasize this kind of thinking pattern are illustrated in Activities 9−3 and 9−4.

In Activity 9−3 the student is asked to determine how many digits would be contained in each answer. Those who *think* about the question and numbers

How Many Digits?

STUDY EACH PROBLEM. *DON'T* ESTIMATE THE ANSWER.
DECIDE *HOW MANY DIGITS EACH ANSWER* WOULD CONTAIN.

	Problem	Number of Digits
1)	134 + 689	_____
2)	134 + 989	_____
3)	716 + 305	_____
4)	455 + 327 + 284	_____
5)	2046 − 128	_____
6)	1764 − 783	_____
7)	12 × 234	_____
8)	5 × 689	_____
9)	9 × 38 × 19	_____
10)	4)‾2345	_____
11)	14)‾2345	_____
12)	468)‾32,476	_____

**ACTIVITY 9–3
Number sense
activity**

**ACTIVITY 9–4
Number sense
activity. From
*Computational
Estimation, Grade 6*
by Robery Reys,
Paul Trafton,
Barbara Reys, and
Judy Zawajewski.
Copyright 1986 by
Dale Seymour Pub-
lications. Reprinted
by permission of the
publisher.**

GET YOUR MIND IN GEAR

WHAT'S SENSIBLE?

Choose the reasonable number:

A NEW BASEBALL GLOVE COSTS:
    $1.40 $14.00 $140.00

THE NUMBER OF STUDENTS WHO ATTEND WASHINGTON SCHOOL IS:
    5   50   500

THE GONZALES FAMILY OF 4 WENT TO SPEEDY BURGER FOR LUNCH.
THEY SPENT ABOUT:
    $8.00 $48.00 $80.00

Fill in a reasonable amount:

IT'S ABOUT _____ MILES FROM HERE TO CALIFORNIA.

A SMALL COMPACT CAR GETS ABOUT _____ A GALLON.

THERE ARE ABOUT _____ STUDENTS IN OUR SCHOOL.

THE AVERAGE NUMBER OF PEOPLE IN A FAMILY IS _____.

THERE ARE ABOUT _____ PEOPLE LIVING IN THE UNITED STATES.

involved rather than compute can answer the question quickly. In Activity 9−4 students are asked to state a "sensible" answer from the list. Additional questions such as "About how many people go to my school?" and "About how much money does a bike cost?" will encourage students to think about numbers in a different context than is typical in school mathematics. In the second half of Activity 9−4, students are asked to create appropriate numbers rather than work with numbers supplied to them.

Developing Number Concepts

Conceptual errors involving numbers are often revealed in estimation. These errors may have existed for a long time, but have gone undetected. For example, when asked to estimate the sum of two fractions, such as 12/13 + 7/8, many students added numerators and denominators and reported either 19 or

ACTIVITY 9−5
Sorting fractions to 0, 1/2, and 1. From *Computational Estimation, Grade 8* **by Robert Reys, Paul Trafton, Barbara Reys, and Judy Zawajewski. Copyright 1986 by Dale Seymour Publications. Reprinted by permission of the publisher.**

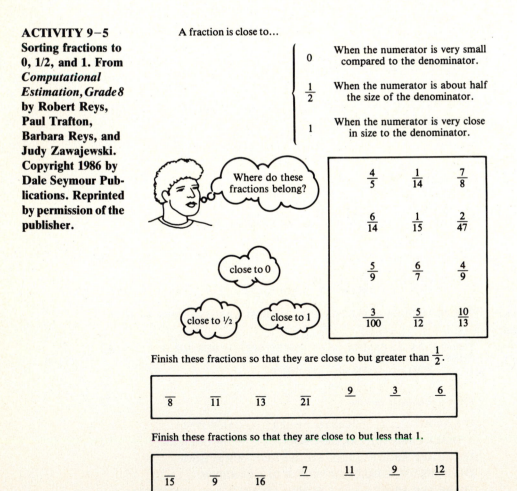

A fraction is close to...

0   When the numerator is very small compared to the denominator.

$\frac{1}{2}$ When the numerator is about half the size of the denominator.

1   When the numerator is very close in size to the denominator.

Where do these fractions belong?

close to 0

close to ½   close to 1

$\frac{4}{5}$ $\frac{1}{14}$ $\frac{7}{8}$

$\frac{6}{14}$ $\frac{1}{15}$ $\frac{2}{47}$

$\frac{5}{9}$ $\frac{6}{7}$ $\frac{4}{9}$

$\frac{3}{100}$ $\frac{5}{12}$ $\frac{10}{13}$

Finish these fractions so that they are close to but greater than $\frac{1}{2}$.

$\frac{}{8}$ $\frac{}{11}$ $\frac{}{13}$ $\frac{}{21}$ $\frac{9}{}$ $\frac{3}{}$ $\frac{6}{}$

Finish these fractions so that they are close to but less that 1.

$\frac{}{15}$ $\frac{}{9}$ $\frac{}{16}$ $\frac{7}{}$ $\frac{11}{}$ $\frac{9}{}$ $\frac{12}{}$

21 as the sum (Carpenter, Corbitt, Kepner, Lindquist, & Reys, 1981). Unless such conceptual errors are corrected, students will continue to struggle with estimating as well as many other mathematical topics.

Estimation offers an alternative way of developing the concept of fraction. For example, Activity 9−5 encourages students to compare numerator and denominator to get an estimate for fractions less than one. This type of presentation can be done before computation with fractions is introduced. The work done developing estimation with fractions will complement and support later work with computation. Once this basic conceptual development is established, exercises such as estimating 12/13 + 7/8 become very simple. Activities 9−6 and 9−7 present some follow-up estimation problems.

ACTIVITY 9−6 Adding fractions near 1. From *Computational Estimation, Grade 8* by Robert Reys, Paul Trafton, Barbara Reys, and Judy Zawajewski. Copyright 1986 by Dale Seymour Publications. Reprinted by permission of the publisher.

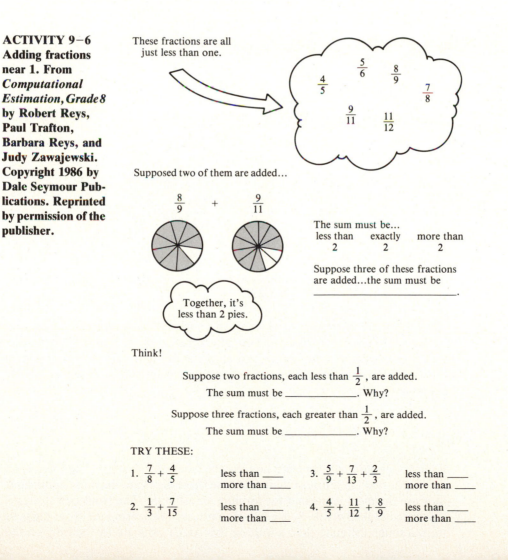

These fractions are all just less than one.

$\frac{4}{5}$ $\frac{5}{6}$ $\frac{8}{9}$ $\frac{7}{8}$ $\frac{9}{11}$ $\frac{11}{12}$

Supposed two of them are added...

$\frac{8}{9}$ + $\frac{9}{11}$

The sum must be...
less than   exactly   more than
    2   2   2

Suppose three of these fractions are added...the sum must be

_____.

Together, it's less than 2 pies.

Think!

Suppose two fractions, each less than $\frac{1}{2}$, are added.
The sum must be _____. Why?

Suppose three fractions, each greater than $\frac{1}{2}$, are added.
The sum must be _____. Why?

TRY THESE:

1. $\frac{7}{8} + \frac{4}{5}$ less than ____
                    more than ____

2. $\frac{1}{3} + \frac{7}{15}$ less than ____
                    more than ____

3. $\frac{5}{9} + \frac{7}{13} + \frac{2}{3}$ less than ____
                    more than ____

4. $\frac{4}{5} + \frac{11}{12} + \frac{8}{9}$ less than ____
                    more than ____

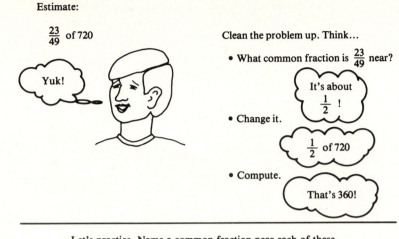

Estimate:

$\frac{23}{49}$ of 720

Yuk!

Clean the problem up. Think...

• What common fraction is $\frac{23}{49}$ near?

It's about $\frac{1}{2}$!

• Change it.

$\frac{1}{2}$ of 720

• Compute.

That's 360!

Let's practice. Name a common fraction near each of these.

$\frac{4}{9}$ $\frac{5}{14}$ $\frac{17}{18}$ $\frac{14}{45}$ $\frac{7}{29}$ $\frac{16}{30}$

ACTIVITY 9–7
Estimating a fraction of a number. From *Computational Estimation, Grade 8,* **by Robert Reys, Paul Trafton, Barbara Reys, and Judy Zawajewski. Copyright 1986 by Dale Seymour Publications. Reprinted by permission of the publisher.**

TRY THESE:

Estimate...

$\frac{4}{9}$ of 679 $\frac{14}{45}$ of 3219

$\frac{5}{14}$ of 889 $\frac{7}{29}$ of 878

$\frac{17}{18}$ of 4204 $\frac{16}{30}$ of 840

DEVELOPING ESTIMATION STRATEGIES

Although there are many components to a complete estimation program, one of the most important is the teaching of estimation strategies. Skilled estimators choose strategies to fit the context of the problem including the specific numbers and operations involved. Several important strategies will be briefly explained.

Front-End Strategy

Even young students can learn and use the front-end strategy. The focus is on the "front-end" or leftmost digit. Because these digits are the most significant, they are the most important for forming an estimate. The front-end strategy, illustrated in Activity 9–8, is a two-step process, first using the front digits to form a rough estimate then adjusting this rough estimate by focusing on the

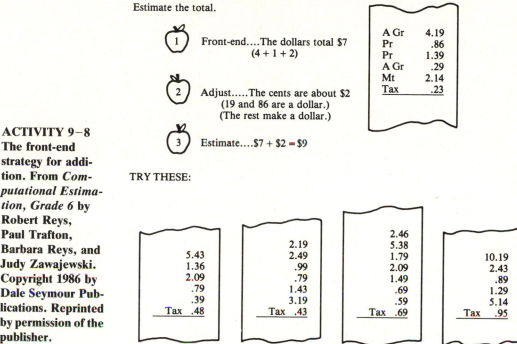

This is a grocery store ticket where the amount has been torn away.

Estimate the total.

A Gr	4.19
Pr	.86
Pr	1.39
A Gr	.29
Mt	2.14
Tax	.23

1 Front-end....The dollars total $7
   (4 + 1 + 2)

2 Adjust.....The cents are about $2
   (19 and 86 are a dollar.)
   (The rest make a dollar.)

3 Estimate....$7 + $2 = $9

ACTIVITY 9−8
The front-end strategy for addition. From *Computational Estimation, Grade 6* **by Robert Reys, Paul Trafton, Barbara Reys, and Judy Zawajewski. Copyright 1986 by Dale Seymour Publications. Reprinted by permission of the publisher.**

TRY THESE:

5.43	2.19	2.46	
1.36	2.49	5.38	10.19
2.09	.99	1.79	2.43
.79	.79	2.09	.89
.39	1.43	1.49	1.29
Tax .48	3.19	.69	5.14
	Tax .43	.59	Tax .95
		Tax .69	

back digits. The amount of adjustment encouraged will depend on the level of the student. This strategy has the advantage of allowing the user to "see" all of the numbers being operated on, thus making it less mentally taxing than rounding. The front-end strategy can first be introduced using money (see Activity 9−8), then other numbers (whole numbers, fractions, decimals) can be substituted.

Clustering Strategy

The clustering strategy is suited for a particular type of problem, often encountered in everyday experiences, in which a group of numbers cluster around a common value. For example, estimate the total attendance:

World's Fair Attendance (July 1−6)

Monday 72,250
Tuesday 63,819
Wednesday 67,490
Thursday 73,180
Friday 74,918
Saturday 68,490

Because all the values are very close to each other in value, clustering can be used to estimate the total attendance for this time period.

1. Estimate the average attendance.

all about 70,000

2. Multiply the average attendance by the number of days.

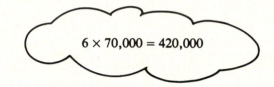

6 × 70,000 = 420,000

The clustering strategy can be used with problems involving whole numbers, fractions, or decimals. It eliminates the mental tabulation of a long list of front-end or rounded digits, creating instead a problem with fewer digits, which are easily computed.

Rounding Strategy

Rounding is a familiar process to students. It is a very efficient strategy for estimating the product of two multidigit factors. The rounding strategy involves rounding numbers and then computing with the rounded numbers. A third step of adjustment can sometimes be added when both factors are rounded in the same direction as illustrated in Activity 9−9.

Instruction should make it clear when rounding can be efficiently used. It should also emphasize that the purpose of rounding is to produce a problem that can be mentally computed. For example, to estimate the product of 23 and 78, several rounding procedures might be employed:

- About 20 × 80 or 1600
- About 25 × 80 or 2200
- More than 20 × 70 or 1400 +
- More than 20 × 78 or 1460 +

Each of these rounded numbers produces a different but reasonable estimate. Students' choice of rounded factors should be dictated by their flexibility and ability to mentally compute, and not by a set of rigid rounding rules.

Students should always remember that the purpose of the rounding strategy is to simplify the numbers and make numbers mentally manageable. They need

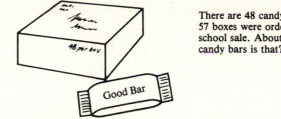

There are 48 candy bars in a box. 57 boxes were ordered for the school sale. About how many candy bars is that?

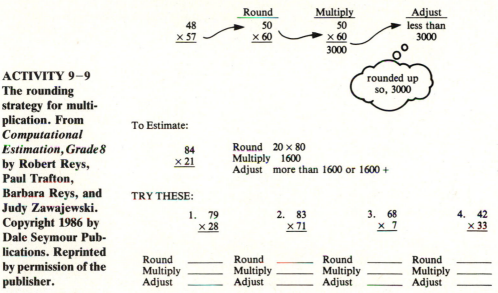

To Estimate:

	Round	Multiply	Adjust
48	50	50	less than
× 57	× 60	× 60	3000
		3000	

rounded up so, 3000

ACTIVITY 9–9
The rounding strategy for multiplication. From *Computational Estimation, Grade 8* **by Robert Reys, Paul Trafton, Barbara Reys, and Judy Zawajewski. Copyright 1986 by Dale Seymour Publications. Reprinted by permission of the publisher.**

To Estimate:

84	Round	20 × 80
× 21	Multiply	1600
	Adjust	more than 1600 or 1600 +

TRY THESE:

1. 79	2. 83	3. 68	4. 42
× 28	× 71	× 7	× 33

Round _____	Round _____	Round _____	Round _____
Multiply _____	Multiply _____	Multiply _____	Multiply _____
Adjust _____	Adjust _____	Adjust _____	Adjust _____

to learn to be flexible in their method of rounding, fitting it to the particular situation, operation, and numbers involved. This experience strengthens understanding that estimation is a simplifying process. Further, it helps students appreciate that individual estimators must decide which simplified problem is most comfortable and accurate for their purposes.

Compatible Numbers Strategy

The compatible numbers strategy encourages more sophisticated rounding. We have been taught round numbers to the nearest multiple of ten, hundred, thousand, and so forth. In the compatible numbers strategy, students are encouraged to round so that the resulting set of numbers can be easily computed. The emphasis is placed on rounding to mentally manageable numbers. This strategy is particularly effective when estimating division problems (see Activity 9–10).

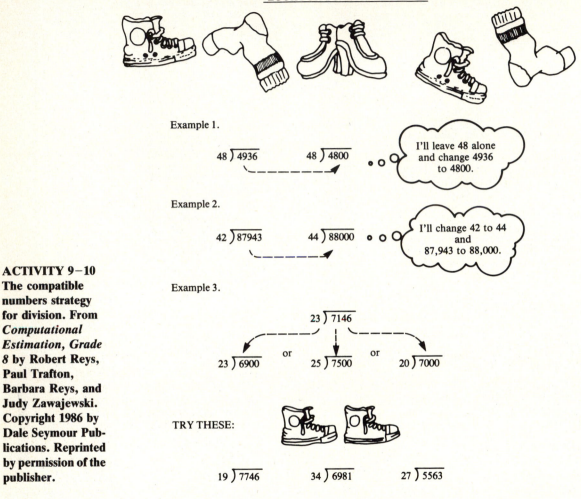

LOOK FOR COMPATIBLE PAIRS

Example 1.

48) 4936   48) 4800   I'll leave 48 alone and change 4936 to 4800.

Example 2.

42) 87943   44) 88000   I'll change 42 to 44 and 87,943 to 88,000.

ACTIVITY 9–10
The compatible numbers strategy for division. From *Computational Estimation, Grade 8* by Robert Reys, Paul Trafton, Barbara Reys, and Judy Zawajewski. Copyright 1986 by Dale Seymour Publications. Reprinted by permission of the publisher.

Example 3.

23) 7146

23) 6900   or   25) 7500   or   20) 7000

TRY THESE:

19) 7746   34) 6981   27) 5563

The compatible numbers strategy can be used for addition problems with several addends. The student learns to look for pairs of numbers that "fit together" to make numbers that are easy to compute mentally (see Activity 9–11).

Special Numbers Strategy

The special numbers strategy overlaps several strategies already discussed. Special numbers include powers of ten or common fractions and decimals. For

This sum can be estimated
by grouping numbers to
form COMPATIBLE sets.

```
   27
   49
   38
   65
   58
 + 81
```

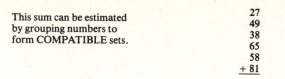

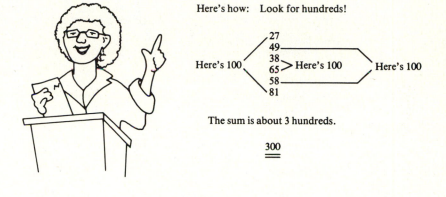

Here's how: Look for hundreds!

Here's 100   Here's 100   Here's 100

The sum is about 3 hundreds.

$$\underline{\underline{300}}$$

ACTIVITY 9–11
The compatible numbers strategy for addition. From *Computational Estimation, Grade 8* by Robert Reys, Paul Trafton, Barbara Reys, and Judy Zawajewski. Copyright 1986 by Dale Seymour Publications. Reprinted by permission of the publisher.

TRY THESE:

1.   37 + 46 + 89 + 24 + 59 + 73

2.   246 + 356 + 689 + 843 + 986 …. | Look for thousands! |

3.
```
   39
   46
   83
   72
   48
   59
 + 46
```

4.
```
  463
  549
  176
  328
  384
  246
+ 684
```

example, each of the following problems involves numbers near "special" values and therefore can be easily estimated.

7/8 + 12/13	Each near 1, so 1 + 1 = 2
23/45 of 720	23/45 near 1/2, so 1/2 of 720 = 360
9.84% of 816	9.84% near 10%, so 10% of 816 = 81.6
436 ÷ 0.98	0.98 near 1, so 436 ÷ 1 = 436
103.96 × 14.8	103.96 near 100, so 100 × 14.8 = 1480

Activity 9–12 further illustrates the special numbers strategy.

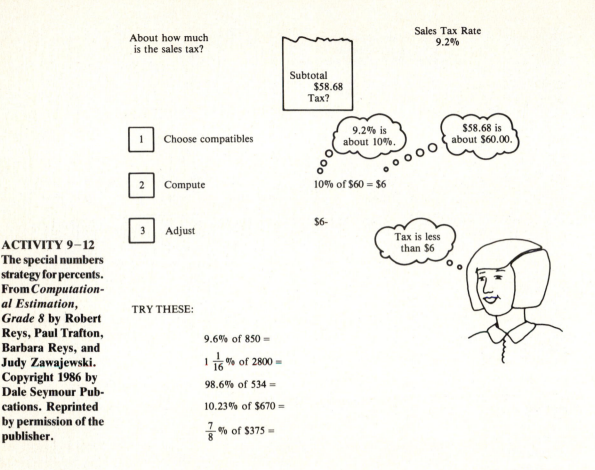

About how much
is the sales tax?

Sales Tax Rate
9.2%

Subtotal
$58.68
Tax?

1 | Choose compatibles

9.2% is
about 10%.

$58.68 is
about $60.00.

2 | Compute

10% of $60 = $6

3 | Adjust

$6-

Tax is less
than $6

ACTIVITY 9–12
The special numbers
strategy for percents.
From *Computation-*
al Estimation,
Grade 8 **by Robert**
Reys, Paul Trafton,
Barbara Reys, and
Judy Zawajewski.
Copyright 1986 by
Dale Seymour Pub-
cations. Reprinted
by permission of the
publisher.

TRY THESE:

9.6% of $850 =$

$1\frac{1}{16}\%$ of $2800 =$

98.6% of $534 =$

10.23% of $\$670 =$

$\frac{7}{8}\%$ of $\$375 =$

ACTIVITIES

1. In your own words, define "number sense."
2. Do the "Try These" exercises in Activities 9–6 and 9–7.
3. Examine the series, "Estimation Materials for Middle Grades" published by Dale Seymour Publications. Make a list of three different activities to help students better understand and appreciate estimation.
4. Consider each of the following problems. Estimate each solution then provide a summary of the strategy you used.
   a. The icemaker on a new refrigerator freezer produces about 27 ice cubes every hour. About how many ice cubes will it produce in a day?
   b. The phone book of a large city contains nines pages of listings of names beginning with the letter Z. If there are over 340 names on each page of the phone book, about how many names beginning with the letter Z are there?

c. At peak hours, the long-distance phone rate is $1.78 for the first three minutes and 38 cents each additional minute. About how much will a 15-minute call cost?

d. The grocery receipt below contains prices for items bought. The total cost has been torn away. Will $15.00 be enough to pay the bill?

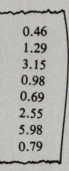

```
0.46
1.29
3.15
0.98
0.69
2.55
5.98
0.79
```

e. The bill for a meal in a restaurant totals $25.45. You want to leave a 15% tip. About how much should you leave?

CHAPTER 9 SUMMARY

Like problem-solving techniques, estimation strategies are developed through careful instruction, discussion, and use. It is recommended that the following three phases be included in your instructional strategy:

Instruction. Unless computation estimation strategies are taught, most students will neither learn nor use them. Prerequisite skills (such as mastery of basic facts and place value) must be reflected in the instructions and development of a strategy. Greater understanding and appreciation of a strategy will result when it is related to different applied situations. Practice is important, but instruction on each of these estimation strategies will complement, direct, and motivate meaningful practice.

Practice: It is important to have a wide variety of practice, preceded by specific instruction. Short practice sessions of five to ten minutes each week are recommended. Such regular practice will help maintain basic facts, improve mental computation skills, and provide opportunities for further development of computational estimation skills.

Testing: Periodic testing provides motivation for developing computational estimation. Each test can include about a dozen similar items. An effective presentation format is to put the items on an overhead transparency and project each problem individually for a short period of time (10 to 20 seconds). Scoring intervals can be set up in advance for each problem. Selected problems and strategies used to solve them can be discussed in class.

Estimation is a rich and rewarding topic to teach. It offers many avenues of discussion with students and overlaps as well as supports many other concepts already being taught.

REFERENCES

Carlton, R. A. 1980, May. *Basic skills in the changing work world.* Monograph, University of Guelph.

Carpenter, T. P., Corbitt, M. K., Kepner, H. S., Lindquist, M. M., & Reys, R. E. 1981. National Assessment: A perspective of students' mastery of basic mathematics skills. In *Eighty-first Yearbook of the National Society for the Study of Education.* Chicago: University of Chicago Press.

Driscoll, M. J. 1981. Estimation and mental arithmetic. In *Research within reach: Elementary school mathematics.* Reston, VA: National Council of Teachers of Mathematics.

National Counciol of Supervisors of Mathematics. 1978. Position paper on basic mathematical skills. *Mathematics Teacher,* 71:147–152.

National Council of Teachers of Mathematics. 1980. *An agenda for action: Recommendations for school mathematics of the 1980s.* Reston, VA: NCTM.

National Science Board Commission on Pre-College Education in Mathematics, Science and Technology. 1982. *The mathematical science curriculum K–12: What is still fundamental and what is not?.* Washington, DC: National Science Foundation.

Reys, R. E. 1986. Evaluating computational estimation. In *Mental computation and estimation: 1986 yearbook of National Council of Teachers of Mathematics.* Reston, VA: National Council of Teachers of Mathematics.

Reys, R. E., & Bestgen B. J. 1981, November. Teaching and assessing computational estimation skills. *Elementary School Journal,* 82:117–127.

Reys, R. E., Bestgen, B. J., Rybolt, J. F., & Wyatt, J. W. 1980. *Identification and characterization of computational estimation processes used by inschool pupils and out of school adults* (Final report, NIE 79-0088). Washington, DC: National Institute of Education.

Reys, R. E., Bestgen, B. J., Rybolt, J. F., & Wyatt, J. W. 1982. Processes used by good estimators. *Journal for Research in Mathematics Education,* 13:183–201.

Reys, B. J., Reys, B. J., Trafton, P. T., & Zawajewski, J. 1987. *Computational estimation grade 6, grade 7, grade 8.* Palo Alto, CA: Dale Seymour Publications.

Reys, R. E., Reys, B. J., Trafton, P. T., & Zawajewski, J. 1984. *Developing computational estimation materials for the middle grades* (Final Report, NSF 81-13051). Washington, DC: National Science Foundation.

Schoen, H. L., Friesen, C. D., Jarret, J. A., & Urbatsch, T. D. 1981. Instruction in estimating solutions of whole number computations. *Journal for Research in Mathematics Education,* 12:165–178.

Seymour, D. 1980. *Developing skills in estimation, book B.* Palo Alto, CA: Dale Seymour Publications.

10 Ratios and Proportional Thinking

ALAN R. HOFFER

Boston University

INTRODUCTION

Proportional reasoning is generally regarded as one of the important components of formal thought acquired in adolescence. Underlying proportional reasoning are the notions of comparison and covariation. These are the conceptual underpinnings of ratio and proportion. Failure to develop in this area by early to middle adolescence precludes study in a variety of disciplines requiring quantitative thinking and understandings, including algebra, geometry, some aspects of biology, chemistry, and physics.

The acquisition of proportional thinking skills in the population at large has been unsatisfactory. Not only do these skills emerge more slowly than originally suggested but there is evidence that a large segment of our society never acquires them at all! These topics are not taught particularly well in schools often fostering meaningless manipulation of symbols and formulas.

This chapter will develop the concepts of ratio and proportion and discuss their role in mathematics and in society. It will provide an overview of the research related to the learning of these concepts and will provide suggestions for effective instruction.

USING RATIOS IN SCIENCE AND SOCIETY

Because the use of ratios and proportional thinking occurs in many practical situations, these skills should be developed carefully in the school program. A knowledge of ratio techniques can be very valuable to students in problem-solving situations as well as in developing general thought patterns. Here are just a few examples of the ways ratio ideas can arise in science and society. As you read these examples try to imagine how your students might encounter situations like these and what manner they might use to solve problems involving these relationships. Only after we have considered several aspects of ratios and proportions will we formally define the concepts.

In Daily Use

- Shopping: There are direct uses of ratios, such as in a grocery store where a single price is given for several of the same item. Examples, three lemons for 89 cents; seven ears of corn for $1.00.

    The shopper associates 89 cents with three lemons and $1.00 with the cost of seven ears of corn. Then the shopper can calculate the cost of one lemon or one ear of corn.

    Also, there are indirect or hidden uses of ratios that occur in shopping situations in which a grocery item may contain several of the units. Example, a seven-ounce can for 80 cents; 18-inch pizza for $6.89.

    The shopper associates 80 cents to the can and may not notice how much is contained in the can. Another brand might charge less than 80 cents for a similar product, but the amount contained in the competitive brand may be much more than in the first brand.
- Money: In making change or comparing monetary units, it is helpful to know how the various money units compare: Examples, one dollar equals ten dimes; two quarters equal ten nickels.
- Recipes: For most recipes the amount of the ingredients depends on how many people are to be served: Examples, 1.5 cups of flour to serve four people; ten ounces of milk for four portions.
- Do-it-yourself: Home remodeling or maintenance uses guidelines to determine how many of an item to purchase. Examples, one gallon of paint to cover 400 square feet; 15 boards to replace two sections of a wall.
- Automobiles: Certain single numbers are guidelines for operating vehicles. Examples, 55 mph; 42 miles per gallon; 3000 miles for each quart of oil. In a sense these are suppressed uses of ratios because people usually do not think of comparing 55 miles with each hour traveled or 42 miles with each gallon used.

In Changing Between Units

- Changing units in a system: 36 inches to one yard; one meter per 100 cm; two cups for each pint.

- Changing units between systems: 2.54 cm to one inch; 161 km per 100 miles.
- Comparing different types of systems: 180 miles in three hours; 186,000 miles per second.
- Physical comparisons: Four paper clips per crayon; 800 strides to each half mile.

In Scales and Scaling

- Numerical changes: Three times as many; twice as fast.
- Geometric changes: Enlargement of a photograph; reduction of a blueprint or diagram.
- Maps: A scale of 1:1500000.
- Similar figures: Sides in the ratio of five to seven.

In Circle Relationships (see Fig. 10−1)

C (circumference) $= \pi \cdot D$ (diameter)
π (pi) $= C/D$

$$L \text{ (arc length)} = \frac{a}{360} = \frac{L}{C} \text{ or } L = C\left(\frac{a}{360}\right)$$

$$A \text{ (area of a sector)} = \frac{a}{360}(\pi r^2) \text{ or } A = \frac{A}{\pi r^2} = \frac{a}{360}$$

In Other Areas

- Music: Four notes per measure; two beats per note; 12 tones per octave.
- Nature: Golden ratio; nautilus shell.
- Probability: Seven favorable events out of 36 possibilities; three to two odds.
- Variation: Direct, indirect, and joint variation.
- Graphs: Slope of a line; rate of change of a curve or function.
- Indirect measures: Trigonometric ratios.
- Levers: (see Fig. 10−2) $W_1 d_1 = W_2 d_2$.

FIGURE 10−1

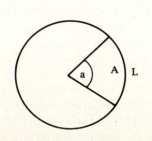

FIGURE 10–2

RATIOS IN THE SCHOOL CURRICULUM

Take a look at some of the old textbooks of a hundred years ago, and you will see how attempts were made to develop proportional thinking then. It was often the case, if we can judge by the printed books, that the teacher would direct the class interaction with sequences of verbal exercises to which the students would respond. There would be a slow development of multiplication exercises (see "Overcoming Obstacles to Learning" later in this chapter) which would gradually increase in difficulty. The students would learn to work with simple proportions and transform them to obtain equivalent proportions, all done through verbalization and whatever physical activities the teachers thought were appropriate to help the students internalize the ratio ideas.

As textbooks evolved through various fads and social demands, the role of proportional thinking changed accordingly. In many foreign countries ratios continued to play a central part in the development of the mathematics curriculum. Unfortunately, in the United States there were social pressures to reduce the reading level of the school books, and one of the consequences was a dramatic decrease in the amount of time and space devoted to ratios as well as to applications and to solving of problems other than nearly rote calculations. The emphasis in this country seemed to be placed on fractions and the associated algorithms. There was and still is, unfortunately, decreased attention to proportional thinking because of the desire to devote more instructional time to fractions. That is altogether fitting and proper; however, there are some significant differences between fractions and ratios and there is the need to devote adequate time to the development of ratios at the school level.

Distinguishing Ratios and Fractions

The fraction notation for ratios may be confusing to students because they may have learned first that fractions are used to refer to or denote parts of a whole object or parts of a set or collection of objects. So the carry-over of the same notation to ratios can cause some learning difficulties. For example, the student can probably recognize the ratio 5/12 (or $\frac{5}{12}$) as a fraction; however, the ratio of 17 girls to 30 students in a class, when expressed in the same notation, would appear as 17 girls/30 students (or $\frac{17 \text{ girls}}{30 \text{ students}}$). To see a ratio in this fraction-like form may be disconcerting to students who are thinking in terms of comparing part of a set to the whole set. The comparison 17 girls to 13 boys in this same class might also add to the confusion. This points out one of the many ways ratios and fractions differ. Here are some other differences:

- Ratios can compare nonsimilar objects, that is, objects measured with different units. Example, 3 lemons for 89 cents.

    Fractions, on the other hand, are used to compare the same type of objects such as "two of the three parts," which is denoted 2/3. The ratio of three lemons/89 cents is not a fraction.
- Some ratios are not represented as fractions. Example, one gallon per 400 square feet. There is no fraction notation needed to convey this relationship although the comparison could be equivalently denoted as one gallon/400 square feet.
- Ratios can be represented by symbols other than fractions. Example, the ratio 4 to 7 may appear as 4:7 or 4 → 7. In the United States the colon notation is the most common way to express a ratio. (In many other countries a colon is used to express division instead of the ÷ symbol.) The arrow symbol → nicely indicates the correspondence aspect of a ratio as a way to compare quantities.
- Ratios can use zero as the second entry. Examples, ten green candies to zero red candies in a particular package. Fractions, on the other hand, are not defined with a zero denominator.
- Ratios are not always rational. Example, for circles the ratio of the circumference to the diameter is equal to π ($C/D = \pi$) and π is not a rational number because it cannot be expressed as a division of two integers. Also, in a square, the ratio of the side length to the diagonal is $1:\sqrt{2}$, and since $\sqrt{2}$ is not equal to the ratio of two integers, it is not a rational number. Fractions, on the other hand, by their very nature are rational numbers because every fraction is equal to the division of two integers.
- Ratios do not combine the same way fractions combine. Example

$$2:5 + 3:7 = 5:12; \text{ however, } \frac{2}{5} + \frac{3}{7} \neq \frac{5}{12}$$

This ratio statement could represent an actual situation: 2 hits out of 5 at-bats followed by 3 hits out of 7 at-bats yields 5 hits out of 12 at-bats. This thinking makes perfectly good sense when applied to certain ratio situations and yet it does not carry over correctly to fractions.

There are wonderful opportunities to fuse proportional thinking together with other topics in the school mathematics curriculum and thereby enrich the learning of several areas. Below we suggest some connections between ratios and other topics. Many of these should start at the first grade and be continued throughout the grades until the students arrive at the formal stage of thinking (see "What We Can Learn from Research" later in this chapter).

Relating Ratios to Other Topics

There are many topics in the school curriculum that have a natural connection with ratios or proportional thinking. In some cases the connections are simply numerical while in others there are bridges between techniques for solving problems and ways to enrich the study of other subjects such as geometry or statistics. Here are some of the connections of ratios with other topics.

Multiplying

In early school work, multiplication occurs as a continuation of adding. Example, if there is a row of 4 objects, then 2 rows have 8 objects, 3 rows have 12 objects, and so forth. Students learn various products this way by counting and eventually finding ways, such as scaling, to figure out the products without counting. This is a natural opportunity to provide more experiences with ratios without using the formal ratio or proportion symbols. Then later, for example when the students encounter a problem that asks how many objects there would be in ten rows (knowing there are four objects in one row), they will be able to build up to an answer.

Applications

Many problem-solving situations can be greatly simplified by using proportional thinking. Example, in expressions such as time-and-a-half hourly wage; the earth weight is six times the moon weight. A problem might request the difference in weight between an object on the earth and on the moon if that object weighs 50 kilograms on the moon. Students could use proportional thinking to determine that the object weighs 300 kg on the earth and so it weighs 250 kg less on the moon than it does on the earth.

Area

Elementary school students usually find the area of rectangles by counting squares. Counting procedures similar to those used in multiplication can help students find the area of rectangles. Example, five squares for each of three rows, the area is 15; seven squares for each of two rows, the area is 14.

Fractions

The fraction symbol 2/3 should be interpreted in the ratio context as two for every three or as two out of three. Several concepts that cause students difficulty with fractions can be greatly simplified by using ratios, such as producing equivalent fractions: two for every three is the same as four for every six, so 2/3 = 4/6. Also, as we pointed out above, the multiplication ideas apply as well to fractions, such as finding 1/2 of 3/5. This view of fractions as ratios takes some of the mystery out of so-called improper fractions, such as 7/3.

Decimals

Decimals can be interpreted as ratios also, for example, students learn that 0.4 is a notation for the ratio of 4 out of 10, and this is equivalent to 40 out of 100, or 0.40. Students can learn to employ the ratio processes when appropriate to solve problems involving decimals. By relating these two concepts the students are armed with more techniques with which to interpret situations and solve problems.

Percents

Percents are of course special ratios in which the second number is 100. Students should be given extensive experiences with scaling up and down with ratios (see "Overcoming Obstacles to Learning" later in this chapter) as preludes to and during the work with percents. Indeed, many problems that involve percents can be solved more easily by using proportional thinking rather than with formal mechanical procedures. As an example, suppose students know that 30% of some amount is equal to $150 and they are asked to find the original amount. Rather than fall into the mode of mindless manipulation of proportions the students can apply ratios as follows: 30% of the amount is $150, so 10% of the amount is $50, so 100% of the amount is $500 ($150 + $150 + $150 + $50). Hence the original amount is $500. In this way the students are thinking their way through problems rather than trying to memorize specialized techniques for a plethora of special problems.

Measurement

We pointed out above how ratios are used to work with units, for example, 100 cm per meter; 2.54 cm per inch, 2 cups for every pint. The transfer of measurements between systems can be a valuable use of ratios. Also measurement applications of ratios can be used to solve problems. For example, suppose some people want to know how much earlier they will arrive at their destination by car if they break the law and drive 65 mph instead of the legal rate of 55 mph. The distance they are to travel is 80 miles. One solution, using proportional thinking, determines that at the 65-mph rate they would cover the distance in about 74 minutes while at the 55-mph rate it would take about 87 minutes. So they arrive only 13 minutes later by adhering to the legal limit and increasing their chances of arriving safely.

Probability

Probabilities are defined initially as ratios. This is clearly seen in examples such as 6 favorable events out of 36 possibilities, which utilizes the ratio 6/36. If ratio concepts and techniques are developed in the students before symbols like

P(7) = 6/36 are forced, there is a greater chance that students will understand and be able to work with probability concepts.

Geometry

Ratios and proportions occur, for example, in scaling figures (see "Instructional Activities" later in this chapter), similarity, arc length for circles, and so forth. In some cases it is useful to employ these topics to increase the level of understanding about ratios as well as to use ratio thinking to more fully understand and apply these topics.

Graphs

Slopes of lines are ratios that provide useful descriptions of the behavior of the lines. It is quite likely that students have difficulty in working with slopes of lines and curves simply because they have not reached a high enough level of understanding and competence with ratios.

Sets

Determining correspondences between sets is one of the valuable techniques used to introduce and develop proportional thinking. Likewise, ratios can provide illuminating examples of set correspondences. Some of the more important applications of sets occur in solving some combinatorial problems which express relationships between various parameters.

Calculators and Mental Arithmetic

With the increasing use of calculators in the school curriculum, there is a need to encourage more mental arithmetic to estimate the answer as an accuracy check. Proportional thinking is needed to scale numbers up and down and make refined estimates in order to check the reasonableness of calculator outputs.

WHAT WE CAN LEARN FROM RESEARCH

Suppose that you have presented the following problem to your students (see Fig. 10–3). How would you expect them to work it?

Mr. Short (shown to the students as a chain of six paper clips) is four large buttons in height. Mr. Tall (not shown to the students) is similar to Mr. Short but is six large

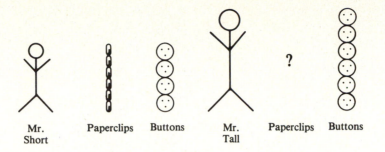

FIGURE 10-3

Mr.
Short   Paperclips   Buttons   Mr.
Tall   Paperclips   Buttons

buttons in height. Predict the height of Mr. Tall if you could measure him in paper clips. Explain your prediction.

If your students are like those in a study that used this problem (Karplus, Karplus, & Wollman, 1974), more than 50% of the fourth graders and nearly 30% of the eighth graders would respond like this:

"Mr. Tall is eight paper clips high. He is two buttons higher than Mr. Short, so I figured he is two paper clips higher."

Try problems like the one above with some students to see how the students react. Compare your results with the study by Karplus (1974). Being able to perform mechanical operations with proportions does not necessarily mean the students understand the underlying ideas of proportional thinking. It is interesting to note that the ability to firmly understand proportionality is a turning point in mental development.

Concrete thought focuses on real objects and events; formal thought can focus on statements about the concrete thoughts. It is this work with thinking and thinking about thinking that relates to proportions. In the Mr. Short—Mr. Tall problem a proportion is an equality between two ratios. Hence, full understanding of proportions appears to require formal thought because it involves thinking about lower level thoughts, namely the individual ratios in a proportion. The results of the Mr. Short experiment support this assertion. Here are two experiments suggested by Piaget.

1. **Similar triangle** (see Fig. 10-4) (Piaget & Inhelder, 1967, chap. 12). Students at the concrete stage are asked to draw a large triangle using PQ as a side with exactly the same shape and position as the triangle PSR. Many students will focus on the difference of six units between PQ and PS and extend the length PR by six units to draw the similar triangle. Admittedly, they often recognize that the result "doesn't look right," but the point is that their natural focus is on the difference rather than on a proportional relationship or angle measure. This same focus on differences rather than proportionality was apparent in the Mr. Short experiment described above.

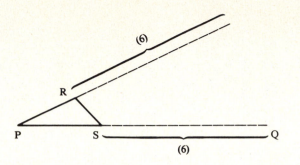

FIGURE 10−4

2. Lever-arm balance (see Fig. 10−5) (Inhelder & Piaget, 1958).   Students at the concrete stage are asked to place a weight on a lever-arm balance so as to balance a weight already on the opposite end (as shown in Fig. 10−5). Some students may count from the ends of the balance arms. Others will have no idea how to predict. Some may focus on the difference in weights (one unit) and feel that the 4-weight should be placed one unit farther out (onto the 9-peg) to adjust for this difference. These experiments have implications for teaching.

Knowledge of Stages

Some knowledge of the developmental stages enables a teacher to be more sensitive to how students may be viewing things and to topics students may not be able to absorb simply by listening to a teacher's verbal explanation. For example, if teachers know some students use the difference relationship instead of proportionality, they would be more likely to provide activities to develop awareness about ratios. The difficulty, of course, is in determining at what stage a student is. Quite often students are in a transitional phase between stages.

FIGURE 10−5

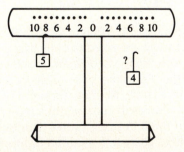

Knowledge of Factors in Development

Included in the natural development of the operational stages are maturation, experience, social transmission (learning from others), and the more technical equilibration. Maturation reminds us not to expect an overnight development of formal thought even though we might give careful verbal explanations of, for example, how to solve a proportion. We should pay more attention to providing physical experiences with proportions.

The importance of social transmission is particularly strong when it comes to students' learning that there are other points of view than their own. Verbal discussions offer an excellent way to hear others' viewpoints. Social transmission also includes information received from the teacher. Students must be in a mental framework and intellectual stage where they can understand and be receptive to new information, otherwise there is a mismatch between the students' ability and the information to be assimilated.

Equilibration seems to explain how one's mental structures change assuming that such changes are not prevented by other factors. As long as new experiences fit into an existing way of thinking, there is no need to change that thought pattern. For example, as long as looking at differences enables students to make correct predictions about proportions, they will continue to use that technique. If, however, the students' thinking leads to an error, as in the Mr. Short experiment, then this discrepancy may cause a change in how the students think. Having students work in situations in which actual observations may be contrary to what some of them predict might effect a change in their way of thinking.

Attention to Foundations

As a general rule, instruction for beginning students should start by making sure the students have some concrete bases for their mental manipulations. This can be done by starting a discussion of a topic as concretely as possible, then moving to drawings or pictures, and gradually including work with abstract symbols.

OVERCOMING OBSTACLES TO LEARNING

As we pointed out earlier and as the research shows, there are natural barriers to learning proportional thinking, especially in moving from the concrete stage to the formal stage. In this section we look first at a way to build upon items familiar to the students and use them to establish some ratios and then show how to scale the ratios up and down to generate equivalent ratios. Then we look at two methods for comparing ratios the students can use to solve problems.

SCALING RATIOS UP AND DOWN

Students do benefit from numerous verbal activities that start with ratios familiar to them and then scale the ratios up and down. It is interesting to watch students as they learn to play the game and use multiplication (sometimes in the form of repeated addition) to produce equivalent ratios. It is best to start with the easiest case and build up slowly. Here are some examples (the blank spaces indicate where the students are to provide the input):

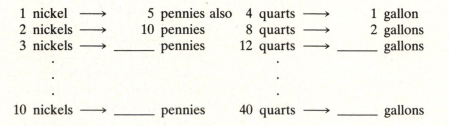

The following topics are familiar to students and can be used to practice scaling up activities:

- *Money:*   1 nickel ⟶ 5 cents; 1 quarter ⟶ 5 nickels, 25 cents; 1 dime ⟶ 2 nickels, 10 cents; 1 dollar ⟶ 4 quarters, 10 dimes, 20 nickels.
- *Time:*   1 hour ⟶ 60 minutes; 1 minute ⟶ 60 seconds; 1 day ⟶ 24 hours; 1 week ⟶ 7 days; 1 year ⟶ 52 weeks; 1 decade ⟶ 10 years; 1 century ⟶ 100 years.
- *Lengths (English):*   1 foot ⟶ 12 inches; 1 yard ⟶ 3 feet; 1 mile ⟶ 1760 yards; 1 mile ⟶ 5280 feet.
- *Lengths (Metric):*   1 centimeter ⟶ 10 millimeters; 1 meter ⟶ 100 centimeters; 1 kilometer ⟶ 1000 meters.
- *Lengths (Converting):*   1 inch ⟶ 2.54 centimeters; 1 centimeter ⟶ 0.3937 inches; 1 mile ⟶ 1.6 kilometers.
- *Weights (English, Metric, Converting):*   1 pound ⟶ 16 ounces; 1 ton ⟶ 2000 pounds; 1 gram ⟶ 100 cg; 1 kilogram ⟶ 1000 grams; 1 pound ⟶ 2.2 kilograms.
- *Capacity:*   1 quart ⟶ 2 pints; 1 gallon ⟶ 4 quarts; 1 liter ⟶ 100 centiliters; 1 liter ⟶ 1.1 quart.
- *Computers:*   1 byte ⟶ 8 bits; 1 kilobyte ⟶ 1024 bytes.
- *Common Units:*   1 dozen ⟶ 12 items; 1 flashlight ⟶ 2 batteries; 1 person ⟶ 2 feet; 1 car ⟶ 5 tires; 1 person ⟶ 10 fingers; 1 person ⟶ 32 teeth.

These are, of course, just a few such items. Students are quite willing to suggest other items of interest to them. Using and scaling up these familiar ratios enhances the notion of multiplication as repeated addition. While this has certain advantages for beginning students, *teachers must help students learn to use multiplication facts directly without always resorting to repeated addition.*

It is not advisable to cover all the scaling activities at once because too much of a good thing can become tedious. Short and easy scaling activities can be used to begin a class session or during a lull in the class such as during a transition from one subject to another or after the school secretary has just finished making an announcement over the public address system. After the students have practiced on various individual items like the ones above, you can provide them with review from time to time with examples like these:

6 nickels	⟶	_____ pennies	7 quarters	⟶	_____ nickels
3 hours	⟶	_____ minutes	18 weeks	⟶	_____ days
12 inches	⟶	_____ centimeters	30 kilometers	⟶	_____ miles

These activities can be part of the students' work in both mathematics and science. For example, when working with areas and volumes, the students can scale up various comparisons like these:

1 square foot	⟶	144 square inches	1 square yard ⟶	9 square feet
1 cubic foot	⟶	1728 cubic inches	1 cubic yard ⟶	27 cubic feet

So far we have suggested scaling up activities in which the numbers increase and can be determined by multiplying. There are several problem-solving situations in which the reverse skill is very useful, namely, to scale down a given ratio. Students seem to have more difficulty with this activity and it is therefore necessary for teachers to choose easy exercises with which to begin. By "easy" we mean first to use numbers that leave no remainder upon division, as in the examples below. After the students gain expertise with the skills involved in scaling down, they can work with numbers that do not necessarily divide evenly because that is usually the situation in practical applications. We emphasize most strongly that children do not need to study division before working on these activities. At the earliest grades children acquire an intuitive feeling for taking half of even numbers and from that time they can practice these scaling down activities. Also we emphasize that these scaling activities should be started when the children are very young and the students should experience them often throughout their school years.

40 pennies	⟶	8 nickels	12 quarts	⟶	3 gallons
20 pennies	⟶	_____ nickels	6 quarts	⟶	_____ gallons
10 pennies	⟶	_____ nickels	3 quarts	⟶	_____ gallons
4 pounds	⟶	64 ounces	4 weeks	⟶	28 days
_____ pounds	⟶	32 ounces	_____ weeks	⟶	14 days
1 pound	⟶	_____ ounces	1 week	⟶	_____ days
6 candy bars	⟶	90 cents	4 gallons	⟶	200 miles
3 candy bars	⟶	_____ cents	_____ gallons	⟶	100 miles
_____ candy bars	⟶	30 cents	1 gallon	⟶	_____ miles

After the students practice the scaling up and scaling down skills sufficiently, it is natural to combine the skills to scale up and then scale down to obtain another equivalent ratio. This combination of the scaling skills is most useful in solving problems and forms the basis of the methods we describe next for comparing ratios. (See also some of the examples at the beginning of this chapter.) Of course, when the students learn about fractions or decimals, it is a natural extension to practice some problems in which the reductions by taking halves, thirds, and so forth do not necessarily come out even, as in most practical problems. This offers an excellent opportunity to use calculators in realistic situations (along with the companion activities of estimation and mental arithmetic). For example,

If $3.25 for 5 cans, then _____ for 3 cans.
Solution $3.25 $\longrightarrow$ 5 cans
                           $0.65 $\longrightarrow$ 1 can (scaling down)
                           $1.95 $\longrightarrow$ 3 cans (scaling up) so 3 cans cost $1.95.

METHODS FOR COMPARING RATIOS

The Unit Method

The unit method consists of scaling both ratios (up and down) to obtain ratios that are equivalent to ones reported in terms of a single unit, if possible. It is because of this technique of scaling down to a single unit that this is called the unit method. In many problems to scale down to a single unit it may be necessary to use fractions or decimals. If the students have not yet studied these topics, the teacher must choose the problems carefully (or the clever teacher can use the problems to introduce the new topics).
   Example:
   Suppose car V can travel 480 miles on 10 gallons of gasoline. Car B can travel 516 miles on 12 gallons. Which of these cars gives the better mileage? The unit method prescribes that we try to scale each of the ratios down to a common unit.

480 miles $\longrightarrow$ 10 gallons   516 miles $\longrightarrow$ 12 gallons

Scale these ratios down to a common unit, namely, one gallon.

48 miles $\longrightarrow$ 1 gallon   43 miles $\longrightarrow$ 1 gallon

Because 48 is greater than 43, car V gets the better mileage.

The Common Multiple Method

This method consists of finding a common multiple of one of the units for both of the ratios involved in the problem; scaling the ratios to utilize that common multiple; and comparing the other values in the two ratios.

Example:

Suppose baseball pitcher A won 18 of 25 games for a particular season. Pitcher B won 15 of 20 games played for the same season. Which of these pitchers has the better rate of pitching for the season? First, we look at the ratios of their pitching records:

A) 18 won $\longrightarrow$ 25 played   B) 15 won $\longrightarrow$ 20 played

A common multiple, in fact the lowest common multiple, of 25 and 20 is 100. We therefore scale each of the ratios so that the second number of each is 100.

18 won $\longrightarrow$ 25 played   15 won $\longrightarrow$ 20 played
72 won $\longrightarrow$ 100 played   75 won $\longrightarrow$ 100 played

Because 75 is greater than 72, pitcher B has the better rate of wins for the season.

The unit method and the common multiple method are very useful in problem-solving situations. Most students need considerable practice to become proficient in these methods. Practicing the scaling activities as well as these methods usually involves mental arithmetic—performing calculations without the use of other tools, not even pencils. Mental arithmetic is an important aspect of the arithmetic program now that calculators and computers are so readily available.

INSTRUCTIONAL ACTIVITIES

Introducing Ratios

In the previous section we looked at how to use the techniques of scaling up and scaling down to develop a feeling for ratios. Now let's consider how you, as the teacher, might introduce ratios and equivalence to your students. Since a picture is known to be worth a thousand words, let's try pictures. This works with students of all ages.

With the pictures shown in Fig. 10−6, and the use of concrete objects to represent the items if you think that is needed, the students can practice scaling the ratios.

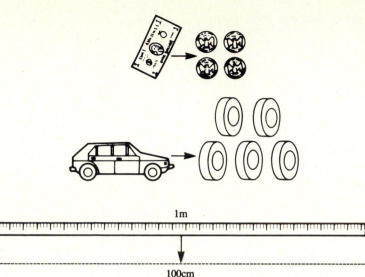

FIGURE 10–6

Dollars – Quarters	Tires – Cars	Meters – Centimeters
1 per 4	5 for 1	1 to 100
2 per 8	10 for 2	2 to 200
3 per 12	15 for 3	3 to 100
4 per 16	20 for 4	4 to 400
.	.	.
.	.	.
.	.	.

Students need practice scaling up and down with various items such as these as well as with items of their own choosing, and these will vary with classes and ages of students.

After the scaling practice, the students should have practice with questions such as these:

- If you have seven dollars in quarters, how many quarters do you have?
- If you have 20 quarters, how many dollars do you have?
- Thirty-five tires can replace the tires on how many cars?
- How many tires do we need to replace the tires on 12 cars?
- Eight hundred centimeters is equivalent to how many meters?

These comparisons and scaling practice can be incorporated into a guessing game. Let the students choose two types of objects or choose them yourself.

Have a box ready to hold some of the objects. For example, use crayons and stones. Place some of each type of item in the box and tell the students what the ratio is, for example, three rocks to five crayons. Now the students are to guess how many of each type of item are in the box. For example, 9 rocks and 15 crayons is a possibility, but 9 rocks and 11 crayons is not possible.

Reducing Ratios

The technique of scaling can be used to reduce ratios. The idea is to have an accepted way to talk about or communicate information about ratios. A ratio is *simplified* or in simplest form if the two numbers in the ratio have no common factor than one. For example, the following ratios are equivalent: 9 rocks to 15 crayons; 6 rocks to 10 crayons; and 3 rocks to 5 crayons. We prefer to use the simplified form 3:5 to talk about the relationship between rocks and crayons in the box.

You can use the guessing game to give the students experience in simplifying ratios. Tell the students how many of each type of item there are in the box and ask them to guess the simplified ratio. When the students agree on a guess, as a class or in teams, take the items out of the box and match them according to the guessed simplified ratio.

Ratios as Rates

We think of a ratio as a pair of measurements. For example, the ratio of five kilometers to three miles involves the comparison between the number of kilometers and the number of miles. This type of ratio is a *rate* because it is a comparison between different units (kilometers and miles.) Some older textbooks refer to rates as rate pairs. A special word like rate is not needed because all rates are ratios; we, however, often encounter expressions such as "the rate of speed is 55 mph," "the rate of pay is $300 per week," and so forth. So it may help students to work with rates if they think of them in the context of ratios.

Let's consider some possible activities to give students practice in working with rates. Again, the students usually are more actively involved if they are allowed to suggest items of interest to them. So ask the students to come to class the next day with examples of rates (for example, fuel consumption, hours slept per night, and so forth) and put these on a bulletin board for the class to look at and possibly add to daily. Older students can look in newspapers, magazines, encyclopedias, trivia books, and the like.

Ratios as Single Numbers

Even though a ratio is a comparison of two measurements, some ratios are reported as single numbers. We have seen several examples of these above.

Here are some others:

Ratio as a Number	First Measurement	Second Measurement
55 mph	55 miles	1 hour
38 mpg	38 miles	1 gallon
26 children per class	26 children	1 class
2.54 cm per inch	254 centimeters	100 inches
π	circle circumference	circle diameter

Here are some activities to give students experience in working with ratios expressed as single numbers.

- Put some single number ratios on the bulletin board.
- Play the guessing game with items in a box.
- Measure the length and width of an American flag; see if the ratio is 1.9.
- Measure the circumference and diameter of circles; see if the ratio is about 3.14 (close to π).
- Measure the diagonal and side of a square; see if the ratio is about 1.4 (close to $\sqrt{2}$).

Notation and Terminology

Students should have extensive experiences with ratios as comparisons and with scaling ratios up and down verbally before they are forced to use formal symbols to represent ratios. All too often the textbooks rush into symbols like 3:5 or 3/5 especially when proportions are introduced, such as 3:5 = 9:15 or 3/5 = 9/15. Most students are not ready to work with these formal symbols until they have sufficient development experiences with concrete and verbal/oral practice with these ideas.

We have seen several examples of the varied terminology used with ratios and proportions. Here is a summary:

Notation	Terminology
$a:b$	a per b
	a to b
a/b or $\dfrac{a}{b}$	a for b
	a for each b

Notation	Terminology
$a{:}b = c{:}d$	a is to b as c is to d
$a{:}b{::}c{:}d$	the proportion a/b to c/d
$\dfrac{a}{b} = \dfrac{c}{d}$	the equal ratios a/b and c/d

We noted above that the ratio concept is more general than the fraction concept. Fractions are ratios but the reverse is not true. Actually children's early experiences are with ratios as they compare different types of objects and learn to find equivalent ratios by scaling up and scaling down. Children learn to use fractions to compare part of a set with the whole set. In Fig. 10–7, 3/12 of the objects are black. Thus the fraction 3/12 is used to compare a subset of the set to the entire set. Students can benefit from numerous counting exercises such as this in which the figure may be organized for them at first, such as in a rectangle, and later presented in irregular forms where counting techniques are necessary.

Children learn that in some situations ratios can be replaced by fraction statements. In the example above, the ratio of three black objects to nine white objects was reported as a fraction, namely, that 3/12 of the objects are black. The two types of objects are combined into a large set and the number of elements in one of the sets is then compared to the total number of elements. Once again, the children need numerous practice exercises in first recognizing when such a translation from a ratio statement to one with fractions is appropriate. Then the children need experience in actually performing the translations. Here are some more samples for student exercises:

- There are 16 girls and 14 boys in the class; girls make up 16/30 of the class.
- The ratio of patients in the hospital with type AB blood is 3 to 2; 3/5 of the patients have type AB blood.
- The odds on our football team winning are 1 to 3; so if the team wins, each dollar bet earns three dollars. As a fraction the team has 1/4 chance of winning, not 1/3.

FIGURE 10–7

By giving students sufficient experiences with the very important notion of ratio we can increase the students' abilities to understand and resolve many problem-solving situations.

Introducing Proportions

As students learn to scale ratios up and down to obtain equivalent ratios they are in effect forming proportions. A proportion is a statement of equality between two ratios, such as

$a:b = c:d$

This is read as "the ratio of a to b is equal to the ratio of c to d" or "a is to b as c is to d."

When the students know three of the numbers in a proportion they need to to have methods to find the fourth number. Often they can do that by scaling up or down. Ask the students to record their information in a table. For example, suppose they encounter a question like this: if the cost of electricity is five cents for two kilowatt hours, how much will eight kilowatt hours cost? Instead of having the students rush into the formal stage of using a proportion, they can set up a table like this:

Number of Kilowatt Hours	Cost (cents)
2	5
4	10
6	15 and so forth

To help students have a pictorial image of the relationship ask them to graph the data they generated in their table (see Fig. 10−8). Graphing activities like this are quite appropriate and desirable at the earliest possible grades, just as soon as the students are able to understand the numbers involved. In fact, the graphs could lead into or be a part of lessons on statistics at most grade levels.

After developing the ability to solve proportions by scaling (using extensive mental arithmetic) and graphical means the students can move into the formal stage of working with the symbols in a proportion. In the form $a:b = c:d$, the first and fourth numbers (a and d) are the *extremes,* and the second and third numbers (b and c) are the *means*. The ratios are equal if the product of the

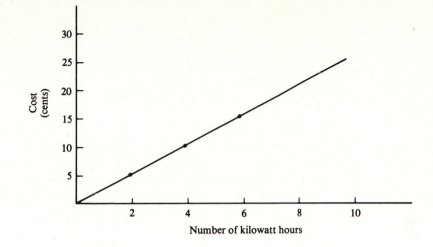

FIGURE 10-8

means is equal to the product of the extremes; that is $bc = ad$. This idea can be displayed in the following way:

$$a:b = c:d \text{ when } \frac{a}{b} = \frac{c}{d} \text{ when } ad = bc$$

The products bc and ad are referred to as the *cross products*. Students can use a visual memory device like this:

Here are some sample exercises that use the formal approach to proportions. As usual students need numerous exercises like these in which the numbers and level of difficulty of the exercises are appropriate to the experience of each student.

Example.

If an airplane can travel 675 kilometers in three hours, how far can the plane travel in five hours traveling at the same average rate?

The problem gives rise to the proportion

675 kilometers/3 hours = x kilometers/5 hours, or 675/3 = x/5.

This problem illustrates how the test for the equality of ratios can be used to find the fourth number of a proportion when the three other numbers of the proportion are known. The method of cross products is an efficient way to solve many problems. *Be careful not to use this before students are ready for it.*

Example.

A Boeing 747 airplane has a cruising speed of 595 miles per hour. How long will it take to travel 1500 miles at this rate?

It is instructive to first ask the students to try to solve the problem by using a list such as this:

Hours	Miles
1	595
2	1190
3	1785

A little mental arithmetic tells the students that an estimate of the answer is about two and one-half hours. Now let's apply the cross products method. We can choose a letter like t to stand for the unknown time it takes the plane to travel 1500 miles. So $t/1500$ denotes the numerical value of the ratio of the time t (in hours) to the distance 1500 (in miles). This is equivalent to 1/595; namely 1 hour to 595 miles. Hence we have the proportion

$$1/595 = t/1500$$

Using the cross product, we have

$$1*1500 = 595t$$

Then, by division, we find out that

$$t = 2.52$$

So it takes 2.52 hours for the plane to travel 1500 miles, assuming the constant cruising rate of 595 mph.

Various collections of lists or data provide excellent sources for exercises. For example, the *Guinness Book of World Records* offers a wealth of information that can be used for problems in which proportions arise. If the numbers in references such as these are too long or complicated for your students, you can make up some similar situations involving smaller numbers.

There are numerous applications of ratio ideas available commercially for you to use with your students. The collection *Ratio, Proportion, and Scaling* from the Mathematics Resource Project (1978a, b) includes activities that call for students to make measurements and observations dealing with gear ratios on ten-speed bicycles (not all ten-speed bikes are the same); finding heights of objects by using shadows; estimating the Golden Ratio; computing automobile driver reaction times and braking distances; comparing weight and height to standard growth charts; and so forth.

Comparing Ratios

Ratios can be used to compare information about various situations. For example, suppose 2 out every 5 households watched the Super Bowl football game; 1 out of every 3 households watched a World Series baseball game; and 7 out of 25 households watched a basketball playoff game. How can we compare this information? A simple technique is to express each of the ratios as a fraction and compare the fractions. The fraction 2/5 is greater than 1/3 so more households watched the Super Bowl than a World Series game. How did the basketball playoff games compare to the other sports? Notice that an essential feature of using ratios to make comparisons such as these is that in all three examples there is a common standard; namely, the number of households in the country, and we are able to make the comparisons even though we may not know how many households there are. Another technique for comparing ratios would be to convert the fractions to decimals, possibly by using calculators, and comparing the decimal equivalents. As an example, 1/3 is about 0.33 and 7/25 is equal to 0.28 and because 0.33 is greater than 0.28, more households watched a World Series game than a basketball playoff.

Scale Drawings

We used the word scale so far in the context of numerical scaling to obtain equivalent ratios, by scaling up, for example. There are of course other types of scales, such as pay scales, musical scales, scales for weighing, and so forth. When we use scale to refer to drawings and pictures, we mean a ratio. A scale of one centimeter to two kilometers on a drawing or a city map, for example, simply means that each centimeter corresponds to two kilometers. As another example, a scale of 1 centimeter:100 students might be used as a basis for a graph or a number line. The scale tells us how the units are used in the drawing to represent different quantities. When the dimensions of the drawing are equal to the dimensions of the object, the drawing is "in actual size," or "drawn to size with a scale of one to one." An *enlargement* is a drawing in which the scale is greater than one, that is, the dimensions of the drawing are greater than the dimensions of the object. A *reduction* is a scale drawing in which the scale is less than one. Examples of such scale drawings are shown in Fig. 10−9.

The structure provided by the lines of a grid helps students to make scale drawings (see Fig. 10−10). There are two main ways to use square grids to make scale drawings. One method involves using grid paper with different size squares, as in Fig. 10−10, while the other method involves the same size grid paper but using a different number of squares, depending on the desired ratio between the original figure and the scaled drawing. There are numerous examples of these student level activities in *Ratio, Proportion, and Scaling* (Mathematics Resource Project).

Enlargement

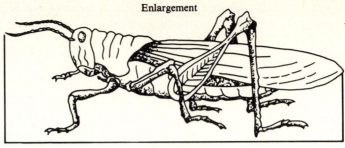

Scale of 2:1

Drawn to Actual Size

Scale of 1:1

Reduction

Scale of 1:2

FIGURE 10-9

ORIGINAL   2:1 ENLARGEMENT

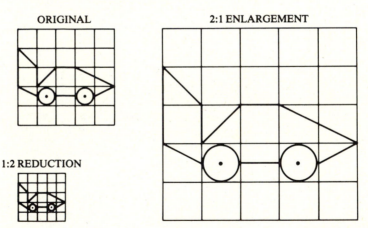

1:2 REDUCTION

FIGURE 10-10

DEFINITION OF A RATIO

So far we have discussed several ideas related to ratios without defining a ratio. We did emphasize that a ratio is not a fraction, although we can interpret fractions as ratios. We considered rates as special types of ratios. The essential ingredients of a ratio involve comparing measurements in an ordered manner, that is, there is a first measurement and a second one, and it is acceptable to compare measurements with different units. For example, the ratio 2.54 centimeters per one inch is different from the ratio one inch per 2.54 centimeter, and the two measurements involve different units (centimeter and inch). We summarize these ideas in the following definition which, as usual, should not be reported to children until they are motivated and receptive to think about the idea at this level.

Definition. A *ratio* is an ordered pair of measurements.

The ratio 250 miles in three hours can be expressed in various ways:

- By showing the correspondence   250 miles $\longrightarrow$ 3 hours
- Using the colon notation   250 miles:3 hours
- As an ordered pair of measurements   (250 miles, 3 hours)

By reversing the order of the two measurements, we obtain a different ratio even though it appears to describe the same comparison. An essential aspect of the ratio concept is the ordering: there is a first measurement and a second one.

We can display the measurements on a graph in which the units along the coordinate axes correspond to the units in the measurements. Two ratios are *equivalent* when one is a nonzero multiple of the other. For example, 2(250 miles, 5 hours) = (500 miles, 10 hours). All ratios that are equivalent to a given ratio lie on a line through the origin of the graph (Fig. 10−11).

A long-range goal (certainly not a beginning one) is for students to learn to express ratios in fractional form such as $\frac{250 \text{ miles}}{5 \text{ miles}}$ and to work formally with proportions such as $\frac{250 \text{ miles}}{5 \text{ miles}} = \frac{500 \text{ miles}}{10 \text{ miles}}$. This should come long after the mental structures of proportional thinking are developed in the students.

FIGURE 10−11

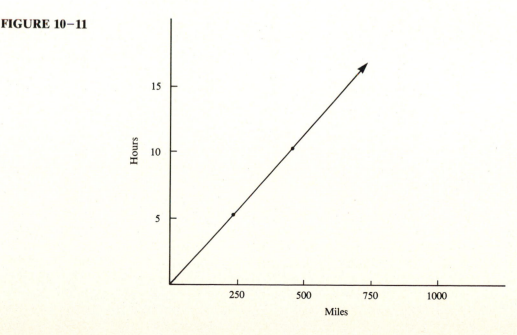

ACTIVITIES

Here are some additional exercises to consider:

1. Make some scale drawings of your own. For example, start with a picture of an interesting object. Make an enlargement with a scale of 3:1, or even 10:1 to put on the bulletin board. Use grids in the two ways suggested in this chapter to make reductions and enlargements. Make a list of places where enlargements and reductions occur in society, such as in photographs, maps, and so forth.

2. After experiencing for yourself some of the scale drawings in Activity 1, design some related lessons for students. Think about how scaling might be used as a continuing theme in teaching concepts involving ratio and proportion.

3. Obtain some maps of your city, county, state, and so forth (maybe even the solar system) and compare the scales on the maps. Make up some activities in which students must deduce information by using the map. For example, finding distances between locations; finding shortest paths from one position to another; changing between metric and English units of measure, and so forth.

4. Use isometric grid paper (with triangles instead of squares) to make some scale drawings of solid objects.

5. Investigate how artists use perspective drawing to represent objects. How are scales used in this type of drawing?

6. Use cubes and blocks to make models of solid objects. Then form similar objects by enlarging the original one with some scale factor. Investigate how the areas and volumes of the similar objects compare and how these relate to the scale factor between the objects.

7. Discuss this quote of Piaget: ". . . there exists a fundamental lacuna in our teaching methods, most of which, in a civilization very largely reliant upon the experimental sciences, continue to display an almost total lack of interest in developing the experimental attitude of mind in our students" (1971, p. 37). (The quote actually dates from 1965.) With regard to proportional thinking what can we do with our students to develop the "experimental attitude" Piaget refers to?

8. Students are not necessarily reasoning at the formal level just because they are expressing themselves verbally. Consider this quote from Inhelder and Piaget: ". . . all verbal thought is not formal and it is possible to get correct reasoning about simple (statements) as early as the 7−8-year level, provided that these (statements) correspond to sufficiently concrete representations" (Inhelder & Piaget, 1958, p. 252). Give the following two problems to an 8-year-old child and a 13-year-old child. How would you expect them to respond?
   a. Jim is taller than Dale. Matthew is taller than Jim. Who is tallest?
   b. Mary runs faster than Ann. Mary runs slower than Jane. Who runs the fastest?

9. Sinclair asserts that excessive emphasis on rote memory could well lead to an underdeveloped self-organized type of memorizing. In addition, ". . . a certain amount of rote learning is, in the present system, inevitable. But as regards mathematics and allied disciplines, it appears that it is the concept formation itself that should be fostered by all possible means . . ." (1971, p. 134).
   a. What aspects of ratios do you think are most efficiently learned through rote?
   b. What are some possible means to foster the formation of the concepts of ratio, proportion, or percent?

10. If a larger unit is used to measure a length, fewer units are required (as in the Mr. Short experiment). Abramowitz [1975] feels students need to have explicit exposure to such "inverse" situations and to contrast problems in which an increase in one thing is associated with an increase in another (for example, things bought and money spent, or speed and distance covered, or time spent on homework and number of exercises finished). Describe how you would handle these inversely related variables:
   a. Size of area unit and number of units required to measure a plane region
   b. Size of volume unit and number of units required to measure a space region
   c. Number of teeth in a gear and number of times it turns
   d. Distance from fulcrum and weight needed to balance a weight, as in a lever-arm experiment.

11. Read the Nelsen article (1969) or Van Engen (1960) article for more on the "are-ratios-the-same-as-fractions" issue. A more technical article is the one by Van Engen and Cleveland (1967).

12. This probability exercise may interest you in trying something similar with your students. Given a spinner like that shown in Fig. 10–12, which is more probable—that the spinner will stop twice on each color with sixteen spins or about one hundred times on each color with eight hundred spins?

FIGURE 10–12

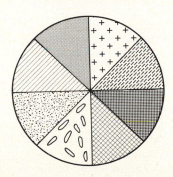

CHAPTER 10 SUMMARY

Ratios and proportional thinking should be introduced to children early and developed throughout successive school years. The formal aspects of proportions should be delayed until the students firmly understand the ideas and reasoning processes inherent in the topic. The activities of scaling up and scaling down should be experienced often and with a variety of applied topics. Eventually the unit method and the common multiple methods of comparing ratios should be mastered and applied to solving problems.

Proportional thinking naturally fits in with several other topics, and it is advantageous to intertwine the development of ratios with development of other basic skills such as the evolution and use of language.

For example, words such as per, for every, out of, same as, more than, less than, compare, correspond, and parts occur with ratios as well as in other topics. These should be used regularly.

Work with equivalent ratios carries over directly to comparing and ordering fractions and decimals, such as 1/6 and 1/8. We can scale these up to 4/24 and 3/24, respectively, and hence see that 1/6 is the greater fraction. Independent of the students' facility with calculators, they should learn how to scale up and scale down and to mentally check their answers.

We must be aware of the level of difficulty of questions we ask of students especially as they begin to study ratios. Without the use of calculators, it appears the level of difficulty depends on divisibility, that is, whether the numbers divide evenly. For example, most students find b) more difficult than a).

a) 8 out of 15   b) 8 out of 15
_____out of 45   _____out of 40.

As in most areas of the mathematics curriculum, calculators can free students to think about the concepts involved in ratio and proportional thinking rather than focusing on complex and time-consuming paper-and-pencil calculations.

REFERENCES

Abromowitz, S. 1975. Adolescent understanding of proportionality: Skills necessary for its understanding (Microfiche. ERIC No. ED 111 690). Washington, DC: Educational Resources Information Center.

Brown, S. I., & Walter, M. 1983. *The art of problem posing,* Philadelphia: Franklin Institute Press.

Fischbein, E., Pampu, I., & Manzat, I. 1970. Comparison of ratios and the chance concept in children. *Child Development,* 41:377–389.

Ford, E. 1974. The spectrum of proportion mastery among New York parochial school children. Columbia University, *Dissertation Abstracts International,* 35A:3573.

Inhelder, B., & Piaget, J. 1958. *The growth of logical thinking from childhood to adolescence.* (A. Parsons and S. Milgram, Trans.). New York: Basic Books.

Karplus, E., Karplus, R., & Wollman, W. 1974, October. Intellectual development beyond elementary school IV: Ratio, the influence of cognitive style. *School Science and Mathematics,* 74:475−482.

Lovell, Kenneth, 1971. Proportionality and probability. *Piagetian cognitive-development research and mathematical education.* M. Rosskopf (Ed.). Washington, D.C.: National Council of Teachers of Mathematics, pp. 136−148.

Mathematics Resource Project 1978. Piaget and proportions. In A. Hoffer (Dir.), *Didactics and mathematics.* Palo Alto: Creative Publications.

Mathematics Resource Project 1978. In A. Hoffer (Dir.), *Ratio and proportion.* Palo Alto: Creative Publications.

National Advisory Committee on Mathematical Education. 1975. *Overview and analysis of school mathematics grades K−12.* Washington, D.C.: Conference Board of Mathematical Sciences.

Nelsen, J. 1969, February. Percent: A rational number or a ratio? *The Arithmetic Teacher,* 16:105−109.

Piaget, J. 1964. Cognitive development in children: Development and learning. *Journal of Research in Science Teaching,* 2(3):176−186.

Piaget, J. 1972. Intellectual evolution from adolescence to adulthood. *Human Development.* 15(1):1−12.

Piaget, J. 1973, October. Piaget takes a teacher's look. (Interview by Eleanor Duckworth, Atlantic Institute of Education, Halifax, Nova Scotia, on special assignment for *Learning*). *Learning,* 2:22−27.

Piaget, J. 1971. *Science of education and the psychology of the child* (D. Coltman, Trans.). New York: Grossman.

Piaget, J. 1973. *To understand is to invest: The future of education.* (George-Anne Roberts, Trans.). New York: Viking.

Piaget, J. & Inhelder, B. 1967. *The child's conception of space* (F. J. Langdon and J. L. Lunzer, Trans.). New York: Norton and Company.

Piaget, J. & Inhelder, B. 1975. *The origin of the idea of chance in children.* (Lowell Leake, Jr.; Paul Burell; and Harold Fisbein, Trans.). New York: Norton and Company.

Portis, T. 1972, May. An analaysis of the performance of fourth-, fifth-, and sixth-grade students on problems involving proportions, three levels of aids, and three I.Q. levels. Indiana University, *Dissertation Abstracts International,* 33A:5981−5982.

Sinclair, H. 1971b. Representation and memory. In Rosskopf, M., et al. (Eds.), *Piagetian cognitive-development research and mathematical education* (pp. 125−135). Washington, DC: National Council of Teachers of Mathematics.

Van Engen, H. 1960, December. Rate pairs, fractions and rational numbers, *The Arithmetic Teacher* 7:389−399.

Van Engen, H., & Cleveland, R. 1967, October. Mathematical models for physical situations. *The Mathematics Teacher,* 60:578−581.

Weeks, R. 1973, November. The relationship of grade, sex, socio-economic status, scholastic aptitude, and school achievement to formal operations attainment in a group of junior high school students. Kent State University, *Dissertation Abstracts International,* 34A:2405.

Developing Relationships Among Mathematics and Other Subjects: An Interdisciplinary Approach

11

ALAN H. HUMPHREYS
THOMAS R. POST
University of Minnesota

ARTHUR K. ELLIS
Seattle Pacific University

INTRODUCTION

Typically school subjects are taught as discrete entities. There are few connections among the teaching of mathematics, the teaching of reading, the teaching of science, and so on. There is little sense of "connectedness" among school subjects or among the parts of the children's day. Children, who come to school with an integrated view of life and of their world, find little to reinforce their notions of the connectedness of things. They are conditioned, in the name of learning, to the idea that knowledge and skills are conveyed through the means of separate subjects. They are told these separate subjects have generalizable applications but do not experience it for themselves.

It is taken for granted, apparently, that in time students will see for themselves how things fit together. In truth children learn what we teach. If we teach connectedness and integration, they learn that. If we teach separation and discontinuity, that is what they learn. To suppose otherwise is inconsistent with principles of learning.

The goal of this chapter is to encourage you to consider the idea of integrated instructional goals. Several general themes that lend themselves to integration will be illustrated. In each instance, topics for the themes incorporate the humanities and communication arts, the natural sciences, mathematics, and social studies. There are even suggested linkages with music and art.

Not everything, however, can or should be taught to students in an integrated fashion. There are many mathematics skills and other subjects you will continue to teach formally. A thematic approach encourages children to change the focus of their knowledge, skills, and values from individual subjects to the problems and challenges encountered within the context of an integrated unit.

THE ROLE OF INTEGRATED STUDIES IN THE SCHOOL MATHEMATICS PROGRAM

An integrated study is one in which children explore aspects of their knowledge of various subjects. The introduction or focus of integrated study comes, therefore, from the student's environment (Humphreys et al., 1981). You may find it desirable to start a particular unit of study with a visit, a film, discussion, or selected readings. These common experiences provide the nucleus from which the child's investigations arise. Select activities are balanced in their educational content so that each child does some work within several broad subjects. Allow children to work individually or as part of a larger group. Generally students will develop a wide variety of materials that depict various stages in their investigations. Encourage students to save this work as it will be useful later for group presentations, classroom displays, and parent—teacher discussions. Set up a file for each child.

Much of your success depends on your care in planning. Collect books about the topic; acquire films, slides, film loops; contact possible speakers; and plan relevant field trips. Once the study is underway, play the role of facilitator. You are not expected to know answers to all questions students may initiate. Rather, your role is that of promoting student learning through encouragement and the establishment of appropriate learning conditions. This is a substantive departure from traditional views of the school curriculum and of appropriate teacher behavior. A single integrated study lasts five to seven weeks. Teachers must plan carefully and think through the procedures for dealing with such an approach.

Your first theme should be a short one—two or three weeks. The appropriate length of a single study should generally be based on four considerations: a) the age and developmental level of the children involved; b) the children's interest; c) your enthusiasm; and d) your initial preparations. Children can often be encouraged to pursue various aspects of a theme at home.

Divide children into work areas and groups. The groups invariably address different aspects of the problem. It is important that children of different abilities and attainment levels work cooperatively on a common problem or theme (Malone et al., 1984). You will find it useful to plan a number of assignments for each working group. These assignments can be designed in cooperation with students or they might be suggested by textbooks or other published materials. Such individualized assignments have many advantages. (One is that resources are needed only for a small group of children rather than for an entire class.) In time you will develop a wealth of classroom resources that can be kept and stored for use from year to year. These resources can be shared with other teachers.

Upon completion of an integrated unit, the children's work should be displayed. The display can be undertaken for the benefit of other class members and also for the information of other children and teachers in the school. Such a display is an invaluable stimulus to worthwhile discussion at a parent–teacher meeting. As a general rule, children who have expressed themselves to the best of their ability on paper or through some other medium should have their work displayed (Johnson, 1983). These displays can then serve as motivators for additional investigations.

Generally, an integrated study is successful when the work is well prepared, assignments are ready and varied, and you are enthusiastic and willing to be very directive but able to sit back and "see what develops."

Investigations call for the collection of data and analysis of those data consistent with the problem. Whether children are constructing a birdhouse, taking a survey, or learning about the structure of a poem, they are faced with using mathematics as it relates to problems of measurement, fit, symmetry, or analysis. They soon find that numbers are a convenient and powerful way to represent and manipulate vital information related to their task. Mathematics, in a utility context, is known as applied mathematics. It is a tool that allows students to quantify data and relationships, to measure and deal meaningfully with measures, and to put procedures, rules, theorems, and axioms into daily problem-solving contexts.

Mathematics is a language and once students gain some skills in its use, it becomes a very efficient, straightforward, unambiguous way of describing elements of a problem, dealing with these elements, and (assuming the problem is within the knowledge frame of the student) solving the problem. For example, in the case of the student building a birdhouse, the student can refer to standard birdhouse size tables. These tables tell how large the bird is, how large the birdhouse must be to accommodate the bird, and how large the hole must be for the bird to enter. On the other hand, the tables do not always tell what materials should be used or what the shape or color of the birdhouse should be. The student's problem is twofold: (1) to make material, shape, and color selections, and (2) to design the birdhouse to accommodate the bird and to please both the bird and the student.

The language of mathematics is specialized and precise. This language demands that words, phrases, and procedures be stated in precise and logical forms. To say that a wren house should be fairly small and have a small, round opening leaves much to the imagination. To say that the inside floor of the wren house should be 10 centimeters by 10 centimeters, the inside height should be no less than 12 centimeters and no more than 16 centimeters, and the hole through which the wren enters should be 2 centimeters in diameter, centered, and between 6 and 10 centimeters from the floor provides the student with a precise description of the essential dimensions of the wren house (Fig. 11–1).

In today's elementary school classrooms a substantial part of each day is devoted to the teaching of mathematics. All too often, at any given time, the development of a specific arithmetic algorithm is the topic for the day. Even though the text may suggest problem examples, the student may not see how this algorithm can be useful. For example, a large portion of grade four (and five) may be devoted to long division, and the textbook will include problems in which long division may be applied. On the other hand if the teacher decides to devote several afternoons to the construction of birdhouses, the students are faced with task-centered problems. Some require long division, and some may require fractions, subtraction, addition, in fact a whole repertoire of mathematical skills.

The creative teacher must use a bit of imagination to see how such an activity can (1) facilitate the application of mathematics skills to other disciplines and life contexts and, (2) build connections among many subjects wherein the power and precision of enumeration, measurement, and the logical processes of mathematics add meaning and understanding to the student's problems.

We contend that problem solving must be preceded by problem finding. Problem finding can be defined as a synthetic process in which the student becomes aware, within a learning or doing context, that a problem exists and that some process can be applied to solve it. Young children are often seen applying a trial and error process to a situation. A young child attempting to catch an active frog chases, grabs, slowly reaches and finally discovers that one successful procedure is to wait patiently until the frog is motionless and then slowly to place a hand over the frog from the rear. Through experience, as the child matures, the child realizes some procedures work better than others. Part

**FIGURE 11–1
A wren house: How
much wood is
needed?**

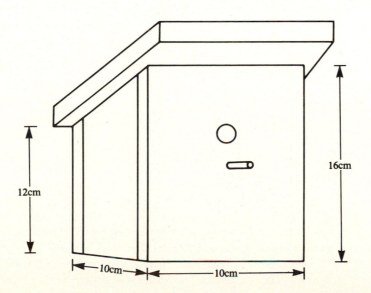

of this learning comes from experience and part comes when the student discovers that most problems can be stated in numbers and mathematical terms and can be solved. In the event that the problem requires a mathematics skill for solution the statement of the problem may well reveal an appropriate mathematics process. Consider this somewhat more complex context: a student plans to build a board fence out of boards that are five and one-half inches wide. The problem that the student finds is that the fence must be ten feet long and the student plans to use exactly 21 boards. The problem is further resolved to the point where the student realizes the total length must equal the sum of the widths of the boards plus the sum of the spaces between the boards. Finally the student realizes there will be one less space than there will be boards. The more sophisticated student will finally construct a mathematical statement that precisely reflects all of these conditions. The number of boards (N) times the width of each added to the number of spaces ($N - 1$) times the width of each will be equal to the total length. Symbolically then,

$$N \times \text{board width} + (N - 1) \times \text{space width} = \text{total length}$$

THE TEACHING OF INTEGRATED STUDIES IN HISTORICAL PERSPECTIVE

It is said that half of a typical human's lifetime learning occurs before a child begins school! It has also been reported that only one and one-half hours of a child's school day involves direct teacher teaching and direct child learning. The remaining time is spent by the child working independently. One conclusion we can draw is that children, by themselves, are efficient learners and that given the encouragement, materials, stimulating environment, and reasonable reward structure, children would be actively involved and learning would continue. This conclusion was given an unexpected test a half century ago.

During World War II, children by the thousands were moved from British cities that were under bomb attack to the country where it was thought they would be safer. Rural public buildings, churches, and other available shelters were hastily converted into makeshift school rooms. Teachers, accustomed to teaching with books, pencils, paper, chalkboards, and other standard equipment of the classroom, found themselves with little or no teaching equipment and with many children anxious about the move and who somehow expected the teacher to restructure security and order just like the classrooms they had left in Coventry or London.

The field became the laboratory. Children studied bridges, buildings, roadways, hedgerows, parks, brooks, even cemeteries! In a park study, children divided into small groups and were assigned to investigate particular features: a gate, a tree, a building, or a marker. They were challenged to find out as much as they could. Later they told other class members about their discoveries.

When the war was over, children returned to their homes and their home schools. The returning teachers incorporated the new methodology of the makeshift country school into the school curriculum. This instructional procedure, born out of necessity and crafted by skilled teachers, came to be known as the British Primary Program.

From these beginnings, thematic or interdisciplinary instruction has, through many years of use, evolved to a very humane, efficient, and exciting instructional methodology. There are several compelling reasons to consider the use of thematic instruction as a part of the daily repertoire of instructional activities.

First, children learn how to apply skills learned in one subject to another subject. They learn about whole structures, not just about parts. They learn to apply ideas gained in one area to the solution of a problem from another area.

Second, the focus of a thematic activity can be child-centered and of high and immediate interest to the child. Thematic instruction often involves grouping children using specific interests as the group membership criterion. Children choose particular subtopics of the theme for intensive study and later report their findings to the class or to a larger group.

Third, thematic instruction affords the teacher a natural, logical way to incorporate instructional techniques that research studies have demonstrated to have a strong positive effect on interest and achievement. Two of these techniques are *cooperative grouping* and *wait-time*. Both of these techniques have been demonstrated to involve all children in the learning activity and to cause achievement gains, particularly among slower or less interested children.

In a cooperative grouping arrangement, children work in small groups. (Johnson & Johnson, 1975). The number may vary, but four or five children seems to be a good working size. Each group is given a set of written tasks and is told when they will be expected to report the outcomes of their investigations. Each student in the group is assigned a task (chairperson, investigator, or recorder; any one or several in the group may be called on to make the report). It is, thus, essential that the chairperson make sure each group member understands and can report the group findings.

Wait-time is the name given to a questioning strategy. Without training, teachers usually wait a very short time after asking a question—usually less than one second! (Budd-Rowe, 1978a, b, 1979). If children don't respond, the teacher often rephrases the question, gives hints, or answers the question. When teachers extend after-question wait time to as little as three to five seconds, the responses children give are longer, more complete, and frequently reflect greater understanding. Moreover, far more children respond. A second part of the process is to wait again after the first child has responded. Slowly, other children suggest variations or alternative explanations. Studies indicate that this technique involves more children, causes the teacher to ask less direct recall and more complex questions, and results in better student attitudes and achievement.

DEVELOPING YOUR OWN THEME

Many successful themes originate with individual teachers. Here is a step-by-step encapsulation of how a teacher develops a thematic unit.

1. The teacher challenges—identification of the topic. (Note: The teacher selects the topic.)
2. The initial discussion, brainstorming, recording session
3. The teacher takes this information and groups it into subtopics.
4. The teacher assigns subtopics to groups: instructions and assignments for the group and for individuals within the group.
5. The teacher carries out small group and whole class skill sessions.
6. The teacher explains how the groups report.
7. The teacher leads group discussion (information-organizing skills and wait-time techniques).

And here are some possible outcomes:

1. Group reports
2. Group posters
3. Group booklets
4. Group actions (report to principal, class outing or picnic, field trip, kite contest, letters to appropriate individuals).

The following paragraphs represent a hypothetical "walk through" with a teacher beginning a simple thematic unit dealing with camping.

The class will be going on an overnight camping trip to a nature center soon. The teacher tells the students about the proposed trip and may even show some slides taken at the center. The teacher then asks the children what they know about camping and what they will need to know to make the camping successful. The word camping is written boldly on the chalkboard. As students suggest ideas, these are written on the board with little or no teacher input. In about ten minutes the board will be filled with ideas, suggestions, things to do, things to take, and so forth (Fig. 11–2).

The teacher then, with the continued help of children or at a later time alone, sorts the suggestions into five or six related categories.

FIGURE 11–2

Food	Camping Equipment
How, what to cook	Tents, sleeping bags
Cooking utensils	Flashlights
Eating utensils	Matches
Paper cups and plates	

Personal Items:	
Clothing	
Rain gear	

Activities:	Daily Schedule:
Campfire skits	Planning
Hikes	Groups
Swimming	Meals, activities
Songs	Calculating cost per person
Baseball	
Scavenger hunt	

The following day the teacher puts the categories on the board and asks children to choose in which group they would like to work. In this way the teacher is assured the children will be working on topics of high interest to them.

The teacher makes specific group assignments. The tasks the children are to undertake are carefully described. Children are told how much time they will have to work on the task. Various children are assigned specific group tasks such as chairperson, recorder, librarian, and so forth. The teacher then moves from group to group, interacting in a supportive, facilitative way rather than telling children how to go about accomplishing the task. When asked, the teacher gives suggestions for resources, how to get specific information, and how the final report to the class might be assembled.

Assignment: Equipment group

1. Make a list of things each person should take.
2. Make a list of things to take by tent groups.
3. Make a list of other equipment needed for eating, investigating, collecting, game playing.

The teacher makes concerted efforts to see that the tasks of the various groups demand skills and lead to expanded understanding in a variety of curricular areas. Virtually any measurement activity will involve mathematics.

The unit should culminate in the camping trip carrying out the predetermined measurements, experiments, and activities. Upon return to the classroom discussions of results should be held. These discussions should include data collected, how data were analyzed, graphs of appropriate phenomena, and so forth. Such a camping trip is very likely to be successful because nearly all of the elements of the trip have been planned and implemented by the children.

It is important for the teacher to rethink the instructional, thematic unit in terms of curriculum and student needs. Because thematic units appear innovative, questions will be asked about what learning has occurred and how curriculum demands have been met. A combination of narrative statement and checklist is one sound way of discharging this dual responsibility.

RESEARCH

Deciding what is basic in education is deceptive. The basics traditionally do not encompass the breadth of the school's curriculum, but only the "three Rs." Various groups approach this issue in decidedly different ways. The traditionalists promote those things that are familiar and well understood. Other groups have come to a decidedly different consensus when asked to identify the basic skills. Parents, teachers, administrators, and university professors do not necessarily agree on exactly what the basic skills are or should be. This causes problems because these groups can misunderstand and misrepresent one another.

At a conference sponsored by the National Institute of Education (NIE) in Euclid, Ohio (NIE, 1975), mathematics educators were asked to define the basic skills in mathematics. Their lists reveal a concern for issues beyond the development of simple arithmetic. Participants suggested that objectives such as estimation, collection, and interpretation of data, rational decision making, generalization, and graph analysis techniques, along with appreciation of the sheer power of the subject, rates of change, measure, equilibrium, the use of the calculator, and, of course, problem solving, are basic and should be part of the school mathematics agenda.

Implementing such objectives may require a redefinition of school mathematics. The same applies to science, social science, and language arts. The basic needs today are different than the basic needs of our parents. The school program should (must) reflect those differences. In many cases it does not.

One could argue that much of the school curriculum exists now because it has always been there and not because it is the most important or the most relevant to the child's life and future needs. The amount of time devoted to the development of speed and accuracy in the mathematics program is a case in point here. Never again will individuals be employed to do long complicated calculations by hand. So to argue that speed and absolute accuracy in hand calculation is all (or most) of what an individual must know to survive in tomorrow's world is simply not true. Why then do most schools spend so much time on the development and maintenance of these skills?

It seems more reasonable to devote at least a portion of the child's time to estimation, approximation, interpreting, hypothesizing, and classifying, to name but a few. These topics are more likely to serve our students well in tomorrow's world. These, incidentally, are also the topics that can be effectively developed through an interdisciplinary approach.

We need to rethink the foregoing issues and attempt again to answer the question, "What really are the basics?" This discussion should involve people from all educational strata who have a basic interest in this issue. The fact that the answers will not be the same ones that would have evolved a generation ago is to be expected. The world and its demands are not the same as then and never will be again.

One attempt to redefine the basics resulted in the development of the following four categories:

1. Coping skills (including various academic disciplines and their interrelationships)
2. Social and character development
3. Citizenship and social responsibility
4. Private realization skills

What is your reaction to this list? Do you think most school curricula consciously address each of these areas? What do you want your students to be like at age twenty? List five desirable characteristics.

A thematic approach has the potential of addressing not only the basic skills as traditionally defined but also the more open-ended process objectives, which are often ignored. Such thematic units should relate basic concepts to children's interests and problem situations that naturally arise in the course of their activities.

PROVISIONS FOR INDIVIDUAL DIFFERENCES

Within each classroom we encounter children whose needs and abilities vary. Within the context of an integrated unit children make choices, learn within groups, and can be asked to pursue activities selected by the teacher as appropriate to needs and abilities. Children can select quiet, individual tasks or participation in group investigations. Children who have handicaps can be helped as needed by other members of the group. Quiet talk within groups can help children understand the nature of the problem because each member of the group is accountable not only for his or her own learning but for the learning of all other group members.

The following section, entitled "Parkland," describes an investigation of a class of British junior school (intermediate grades) students as they study a neighboring park.

The section entitled "Flight" is presented in more of a lesson plan format describing objectives, student activities, procedures for evaluation, and a series of suggestions for the teacher.

Each format has both advantages and disadvantages.

Parkland*

A trip to the park resulted in an incredible variety of student-generated investigations. A British teacher describes, with clarity, insight, and sensitivity, an illustrative sample of those investigations.

Parkland as presented here is a narrative account of a thematic unit conducted during the spring and summer months in an English country school. Twenty-six children, aged seven to eleven, participated in its development. The teacher's log has been reproduced here. It provides keen insight into the malleable nature of a theme, ever growing, contracting, and extending into new and different areas of interest and appeal.

Procedure

The first visit to the park was by the whole class and was used to decide what should be studied. They quickly concluded that there was far more material than they could deal with, and that it would be better to restrict their attention to trees. The first task was to count and identify the trees, as far as they were able. In fact, they had doubts about the identities of only two trees, and their suspicion that these were Norway Maple and Turkey Oak proved to be correct. This visit led to the decision to keep field diaries and to draw block graphs showing the numbers of trees.

Back in the classroom, the children argued out how to make a start on the problem, and they determined to work in small groups, each group including children of various ages. This decision was based on the belief that the older children would be able to help the younger ones, whereas a group made up entirely of young children started to collect twigs, but would be faced with too many obstacles.

Some of the children started to collect twigs, but when they felt that the twigs themselves were not a satisfactory form of recording, they decided to make plaster casts. This was not without its problems, with early mixes being too wet and later ones setting too quickly, and one boy was asked to find out what proportions of plaster and water gave the most satisfactory consistency.

Records took the form of plaster casts, drawings, and paintings. The children used reference books extensively to discover the names of many of the structures. Much detail was also supplied by these methods.

Work continued during the Easter holiday when a large proportion of the class visited the park. Attention now focused on seeds found under the trees, and back at school a selection of seeds was planted in pots and boxes and allowed to germinate.

Nuffield Junior Science Project, Teacher's Guide 2 (pp. 74–79) E. R. Wastnedge (Ed.), 1967, London: Collins Publishing Co. Copyright 1967 by Nuffield Chelsea Curriculum Trust. Reprinted by permission.

This was to determine what kinds of seeds they were and what proportion of them was capable of germination.

At the beginning during the summer term, several children were surprised to see that some of the trees were flowering, even though they had no leaves. They were now keeping field diaries, and began to compile progress reports on foliage to enter in these. The facts were assembled formally at a certain time each week, but the entries were written freely by the children.

It was at this point that two boys who were studying ash trees in widely different positions in the park realized that one tree had flowered two weeks before the other. Tommy thought that it was related somehow to temperature and that it would be useful to know something about ground and air temperatures. These were measured.

By now, the leaves were opening and there was a general interest in the changes occurring during growth. Leaf shape and details of veins and margins were examined. The class decided as a whole to keep a record of the leaves, but one group in particular was dissatisfied with the method of pressing or of sticking leaves on cards, since the results were fragile and short-lived.

This group investigated the relative values of different materials and methods of recording. They were given a free hand and a wide range of materials in their efforts to find the best way of taking permanent leaf impressions. These included rubbings, pressings, and spatter prints.

At about this time, there was a period of strong winds, and during one of their visits to the park the children found a branch lying on the ground under the tree. Interest was high. Why had it broken off? Examination showed that it was not rotten. Could it be the wind? They were not very convinced of this. The most popular idea was that the weight of leaves had caused it to fall.

What was the weight of leaves? Indeed, what was the weight of leaves on the whole tree? The children decided to count the leaves on one section of the branch, and weigh them. Then, by estimating how many similar sections there were, they could calculate the total weight.

The leaves from the broken branch were tied into a bundle for weighing, and it was a matter of interest that when they were weighed again, they had lost weight. By now, several new lines of investigation had been opened up. The children had determined the weights of equal numbers of leaves from different kinds of trees, and drawn graphs of their findings.

There were also graphs showing the relationship between leaf size and weight, and between size and kind of tree. Other graphs showed rate of loss of weight due to drying. All these graphs were compared.

Finally, one boy calculated the total leaf area on a tree. To do this, he used $0.1''$ squared paper, thus getting his introduction to decimals.

There were other measurements being made, too. The children had decided to measure the height of each tree, first using a stick placed against the tree and estimating how many times it would go into the height. They measured girths and also diameters, noting the simple relationship. The girth at different heights was related to the height of the measurement from the ground, and hence indirectly to the vertical growth of the tree.

The group noticed the vegetation under the tree and compared it with that under others but, unfortunately, this study ended when the farmer applied weedkiller. It was noted, however, that nettles and chickweed grew under the trees, but not in the open; and that there were bare uneven patches under the conifers, and that these were related to the varying extent of the canopy which in turn depended on the prevailing wind.

One group collected insects from the foliage by rapping a branch smartly with a stick, or by shaking. These had to be housed and this meant making cages from cardboard boxes, muslin, and cellophane. The children learned to recognize the creatures they collected and compared them with those they found on a dead tree stump. The eggs collected from the stump were kept and eventually proved to be those of a spider. From these collections, the children were able to observe life cycles in a number of cases.

Stephen collected insects from the trunk and branches. David became interested in timbers and collected and compared twigs from the trees. He also corresponded with the Forestry Commission, and started to enquire into the properties of different woods. For example, he investigated hardness by seeing how many strokes of the hammer were needed to knock a large nail into different kinds. He learned to tell the age of twigs by counting rings. To do this more efficiently, he decided to saw a twig at an angle. He then discovered that the cross section was elliptical instead of circular. The teacher used this as the basis for a general class discussion on shapes, especially those obtained by sectioning and also by rotating common objects such as pennies, books, and cards. David also noticed that the distance between rings varied from year to year and wrote away for details of weather records over the years to see if there was any connection.

The study had now reached a stage where it had a bearing on all parts of the school curriculum. The children did a great deal of computation and making graphs, and learned numerous new words. Philippa compiled a dictionary. Another group collected poems about trees and then took to writing their own. Art work grew out of the twig and leaf records. Leaves provided stencils for patterns and the children made leaf and bark rubbings. The teacher brought into the classroom a fantastically shaped piece of wood that he had found and they used their imaginations about it eagerly, discovering weird monsters in the shapes. The study also gave rise to geography and added to the children's interest in the history of their village.

Sometimes the children made tape recordings describing the work they were doing. They exchanged these with tapes made by a similar school some thirty miles away, and this led to one school visiting the other.

Flight

The flight unit is presented in a form different from the Parkland theme. It was selected to illustrate two major points.

1. The variety possible in the manner in which the themes can be constructed, implemented, and displayed
2. The relative ease with which individualized student projects can be assembled and conducted.

The body of this unit consists of a student contract outlining projects for individual students. It serves as an example of one way in which interdisciplinary units can be handled in a largely individualized format. Birds, airports, people, careers, and flying machines all play an important role in this theme, which is rich in the diversity of possible extensions.

The theme consists of a brief overview, by curricular area, of some of the potential activities that can be pursued within the unit. Some of these are intended to be carried out with the whole class as part of your instruction concerning basic principles of flight. The remainder of the activities presented in the overview are found within the individual Flight Contract, which you may wish to reproduce for use in your classroom. These activities are intended for the most part to be completed by individual students. You should find the contract system to be helpful in providing some basic structure for student use of class time; however, it allows for flexibility and tends to encourage the production of high quality work because of the high degree of individualization provided.

Resources and materials are easily obtained and inexpensive. These materials, which will be used extensively, include paper, cardboard, wire, sticks, and cloth. Guest speakers and field trips can also be an important part of the classroom activities, but films and filmstrips can be substituted if necessary. You might also be lucky enough to find documentaries on television to provide out-of-the-classroom experience. Other supplementary materials should be readily available through various local and school libraries.

Unit Objectives

The student will:

1. Learn some basic principles of flight.
2. Complete at least one project outlined in the Flight Contract.
3. Gain skills relative to independent goal setting and work completion.

Appropriate grade levels: Sixth grade to eighth grade.

Suggested Activities by Discipline

Literature and language arts

1. Read *The 21 Balloons* by Pere DuBois.
2. Fly a helium balloon. Send a message or self-addressed postcard.
3. Read flight-related poetry.
4. Read *A Bride for Pegasus* by K. Shippen out loud.
5. Write a description of an aerial view.
6. See Walt Disney's film "Man in Flight."
7. Read about famous flight contributors such as Lindbergh, Earhart, and the Wright brothers.
8. Write flight-related short stories.

Music and drama

1. Sing "Up, Up, and Away," "Fly Me to the Moon," and "Leaving on a Jet Plane."
2. Put on a dramatic skit of the life of a famous person in the field of flight.

Math

1. Measure the distance of a flight with paper planes by calculating time and distance.
2. Figure the cost of airplane tickets.
3. Design flight plans and routes.
4. Build models of famous planes and airports using ratio and proportion.

Field trips, guests

1. Visit an airport.
2. Invite a pilot to speak to the class.
3. Invite a hang-gliding expert to speak to the class.
4. Visit a science museum.

Social studies

1. Learn the history of flight. See Walt Disney's "Man in Flight."
2. Research famous people in the field of flight.
3. Study the countries producing contributions to flight.
4. Study how aircraft changed wars and developed military warfare.
5. Study how aircraft changed people, politics, and so forth.
6. Research how airports are organized and built.
7. Explore careers related to flight, ornithology, and engineering.
8. Write to NASA about its history and future work.

Science

1. Develop a basic understanding of the principles of flight by using paper airplanes in simple experiments.
2. Name the parts of the plane.
3. Name the parts of the rocket.
4. Compare the parts of the bird to the parts of the plane.
5. Build kites.
6. Complete the science contract.
7. Study both current and early flying machines.
8. Study about rockets, satellites, and space exploration.

Art

1. Display the best student plane design.
2. Build and design kites.

3. Display research information with posters.
4. Draw a map from an aerial photograph.

Contract for flight unit.
Name
You will have class time to work on this from ___ to ___ (approximately 2 1/2 weeks). Reporting time will be every Friday.

Minimum requirements (C grade)

- Know the basic principles of flight we worked on together in class.
- Be able to pass the test on flight.
- Complete one of the projects listed below.

Above average or (B grade)

- Know basic flight principles.
- Be able to pass the test on flight.
- Complete two of the projects listed below.

Top quality work (A grade)

- Know basic flight principles.
- Be able to pass the test on flight.
- Complete three of the projects listed below.

Sample Flight Projects

1. Read about the flight of the Double Eagle II (balloon). Write a one-page report summarizing its flight and problems. Draw a map of where it was launched and where it landed.
2. Research how the invention of the airplane affected wars, particularly World War I. Starting points might be to find out something about Count Zeppelin and his invention and how it was used in the war. Other research topics might be pilots such as Anthony Fokker or a flying "ace" such as Oswald Boelcke. Write a two-page report.
3. Write a paper on the flying ace of World War I, Baron von Richthofen—the "Red Baron." Report on his role in World War I. Maps or drawings can be included.
4. Research planes of World War II. Present pictures or drawings of each with their names.
5. Research the life of Orville and Wilbur Wright. Write a two-page report. Include information about where and when they lived and worked, and the problems they overcame in order to build the first successful plane. Build a model of their first plane.

6. Make a booklet of at least five early flying machines or inventions. Explain when, by whom, and where they were invented. Draw a picture of each. Examples might be Montgolfer, da Vinci, Lillienthal, Cayley, or any of the names from the list given in class.

7. Make a study of birds' anatomy (body structure) and make drawings showing the parts of the birds, particularly the wings. Explain in your report how a bird's anatomy is similar to airplane design and also how birds control their flight pattern. Gather feathers of different birds.

8. Research the history of the parachute. In a one- to two-page report tell who invented it, when, and how they were perfected. Explain how parachutes work today. Build a simplified model to explain what you learned and demonstrate this in class.

9. Make a poster or bulletin board of how aircraft has changed and developed in recent years. Include pictures or drawings of each type of aircraft and a paragraph about each.

10. Research the history of gliders. Who invented and perfected the first successful gliders? Build a cardboard glider with essential parts.

11. Read the book *Five Weeks in a Balloon* by Jules Verne. Report to the class about it. Use a visual medium such as a poster or diagram as part of your report. Discuss with teacher.

12. Learn more about how airplanes are designed. Write to airports and airport designers to obtain information and report your findings. Write a one-page report. Build a model of an airport.

13. Write about the history of both hot air and gas ballooning. Include the inventors and be able to explain how balloons work. Design a hot air balloon of your own on a poster and label parts, or build a hot air balloon and we'll attempt to fly it. (This is a difficult project.)

14. Make a large time line, to be put up in the room, of the most significant events in the history of flight starting when Montgolfer invented ballooning.

15. Research the history of rocketry beginning in America with Robert Goddard. Explain in your report how rockets work and include a diagram with parts labeled. You can demonstrate simple experiments or build a model. (There are kits for this but they cost money.)

16. Research the history of helicopters in a report and build a simple model to demonstrate (not paper).

17. Explain the principles of kite flight. Make a kite to demonstrate (not from a kit unless it is unique).

18. Research the space race between the United States and the Soviet Union. Include information about Sputnik I and II. Discuss United States achievements in the early 1960s.

19. Report on the Apollo II landing on the moon: who the astronauts were, how they accomplished their mission. Interview three people who watched the landing on television and write about their reactions at the time. Or make a poster or bulletin board about how people felt about the space race.

20. Write a complete biography of Charles Lindbergh or Amelia Earhart. Be sure to explain their greatest feats in flight history.
21. Get background information about person(s) connected with flight and write a dramatic skit about them to be presented to the class. Minimum time: five minutes. (Four people may work on this project.)
22. Read the short story by Edgar Allan Poe entitled "The Unparalled Adventure of One Hans Pfaall." Write your own short story concerning flight and illustrate it. Be ready to use it in class.
23. Research and gather songs about flying. Get the lyrics, titles, copyrights, and a recording if the library has it. Perform one for the group. (Three people may work on this project.)
24. Conduct an interview with a pilot, flight attendant, or any other person whose career is associated with flight and report to the class.
25. If there is another project you are interested in, you may discuss it with your teacher.

There have been a large number of publications that relate explicitly or implicitly to integrated approaches to learning. Several that we have enjoyed include: Baratta-Lorton, 1976; Bosstick & Cable, 1975; Burns, 1976; Cardozo & Menten, 1975; Ellis, 1986; Fennell, 1982; Forseth, 1984; Goldberg, 1983; Hansen, 1983; Harmensen, 1983; Harmin et al., 1973; Melle & Wilson, 1984; Merkle, 1984; Shaw, 1984; Pereira-Mendoza, 1983; Weber 1971. As you further contemplate your role you will find these references useful.

SOME CLOSING THOUGHTS

Some teacher behaviors have proven effective in the past and are worth remembering as you embark on this new teaching and learning experience.

1. Introduce the theme in a flexible manner. This not only allows the children to relate it to their particular situation but also opens up various avenues of potential investigation.
2. Serve as a coordinator and collaborator. Assist, rather than direct, individuals or groups of students as they investigate different aspects of the problem.
3. Involve students regularly in project or theme activities. This regularity will allow the children to have a chance to become involved in the challenge and carry out comprehensive investigations.
4. Provide the tools and supplies necessary for initial hands-on work in the classroom. Later on, children can become partially responsible for the location, procurement, and development of needed materials.
5. Be patient. Allow the children to make their own mistakes and to find their own way. But do offer assistance and point out sources of help if the children become frustrated in their approach to the problem.

6. Provide frequent opportunities for group reports and student exchanges of ideas in class discussions. In most cases, students will, by their own critical examination of the procedures they have used, improve or set new directions in their investigations.

7. Ask higher level questions (questions not answerable with a single word or fact) to stimulate thinking.

8. Make sure that groups are appropriately constituted and that the criteria for group development are continually varied. This will ensure the broadest possible set of experiences for each individual.

9. Remember that success can be defined in many different ways. It is not simply the mastery of specific bits of knowledge, although this is sure to occur. It is not only the following of a particular line of investigation predetermined by the teacher. Success in an integrated study is defined by the progress students make toward the solution of a particular problem or concern. Success is defined in terms of process as much as it is defined in terms of specific product outcomes. Evaluate accordingly!

CHAPTER 11 SUMMARY

A school day is often divided into reading time, recess, more reading, spelling, lunch, arithmetic, recess, clean-up, and go home. A child's day may be made up of thoughts of play, conversations, pretending, watching the custodian or the painter, constructing forts or making cookies, and looking forward to family sharing time. The former seems efficient and logical, the latter disorganized and illogical.

The thesis of this chapter is that the latter day, the child's day, may be a better model on which to develop thinking abilities, problem-solving abilities, and conceptual structures. If children are to learn how their world works, they must interact with it. And their world is not like an assembly line. An integrated theme begins within the child's environment and expands to include elements of reading, arithmetic, science, social studies, and many other topics. You, the teacher, build the theme around the child's interests and slowly facilitate conceptual development through the challenges you offer, the questions you pose, and the investigations you initiate.

Conceptually this approach is fairly simplistic; it does make sense and it can be defended from a number of perspectives. Its difficulty lies in the fact that there are literally an infinite number of permutations this approach can take, and no one can ever really master all of the whats, whys, and wherefores. There will always be that simple investigation that could have been carried out and for one reason or another never was, or those general directions not pursued which might have improved the overall quality of the theme.

Teaching involves a great deal of judgment. Good teachers make good judgments more than they make bad ones. Comfort with this approach grows, and with experience you make better judgments.

REFERENCES

Baratto-Lorton, M. 1976. *Mathematics their way*. Reading, MA: Addison-Wesley.

Bosstick, M., & Cable, J. L. 1975. *Patterns in the sand: An exploration in mathematics*. New York: Macmillan.

Budd-Rowe, M. 1978a. *What research says to the science teacher: Vol. 1*. Washington, DC: National Science Teachers.

Budd-Rowe, M. 1978b. *Teaching science as continuous inquiry: A basic 2-E*. New York: McGraw-Hill.

Budd-Rowe, M. 1979. *What research says to the science teacher: Vol. 2*. Washington, DC: National Science Teachers.

Burns, M. 1976. *The book of think*. New York: Little, Brown, and Co.

Cardoza, P., & Menten, T. 1975. *The whole kid's catalog*. Bantam Books.

Ellis, A. K. 1986. *Teaching and learning elementary social studies* (3rd Ed.). Boston: Allyn and Bacon.

Fennell, F. 1982, October. Newspaper: A source for applications in mathematics. *Arithmetic Teacher*, 30:22−26.

Forseth, S. D. 1984. *Creative math-art activities for the primary grades*. Englewood Cliffs, NJ: Prentice-Hall.

Goldberg, D. 1983, November. Integrating writing into the mathematics curriculum. *Mathematics Journal*, 14:421−424.

Hansen, V. P. 1983, September. Using media to teach math. *Instructional Innovator*, 28:25−26.

Harmensen, B. 1983. Using the front page news to teach mathematics. In *National Council of Teachers of Mathematics Yearbook*, (105−9). Reston, VA: National Council of Teachers of Mathematics.

Harmin, M., Kirschenbaum, H., & Simon, S. 1973. *Clarifying values through subject matter: Applications for the classroom*. Winston Press.

Humphreys, A., Post, T., & Ellis, A. K. 1981. *Interdisciplinary methods: A thematic approach*. Glencoe, IL: Scott, Foresman and Company.

Johnson, D. W., & Johnson, R. T. 1975. *Learning together and alone: Cooperation, competition, and individualization*. Englewood Cliffs, NJ: Prentice-Hall.

Johnson, M. L. 1983, Fall. Writing in mathematics classes: A valuable tool for learning. *Mathematics Teacher*, 76:117−119.

Malone, J., & Dekkers, J. 1984, March. The concept map as an aid to instruction in science and mathmatics. *School Science and Mathematics*, 84:220−231.

Melle, M., & Wilson, F. 1984, April. Balanced instruction through an integrated curriculum. *Educational Leadership*, 41:59−63.

Merkle, D. R. 1984, Winter. Thematic units for the classroom. *Reading Association Journal*, 19:12−17.

National Institute of Education. 1975, October. *NIE Conference on Basic Mathematial Skills and Learning*, Volumes I and II. Euclid, OH: NIE.

Pereira-Mendoza, L., & May, S. 1983, January. Environment—a teaching aid. *School Science and Mathematics*, 83:54−60.

Shaw, J. M. 1984, April. Newspapers add spark to mathematics activities. *Arithmetic Teacher*, 31:8−13.

Weber, Lillian 1971. *The English infant school and informal education*. Englewood Cliffs, NJ: Prentice-Hall.

12 Calculators and Computers

RICHARD J. SHUMWAY

*The Ohio State University and Centro de
Investigación en Matemáticas,
Guanajuato, Mexico*

INTRODUCTION

Calculators and computers play a major role in the numeric and symbolic computations of adults in our society. Fully 98% of adults were using calculators to do mathematics by 1979 (Saunders, 1980). Computers are used in laboratories, supermarkets, auto parts stores, ticket sale booths, banks, schools, space vehicles, and most places of business. Calculators and computers are used in automobiles, sewing machines, telephones, watches, heating systems, and toys. Since 1977, when Radio Shack, Commodore, and Apple began selling inexpensive microcomputers (Ahl, 1984), the increased use of calculators and computers has been remarkable. Technology is continuing to improve and costs are still going down. Computers with extensive capability and large memory are likely to match the size and cost of calculators now. Calculator and computer use will continue to increase in all phases of our society.

What role should these devices play in doing mathematics? Calculators are used to do almost all simple, numeric computations. Computers have played critical roles in mathematics. During World War II, computers aided mathematicians at Los Alamos to do computations related to the atomic bomb and also allowed British mathematicians to break German secret codes (Ulam,

1980). The National Council of Teachers of Mathematics (NCTM) has recommended that "mathematics programs take full advantage of the power of calculators and computers at all grade levels" (NCTM, 1980). The position of the NCTM has been met with enthusiasm with regard to computers and systematically ignored by almost all schools with regard to calculators (Meissner, 1984).

One summary of the most recent International Congress on Mathematical Education recommends (Shumway, 1985a):

1. There is no circumstance in mathematics instruction or testing when the use of calculators should be restricted.
2. All teachers of mathematics (K−16) should have access to computers and calculators to plan and carry out the teaching of mathematics.
3. Inexpensive computers and short programs can effectively lead students to significant mathematics. We must move to the idea that computers should be as common as textbooks in the studying and learning of mathematics.
4. We need to make deep and significant revisions of the school mathematics curriculum—because of the new developments in computing technology.

The purpose of this chapter is to examine the available evidence about technology and mathematics learning and attempt to determine the appropriate response to such dramatic and far-reaching recommendations. Appropriate models for calculator and computer use are discussed, along with activities for the student and suggestions for the teacher.

THE ROLE OF CALCULATORS IN SCHOOL MATHEMATICS

Computing has always been a part of school mathematics. Early mathematical education involved number computations with numeration systems such as Roman numerals and symbolic computations involving words rather than letters. The modern version of the Hindu-Arabic numeration system was not extended to decimals until 1585 by Simon Stevin. Algebraic symbols as we know them, for example, $x + 2y = 7$, were used by Wallis in 1693. Naturally, the "modern" paper-and-pencil algorithms for computations with numbers and symbols were not developed until after these modern symbols were developed. It is very interesting (and difficult!) to try to multiply or divide two Roman numerals (say, XXVI and CCIX) without translating the numbers to our Hindu-Arabic symbols (that is, 26 and 209).

Modern algorithms for number computations involve calculators and became widely available in about 1976 (inexpensive calculators). Modern algorithms for symbol computations became widely available for small computers in about 1981 (muMath/muSIMP-80, or MACSYMA in the 1970s on large computers) and for graphics calculators in 1987 (Tucker, 1987).

Fundamental questions always arise when new and faster algorithms become available. Should the old algorithms be taught? Should the new algorithms be taught? Should both the old and new algorithms be taught?

Knowing the concept of addition means being able to sort problems or situations into those that can be modeled by addition and those that cannot be modeled by addition. Unless the algorithm chosen for addition is the very definition itself (a good conceptual model, but a very inefficient computational algorithm), the algorithm chosen has little to do with understanding the concept or assisting in the choice as to whether or not to use addition. The algorithm "invert and multiply" is another example. This procedure has nothing at all to do with the concept of dividing two fractions. The ability to compute has little to do with the ability to choose what computation is needed. The fear that calculators will somehow do problems for students is unfounded. Calculators cannot chose operations.

We have always expected students to learn to do computational algorithms. We have always expected students to learn concepts. The critical issue is not whether concepts should be taught in schools or whether computational algorithms should be taught in schools. The issues raised is *which computational algorithms should be taught?*

One solution is to teach the quickest, fastest, most accurate, and accessible algorithm. Another solution might be to teach all the algorithms. Or you could teach the quickest, fastest, most accurate, and accessible algorithm together with the algorithms that help students learn mathematical concepts. You could ban all algorithms unavailable before some date, say, 1975. Perhaps you can think of other alternatives. However, *logical analysis of the problem seems to suggest teaching the most practical algorithms and teaching concepts.*

Judging from the behavior of adults, the most practical algorithms are the calculator, the computer, knowledge of basic facts, mental arithmetic, and estimation. We will examine the research evidence regarding the issues raised and illustrate some potential ways calculators and computers can be used to teach mathematics.

RESEARCH RELATING TO CALCULATORS

There have been over 150 studies on the effects of calculators on school mathematics learning (Suydam, 1981b, 1983). The principal focus has been to explore the feared debilitation calculator use might cause. The evidence is overwhelmingly in favor of the use of calculators and provides little evidence of the feared debilitation. Few results in mathematics learning research today have such strong and unequivocal support. We will discuss the research in the contexts of skills, concepts, problem solving, and attitudes.

Skills most likely to be influenced by calculators are knowledge of basic facts ($3 + 4 = 7$, $9 \times 7 = 63$, and so forth) and the ability to do paper-and-pencil algorithms. Calculator use has not had a debilitating effect on knowledge of basic facts. Students recognize that recalling basic facts is quicker than keystroking a calculator. Calculators provide an opportunity to learn basic facts not covered in instruction and provide a memory source to review forgotten facts (Channell, 1978).

The evidence regarding paper-and-pencil algorithms is less clear. No one has experimented with making no effort to teach paper-and-pencil algorithms. Certainly, if you remove long division from the curriculum, students would be unfamiliar with the long division algorithm. When students using calculators are expected to perform the paper-and-pencil algorithms too, they do as well as they would had they not used calculators. Whether or not paper-and-pencil algorithms should be taught is a question of objectives and purpose, not one of research. The research shows adults are not using paper-and-pencil algorithms, but it does not show whether or not we should teach paper-and-pencil algorithms to children.

To summarize, we observe that *calculator use does not debilitate knowledge of basic facts nor the teaching and learning of paper-and-pencil algorithms. Adults use calculators instead of paper-and-pencil algorithms for computations.*

The only question unanswered is why one might wish to teach the paper-and-pencil algorithms. Our historical perspective and logical analysis suggest we retain only those algorithms that model the operations or are most efficient. Our best advice is to *use calculators to do computations.*

However, we must recognize the value of basic facts, mental arithmetic, and estimation. We will illustrate ways to use calculators to support basic facts, mental arithmetic, and estimation in a later section.

Concept learning and problem solving have not been the central focus of many calculator research studies. Calculators may help concept learning because calculators allow one to examine many examples and nonexamples. Because the calculator will perform the needed computations, operation selection can be the major focus of a lesson or series of problems. Determining the mathematics appropriate to model a problem may be the key to using mathematics successfully. Calculators do not determine the mathematics appropriate to model an application. Calculators only assist in computations. Students must learn the concepts necessary to model problems with mathematics. While students can increase their computational scores on tests by using a calculator, their comparable concept scores do not change simply because a calculator is being used (Shumway, White, Wheatley, Reys, Coburn, & Schoen, 1981). Our best advice for concept learning would be to *use calculators to study the definitions of operations and concepts together with the many and varied examples and nonexamples of concepts calculators allow one to consider.*

For example, the calculator can help one look at multiplication as repeated addition by carrying out repeated additions through many examples of skip counting. Problems of great diversity and "realism" can illustrate the many and varied situations that can or cannot be modeled by multiplication. How high a pile would all the mathematics books in the school make if they were stacked, one on top of another, in the playground? It is important to understand repeated addition or multiplication can be used to model the problem of stacking books because the strategy can be generalized to piles or stacks of many things. The computation, 473×2.7 cm, can be carried out on a calculator and is not important for learning the concept of repeated addition or multiplication, or whether or not the multiplication models the problem. Students required to use a paper-and-pencil algorithm can easily be distracted into thinking the problem is to carry out the computation. The algorithm is laborious and time consuming. Using a calculator, as would adults, students focus their attention on the problem as a potential example or nonexample of the concept of repeated addition or multiplication. Further examples of concept learning will be given in a later section.

Problem solving is different than skill learning and concept learning. Solving word problems is typically concept learning or skill learning. Students determine which operation or operations model the problem (concept learning), and then use a computational algorithm (skill learning) to carry out the chosen computation. Problem solving requires students to learn and/or use concepts in new and more complex ways than their previous experience has taught them. Calculators free students to focus on problem solving rather than doing computations. Calculators allow exploration of the many examples and nonexamples needed to develop new concepts and discover relationships between concepts. There is no advantage to avoiding calculators for problem solving. On the other hand, problem solving is difficult. Many factors contribute to successful problem solving. One cannot expect calculators to be the significant, deciding factor. However, *calculators should be standard, available tools for problem solving.*

Many enthusiasts of calculators suggest positive student attitudes result from calculator use in schools. There is evidence children enjoy using calculators (Shumway et al., 1981). One might guess that if students like calculators then they will like mathematics. Current data suggest students do not make such a transfer. Calculators are yet to be perceived by students as a significant part of mathematics. Interview data suggest primary grade children simply enjoy using calculators. Intermediate grade children seem to temper their enthusiasm with a feeling of guilt. The most common view is that calculators are fun to use, but students are unsure calculators ought to be used. Perhaps such guilt is natural. Adults generally oppose calculator use by children. Standardized testing is done without the use of calculators. To relieve such guilt feelings one could either ban the use of calculators or develop a parent education program and *use calculators for all mathematics testing.*

Schools and teachers must begin using calculators for instruction, testing, and standardized testing. Perhaps a needed compromise would be double testing for mathematics on the standardized tests for a few years to develop individual school and district norms for testing with and without calculators. Such double testing would add approximately 75 minutes to the testing program and could be graded by classroom teachers. The data would help parent and teacher understanding and allow the district to continue to describe progress in mathematics in the context of prior years' data. For parents, administrators, teachers, and other adults to ban calculator use in school mathematics learning and testing (1) is not based on rational study of the data; (2) is certainly a double standard; (3) may contribute to guilt feelings of students involved in exemplary programs using calculators; and (4) causes students to waste large portions of valuable mathematics time learning paper-and-pencil algorithms not used by adults.

RESEARCH RELATING TO COMPUTERS

The research on computers in school mathematics can be divided into two sections, earlier studies conducted with large computers (1960–1976), and studies using the more recent microcomputers (1977–present). Results are more tenuous and give less direction than the research on calculators (Suydam, 1981a, 1984). Computer uses that show the most promise are drill and practice for skill learning, and student programming and exploration of simulations for concept learning and problem solving (Suydam, 1984). The use of a computer to simulate teachers is not yet realized and very difficult. Enthusiasm for computer use in schools is usually high when the use is practical, affordable, and allows student control of computers. Before illustrating promising computer uses, we will discuss the research regarding drill and practice, tutorial, management systems, student programming, computation, and simulations.

One of the first uses most teachers make of computers is for drill and practice of skills. The research clearly documents computers to be effective for skill learning when used in the drill and practice mode (Suydam, 1984). The focus is generally on learning facts. The computer can be used to randomly select and sequence the stimuli, collect responses, and provide immediate feedback regarding the responses. A typical drill and practice program for mathematics would simulate basic facts flash cards. The computer would show $4 \times 7 = ?$ on the screen and wait for a response. Such use relieves the teacher of some mundane teaching and drill and practice sessions can be individualized and worked into the school day at any convenient time. Another suitable drill and practice topic is estimation or mental arithmetic. Given the role of calculators and computers, it is inappropriate to use drill and practice to teach paper-and-pencil algorithms.

Use simple computer programs that are easy to write, easily modified,
understandable, and usable by children for drill and practice
of basic facts and estimation.

Teachers should modify simple programs for their students rather than purchase expensive software. An example of a simple BASIC program, which can be easily modified, is in a later section. No course in computer programming is necessary and students can make such modifications.

Tutorial programs are computer programs designed to teach mathematics to children. Student responses to questions are used to provide instruction to students via the computer. Such approaches have yet to show great promise. The difficulty is in the attempt to simulate a good teacher. The interaction between student and teacher is very complex and depends on several forms of simultaneous communication. The creative authoring time needed to program (that is, teach the computer) all the different and appropriate responses to student errors has been monumental. At the present time, such use is limited and unsatisfying.

Do not use a computer to simulate a teacher.

Several management systems have been designed for schools. They are designed to use the computer to do much of the record keeping and clerical duties individualized programs require of teachers, such as managing student records, worksheets, tests, and so forth.

Student computer programming has a long history of favor by mathematics teachers and mathematicians. BASIC and Logo are the most common languages used in elementary schools and generally the languages of research involving student programming (Suydam, 1986). One claim is that student programming requires students to understand the mathematics they are "teaching" the computer (Kemeny, 1966). Because the computer requires specific instructions and has no tolerance for ambiguity, a student programming a computer must develop a clear, exact understanding of the mathematics involved. Whether programming an algorithm or a mathematical concept, the student writing the program must clearly understand the algorithm or concept. Advocates claim student programming assists teaching problem solving and more generalized concepts of mathematical thinking such as variables and generalization (Shumway, 1984c). Correctness of programs seems to be highly related to mathematical proof. Computer programming may help students understand concepts and variables (Shumway, 1984a). There may be a relationship between student programming and problem solving in mathematics (Johnson & Harding, 1979).

Use computers to do mathematics.

The bottom line is computers are powerful tools that should be used to do mathematics. The jury is still out on whether or not computer programming teaches higher level thinking such as concept learning and problem solving, but the chances look good. Such learning would be an added bonus, but not a requirement. A related issue is how early children can profitably program computers. Informal research shows very young children (four and five years old) can program computers (Papert, 1980; Pea, 1983; Shumway, 1984a).

Young children can program computers.

We need further research on children's capabilities for programming and what they learn when they program computers. However, there seems to be no reason not to consider student programming at the earliest school years. We will illustrate a variety of student programming activities using BASIC and Logo.

Computers are designed to do computations. The surprise for mathematics teachers has been that the computers can do symbolic computations as well as arithmetic computations. There are two advantages. First, the computer is often the best algorithm for the computations. Second, examination and study of the computational results done by a computer can result in new concepts and mathematical discoveries. The issues are similar to those of the calculator. A computer is a powerful calculator. If students can use a computer for computations, and the computations can be done more quickly and accurately with a computer, then *use computers to do mathematical computations.*

Simulations are a potential area for effective computer use. Simulations are broadly viewed as situations in which the computer is used to simulate a system of variables and relationships, allowing students to easily modify the variables and relationships in order to see the consequences. Simulations can be used to generate many examples of a phenomenon to allow for concept learning or problem solving. The simulation may be as simple as modeling the exponential growth of bacteria (2, 4, 8, 16, 32, . . .) or as complex as the Turtle Geometry environment in Logo.

Computers can simulate mathematical systems.

There are many possibilities, but so far, research has only generated a limited number of interesting examples of computer simulations of mathematical systems. We do not know much about the potential impact of the use of such examples.

PROVISIONS FOR INDIVIDUAL DIFFERENCES AND SPECIAL PROBLEMS

Student Ability to Use Calculators and Computers

It is appropriate to be interested in student ability to use computing devices for school mathematics. There is little to prohibit their use at all school levels. It is true, we have encountered kindergartners who can't recognize R on a computer keyboard. Nevertheless, these same students ran a computer program whenever asked by pressing the R key (Shumway, 1984a). Whenever computations and letter recognitions are appropriate, calculators and computers can be used by children. Some parents encourage children to use calculators and computers as young as age three. Such use can help children develop familarity with symbols and mathematics.

Can students program computers? Kindergartners seem well able to take programs such as the following, modify the programs, and predict the outcome:

```
10 FOR N = 0 TO 40
20  PLOT 10,N
30 NEXT N
```

or

```
 5 INPUT X
10 FOR N = 0 TO 40
20  PLOT X,N
30 NEXT N
```

or

```
REPEAT 4[FD 70 RT 90]
```

or

```
TO BOX :SIZE
   REPEAT 4[FD :SIZE RT 90]
END
```

The first two programs draw vertical lines using BASIC, the second two programs draw squares using Logo. These programs introduce geometric ideas, the relationship between symbolic forms and the associated geometric figures, the use of variables, and iteration. All of these ideas are important, fundamental concepts of mathematics. It is possible to debate just what is being learned and how much of the programming students can do on their own. Allowing students to explore these ideas in a computer environment leaves room for individual differences and the opportunity for students to grow as they are able. Good teachers have always had high expectations of students, but have tempered these expectations as a result of students' actual performance. All students can use calculators and computers. The extent to which students can conceptualize their own programs will naturally vary. Our first task is to provide children with the opportunity. Examples of introductory programming lessons for young children may be found in Shumway (1983a, 1983b, 1984b, 1984c, 1987) or Johnson (1981).

Learning Disabled

One of the most obvious advantages of using the calculator in teaching learning disabled students is enabling them to compute accurately. Sometimes, students who had never shown interest in mathematics because they always got the computations wrong have shown leadership capabilities in problem solving. Calculators with large keys, large displays, and solar power have facilitated computations for visually and/or physically handicapped students. The computer offers individually paced drill and practice and the ability to produce large displays. Although keyboarding does not require the motor skills of writing legibly, there are such factors to consider for the learning disabled. The lack of printed record of computations can be a limitation. However, the computer and the calculator are powerful tools, and giving the learning disabled access to these devices, in all their forms, can do much to facilitate the learning necessary for survival in the adult world.

New Topics Introduced by Computing Devices

Effective use of calculators and computers is accompanied by the use of decimals, scientific notation, coordinate systems, variables, and logic. Systematic use of computers and calculators can involve topics such as functions, relations, trigonometry, symbolic logic, modular systems, computer arithmetic, iteration, recursion, estimation, approximation, generalization, algorithm design, proof, mathematical concept learning, and problem solving. The impact of computing devices on mathematics is so great we must completely revise elementary school mathematics to account for these new needs and changes (Conference Board for the Mathematical Sciences, 1983). Obviously these changes cannot occur overnight, but we can begin needed modifications at once. Computations with finite decimals and models for finite decimals must be taught as early as possible. Some explanation of decimals through measurement is needed and perhaps much earlier than has been the tradition. Mental arithmetic and estimation are critical skills needed for calculator use. These topics must be introduced and systematically taught beginning in kindergarten. Mental arithmetic and estimation skills should be apparent by third grade. It is possible to consider children in fifth grade using functions such as the sine and cosine defined as coordinates on a unit circle. Computers can provide conceptual models for these functions as well as the computational power needed to use them. As we find student success at doing such mathematics, it will seem natural to expect performance at this level as there are few computational limitations. We will illustrate some of the beginning possibilities in the sample activities in a later section.

Topics to Deemphasize or Eliminate

It is easy to become nonobjective or emotional about topics to be deemphasized or eliminated, particularly when the topics have a long tradition, are well known by teachers, and are easy to teach. The paper-and-pencil algorithms are ideal candidates for elimination, but they also have a long tradition, are well known, and are relatively easy to teach. We must do our best to remain objective.

Paper-and-pencil algorithms, such as long division, are no longer used by adults to do computations. Calculators are the mainstay of adult computations. If we were to allow it, calculators would be the mainstay of children's computational algorithms too. For practical reasons, calculators have replaced the paper-and-pencil computational algorithms for adults. On the basis of preparing children for the adult world, it looks as though the correct algorithm is the calculator algorithm. It is clearly the most powerful one. Suppose we were to propose the elimination of the paper-and-pencil algorithm of long division. It is quite reasonable to do all long division problems with a calculator. For example,

$$
\begin{array}{r}
41.1.\,.\,. \\
53\overline{\smash{)}\,2179.0} \\
\underline{212} \\
59 \\
\underline{53} \\
60 \\
\underline{53} \\
\cdot \\
\cdot \\
\cdot \\
\end{array}
$$

would be replaced by the calculator computation

2179, ÷ , 53, =

giving

41.113207. . .

The question is, what would be "lost"? The long division algorithm has little apparent relationship to the concept of division. Knowing the algorithm does not help one to decide whether or not division is the appropriate operation to model a given situation. However, using the calculator algorithm does not automatically make the problem trivial. One needs to be able to interpret decimals and approximations. The calculator algorithm does not automatically produce the remainder, if a remainder is needed. Some have argued long division is necessary for students to understand how to divide polynomials. Careful study shows the parallel between the two algorithms is not good and it is possible the algorithms interfere as much as they might complement. Of course the other answer is that the computer will be used to divide the polynomials too. The final analysis seems to favor the elimination of the paper-and-pencil algorithms such as long division. This does not mean mental arithmetic or estimation skills should be deemphasized. Such skills are very important and must be added to the curriculum. But one must recognize *the needed elimination of paper-and-pencil algorithms will substantially change the elementary school mathematics curriculum.*

To eliminate or deemphasize paper-and-pencil algorithms removes substantial portions of the third grade to eighth grade mathematics curriculum. Other candidates for deemphasis are the computational algorithms for adding and multiplying fractions because today's calculator and computer world is decimal-based.

Management Problems Associated with Calculators and Computers

Calculator costs are now low enough that it is feasible for schools to announce a list of appropriate calculators for students and provide a calculator for any child who cannot afford to own one. Inexpensive light-powered calculators, which would allow constant addition and multiplication, are appropriate. Intermediate grades could consider scientific calculators and graphics calculators. Most management problems associated with calculators disappear when there is no restriction on their use. Teachers will need a few backup calculators for students who forget, lose, or break calculators. Strategies for pencil borrowing readily generalize to strategies for calculator borrowing. Students should put names on their calculators.

Computer management strategies are more complex because of the size and expense of computers. The problem is a temporary one because computer sizes and prices are rapidly reducing. Soon we may be able to adopt the model of each child having a computer since graphics computers are now calculator-sized and calculator-priced. However, until such time we must accommodate models ranging from one computer per school, to classroom sets of computers, to a computer for each child. As it is possible for a class to do a mathematics problem as a group with the teacher as recorder and moderator, it is also possible for a class to do mathematics on one computer with the teacher as moderator. Some teachers have found with a computer for every student it is difficult to get students' attention on group discussions or teacher exposition. Students are so interested in doing their own problems they prefer to learn through doing rather than listening. Some teachers welcome such involvement and teach students to listen when important. Others devise ways to turn off all monitors at once to gain student attention. Generally, the assumption has been the more computers, the better for learning. Teachers report pairs or triples of students can use computers effectively if they can learn to share responsibilities. Often the interactions between students at different machines is more powerful than interaction between students at the same machine because they are sharing different programs for similar problems.

Sex Differences

Some teachers report or suspect there are sex differences related to the use of the computer. It is possible of course, but it seems more likely the computer is simply revealing differences that exist for other reasons. We suggest you ensure girls and boys have equal access to computers and that using a computer not be stereotyped for either sex. The computer can be used as a motivational tool for both sexes to do interesting, thoughtful mathematics. (See Chapter 14 for a detailed discussion of sex differences, including those potentially involving the computer.)

Machine Capabilities and Needs for Learning Mathematics

There is a balance of cost and capabilities for doing mathematics which works in favor of inexpensive computers and graphics calculators for mathematics. Whereas graphics and a language such as BASIC or Logo are required for doing mathematics, word processing, color, sound, disk drives, and expensive printers are not necessary. Many effective uses of computers to do mathematics involve very short programs (less than ten lines) written by students or the teacher. Consequently there are inexpensive machines that will serve mathematics students well. One can buy one expensive machine or 35 inexpensive machines (less than $50). The need for student access speaks well for inexpensive machines. You should consider purchase of a computer to learn how to do mathematics and how to teach mathematics using a computer. Almost all the programs illustrated in this chapter can be done on an inexpensive computer or graphics calculator.

TEACHING MATHEMATICS WITH CALCULATORS

Calculator Activities for Skills

One skill of great concern is knowledge of basic facts. The natural use and encountering of basic facts while using a calculator seems to teach many basic facts. However, a calculator can be used very directly to teach, practice, and reinforce basic facts. Find yourself a calculator that will count by ones if you press 1, +, =, =, =, . . .(or on some machines, 1, +, +, =, =, =, . . .) that is, the calculator will show 1, 2, 3, ... Now try the following activity. For instructions, read the text material as you begin the activity.

Basic Facts Drill
(Grades 1 through 6)

	5				
	+		—		—
	—		—		—
6	✓	6	—	0	—
2	✓	8	—	8	—
4	x	1	—	3	—
1	—	4	—	0	—
0	—	7	—	8	—
3	—	9	—	0	—
0	—	0	—	1	—
6	—	2	—	4	—
4	—	6	—	8	—
5	—	9	—	6	—
2	—	7	—	2	—
9	—	6	—	9	—
5	—	8	—	3	—
2	—	9	—	5	—
2	—	7	—	5	—

4 __	3 __	0 __
0 __	3 __	3 __
4 __	9 __	0 __
9 __	5 __	3 __
5 __	2 __	6 __

Instructions: The 5 and the + tell us to press 5, +, =, = to set up the calculator to add 5 to any number we enter. Thus, after pressing 5, +, =, =, we press 6, pause with our finger ready to press =, and guess the sum of 6 + 5. We think 11, press =, and verify the answer 11 on the calculator, and put a check in the blank next to 6. Now, *without clearing the calculator,* we press 2, pause with our finger ready to press =, and guess the sum of 2 + 5. We think 7, press =, and verify the answer 7 on the calculator, and give ourselves another check. Now, we press 4, pause with our finger over the = and guess the sum 4 + 5. We think 8, press =, and discover we are wrong, the answer is 9, so we give ourselves an x, and continue to 1 + 5, and so forth.

Before the first column is completed we will have practiced 20 addition facts about 5 and other random numbers, never having written down an incorrect answer, and having received immediate reinforcement of each fact with a correct answer. Students can review facts they miss by repeating those with an x, or you, as the teacher, can ask them the fact again, and there are no give-away clues on the sheet. Spot checking will keep students honest and in most cases, students will know the fact the second time. You can fill in other numbers at the tops of the other two columns. In about five minutes, children can practice about 60 basic addition facts. The sheet can be used over and over again with different numbers at the tops of the columns. Knowledge of basic facts is critical for mental arithmetic and the number sense necessary to detect errors in calculator and computer computations.

Our strategy of the Basic Facts Drill is to run off 1,000 copies of the sheet and vary the numbers of the operations at the top. You can use the same sheet for multiplication facts too. (Press 5, ×, =, = instead of 5, +, =, = to set up the calculator for the column headed by 5, ×.) For older children you can put numbers like 0.5 or 0.03 at the top and other bigger numbers along the side so students can practice basic multiplication facts, mental arithmetic, and estimation skills with decimal multiplication as well.

There are several advantages to the activity. First, the numbers on the left are randomly ordered and selected so students will not use unrelated patterns or ignore certain special numbers such as 0 or 1. Second, the learning theory is excellent. The reinforcement is immediate, and provides the correct answer. Students do not write down wrong answers, thus reinforcing wrong answers, nor do they wait for feedback. Students learn to respond quickly, accurately, and automatically. Third, class time for the activity is less than five minutes, including the self-assessment. Fourth, the same material and strategy can be used for basic fact activities throughout the year.

While we have illustrated a specific, basic fact activity, research suggests basic fact learning occurs when calculators are used for mathematics or play (Channell, 1978). Basic facts not normally part of teacher and text plans become known to students through calculator use. A combination of such informal learning together with the proposed Basic Facts Drill could provide unpressured learning opportunities together with systematic check of the full range of needed facts.

For very young children (Grades K through 2), using the calculator by pressing, 1, +, =, =, =, =, =, . . ., to count by ones allows students to practice naming numbers in sequence. Children enjoy such counting because it reinforces their counting, it is interesting to see the numbers, and it reinforces number names.

Calculator Activities for Concepts

It is natural to generalize the counting by 1s activity to counting by 2s or 5s (Grades 2 through 4). If children press 5, +, =, =, =, =, . . ., the multiples 5, 10, 15, 20, 25, 30, 35, . . ., appear and children can count the sequence on the calculator over and over. The numbers that appear result from the repeated addition of 5. Thus, one model for the relationship between repeated addition and multiplication is illustrated. Counting by 5s is most helpful in counting money and telling time (on old fashioned analog clocks). The plot can thicken if you ask students if they can count by 5s and stop on 175? 260? Or 183? What number do you have to start with to land on 183? Or 207?

How big is 100? How big is 1,000? How long would it take to make the calculator count to 100 by pressing 1, +, =, =, =, =, . . . ? Try it. To count to 1,000? Try it. Here is an interesting, different way to explore the meaning of big numbers (Grades K through 6): As students count to 1,000 ask questions like: How far from 1000 are you? Are you half way yet? What is the number just before 1,000? How fast do numbers in the ones column change? The tens column? The hundreds column? Suppose you race to 1,000 and half the room counts by 1s and the other half counts by 2s. Who will win? Why? What will the difference in time be? Suppose half the class counts by 9s and the other half by 8s? Who will win? What will the difference in time be to exceed 1,000? Why? Try it. Make some predictions for counting by other numbers. Such activities can involve concepts such as: number size, multiples, patterns in multiples, multiplication as repeated addition, place value, factors of numbers (can you count to 49 by 7s? If so, is 7 a factor of 49?), ratios, and counting money.

Calculator Exercises

1. Set your calculator to count by 1s and count to 100 several times. Watch the numbers carefully and try to imagine what young children would

notice or think about as they did the same counting. Now count to 1000 at least twice. What questions and thoughts might come to mind for first graders? Describe three lessons that could be done with such counting, focusing on: number names, numeration system structure, and number size.

2. Try the Basic Fact Drill yourself using multiplication as the operation, using the numbers 0.7, 0.002, and 0.15 at the top of the three columns, and inserting decimal points in front of the last ten numbers of each column (for example, the last number in the first column, 5, would then become 0.5). How did you do? What caused the errors you made? Did you learn from your errors? Improve the activity by making some of the numbers in the columns larger. (*Note:* Why would it be inappropriate to change a 2 to 256 instead of 200? This could give you an idea for an estimation activity, however.) Notice that multiplying by 0.15 is really the mental arithmetic problem we all face every time we wish to leave a tip after a meal in a restaurant. Now do the activity again with the larger numbers. What errors did you make this time? Why? What was learned?

3. Set your calculator to count by 9s (press 9, +, =, =, . . .). Count by 9s several times and try to imagine what third graders might notice in doing such counting. Make a list of all possible observations. What mathematical ideas are involved in each? What questions could you ask to encourage further thought and exploration? What could be learned? Design an activity for third graders based on counting by 9s with a calculator.

4. Design a counting by 5s activity for second graders. Indicate how three more lessons involving counting by 5s could be used as follow-ups to your lesson. Describe the mathematics to be learned.

5. Can you count by 9s and stop on 261? Why? Can you count by 9s and stop on 114? Why? Press 4, +, 9, =, =, =, . . ., on your calculator. What happens? (4, 13, 22, 31, . . .?) Let's call 4 our start number. What start number less than 9 would you need to use to stop on 114? Try some. Explain. What about if you are to stop on 85 and count by 7s? What start number less than 7 should you use? Suppose you are given any number and some multiple to count by; how can you figure out what start number less than the multiple to use? Can the problem always be solved? What mathematics is needed to be sure there is always a solution? Design an activity for fifth graders using these ideas and mathematics.

6. How do you explain why, in counting by, say, 2s and 3s, there will be large differences in time needed to exceed 1,000, but in counting by 8s and 9s, the differences are much smaller? Try it. Why does this happen? Design an activity for fourth graders to explore such an activity. Provide ample opportunities for counting with calculators but also organize the lesson so children will encounter, explore, and solve the mathematical problems involved.

Decimals are fundamental to most computations done by adults. Calculators and computers are designed to use decimals. We will illustrate three activities to explore fundamental ideas about decimals. The calculator plays an integral part in the activities. As you explore and try the activities, see if you can determine just what role the calculator plays in each activity. We will call the activities Decimal Folding, Zeroing In, and Calculator Arithmetic.

Decimal Folding
(Grades 2 and 3)

This activity was suggested by a second grade teacher. Each child should have a centimeter ruler, a calculator, and a strip of paper 22 cm in length. Measure the strip of paper with the centimeter ruler.
How long is it? _____
Fold the strip of paper carefully in half.
How long is the folded strip now? _____
Using your calculator, compute 22 ÷ 2 = _____ .
Now, without unfolding the strip, fold the strip in half again.
How long is the folded strip? _____
Compute 11 ÷ 2 = _____ .

The purpose of the decimal folding activity is to help students link calculator operations that result in decimal answers with physical situations for which the mathematics is a model. Measurement with the metric system (for example, centimeters) is ideal because decimals arise naturally and with a physical meaning. The folding in half and the corresponding division by two on the calculator provide a needed example of the relationship between arithmetic operations and the physical world. Another issue is the manner in which mathematics models reality. The measurement of the folded strips does not match the precision of the calculator computations. We have an opportunity to talk about the nature of measurement as approximation and the nature of mathematical models as approximations to the real world.

Students need opportunities to model reality with mathematics and explore the advantages and disadvantages of such modeling in order to develop the ability to use mathematics and calculators to solve problems.

Calculator Arithmetic
(Grades 5 and 6)

Mary discovered on her calculator that the number 3.1622776, when multiplied by itself, gives 10. That is: 3.1622776 × 3.1622776 = 10. However, 10 ÷ 3.1622776 gave 3.1622777 instead of 3.1622776. Mary correctly deduced her calculator was not following the laws of mathematics as she knew them.

John divided 2 by 3 on his calculator and got 0.6666666. He then multiplied this answer by 3 and got 2. However, if he just put in 0.6666666 and multiplied by 3, he got 1.9999998.

Rosa divided 2 by 3, multiplied the answer by 3, and got 1.9999998 instead of 2 John got. Because $(2/3) \times 3 = 2$, Rosa correctly deduced her calculator was not following the laws of mathematics as she knew them.

What is going on here? Use your calculator and explore similar problems to see how your calculator behaves. See if you can discover some possible reasons for the results and computational examples to support your ideas.

The calculator arithmetic problem can be explored further. In order to trust calculators, it is important to understand how calculators do mathematics and when calculators may not follow the usual laws of mathematics.

Decimal Counting
(Grades 2 through 4)

Ask students to count by 0.1 by pressing 0.1, +, =, =, ... Such counting can begin to develop intuitions about how decimals work. Try it yourself. Would you be willing to count to 10 by 0.1? How about 100? Why? What about counting by 0.01?

One critical factor in solving problems as adults is to decide what operation models the problem situation. It is appropriate to allow students to use a calculator to allocate most of their problem-solving time to determining the operation to use. Because the computations will be done by calculator, *students can focus their attention on the critical features of the applications; that is, do concept learning instead of algorithm practicing.*

Calculator Activities for Problem Solving

Problem solving usually involves placing a student in a situation where: (1) there is a problem or goal; (2) the solution is not evident; and (3) the student has or can find several possible strategies or alternative, potential solutions. The activity requires a student to commit some time to the problem, accept some failures, and link concepts together in new ways. Word problems in most texts do not require problem-solving behavior from students. Word problems usually involve skill learning and concept learning. (You will be asked to check this statement in a later exercise). Here are a couple examples of problem-solving activities.

Zeroing In
(Grades 2 through 6)

Two people and a calculator are required. The degree of difficulty is associated with the number of digits in the number entered into the calculator. For most students, you may wish to start with a two- or three-digit, natural number. We will illustrate the activity with an advanced example which would normally follow several easier examples. (Some calculators may not handle the repeated division required. School calculators need repeated division as well as repeated addition and multiplication.)

Enter your secret number in the calculator by pressing:
"Secret Number," ÷, =, =
(For example, if your secret number is 32, you press: 32, ÷, =, =)

Pass the calculator to a friend to see if they can discover your number. To guess, they should press:
"Guess," =
(For example, if they wish to guess 45, they would press: 45, =, and the calculator would display 1.40625.)

If the number that appears is 1, then the guess is correct. If the number is less than 1, the guess is too small. If the number is greater than 1, the guess is too big. Using the information, guess again. *Do not clear the calculator or your friend will have to enter the secret number again.* You have the answer when 1 appears on the calculator.

Let's suppose students have played the game for awhile, and one student enters the secret number, 3.1415927. How would an experienced student discover the secret number? The sequence might be as follows:

Guess:	100	Feedback:	31.830988
Guess:	3	Feedback:	0.9549296
Guess:	4	Feedback:	1.2732395
Guess:	3.5	Feedback:	1.1140845
Guess:	3.2	Feedback:	1.0185916
Guess:	3.1	Feedback:	0.9867606
Guess:	3.15	Feedback:	1.0026761
Guess:	3.13	Feedback:	0.9963099
Guess:	3.14	Feedback:	0.999493
Guess:	3.145	Feedback:	1.0010845
Guess:	3.142	Feedback:	1.0001296
Guess:	3.141	Feedback:	0.9998113
Guess:	3.1415	Feedback:	0.9999704
Guess:	3.1416	Feedback:	1.0000023
Guess:	3.14155	Feedback:	0.9999864
Guess:	3.14158	Feedback:	0.9999959

Guess:	3.14159	Feedback:	0.9999991
Guess:	3.141595	Feedback:	1.0000007
Guess:	3.141593	Feedback:	1.0000001
Guess:	3.141592	Feedback:	0.9999997
Guess:	3.1415925	Feedback:	0.9999999
Guess:	3.1415927	Feedback:	1.

Conclusion: The number must be 3.1415927. But wait, we also have

| Guess: | 3.1415928 | Feedback: | 1. |
| Guess: | 3.1415929 | Feedback: | 1. |

Conclusion: The secret number is 3.1415927, 3.1415928, or 3.1415929. However, further exploration verifies the actual solution is 3.14145927.

If the secret number entered does not make full use of all the available digits, the calculator will produce a unique solution instead of three solutions. We have seen intermediate students play the game with as much complexity as the above example. Of course, such a game is the culmination of several games played earlier with fewer digits. In order to see the full scope of mathematical ideas possible with such an activity, we are examining the most complex example of a guessing sequence by an experienced student.

The student began with a guess of 100. Given the total range of numbers possible, a better guess might have been 10000000 or 50000000, since numbers as large as 9999999 could have been possible. Such a guess would divide the range in half. (If the secret number was negative, the feedback would be negative also.) However, the student tried 100 and discovered the number was between 0 and 100, or using the value of the feedback, 31.8 . . ., discovered the number was a little more than 3 (because $100 \div 31.8$ is between 3 and 4). The second and third guesses were made to verify the solution was between 3 and 4. Next, the student tries to identify the second digit of the solution. This was done in three guesses, and the process was continued, until all the digits were determined. The first idea used was that a digit can be put between two numbers close enough together to uniquely determine each successive digit. The fundamental idea that each point on a number line has a unique decimal representation uses this same approach. (If you know sophisticated mathematics, the explanation is that all Cauchy sequences converge, because the real numbers are complete, and a Cauchy sequence of intervals of widths $1/10^n$ converges to a unique point.)

The second important idea is the binary search strategy, which suggests dividing the universe of possibilities in half by each approximation. The student uses a modified form of the binary search by choosing a digit close to the middle of the range at each new choice. For example, having verified the number was between 3 and 4, the student selected 3.5 for the next guess. Then, having verified the number was between 3 and 3.5, the student selected 3.2 (rather than 3.25 which would have been exactly halfway, but involved guessing two digits instead of just one).

The third important idea is that there may be more than one solution. The student did not assume the algorithm used would produce a unique answer and found two other apparent solutions. However, because the game required a uniquely entered number, the student took the three solutions produced by the algorithm and determined which number actually was entered to start the game. We leave discovery of the technique used by the student as an exercise for you. Of course, there are students who discover how to find the solution after just one guess. We also leave this discovery as an exercise.

**The Full Display Problem
(Grades 5 and 6)**

Compute the following exercises using your calculator:

1/2   _____

1/3   _____

1/4   _____

1/5   _____

1/6   _____

1/7   _____

1/8   _____

1/9   _____

.   .

.   .

Notice that for some problems, the whole display of the calculator is filled, but for others, the display is not completely filled. For example, $1/2 = 0.5$, and does not fill the whole display. On the other hand, $1/3 = 0.3333333...$, and does fill the whole display. Can you predict when the full display will be used and when it will not? Describe and test your conjectures. Keep a record of your results.

One common proposal for solution is to claim that odd numbers fill the screen or prime numbers fill the screen (a counterexample for both hypotheses: 5 neither fills the screen as an odd number nor as a prime number). Another hypothesis is that, if the number is a prime number greater than 5, then the screen fills. Such a hypothesis appears correct, but it does not deal with the converse issue, that is, why does 1/12 fill the screen when 12 is neither prime nor contains primes greater than 5? We leave the resolution of this problem to you. Under exactly what conditions for n will $1/n$ fill the screen?

Calculator Exercises

1. In the lesson called Decimal Folding, what happens when the folded strip of length 5.5 is folded again? How does the measured length compare with the calculator value when 5.5 is divided by two? It would be easy to argue that such repeated division beyond 5.5 confuses more than it helps as an initial experience. On the other hand, there may be a good mathematical lesson in the continuation. Argue for the second view, design a brief outline of a next lesson, and discuss the mathematics encountered.

2. Play the Zeroing In game with a friend. Start with a number between 0 and 99. In how many guesses can you always ensure that a solution can be found? Why? Make the number of guesses needed as small as possible.

3. How do you know you can always find the solution in the Zeroing In game? Can you always find a solution? Why? Explain.

4. How can there be three solutions to the Zeroing In example? Explain. How did the student in Zeroing In choose and verify the actual solution from among the three apparent solutions? Can the student be sure? Why?

5. If the student has a calculator, can the Zeroing In game be solved after one guess? Why? Illustrate.

6. In the Calculator Arithmetic example, what is the difference between John's calculator and Rosa's calculator? Explain. Why do they behave differently? Which one has the more desirable procedure? Why?

7. Explain the behavior of Mary's calculator in the Calculator Arithmetic example.

8. Design a lesson for third-grade students using a calculator to count by 0.1. What concepts might be encountered (learned)?

9. Show how word problems and a calculator can be used to teach concepts.

10. Work on the The Full Display Problem. Imagine some of the conjectures fifth graders might propose as a solution. Give the conjecture and the appropriate counterexamples to help students see the limitations of the conjecture. Continue conjecturing and counterexampling until you believe you have solved the problem. Are there any limitations to your solution? What? (Hint: Calculator arithmetic?) What do you think is learned from this problem? Explain.

Calculator Activities for Simulations

As a generalization of the simple counting programs we used for concept development in young children, we can simulate the effects of extra eating on total body weight. This is an activity for teachers which we will ask you to translate into activities for children later in this chapter.

For Teachers (Ages 15 and older)

Suppose you weigh 50 kg (110 lbs. if you must know) and eat 100 calories of food too much each day. Assume each 7700 calories of extra consumption results in a weight increase of 1 kg. Use simple counting on a calculator to illustrate the total body weight, day by day. You want to produce the sequence 50, 50.012987, 50.025974, 50.038961, 50.051948, . . ., or, if you must know in pounds, 110, 110.02857, 110.05714, 110.08571, 110.11428, . . .,.

To produce the desired sequence, you must determine the weight increase per day and then cause the calculator to count by the increase per day starting with the desired beginning weight. (*Hint:* You want your calculator to count by 100/7700, starting with 50, or by (100/7700) × (2.2), starting with 110. Keystroking 50, +, .01297, =, =, =, . . ., does the trick for kilograms with most calculators.)

Would your bathroom scale reveal the weight gain after 1 day? 10 days? 30 days? 100 days? 365 days? What are the total weight and weight gain at each of these stages? Comment on problems of weight control and what one might learn from examining such a sequence.

What mathematics is needed to understand and produce this weight gain simulation? Should adults be able to do this problem?

The above activity illustrates an arithmetic sequence. Such sequences can model or simulate many forms of growth common in our world. However, there is another form of growth called exponential growth which is also common and of a rather dramatic, different, nature. The following activity for kids introduces the simulation:

Folding Paper (Grades 2 through 6)

Take an ordinary sheet of typewriter paper and fold it in half. After one fold you should have two thicknesses of paper. Now, without unfolding, fold the paper in half again. After two folds, you should have four thicknesses of paper. Again, without unfolding, fold the paper in half again. After three folds, how many thicknesses of paper do you now have? How many thicknesses after four folds? Make a table of the number of folds, and the number of thicknesses from one fold to ten folds of the paper.

Now, use your calculator to simulate the paper-folding problem. Press:

2, ×, =, =, =, . . . ,   (on some calculators, 2, ×, ×, =, =, =,)

You should get the sequence:

2, 4, 8, 16, 32, 64, 128, 256, 512, 1024, . . ., .

If a ream of paper is 500 sheets, when does your paper-folding problem become as big a problem as folding a ream of paper?

The same sequence can be used to simulate the growth of bacteria. Suppose you start with one bacterium and bacteria divide every 20 minutes. After one hour, how many bacteria will you have? After two hours, how many bacteria will you have? After eight hours, how many bacteria will you have?

Would this result be related to brushing teeth?! Comment.

We will see several more examples of arithmetic and geometric growth in the following exercises. The computational power of the calculator allows one to examine a wide variety of such examples and generalize from the examples the essential similarities and differences between arithmetic and exponential growth patterns and the implications for society.

Calculator Exercises

1. Redo the For Teachers activity so it is appropriate for fourth graders. Do you think weight gain in children is the same as for adults? What other examples of arithmetic growth could be used with children? Choose an example you think would be particularly meaningful for fourth graders and design a lesson. Solve the problems you give and talk about the mathematics involved. Describe what is needed to set up the calculator to simulate the activity.

2. Keystroke 100000, ×, 1.05, =, =, = (or whatever is needed to get your calculator to repeatedly multiply by 1.05. For some, it is 1.05, ×, 100000, =, =, =). The result should be

100000, 105000, 110250, 115762.5, 121550.62, 127628.15, . . .,

Thus, if a city of 100,000 grows by 5% each year, what will be the approximate population after 5 years? After 10 years? After 15 years? After 20 years? Does each five years add the same number of people? Why? How would you set up your calculator to add 5,000 people each year? How does such a sequence compare to the 5% growth sequence? What is the difference?

3. Find two countries with very different population growth rates, and chart the population figures for each country for the next 20 years, assuming the growth rates do not change. Comment. Take the world population and assume an annual growth rate of 4%. What is your prediction of the world population after 10 years? After 20 years? After 30 years? After 50 years? Comment.

4. Suppose you put $10,000 in a bank and 8% interest is added to your account each year. What will be the value of your account after 5 years? After 10 years? After 15 years? After 20 years?

5. Suppose you feel you could live comfortably in retirement for $25,000 per year today. If our economy experiences 10% inflation per year, how much money will be needed in 20 years to buy what $25,000 would buy today? Solve the same problem for 5%, 15%, and 20% inflation rates. Comment.

6. John is overweight by about 20%. He weighs 235 pounds. He decides to go on a diet that will reduce his weight by 5% per year. Will he reach his desired weight in four years? Why? (*Note:* $1 + 0.05 = 1.05$ and increases factor by 5%, thus, $1 - 0.05 = 0.95$ decreases factor by 5%.)

TEACHING ABOUT MATHEMATICS WITH COMPUTERS

Computer Activities for Computations

We have used the following program to introduce children as young as kindergarten to writing and modifying computer programs.

Getting Started with Computers (Grades K through 6)

```
10 FOR N = 1 TO 12
20   PRINT N, N + N
30 NEXT N
```

We discuss the role N plays in the various lines of the program. Lines 10 and 30 tell the computer to "set up an N-box" and choose the values 1, 2, 3, . . ., 11, 12 for N, one at a time. After each value for N is chosen, line 20 tells the computer to print N and $N + N$. Then the next value of N is chosen, and the program continues. The output is as follows:

```
 1  2
 2  4
 3  6
 4  8
 5 10
 6 12
 7 14
 8 16
 9 18
10 20
11 22
12 24
```

Children of various ages recognize several features of the above program. All recognize the two sequences in the output. Many realize that by varying the last number in line 10 it is possible to give the computer a great deal more work to do. You will find counting to 100 or 1000, or . . ., is very likely. The generalizability of the above program is remarkable. For example, consider the following minor variations:

```
10 FOR N = 1 TO 12
20   PRINT N, N*N
30 NEXT N

10 FOR N = 1 TO 12
20   PRINT N, N^N
30 NEXT N

10 FOR N = 1 TO 12
20   PRINT N, 1.98*N
30 NEXT N

10 FOR N = 1 TO 12
20   PRINT N, SQR(N)
30 NEXT N

10 FOR N = 1 TO 12
20   PRINT N, ATN(N)
30 NEXT N

10 FOR N = 1 TO 12
20   PRINT N, SIN(EXP(N))
30 NEXT N
```

The programs range in mathematical sophistication from first grade mathematics to eleventh grade mathematics (Grades K through 11). ($N*N$ stands for $N \times N$, $N\hat{}N$ stands for N^N, SQR(N) stands for $\sqrt{N}$, ATN(N) stands for the arctangent of *N*, and SIN(EXP(*N*)) stands for sin (e^n).) The point of these more advanced examples is to illustrate that the programming ideas may stay very simple while the mathematics becomes quite advanced. *Providing young children with such computational programs that generalize and continue to be useful throughout their mathematical careers seems very appropriate and efficient.*

As the calculator can be used to reinforce basic facts, so can the computer. The following program is designed to give students ten randomly generated basic facts. Wrong answers are corrected, and correct answers are reinforced.

**Computer Basic Facts Drill
(Grades 1 through 6)**

```
10 FOR N = 1 TO 10
20 LET A = INT(10*RND(1))
30 LET B = INT(10*RND(1))
40  PRINT A; "+"; B;" = ";
50  INPUT C
60 IF C = A+B THEN GOTO 90
70  PRINT "NOPE, "; A;" + "; B; " = "; A+B;"."
80  GOTO 100
90 PRINT C; "YES!"
100 NEXT N
```

Lines 10 and 100 tell the computer to do the statements between 10 and 100, 10 times. Lines 20 and 30 randomly choose two digits from 0 to 9, line 40 prints the question, line 50 accepts the student's response, line 60 checks the student answer to see if it is correct, and lines 70 and 90 give the appropriate feedback. (*Note:* RND(1) is to be a random decimal between 0 and 1. Some computers use RND or RND(0) for the RND(1) in the above program. INT(□) means to take the greater integer less than the number inside the parentheses (□). For example, INT(2.71236) = 2.)

Most teachers and students can take a program similar to the one above and modify it to suit their own needs. For example, the feedback can be improved, the problems can be changed to multiplication, or the range of numbers can be increased or decreased. Try the program and see what modifications you can make. For a challenge, see if you can modify the program for subtraction and division. (*Hint:* For subtraction, make the problem $(A + B) - B$, so you can be sure the answer is in the range you desire.)

Computer Activities for Estimation

Estimating is very important for doing mathematics with calculators and computers. The most common errors using calculators and computers are errors easily detected with mental arithmetic and estimation skills. Whenever calculators and computers are being used, be sure you encourage students to use estimation skills. The following program is a generalization of the basic fact program to estimation problems:

Estimation Practice
(Grades 3 through 6)

```
 5 PRINT "ESTIMATE:"
10 FOR N = 1 TO 10
20  LET A = INT(99*RND(1)) + 1
30  LET B = INT(99*RND(1)) + 1
35  PRINT
40  PRINT A; " * "; B; " (=) ";
50   INPUT C
60 IF ABS(C-A*B)/(A*B) < = .2 THEN GOTO 90
70  PRINT "NOPE,";(INT(C/(A*B)*10000))/100;
    "PERCENT."
80   GOTO 100
90 PRINT C; " GOOD ESTIMATE!"
100 NEXT N
```

This program randomly generates values for *A* and *B* ranging from 1 to 99, asks for an estimate of the product $A \times B$, judges estimates within 20% to be correct, and gives feedback about the percent error for those estimates outside of the 20% range. As with the basic fact program, teachers and students can modify the program to fit their particular needs.

Using the computer for drill and practice of basic facts and practice with estimation skills can be effective. However, little capability of the computer is being used for such activity and judicious use of computers would suggest inexpensive computers be used for drill and practice. Also, don't forget some of the advantages of flash cards for drill and practice. For example, flash cards require no electricity, are very portable, can be constructed by the learner, and cost next to nothing. Use the most appropriate tool for the job. Sometimes the answer will be flash cards, other times the answer will be a computer.

Computer Activities for Concepts

Computer programming to teach concepts of mathematics appears to be one of the computer's most powerful uses. We will give several examples to give you a feeling for the variety possible. The first example involves using the computer for graphing. One of the most practical and powerful discoveries of mathematics was developing a relationship between symbolic representations and geometric representations. The following program illustrates the development of such relationships:

**Graphing
(Grades K through 6)**

```
10 FOR N = 0 TO 40
20  PLOT 0, N
30 NEXT N
```

The above program draws some sort of a vertical line on almost all computers. The language is BASIC, a language available on almost all microcomputers.

(*Note:* For an Apple computer, you must add lines: 5 GR and 6 COLOR = 7 and change the number 40 to 39. For Radio Shack computers, you must change line 20 to: 20 SET(N, N). Other computers may require commands similar to the Apple to start the graphics, or PSET(N, N) in place of PLOT N, N. If your computer is using high-resolution graphics and you got a very short line, you can change the 40 in line 10 to 160 or more. Such variations are irrelevant to the mathematics learned so we will illustrate and discuss programs without the machine-specific minor variations.

The mathematical ideas of the above program are powerful, significant, and important for the mathematical development of children. First, in lines 10 and 30 we find the letter N used to represent not only one number, but to systematically vary over a set of numbers. While apparently understood and used by children, these fundamental notions about mathematical variables and the use of quantifiers usually are associated with high school and college mathematics. Line 20 involves the Cartesian coordinate system, a marvelous invention of the seventeenth century that allows algebraic or symbolic representation of points in the plane. Line 20 goes further than simply plotting ordered pairs, however, because line 20 also involves the use of a variable, and very shortly, two variables. The correspondence between symbolic representations and geometric figures, and the use of variables to represent numbers are two of the most practical and powerful ideas of mathematics. There are many natural extensions of the above program that introduce further mathematical ideas. For example, change line 20 to: 20 PLOT N, 2*N or 20 PLOT N, .5*N and you will encounter the ideas of geometrical representation of multiplication, slope, domain, range, and function.

The above program allows children as young as kindergarten age to begin to explore and develop some important ideas of mathematics. As we deemphasize paper-and-pencil skills and begin using calculators and computers as tools to do mathematics, we have the time and opportunity to begin developing mathematical thinking in children.

Now consider the following generalization of the graphing program:

```
 5 INPUT A
10  FOR N = 0 TO 40
20    PLOT N, A*N
30  NEXT N
40 GOTO 5
```

(*Note:* Remember to add the special graphics command required by your computer. The Casio graphics calculator (fx-7000G) program is simply: ? ⟶ A: Graph Y = AX.)

Now we are able to explore the effects of varying *A* and the impact on the graph. Through the use of a variable we have generalized the program for an active exploration of a model for multiplication which is very intuitive, but not commonly seen by elementary school age children. The program is important for two reasons: (1) the program allows an active exploration of a model for multiplication; and, (2) the program illustrates the important and powerful idea of mathematical generalization. We encourage similar generalizations in programs the students write or modify.

Another effective graphics languages is Logo. Logo is not available on every microcomputer, but when available, is easily accessible by children. The following program illustrates Logo:

```
TO BOX
 REPEAT 4[FD 60 RT 90]
END
```

The program defines a procedure called BOX. Whenever called, BOX draws a square, 60 units on a side. The middle line contains the critical code. The computer is directed to, 4 times in a row, move forward 60 units and turn 90 degrees to the right. The result is a square. In Logo, the approach to symbolization and geometry is through the vehicle of what one might call local vectors. The symbolism specifies a length and a direction. Of course, to draw a square one must essentially know and specify the definition; that is, there are four equal sides and four right angles. As with BASIC, the program can easily be generalized as follows:

```
TO BOX :S
 REPEAT 4[FD :S RT 90]
END
```

Now the square can be of any specified size *S,* subject to the limitations of the screen. Thus, if one types BOX 20, the computer draws a square of 20 units on a side. It is natural to ask students to write a program for triangles. In fact, it is natural to write a program for any equal-sided figure. Choosing the correct angle is an interesting problem. Logo is ideal for such a vector-based exploration of geometry. One of the advantages of computer programming in any language is that it encourages, or allows a teacher to encourage, mathematical generalizations in a natural way.

An added advantage of Logo is the ease with which one can use procedures (like BOX) and the ability to call a procedure within the procedure itself. The following program defines BOX and shows an example of the procedure being called within itself.

```
TO BOX :S
  IF :S < 2[STOP]
  REPEAT 4[FD :S RT 90]
  BOX :S - 4
END
```

The program draws a set of nested squares that get smaller and smaller until the value of *S* is less than 2. Each square could be thought of as a new iteration of BOX with a smaller value for *S.* Children find such techniques for making the computer do a lot of work very stimulating. Of course, our goal is to ensure mathematics and mathematical thinking are the focus. The use of variables and the recursive nature of the program (BOX calling itself) ensure the mathematics involved in writing and modifying such programs is excellent.

We would be remiss if we did not illustrate the deeper form of recursion possible in Logo. The following two programs illustrate the difference between iteration, a common computer programming strategy possible in most languages, and recursion, an important idea difficult to illustrate in languages such as BASIC, but quite feasible in Logo. The programs are quoted from Abelson (1982, p. 37).

```
TO COUNTDOWN :NUMBER
  IF :NUMBER = 0 [STOP]
  PRINT :NUMBER
 COUNTDOWN :NUMBER - 1
END
```

Output for COUNTDOWN 3:

```
3 2 1
```

```
TO MYSTERY :NUMBER
  IF :NUMBER = 0 [STOP]
  MYSTERY :NUMBER - 1
  PRINT :NUMBER
END
```

Output for MYSTERY 3:

```
1 2 3
```

Understanding the differences between COUNTDOWN and MYSTERY is very subtle and may or may not be within reach of elementary school children. Some argue the opportunity should be available and others indicate there is no evidence the concepts can be appreciated at such a young age. However, because the Logo graphics are accessible to young children, we believe children's abilities can become apparent through making Logo and programs available and sensible teacher interaction with children. The reader is invited to consult Papert (1980) and Abelson & diSessa (1980) for further information regarding Logo as a mathematics learning environment for young children.

Computer Exercises

1. Write a computer program to count to 100. How long does it take? Now count to 1,000, 10,000, and 100,000. How long did each take? Do you get the results you expect, that is, does it take ten times longer to count to 1,000 than to count to 100, etc.? Is it possible to give the computer a job bigger than you want to wait for? Run the program(s) again. Watch the number patterns and discuss what you think children might notice or what you might ask them to notice. Describe the mathematics involved in the patterns.

2. Write a drill and practice program for multiplication of basic facts. Write down a sample of the interaction you get. Now write programs for subtraction and division. Fix the program so the answers are whole number answers. Show samples of the interaction. What were the difficulties you encountered in writing these programs?

3. The computer estimation program is probably pretty easy for you to interact with. Change the program to give harder problems. Show the

interaction and your calculator computations used to be sure the program is working properly.

4. For a real challenge, change the estimation program so that it asks you to estimate A^B for values of A ranging from 0 to 100, and values B ranging in decimal values from 0 to 10. Show the interaction and your calculator computations used to be sure the program is working properly. (Extra for experts: Let B vary from -10 to 10.)

5. Write a program to allow you to draw vertical lines anywhere you wish on the screen. Now draw horizontal lines. Write two programs, one in BASIC and one in Logo, to draw squares. What are the differences between the two programs and what different learning occurs? Write a program in Logo that draws a pinwheel of squares, each turned 9 degrees at a vertex from the one before.

6. Run the programs COUNTDOWN and MYSTERY and solve the mystery as to why the results are different.

Number Concepts
(Grades 3 through 6)

The least common multiple (LCM) of two numbers, *a* and *b,* is the smallest number divisible by both *a* and *b*. So for example, the LCM of 6 and 4 is 12. Other common multiples of 6 and 4 would be 24, 36, ... Children often explore such a concept with the following computer program:

```
10 INPUT A
20  FOR M = 1 TO 30
30   PRINT A*M; " ";
40  NEXT M
50 GOTO 10
```

For any value of A you get the first 30 multiples of A. By inputting 4, you get 4, 8, 12, 16, 20, 24, . . ., 120. By inputting 6 you get 6, 12, 18, 24, . . ., 180. The common multiples can be found by comparing lists and choosing the common numbers; namely, 12, 24, 36, 48, . . ., . The least common multiple can be found by observing 12 is the smallest common multiple. Such work involves children in the use of variables, a precise definition of the multiples of a number, and exploration of the meaning of least common multiple. Third graders might stop at this point, but fifth graders think it is reasonable to ask the computer to search the lists and are ready and willing to tackle programs that give the LCM of two numbers directly. One such program is the following:

```
10 INPUT B,C
20  FOR N = B TO B*C STEP B
30   IF N/C = INT(N/C) THEN GOTO 50
40  NEXT N
50  PRINT B; " "; C,N
60 GOTO 10
```

Students who have written such a program have given powerful evidence of deep understanding of several important mathematical concepts. For example, line 20 illustrates the understanding candidates for the LCM of B and C must be multiples of B less than or equal to $B*C$. Line 30 illustrates a definition of what it means for C to divide N, and uses the fact that as long as B and C are positive, the LCM of B and C will be the first value of N divisible by C. (Of course, one should ask students to follow up this program with a consideration of the consequences of B and/or C being less than zero.) A similar program on the Casio graphics calculator would be as follows:

```
? → B: ? → C
0 → N
Lbl 1: N + B → N
N ÷ C ≠ Int (N ÷ C) => Goto 1
N
```

Writing such computer programs requires complete, detailed understanding of the concept of least common multiple. The language used is not critical, but all the relevant attributes of the concept must be identified as must the logical rules connecting the relevant attributes. The complete analysis of the concept is required to write the program. Once the program is written, one can explore a host of examples of LCMs in an effort to find potential bugs in the program and to develop good intuitions about the nature of least common multiples.

In the interest of space we will stop providing examples. Others can be found in Shumway (1987), Johnson (1981), and other sources. Our experience has been that almost any mathematical concept learning can be significantly enriched by the writing of computer programs to define or use the concept to do mathematics.

Computer Activities for Problem Solving

Driscoll (1982), in an analysis of the research on problem solving, identifies several traits associated with successful problem solvers.

Successful problem solvers. . .

1. do more . . . rereading, rechecking, reviewing.
2. are able to pull key ideas from a problem, to distinguish between relevant and irrelevant information, and to bring relevant information to bear on a problem.
3. exhibit goal-oriented planning—that is, they identify a solution and a plan of attack.
4. use a wide variety of problem-solving processes, including estimation, recalling similar problems.
5. perceive the mathematical structures of problems.
6. can remember the mathematical structure of problems.
7. can generalize across problems, seeing mathematical threads. (Driscoll, 1982, p. 71)

Those familiar with computer programming often claim the above are just the attributes required to write successful programs to solve problems in mathematics. Johnson and Harding (1979) found significant correlational relationships between students who elected computer programming and success in mathematical problem solving. While good, solid, cause-and-effect relationships have yet to be demonstrated, most researchers agree the potential impact for computer programming on mathematical problem solving looks promising (Suydam, 1986). It is appropriate for teachers to begin exploring such relationships through computer programming concepts and problems in mathematics. Before we look at a mathematical example, let's examine a problem in language arts:

Plurals
(Grades 3 through 6)

The general problem is to teach the computer to form the plural of any word. The following program will get you started:

```
10 INPUT A$
20  PRINT A$, A$ + "S"
30 GOTO 10
```

Try the program with the following words: CAT, HAT, BAG, ALLYN, your name, RUN, TALK, WORD, SKY, TRY, IMPLY, ... How did the program do? What percentage of the plurals do you think the computer would get right with this program? (You could get an estimate by randomly selecting about 30 words and seeing how many plurals would be correct by simply adding an "s.") In the list we suggested, the computer would fail with those words ending in Y. Suppose we were to fix the program so that if a word ended in Y we would drop the Y and add IES. How would the new program do on CAT, BAG, SKY, TRY, IMPLY, REPLY, FLY, STRAT-

EGY, SPY, MARY, BOY, KEY, FOX. Are you going to spring some new rules on us?

Children will start scrambling for dictionaries to try to figure out how this forming plurals business works. The rules for forming plurals in English are rather tricky. Even after you deal with the problem of vowels preceding the final Y, you still have difficulties with words such as: LEAF, SELF, LIFE, CHILD, MOUSE, GROUSE, INDEX, OPUS, ANALYSIS. (Note: the plural of opus is not opi, but opera, for you music lovers.) Computer programming problems cause students to learn new concepts and combine those concepts in new ways. The problem of specifying an algorithm for the computer reveals to the students the complexity of the problem and the many factors involved in telling the computer exactly how to solve the problem. Students are rarely interested in the rules for forming plurals, but in the context of programming the computer to solve the problem, interest is very high.

We now turn to a mathematical example, which remains, at press time, an unsolved problem:

Wondrous Numbers
(Grades 3 through 6)

Choose a number between 2 and 10 and write it down. We are going to pick 10, you choose another number. If your number is even, divide by two and write down the result. If your number is odd, multiply by three, add one, and write down the result. Now, follow the same procedure with the result you just wrote down. Continue this process and see if you eventually reach one. If you do, you have found a wondrous number (Hofstadter, 1979, p. 400). Here is how our choice of 10 worked out:

10	5	16	8	4	2	1	Wondrous!
$n/2$	$3n+1$	$n/2$	$n/2$	$n/2$	$n/2$		

The computation at each stage is shown below the numbers. Here is another example:

7 22 11 34 17 52 26 13 40 20 10 5 16 8 4 2 1

So both 10 and 7 are wondrous. Summarizing the rule:

1. If n is even, let the next value be $n/2$;
2. If n is odd, let the next value be $3n + 1$;
3. If the sequence reaches 1, the number is wondrous.

See if 27 is wondrous. The sequence would start: 27, 82, 41, 124, 62, 31, 47, 142, 71, 214, 107, 322, ... If you get tired, try the following program:

```
10   INPUT N
20   PRINT N; " ";
30   IF N = 1 THEN GOTO 90
40   IF N/2 = INT(N/2) THEN GOTO 70
50   LET N = 3*N + 1
60   GOTO 20
70   LET N = N/2
80   GOTO 20
90   PRINT "WONDROUS"
100  GOTO 10
```

or, if your computer language has the ELSE command:

```
10   INPUT N
20   PRINT N; " ";
30   IF N = 1 THEN GOTO 60
40   IF N/2 = INT(N/2) THEN LET N = N/2
     ELSE LET N = 3*N + 1
50   GOTO 20
60   PRINT "WONDROUS"
70   GOTO 10
```

The above programs compute the sequences necessary to determine whether or not a number is wondrous. You can tell by the variable spacing the programs are more disjointed than others we have written. This is due, in part, to the nature of BASIC, and in part, to our interest in keeping the program short and focusing on the results of the computations. The basic problem is to investigate wondrous numbers. Will all numbers be wondrous? (Mathematicians think so, but there is no proof.) How can you determine when it will take many steps to determine whether or not the number is wondrous and when it can be done quickly? Make a table of numbers and the number of steps required to verify that each is wondrous. Can you change the computer program to count the number of steps for you?

Computer Activities for Simulations

The computer can be an ideal tool for simulating some mathematical concepts or problems because of its great speed and computational power. For example, the following program simulates the paper-folding or the bacterial growth problem:

Growing Numbers
(Grades 2 through 6)

```
10 LET G = 1
20 PRINT G
30  LET G = G + G
40 GOTO 20
```

The output is as follows:

```
1
2
4
8
16
32
64
128
256
512
.
.
.
2097152
4194304
8388608
16777216
33554432
67108864
1.3421173E+8
.
.
.
8.5070592E+37
OVERFLOW . . .
```

As you can see, the program simulates the growth of bacteria, illustrates an elementary form of recursion (LET $G = G + G$), large numbers, scientific notation, computer arithmetic, and computer overflow. In order to generalize the program and keep track of the number of terms, the following program can be developed (Grades 5 and 6):

```
10 INPUT M
20 FOR N = 1 TO M
30  PRINT N, 2^(N-1)
40 NEXT N
```

The development of this program results in the ability to see the number of each term and requires the mathematical generalization that the nth term of the sequence is $2^{(n-1)}$. Then you can print the number of hours and the number of bacteria by modifying line 30. (One would assume bacteria divide every 20 minutes, so $N/3$ would give the number of hours.)

Another form of simulation takes advantage of the random number generator of the computer. For example, the following program simulates flipping a coin:

Coin Flip
(Grades 2 through 6)

Probability plays an important role in decisions we make daily. Most of us are not particularly aware of our use of probability and we tend to develop intuitions which are often subconsciously used to make decisions. For both adults and children it is important to develop realistic intuitions that can form the basis for good decision making. We begin with a situation most adults and children feel is quite straightforward and simple, namely, flipping a coin. Take a coin and flip it ten times. Record the results of each flip as follows:

H H — H — — — H — —

The record shows the first flip was heads (H), the second was heads, the third tails (—), the fourth heads, and so forth. (Imagine doing this for 30 minutes with a roomful of children!) After we get an idea of what coin flipping is like, we can turn to the computer to help simulate a large number of flips.

```
10  INPUT P
20  FOR N = 1 TO 10
30  IF RND(1) < P THEN GOTO 60
40  PRINT "- ";
50  GOTO 70
60  PRINT "H ";
```

```
70  NEXT N
80  PRINT
90  GOTO 20
```

or, if your BASIC allows ELSE:

```
10  INPUT P
20  FOR N = 1 TO 10
30  IF RND(1) < P THEN PRINT "H "; ELSE
    PRINT "- ";
40  NEXT N
50  PRINT
60  GOTO 20
```

Line 10 allows one to choose any probability level for *P*. For the coin flip problem, we set the probability of a heads at 0.5 so there is an equal probability of heads or tails on each flip. Line 20 tells the computer to plan to do and print out rows of ten flips. In line 30, the computer randomly generates a decimal between 0 and 1 and checks to see if the value is less than *P*. If so, an "H" is printed. Otherwise, a "—" is printed. Type RUN and input 0.5 for *P*. Your output should look similar to the following:

```
H — — — H — H H — —
— H H H H H H — H H
— — — — — — — H H —
H — — H — — H — — H
H H H H — H H — — —
— H — H — — — — — H
— — H — H — H H — —
H H H — — H H H H —
— H H — H — H — H H
```

Ask students to count the heads in each row. Are there always 5? What is the fewest number of heads in a row? The most? Run the program long enough so you get a row with only one head. How long did you have to wait? If you flip a fair coin 10 times, is it possible to get 9 tails out of 10 flips? How often do you think it would happen? Such programs are also possible on graphics calculators.

There are many misconceptions about events such as coin flipping. One view is, somehow, the coin remembers what has come up before, and if you get a string of several tails, heads is more likely than 0.5. This simulation allows one to explore such a misconception and see why it is false. Another misconception is that the pattern H — H — H — H — H — should be more likely than others. Is it? How often does it show up in the simulation? How often do you think you will get exactly 5 heads in a row? Other values for *P* such as 0.3, 0.1, or 0.01 can simulate events such as hits for a good major league batter, the chances of getting a job at an interview, or the chances of a star athlete making it in professional sports. Such explorations can begin to develop more realistic and accurate intuitions about probability and our daily decision making. For more classroom examples of these important ideas, see Shumway (1987).

Computer Exercises

1. Using the LCM program for clues, write a program to find the greatest common factor (GCF) of any two numbers. Discuss the problems you encounter, the mathematics you learn, and what experiences you think fifth graders have when they solve this problem.

2. Find some wondrous numbers less than 100 that require over 100 steps to show they are wondrous. What was the largest number in the sequence? What is so special about 9232? How often does it appear and for what numbers? What sorts of numbers can be shown to be wondrous very quickly? Why? What would students learn from exploring wondrous numbers? Make up some other questions about wondrous numbers you think children might consider.

3. The computer programs that simulate paper folding or bacterial growth soon move to scientific notation to represent numbers. Why? Write out, without scientific notation, the largest number in the output before the computer overflows. What do you think would happen if you added 1 to this number on the computer? (Just say PRINT ____ + 1, and fill in the blank with the largest number.) How big a number would you have to add to have the result show a change? Illustrate.

4. The use of $2^{(n-1)}$ to simulate bacterial growth can be generalized to other forms of growth rates than 200% (doubling each time). For example, $(1.05)^{(n-1)}$, or (1.05)^(N−1), simulates a growth rate of 5%. Write a program to simulate a city population growth rate of 5% beginning with 100,000 people and continuing for 50 years. Check with your calculator. Generalize the program so that any growth rate may be input. Try rates of 2%, 5%, 10%, 25%, −15%, and 50%. Comment. What social implications do you see?

5. Using the coin flip problem, simulate a good baseball player with a batting average of 0.3 (in the sports page this is written as .300 or sometimes even 300.). Suppose Julie Casey "goes ten at bats without a hit," but expects to bat 0.3. Should she start worrying about her batting stance or changing her swing? Why? Who is more likely to consider a change, a rookie or an old pro? How would both players develop a better sense of the nature of the 0.3 distribution? If your school writes proposals for funding and they think their chances of being funded are about 10%,

how many times should they submit a proposal before being discouraged by repeated rejection? Use the coin flip program to investigate.

6. Write a program that will print N, $N \times N$, N^2, and $N^2 - N \times N$ whenever the computer thinks $N \times N \neq N^2$ ($N*N <> N^2$), for, say N from 1 to 70. Are you surprised? Why do you suppose this happens? Comment.

There are some observations one might make in reviewing the various computer programming activities illustrated. One way to categorize the observations would be in terms of levels of learning.

Computer Literacy

The commands FOR, TO, PRINT, NEXT, LET, INT, RND, INPUT, IF, THEN, GOTO, ABS, PLOT, REPEAT, FD, RT, END, STOP, A$, ELSE, RUN, LIST, and BREAK and ideas such as loops, iteration, recursion, and procedures were encountered, used, and understood in the context of very short programs which nevertheless illustrated big, important ideas. None of the programs is silly, and none is just an example to show how commands work. All the programs do real work in mathematics. Most programs in BASIC use a few more commands than have already been encountered. Several limitations of computers have become apparent. Computers do only what they are told to do, they have only a finite number of numbers, they are fast, but not *that* fast, and they do not think. Children will be well on their way to learning a computer language and becoming computer literate.

Specific Mathematics

The list of mathematical topics encountered in the programs illustrated includes counting, place value, basic operations, exponents, random, greatest integer function, basic facts, large numbers, decimals, estimation, absolute value, relative error, percent, Cartesian plane, graphing functions, vector geometry, multiples, least common multiples, sequences, and geometric growth. The set of topics is impressive, but of course, if your favorite is missing it is generally a matter of omission on our part rather than that the topic cannot be studied using computers.

General Mathematics Concepts

The following unifying concepts of mathematics are an important part of the computer activities illustrated; namely, variables, operations, functions, approximation and error, numeration systems, recursion, sequences, and number theory.

Mathematical Thinking

Important general ideas and strategies such as: the power of using variables for generalization (for example, writing a program that counts to any input value instead of just 100), using the computer to teach one's self mathematics, the linking of arithmetic and symbolic code with the geometry of the plane, different models for the geometry of the plane (Cartesian or local vector models), procedures and algorithms, attention to details (almost any minor change in a program changes the results), mathematical modeling, computational exploration of mathematics, and correctness of programs.

Problem Solving

The writing of extensions of computer programs represents rather sophisticated problem solving of the type likely to be a part of the adult world of children today. Because the computer allows student-directed exploration of mathematical concepts and problems it is an ideal environment to encourage problem solving at all levels by all students.

Logical Reasoning

It is difficult to make direct claims, but programming activities involving IF, THEN, procedures, generalized algorithms, problem solving, strict logical code, and computer modeling of mathematics and the "real" world are rich in developing logical reasoning. One impact of computer programming is the fact that when a computer program does not work as the student had planned, the counterexample of the concept or principle the student is attempting to program is the very counterexample that matches the student's specific misconception and is therefore a powerful example for the student to be examining.

Substantial changes in our curriculum can be made as young children have the opportunity to write and explore computer programs. Programming can be an integral part of the daily study of mathematics. The richness of the mathematics encountered will be multiplied dramatically; more young children will see mathematics as a dynamic, creative activity; and teaching and learning mathematics will be a lively, active sport.

Overview

The potential for calculators and computers in school mathematics is dramatic and far-reaching. For example, in elementary schools, while children must continue to learn basic facts and mental arithmetic skills, the paper-and-pencil algorithms for addition, subtraction, multiplication, and division should be replaced by calculator algorithms. All testing, learning, and instruction in elementary school mathematics should be done with calculators readily available and used. There must be a focus on the skills, concepts, and problems that will accompany the use of calculators and computers to do mathematics. Such action will remove a significant number of pages of current mathematics texts and introduce many new mathematical concepts and skills currently unfamiliar to elementary children and teachers. (Secondary and college teachers are not immune from these changes because graphics calculators will have a similar impact on secondary and college level mathematics (Fey & Heid, 1984; Tucker, 1987; Wilf, 1982).) Some delay in the implementation is appropriate while research and curriculum results are developed. However, the research and curriculum results relative to calculators are well-known and readily available (Meissner, 1984). Changes in curriculum due to calculators should be implemented immediately.

Suggestions

In implementing calculator use in all elementary school mathematics, there are several factors to consider. First, it must be made clear to all persons interested in education that knowledge of basic facts and mental arithmetic are goals completely consistent with widespread use of calculators. For example, ask someone to read you basic fact questions (for example, $5 \times 7 = ?$) with a five-second delay for responding. It is impossible to use a calculator effectively to respond to such questions, but such testing represents an appropriate goal for mathematics instruction with calculators available. Consequently, all testing should be done with calculators freely available. Students quickly realize when they will want to use calculator and when they will not. The importance of testing with calculators is critical when you consider the impact on teachers and students if they anticipate being evaluated without calculators. Such testing implies the use of calculators for mathematics is inappropriate and puts unwanted pressure on teachers and students attempting to devise appropriate mathematics programs using calculators.

To implement the use of calculators for testing we suggest a period of two or three years in which the standardized mathematics tests are taken twice, once without a calculator and again with a calculator. Such temporary double testing would allow students, teachers, parents, and administrators to assess the impact of calculator use on achievement in their own district, yet allow a modern curriculum to be used. Teachers can grade the calculator version by hand. The task is small and the interest in getting immediate results will compensate for the extra time required. Research suggests computation scores will be higher; concepts and problem-solving scores will be the same, at least until the time freed from the removal of paper-and-pencil algorithms is made available for learning concepts and problem solving. It will not work to wait for calculator-based tests to be developed by publishing companies. The production of such tests will not occur until there is a market, and the market assessments are based on actual calculator use.

Computing and Mathematics

One fundamental goal of mathematics instruction in elementary schools is to prepare students for the adult world of some 15 to 20 years in the future. It is clear, by even today's standards, the calculator and computer will play a significant role in the lives of every adult (Saunders, 1980). It is mandatory children learn how to use these devices for computations. Does the introduction of powerful computing devices distract from the learning of mathematics or support the learning of mathematics? The mathematics being replaced by calculators and computers is the nonthinking, boring, time-consuming computations. The ability to do the computations quickly, accurately, and without boredom allows more examples to be considered and more opportunity to study the decisions necessary to use mathematics effectively to solve problems.

Material Selection

The basic philosophy expressed is calculators and computers should be used throughout the elementary mathematics curriculum. Involvement in research projects with children and teachers (Shumway, 1976; Wheatley & Shumway, 1978; Shumway et al., 1981; Shumway, 1984a) and the development of curriculum materials for children and teachers (Reys, Bestgen, Coburn, Schoen, Shumway, Wheatley, Wheatley, & White, 1979, 1980; Shumway, 1983a–e, 1987) have led to the following suggestions for all grade levels K through 6:

1. Calculators should be used as regularly and commonly as paper and pencil for doing mathematics. Expect children to have and use calculators. Do not restrict the use of calculators.
2. In order to effectively plan for instruction, you, as a teacher, must use a calculator, both personally and as a device for exploring and developing mathematics lessons for your students. Expect dramatic changes in your planned activities for students.
3. There will be opposition to calculator use. You must understand the issues yourself and be prepared for honest, concerned questions from parents, fellow teachers, and administrators. Be confident, well-informed, and patient.
4. There are calculator materials available, but your best solution is to purchase single copies and produce your own student materials. Such a strategy is more work, but makes you well prepared to teach and modify the lessons as needed for your students, school, and curriculum.
5. Computers should be available for students to do mathematics. Students of all ages (K through 6) can program computers and should be encouraged to do so.
6. You must have a computer available wherever you plan instruction for your students. Your thinking about mathematics must routinely involve a computer.

7. There will be little opposition to the use of computers for mathematics by parents. Fellow teachers may resist changing programs because of anxiety and lack of information and some administrators may resist added costs, but generally, there will be support for your planned computer activities.

8. There are a very large number of texts and software disks available for computer use in elementary schools. Assessments of the quality vary, but the most common figure is that about 95% of the material is of very poor quality. Student programming texts have improved. Purchase several that match your philosophy of short, mathematically important programs and develop programming problems for your classes to support and extend your goals for mathematics instruction. Resist software that attempts to simulate teachers. Look for software that simulates decision-making environments and allows children to control the computer. Examples are other programming languages such as Logo, simulations of probability situations, and graphics programs that allow students to explore geometric transformations.

9. The research data are not yet strong, but we would be remiss if we did not suggest students with a history of disappointment in mathematics often show new mathematical life when given the opportunity to use calculators and computers. They seem to feel past failures will not influence their chance for success. Programming also seems to improve reading skills.

10. A word about equipment: Calculators should be capable of repeated addition and repeated multiplication, can be light powered, and very inexpensive. Inexpensive computers and graphics calculators are quite capable of doing all the computer programs we have illustrated. To ensure student access, the use of such inexpensive machines should be encouraged. Only a few machines need the added power of large memory, disk drives, and so forth.

In summary, we are placing a heavy burden for successful curriculum implementation of calculators and computers on individual classroom teachers. We believe teachers must accept responsibility for the decisions and the nature of the changes and use. Use the advice and help of others, but you are the professionals who must make the decisions.

School Policies

Because schools in the United States are under local control by school boards it is absolutely mandatory that policy changes regarding computing devices be the result of broad, community-based committees fully examining the evidence and making recommendations to local school boards. The decisions will need to be made over and over again in every district. Teachers (you) must be prepared to assist in the formation of such committees and act as resource persons to assist committees in obtaining the relevant research evidence on which to base their decisions.

The Future

What will the impact of computers really be? History can give us some clues. The invention of the printing press made libraries and books available to everyone. Many feared students' minds would become weak because everything could be looked up. We soon found books to be powerful devices that could extend our memories. Books made significant changes in students' opportunities to learn independently. Books required new knowledge and abilities such as reading. Unfortunately, books did not solve problems, they were only useful tools to aid in solving problems. One still had to be able to think, but one could think with much more power and diversity.

Computers and calculators raise some of the same fears. Some believe students will no longer have to think, they will be unable to compute, and will not need to know anything. Reality suggests students will be free from many skills and demands on memory. Calculators and computers are powerful tools for extending our memory, our skills, and our ability to learn independently. Computers and graphics calculators require new knowledge such as programming languages and using variables. Unfortunately, computers do not solve problems, they are only useful tools to aid in solving problems. One still has to think, but one can think with much more power and diversity.

Exercises

1. At the very beginning of this chapter there are five statements summarizing the National Council of Teachers of Mathematics recommendation on calculators and computers (NCTM, 1980) and a summary of the International Congress on Mathematical Education (Shumway, 1985a). Take each of these statements, defend them, and give examples to illustrate your points.
2. Choose one calculator activity that you feel teaches important mathematics. Defend your choice with a complete discussion, including references to other chapters.
3. Choose one computer activity that you feel teaches important mathematics. Defend your choice with a complete discussion, including references to other chapters.
4. The goals and objectives for this chapter were to: develop a perspective on the potential roles of calculators and computers in school mathematics; know, understand, and apply the research on calculators and computers for the learning of mathematics; develop sufficient calculator and computer capability to make such computing devices a part of your regular planning for the learning of mathematics; and describe, illustrate, and design for children significant calculator and computer activities for the learning of mathematics. Discuss your own learning about calculators and computers with respect to these goals. What activities do you still need to engage in to meet the goals?

CHAPTER 12 SUMMARY

Changes in curriculum due to calculators should be implemented immediately. In elementary schools, while children must continue to learn basic facts and mental arithmetic skills, the paper-and-pencil algorithms for addition, subtraction, multiplication, and division should be replaced by calculator algorithms. All testing, learning, and instruction should be done with calculators readily available and used. There should be a focus on the skills, concepts, and problems that will accompany the use of calculators and computers when students do mathematics. The topics being replaced by calculators and computers are those involving time-consuming computations and graphics. The ability to do the computations and graphics quickly and accurately allows more opportunity to study the structures necessary to use mathematics effectively to solve problems.

The basic philosophy expressed is that calculators and computers should be used throughout the elementary mathematics curriculum. We are placing a heavy burden for successful curriculum implementation of calculators and computers on individual classroom teachers. We believe teachers must accept responsibility for this decision and for the nature of the changes to be made. Use the advice and help of others, but you are the professional who must make the decisions.

Today is an exciting time for mathematics teaching and learning. We have powerful new tools that will make dramatic changes in mathematics and how students learn mathematics. The tools are inexpensive and can be as available as books. There are still many questions, but, it is clear, our responsibility is to promote the use of these powerful tools to do mathematics. This most certainly will be required of today's students as tomorrow's adults.

REFERENCES

Abelson, H. 1982. *Apple Logo.* New York: BYTE/McGraw-Hill.

Ableson, H., & diSessa, A. 1980. *Turtle geometry: The computer as a medium for exploring mathematics.* Cambridge, MA: The MIT Press.

Ahl, D. H. 1984. The first decade of personal computing. *Creative Computing,* 10(11): 30−45.

Channell, D. W. 1978. *Basic facts and the use of calculators in second grade mathematics.* Working paper prepared for ERIC Clearinghouse for Science Mathematics and Environmental Education. Columbus, OH: Ohio State University.

CBMS. 1983. *The mathematical sciences curriculum K−12: What is still fundamental and what is not.* Report to the National Science Board Commission on Precollege Education in Mathematics, Science, and Technology. Washington, DC: National Science Foundation.

Driscoll, M. 1982. *Research within reach: Secondary school mathematics.* Reston, VA: National Council of Teachers of Mathematics.

Fey, J. T., & Heid, M. K. 1984. Impact of computing on calculus. In J. T. Fey (Ed.), *Computing & mathematics: The impact on secondary school curricula.* Reston, VA: National Council of Teachers of Mathematics.

Hofstadter, D. R. 1979. *Gödel, Escher, Bach: An eternal golden braid*. New York: Basic Books.

Johnson, D. C. 1978, December. Calculators: abuses and uses. *Mathematics Teaching,* 80:50−56.

Johnson, D. C. 1981, June. Calculators: Exploration for concept reinforcement. *Mathematics Teaching,* pp. 28−29.

Johnson, D. C. 1983. *Explore math with your micro: A book for kids aged 9−90*. London: Heinemann Educational.

Johnson, D. C., & Harding, R. D. 1979. University level computing and mathematical problem-solving ability. *Journal for Research in Mathematics Education,* 10: 37−55.

Kemeny, J. 1966. The role of computers and their applications in the teaching of mathematics. In H. F. Fehr (Ed.), *Needed research in mathematics education*. New York: Teacher's College Press.

Meissner, H. 1984. *Calculators for developing countries and for developed countries*. Draft of International Congress on Mathematical Education report of working group 1.1/1.2, Münster, West Germany: Universität Münster.

National Council of Teachers of Mathematics. 1980. *Agenda for Action*. Reston, VA: NCTM.

Papert, S. 1980. *Mindstorms: Children, computers, and powerful ideas*. New York: Basic Books.

Pea, R. D. 1983. *Logo programming and problem solving*. (Technical Report No. 12). New York: Center for Children and Technology, Bank Street College of Education.

Reys, R., Bestgen, B., Coburn, T., Schoen, H., Shumway, R., Wheatley, C., Wheatley, G., & White, A. 1979a. *Keystrokes: Addition and subtraction*. Palo Alto, CA: Creative Publications.

Reys, R., Bestgen, B., Coburn, T., Schoen, H., Shumway, R., Wheatley, C., Wheatley, G., & White, A. 1979b. *Keystrokes: Multiplication and division*. Palo Alto, CA: Creative Publications.

Reys, R., Bestgen, B., Coburn, T., Marcucci, R., Schoen, H., Shumway, R., Wheatley, C., Wheatley, G., & White, A. 1980. *Keystrokes: Counting and place value*. Palo Alto, CA: Creative Publications.

Reys, R., Bestgen, B., Coburn, T., Marcucci, R., Schoen, H., Shumway, R., Wheatley, C., Wheatley, G., & White, A. 1980. *Keystrokes: Exploring new topics*. Palo Alto, CA: Creative Publications.

Saunders, H. 1980, January. "When are we ever going to have to use *this*?" *Mathematics Teacher,* 73:7−16.

Shumway, R. J. 1976. Hand calculators: Where do you stand? *The Arithmetic Teacher,* 23:569−572.

Shumway, R. J. 1983a, February. Let kids write programs. *The Arithmetic Teacher,* 30:2, 56.

Shumway, R. J. 1983b, September. Try this. *The Arithmetic Teacher,* 31:52−53.

Shumway, R. J. 1983c, October. What machine? *The Arithmetic Teacher,* 31:54−55.

Shumway, R. J. 1983d, November. Simulation. *The Arithmetic Teacher,* 31:52−53.

Shumway, R. J. 1983e, December. Growing numbers. *The Arithmetic Teacher,* 31:38−39.

Shumway, R. J. 1984a. Exploring computer programming in BASIC with kindergartners. In J. Moser (Ed.), *Proceedings of the Sixth Annual Meeting of PME-NA*. Madison, WI: PME.

Shumway, R. J. 1984b, January. Graphing. *The Arithmetic Teacher,* 31:56−57.

Shumway, R. J. 1984c. Young children, programming, and mathematical thinking. In V. P. Hansen & M. J. Zweng (Eds.), *Computers in mathematics education*. Reston, VA: National Council of Teachers of Mathematics.

Shumway, R. J. 1985a. A perspective on ICME-5. In W. Page (Ed.), *American perspectives on the Fifth International Congress on Mathematical Education*. Washington, DC: The Mathematical Association of America.

Shumway, R. J. 1985b, May. Why Logo? *The Arithmetic Teacher,* 32:18−19.

Shumway, R. J. 1987. *101 ways to learn mathematics using BASIC (K−8)*. Englewood Cliffs, NJ: Prentice-Hall.

Shumway, R. J., White, A. L., Wheatley, G. H., Reys, R. E., Coburn, T. G., & Schoen, H. L. 1981. Initial effects of calculators in elementary school mathematics. *Journal for Research in Mathematics Education*. 12:119−141.

Suydam, M. N. 1981a. *Microcomputers and mathematics instruction*. ERIC/SMEAC Mathematics Education Fact Sheet No. 4, ERIC, 1200 Chambers Road, Columbus, OH 43212, USA.

Suydam, M. N. 1981b. *The use of calculators in pre-college education: Fourth annual state-of-the-art review*. Columbus, OH: Calculator Information Center.

Suydam, M. N. 1983. Achieving with calculators. *The Arithmetic Teacher,* 31(3):20.

Suydam, M. N. 1984. Microcomputers in mathematics instruction. *The Arithmetic Teacher,* 32(2):35.

Suydam, M. N. 1986. *An overview of research: Computers in mathematics education, K−12*. Mathematics Education Digest No. 1, 1986. ERIC Clearinghouse for Science, Mathematics, and Environmental Education. Columbus, OH: Ohio State University.

Tesler, L. G. 1984. Programming languages. *Scientific American,* 251:70−78.

Tucker, T. 1987. Calculators with a college education? *Focus, The Newsletter of the Mathematical Association of America,* 7(1):1−5.

Ulam, S. M. 1980. Von Neumann: The interaction of mathematics and computing. In N. Metropolis, J. Howlett, & G. C. Rota (Eds.), *History of computing in the twentieth century* (pp. 93−99). New York: Academic Press.

Wheatley, G. H., Shumway, R. J., et al. 1979. Calculators in elementary schools. *The Arithmetic Teacher,* 27:18−21.

Wilf, H. S. 1982. The disk with a college education. *The American Mathematical Monthly,* 89:4−8.

13 Moving to Algebraic Thought

ALAN OSBORNE

Ohio State University

PATRICIA S. WILSON

University of Georgia

INTRODUCTION

It is not enough to teach children numerical computation. At least 75% of the children exiting elementary school mathematics programs progress to the study of algebra. A comprehensive mathematics program must help students get off to a good beginning in algebra.

A key factor in getting ready for algebra is developing an understanding of variable. Our experience in three years of work with seventh graders in the Approaching Algebra Numerically Project materials (Leitzel, Demana, & Osborne, 1985) convinces us that children can acquire the idea of variable from numerical experiences.

The goal of this chapter is to examine several factors we have found that help children learn about variables. We will look at the relationship between arithmetic generalizations and the concept of variable, as well as the stages learners progress through in learning about variables. Then we will develop the idea of variable from a base of numerical problem-solving techniques applicable to the classroom teacher. We will consider the nature of equations and relevant research about children and equation solving. The final and major section discusses the key role language plays in learning mathematics and gives particular attention to the interactive role of the calculator in classroom talk.

GENERALIZATIONS AND VARIABLES

Experiences in arithmetic are critical in preparing for study in algebra. Early experiences with algebra typically are nothing more than generalized arithmetic. The concept that enables generalizing of arithmetic is that of variable.

The use of a variable, such as the X and Y in the statement $Y = 5X + 12$, is nothing more than the generalization of an arithmetic relationship. Y is a number that is 12 more than 5 times another number. If you state a number, say 6, multiply it by 5, and add 12, then you produce a number, 42, that is the Y. A huge number of such related pairs of numbers exist. We could begin to list the pairs as in Table 13−1. In fact, you could continue listing such pairs of numbers throughout your life. The use of variables allows you to stop the listing; the statement $Y = 5X + 12$ "captures" all such pairs. It generalizes the numerical relationship one number is 5 times a number plus 12.

The use of variables is the single characteristic that determines whether you are doing algebra or doing arithmetic. For beginners in algebra it is hard to determine where the work in arithmetic ends and the fun of algebra begins. All one needs to do is to try to capture the arithmetic in a more generalized form with variables.

We have considerable experience in working with older students who have had trouble on university entrance examinations because of deficiencies in mathematics. Experience and data indicate the lack of understanding of variable accounts for a significant portion of their difficulties (Leitzel & Osborne, 1985; Rhodes, 1982; Wagner, 1983). Our experiences indicate that techniques of numerical problem solving can focus instruction on variables. Younger students can generalize arithmetic relationships and acquire an understanding of variable which enables success in algebra.

We view the teaching of arithmetic to be incomplete and deficient if it does not have an orientation to generalization. Using variables shifts attention from algorithmic computation to generalization. Stopping instruction in arithmetic with the how-to rules for algorithmic computation provides children with a limiting liability when they study more advanced mathematics.

Variables are symbols that indicate you are operating in the mathematical language of algebra. Children bring experience with ordinary language to the

TABLE 13−1
The numerical
relationship
$Y = 5X + 12$

X	6	5	8	10	37	2.3	229	0
Y	42	37	52	62	197	23.5	1157	12

learning of the new language of algebra. As in learning any second language, talk plays an important role. Problem situations and the generalization processes featured in this chapter stimulate talk using the language of algebra.

STAGES IN UNDERSTANDING VARIABLES

Learners at any age progress through distinct stages in acquiring understanding of the concept of variable. Kuchemann (1981), Hart (1980), and Booth (1984) documented a progression through stages of letter use. They interviewed and tested English school children aged 11 through 16. The stages in letter use described below are adapted from Kuchemann (1981).

Stage 1: Letter Evaluated

At the outset of a problem, the child assigns the letter a value. Given the problem "If $5 + 2X = 13$, then what is X?" a child at this stage might say X is 4 or 6. They simply recall a familiar, "comfortable" number. Only one value is considered. The child's logic may produce an incorrect response. No manipulation of the variable is required by the problem. For the young child at this stage, an exercise like $11 - Y = 6$ is handled by the recall of the subtraction fact $11 - 5 = 6$ or realizing that $6 + 5 = 11$.

Stage 2: Letter Not Used

The letter is ignored or is given no meaning. If asked to find the value of $A + B + 2$ when it is known that $A + B$ is equal to 27, the child can respond 29 without ever thinking about the A, the B, or $A + B$.

Stage 3: Letter Used as an Object

The letter is regarded as an object in its own right. The mathematical phrase $3A + 7A$ and the English phrase three apples and seven apples are considered as equivalent; the A in a sense labels the numbers so the child knows they stand for apples. This is very similar to the thinking about denominate numbers used in teaching measurement a century ago.

Stage 4: Letter Used as a Specific Unknown

Children assign a letter a specific though unknown value which can be operated with even when the value is not known. Kuchemann (1981) asked children to find R with the following conditions stated:

$R = S + T$ and $R + S + T = 30$

A frequent response was that R was 10. The children worked with the situation even before they arrived at a specific value for the variable.

Stage 5: Letter Used as a Generalized Number

A letter is seen as representing several different values instead of only one. Suppose children are asked to list all the values of Q when $Q + R = 10$. After some experience they will list more than one of the whole numbers that satisfy the conditions rather than only one such number. But they want specific numbers that satisfy the conditions and do not realize that all numbers that make both statements true are needed.

Stage 6: Letter Used as a Variable

The letter is seen as representing a range of unspecified values and a systematic relationship is seen as possible between two such sets of values. Consider the question: Which is larger: $3K$ or $K + 3$?

If children think in terms of testing with a single number, say 5, or perhaps three or four such specific numbers, then they are operating with the letter as a generalized number as in Stage 5. If they consider the relationship in terms of all numbers, perhaps even using some specific instances to help them decide, then they are at Stage 6.

The stages in using letters represent part of the understanding and use of variable you can expect children to progress through prior to studying algebra. The idea of variable ultimately involves more than using letters to indicate numbers. But for that more sophisticated learning, children need a thorough experience with letters that have numbers as replacements.

Assignment: Interview children at different ages to see where they are in progressing through stages in learning about variables. Note that if their curriculum provides no experience in using variables, they may be at Stage 1 even if they are 12 or 13 years of age.

The level of letter usage attained is determined by the types of mathematical experiences children have in school. We think current emphasis on solution of equations and on substitution in formulas delays students from acquiring the idea that a variable can have many replacements. Providing experiences that encourage many different replacements of a variable is an important step in helping students attain Stage 5 or 6 usage. A second step is to talk about equation solving or formula substitution so that children think it is okay to have more than one replacement for a variable.

ESTABLISHING THE CONCEPT OF VARIABLE

Children can encounter many problem settings that extend computational proficiency in arithmetic while at the same time extending the idea of letter usage. Problem settings that suggest building tables and using them to find a solution provide a natural base for building the idea of letter usage. The following example indicates a type of problem that helps establish an expanded concept of letter usage.

> Farmer Brown noticed when he collected eggs each evening that for every three brown eggs he gathered, he had two white eggs. Find the number of white eggs he collected several different evenings.

Have the students construct a table like Table 13–2. Children become quite proficient at completing such tables.

Modify the problem slightly by changing the exercise (see Table 13–3) to the following: Complete the table to show how many brown eggs and how many white eggs Farmer Brown collected.

Instead of asking the children to find the number of white eggs when given the number of brown eggs, this table modification requests the reverse: How many brown eggs are there if there is a given number of white eggs? This reverse problem stimulates student talk to facilitate the generalizing process.

The students acquire enhanced skills in computing, in observing patterns, and in expecting one number in the table to be related to another with table-building activities. The repetitive computations are facilitated by use of a calculator.

The next step is critical in establishing the idea of variable as a letter having many replacements. Ask the children to give a verbal rule for calculating the

TABLE 13–2
Farmer Brown's eggs

Brown Eggs	30	12	15	24	27	30	33	36
White Eggs	20	8						

TABLE 13–3
An extension for a reverse problem

Brown Eggs	30	12	15		27	30		36
White Eggs	20	8		28			44	

number of brown eggs if they know the number of white eggs. Solicit different rules from the children. Turn the problem around: Give a rule to find the number of white eggs if the number of brown eggs is known.

Some children find verbal rule giving easy; others do not. It represents a push for generalization. The generalization is the essence of using a letter to represent many different replacements. Realize that the number work is relatively concrete but requesting the verbal rule, the generalization, ups the ante for some children. Repeated opportunities with problems that allow such verbal generalizations are needed by children before they are comfortable with the next step.

The next step establishes the idea of variable as a means of capturing a generalization. Again, it is a minor modification of the first problem with an additional feature added in Table 13—4.

The difference is in adding a variable to the table. With the addition of the B, you are asking the child to think in terms of the verbal rule or generalization again but to think of B as a specific number of brown eggs. The child who thinks in terms of taking one third of the top number and doubling it finds it relatively easy to move to $2 \times (1/3) \times B$. A good teaching strategy is to write the oral statement of the computational rule on the board and immediately below it to write the rule involving the variable:

$$\text{Take } \underbrace{\text{two}}_{} \underbrace{\text{times}}_{} \underbrace{\text{one third}}_{} \underbrace{\text{of}}_{} \underbrace{\text{the number of brown eggs.}}_{}$$

$$
\begin{array}{ccccc}
\updownarrow & \updownarrow & \updownarrow & \updownarrow & \updownarrow \\
2 & \times & 1/3 & \times & B
\end{array}
$$

Then, write the expression involving the variable B that tells how to find the number of white eggs in the tables. Discuss the correspondence between the verbal and symbolic phrases.

Our experience in working with seventh graders indicates talking about the correspondence of the ideas is better than referring to it as a translation. Children expect translation to be exact and precise. This puts a blanket on creativity and keeps children from recognizing other legitimate phrases. Do ask the children to give alternative mathematical phrases.

Some children gravitate naturally to using a mathematical phrase to capture the generalization. Others need repeated encounters with problems of this type over an extended period of time before they use variables with ease. The computation in the table building is a tangible activity which allows the students who do not have letter usage under control to feel successful.

TABLE 13—4
An extension to use a variable

Brown Eggs	30	12	15		27	30	39	36	B
White Eggs	20			18					

Many problem situations are similar to the egg problem in that they are based on rules. Rule-based problem situations vary in the mathematical demands they place on children. We find it best to do many table-building problems that use skills of computation the children already know. Many ordinary and commonplace situations serve quite well as a problem base. Here are two examples:

Exercise: Jimmy has three more dimes than quarters in his piggy bank. Build a table to show possible combinations of dimes and quarters in his bank.

Exercise: Andre's grandmother lives 24 miles from his home. Andre and his cousin are going to ride their bikes to visit her. Make a table to show different combinations of speed and time for the bike trip.

Each of these situations can be used to establish a problem. You could ask, for example, how many dimes Jimmy has if there are 127 coins in his bank. Or, how long would it take Andre and his cousin to get to grandmother's home if they averaged six miles per hour. Children become quite skilled at observing patterns in the tables and using these to guide guess-and-check procedures to refine their guesses until they produce a correct answer. Of course, a calculator greatly facilitates such processes.

The essence of the table-building activity is to lead children to make a verbal generalization, and then capture the generalization with a mathematical phrase that uses a variable or letter. Several encounters with table building create the idea that a letter can have many different replacements. You will enjoy better success with this method if you scatter table-building activities over several weeks. Move from situations in which the students just build and use the tables, to those in which you ask for the verbal description of the computational rule, and finally, to situations in which children express the verbal rule with variables.

Generalization and the use of variables are both major domains of learning. Some children take longer than others to acquire the salient behaviors. Wait to expect children to use variables until many individuals in your class can make the verbal generalization. Be patient; allow time for the ideas to germinate.

Assignment: Find and describe a problem situation based on a rule that can be used to create a table with children in second grade, fourth grade, sixth grade.

Rule-based problem situations provide an excellent context for establishing the idea of many replacements for a variable. The context of equation solving is more complicated mathematically. Children have more difficulty in learning about variables in equation solving than in table-building activities.

HOW TO TALK ABOUT EQUATION SOLVING

The learning difficulties children exhibit when trying to understand variable in a context of equation solving stem from interpretations they make for the concept of equals and the equality symbol. Equality involves abstract ideas from the foundations of mathematics about what a mathematical sentence is and when a sentence is true or false. Using rule-based problem situations allows children to acquire the idea of a letter having many replacements before encountering the sophisticated interaction with ideas of equation, equivalent equations, solution algorithms, and how mathematical sentences may be true or false.

The fundamental characteristic of a variable—its having many different replacements—differs from the orientation to variables that develops with initial experiences in equation solving. To solve an equation children manipulate or operate on variables as if they were numbers. Often this is before they attain an appropriate level of letter usage to allow them to understand what they are doing with variables.

Equation solving is a major feature of most secondary school mathematics programs. The skills and understandings involved are important. However, providing experiences that exclusively anticipate equation solving without establishing a fundamental understanding of variable limits children's learning. In this section evidence concerning how children behave in equation solving is presented. Then analyses of the complexity of what "equals" and "equation" mean and how these meanings interfere with developing a concept of variable are provided. A concluding segment suggests appropriate equation-solving activities for children.

Children's Understanding of Equations and Equals

Several studies reveal children's interpretations and understandings of the = symbol and of equation differ from what might be expected from their experience in the classroom. Consider the following:

- Children believe the principal use of the equal sign is to separate the problem from the answer (Van de Walle & Thompson, 1981).
- When seventh graders were asked to give an example using an equal sign, they all offered examples with a number, one operation ($+$, $-$, $\times$, $\div$), and another number on the left, the equals symbol, and the result of the computation on the right (Kieran, 1979).
- Children being interviewed interpret = as a direction to operate or compute. For example, $2 + 5 = 7$ is interpreted (read) as "2 plus 5 makes 7" (Ginsberg, 1975).
- Junior high school students think changing the letter in an equation may

change the solution. If the two equations $7W + 3 = 38$ and $7B + 3 = 38$ are written in close proximity, students may give different answers. Some students believe W is larger than B because W is farther along in the alphabet (Wagner, 1981).

- When nine year olds were given equation of the type $\square - 19 = 32$ and asked what should go in the box to make the equation true, 15% of the National Assessment sample responded correctly (Carpenter, Corbitt, Kepner, Lindquist, & Reys, 1981). Thirteen percent of the 13-year-old children sampled could write an equation to find the answer to the problem: "Janelle had 173 matchbook covers in her collection. Her aunt sent her some more. She now has 241 matchbook covers." Interestingly, 63% could solve the equation that matched the problem.

- Children find equations like $\square = 12 + 59$ more difficult to solve than $12 + 59 = \square$ (Denamark, Barco, & Voran, 1976).

- Thirty-seven percent of the students in an introductory college engineering class could not write an equation expressing the idea that a school has six times as many students as professors (Clement, 1982; Clement, Lockhead, & Monk, 1981; Rosnick, 1981). The most common error was to write the equation $6S = P$. Follow-up interviews and retesting demonstrated this was not a careless mistake but a strong misconception that had developed over time. Do note that because of self-selection and entrance testing the engineering class was composed of mathematically talented students. The students apparently viewed the equals as a kind of correspondence indicator and used the variable as a label rather than thinking through the equality.

These studies indicate misconceptions and meanings of equals and equation quite different than what is preferred or correct.

Meanings of Equals and Equation

An equation is a sentence written with an $=$ symbol. This deceptively simple statement does not indicate how much a child must learn to use equals correctly and to have a full-blown concept of equation. Conceptual expansions through which the child must progress in the gradual shaping of meanings of equality and equation are listed below.

The initial encounter of most young children with an equation is as a means of recording the results of early computation. A first grader combines three chips with one chip and observes there are four chips altogether. The first grader and the teacher record this result as $3 + 1 = 4$. The teacher makes a big fuss about the "+" and the idea of combining. Few first graders have the language perception necessary to observe that $3 + 1 = 4$ is a sentence. Nonetheless, $3 + 1 = 4$ is a complete recording of the combining action and its result.

True/False Expansion

Most teachers and text materials progress next to equations with a box in the instructional sequence. For example, the equation $3 + \square = 5$ might be posed in a lesson concerned with addition. The instructional intent may be to focus on what numbers add to make 5, the combination of 3 and 2, rather than to introduce the idea of variable.

The teacher has a major choice in how to talk about this situation, which is both subtle and important to children in developing a second concept.

Choice 1: Talk exclusively about finding the unknown number.
Choice 2: Talk in terms of some choices making the statement true and others making it false.

The first choice emphasizes that a variable has a single replacement; this is a misconception. The second choice establishes the important ideas that (1) an equation, like any other sentence, can be true or false, and (2) many different numbers can be placed in the box. And it helps disavow students of the idea that = is simply an indication to perform a computation as reported in the first three research studies cited in the previous section.

Fill-in-the-box exercises are valuable in focusing attention on the number triple association of 2, 3, and 5 which you want students to make. Simply associating 5 with $2 + 3$ is not enough. Children need to think in terms of what number added to 2 gives 5 and what number added to 3 gives 5. Fill-in-the-box exercises are a sensible drill activity allowing the expansion of the idea of equation to include equations that are false as well as true. The use of language consistent with a variable having many different replacements is an important secondary outcome of instruction shaping children's understanding of variable and of equation.

Equivalent Equations Expansion

Many teachers and texts try to establish the idea of inverse operations and families of related sentences. For the operations of addition and subtraction, the sentences $9 + 8 = 17$, $8 + 9 = 17$, $17 - 9 = 8$, and $17 - 8 = 9$ are a family of sentences about the number triple 17, 8, and 9. Similarly for division and multiplication, four sentences can be written for the number triple 7, 9, and 63. Emphases on inverse operations and families of number facts appreciably strengthen children's control and understanding of computation.

An important secondary goal can be emphasized in teaching about inverse operations. Children can be urged to look outside of a numerical statement to find more information to solve a problem. Suppose a second grade student does not yet know about regrouping for the problem of subtracting 22 from 31 but is given the information $9 + 22 = 31$. If the child has been working with inverse operations and families of number sentences, the child can solve the problem of the subtraction easily. To encourage looking beyond the problem statement of $31 - 22 = \square$ for other information to use emphasizes a behavior that should become habituated in problem solving: Use what you know whether within or outside of a problem statement.

Teachers who use inverse operations in this manner are emphasizing fundamental algebraic concepts. To use the sentence $22 + 9 = 31$ to solve the equation $31 - 22 = \square$ is a more meaningful way to communicate that the sentences are equivalent than simply to tell a class they are equivalent. It anticipates the extensive emphasis in algebra on equivalent equations by providing a framework for children's intuitions.

Number Sorter Expansion

An equation with a variable can be thought of as a number sorter. Equations without a variable are either true or false. However, the truth or falsity of an equation with a variable typically is not known until a replacement is considered. In some senses the variable serves the role in an equation of a pronoun in an ordinary English sentence. The sentence "He is currently president of the United States" is neither true nor false until you know the replacement or referent for "he." Mathematical sentences with variables are often called open sentences to indicate the truth status is open until the replacement of the variable indicates the truth or falsity of the sentence.

The sentence "He is currently president of the United States" serves to sort the set of men into two sets, one containing all men except the one who is currently president and the other containing the one man who is president. (How would you analyze the sentence if the president were female?) Similarly, the sentence $3Y = 24$ serves to sort numbers into the set of all numbers making the sentence false and the one number, 8, which makes the sentence true. Some sentences are made true by more than one number: $X^2 = 9$ sorts the numbers 3 and -3 from the remainder of the numbers.

Some special sentences warrant attention. Equations like $A + 5 = 5 + A$ sort out all numbers because they are made true by any replacement. Such equations are called identities.

Other equations are made true by no number, consider $7 + B = 2 + B$, and sort out no numbers. Suppose B were replaced by 8, then $7 + 8 = 2 + 8$ or $15 = 10$. Some children resist calling a statement like $7 + 8 = 10$ or $15 = 10$ an equation; earlier encounters with equation solving did not emphasize multiple replacements for a variable.

Talk about equations happens as you help children record their computations. The meanings for equality are shaped gradually and expanded by your using the language correctly. Most fundamental concepts of algebra develop out of numerical problems and concepts. Recognize that how you talk about numerical equations anticipates learning in algebra.

Activities With Equations

Herscovics and Kieran (1980) describe a program that builds on children's knowledge of arithmetic. The activities provide practice of arithmetic skills but restructure ideas about equation. Students are asked to write an arithmetic identity with an operation on each side of the equal sign. Students might write

$$5 + 2 = 2 + 5$$
$$3 + 6 = 3 \times 3$$
$$18 - 8 = 2 \times 5$$

Ask students to replace the phrase on one side of the equals symbol with another that names the same number. For example, in the last sentence the 2×5 might be replaced by $3 \times 3 + 1$ or $2 + 2 + 2 + 2 + 2$. Students develop a large number of arithmetic identities and begin to behave as if the equals sign is more than a direction to compute.

You may continue the program by

1. Writing an identity on the board and asking children to convince you it is an identity.
2. Covering a number of the identity with your hand. Ask children what number(s) could be hidden under your hand that would make the identity true.
3. Replacing the "hand covering" with the traditional box □. Continue talking about numbers that make the identity true and others that make it false.
4. Using a letter—a variable—to replace the empty box.

This progression of activities should not happen in a single day but should span four or five days of lessons. Emphasize that the equal sign indicates the same number on both sides but that an equation can contain a variable.

Van de Walle and Thompson (1981) suggest using a scale balance in the same vein. Draw a picture of a balance on posterboard (see Fig. 13-1) and place cards representing numbers and operations on each side of the balance in paper pockets. Stress the concept of equality by asking if the scale balances. For example, will the cards 5, +, and 3 on one side balance 10, -, and 2 on the other? This stresses that phrases such as $5 + 3$ and $10 - 2$ are numbers instead of things requiring an answer. Do not refer to one side of the equation as the

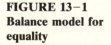

FIGURE 13-1
Balance model for equality

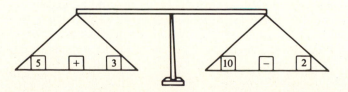

problem and the other side as the result. Record the mathematics of the balance activity as an equation.

Students soon establish a working definition of equation. Then shift investigation to ways of maintaining equality. Ask what would happen, for example, if 10 were added to one side of the equation. Would the balance of the scale be preserved? Students can try different ideas to reestablish the balance. They might add 2×5 or $12 - 2$ to the other side. Acceptable answers preserve equality and balance.

This approach is different from the traditional rule, "Whatever you do to one side of an equation you must do to the other side." The stress is on maintaining equality and what the numbers and operations mean. Many students blindly use the do-the-same-thing rule and find themselves in trouble. Suppose a student changes the sign of the first number on both sides of an equation, is equality preserved? For many students, doing the same thing to both sides of an equation is mechanical, meaningless, and rote. Students frequently close on this rule prematurely before having an adequate understanding of number, operation, variable, and equality.

Another activity appropriate for middle school-age children is to approach solving an equation as an unpacking operation. Consider the equation $2X + 3 = 7$. Think of the phrase $2X + 3$ in terms of a box. The first item placed in the box is the X. The order of operations indicates the order of placing other items in the box. That is, what happens next to the X?

First: X was multiplied by 2.
Second: 3 was added.

To solve the equation, unpack the box by reversing with the inverse operations but use the 7, which also indicates what is in the box:

First Unpacking: $7 - 3 = 4$.
Second Unpacking: $4 \div 2 = 2$.

Therefore, 2 is a solution of the equation. This process works well with equations with a variable only on one side of the equals symbol.

A word of warning: Some children will describe the solution process by writing

$$7 - 3 = 4 \div 2 = 2$$

This is mathematical gibberish: $7 - 3$ does not equal 2. It is ungrammatical. Concentrate on recording each step of the packing or unpacking process separately instead of using a single statement.

Assignment: Write an equation that involves a variable and at least two operations. Solve it by the packing/unpacking method. Rehearse how you might talk about the packing/unpacking approach with children.

Children respond well to the imagery suggested by the packing/unpacking analogy. It has the advantage of focusing attention on operations and the numerical relationships in the phrase containing the variable.

The word "unknown" has been used only once in this chapter. This was not as a synonym for the word variable. This choice was purposeful. Use of the word "unknown" suggests a single replacement for a variable, an idea in conflict with the idea of variable that children should have. Consider the word "unknown" as unfit for the ears of children.

SAYING WHAT YOU MEAN IN MATHEMATICS

A key element in understanding mathematics is gaining control of the language of mathematics. Whether the language setting is written or oral, the observation applies. It is too easy to dismiss the problem with the observation that children need to be precise. The learning of precision is quite complex, a skill acquired in small increments that both bolster understanding and make learning more efficient.

Algebraic concepts and skills serve to refine and generalize arithmetic concepts. They are described with the language both of mathematics and of ordinary discourse. The learner and the teacher both must move back and forth between mathematical language and ordinary discourse. This aspect of precision in the mathematics classroom adds complexity to the teaching task.

In acquiring language, children who gain control of the symboling process early tend to learn faster and with greater depth. The research concerning language arts offers some guidance for mathematics teachers but parallel studies in mathematics have not been completed. The work of the linguist DeStefano (1977) highlights the role of those words—and the conceptual base for those words—that describe the objects of and in language, such as phrase and verb, for learners of language. The concept that describes these special words and concepts of language is called register.

The idea can be described more generally by noting that some children learn to speak "school" quite rapidly compared to their peers. When the first grade teacher says, "Line up for lunch," they react quickly to the direction. But others do not; they are not aware, if you will, of the relation between the school setting and their language. The children who acquire the official lexicon of school words—the school register—quickly and early progress through school with greater ease and learn more efficiently than their peers.

It is but a short step from the role of register in learning language to the nature of linguistic processes supporting thinking. Coherence, the structure of arguments, and other linguistic aspects of discourse examined by Halliday and Hasan (1977) indicate the role of the structure of language in understanding language learning.

We suspect a mathematical register operates for learning in mathematics. The research about mathematical register is sparse. Based on research conducted mostly in Third World countries or countries with an indigenous culture that provides a contrasting language setting (often with schooling conducted in a second language), the report of a UNESCO-sponsored conference in Nairobi (UNESCO, 1974) provides one of the few collections of essays concerning the paralleling concept of mathematical register. The research does not yet offer definitive guidance for teaching mathematics (Halliday, 1974). However, if a learner gains the capability to describe the objects and processes of learning, then the learner can be reflective, can evaluate what is being done, and can make decisions about what is fundamental and important.

An important aspect of mathematics is symboling. Dealing with a variable is the ultimate in symboling behavior. Mathematics shares many aspects of language. It has symbolic equivalents of verbs, nouns, phrases, and sentences. Most verbs are variants of the word equals; of course, symboled differently with the = and < and other such relational symbols. But mathematics differs considerably from other languages in several fundamental ways. Halliday and Hasan (1977) and King and Rentel (1981) used the built-in redundancy of language to examine sentences and prose passages for characteristics of coherence. Consider the passage:

> John went to the store to buy candy. Spending 45 cents on hard candy and 55 cents on candy bars, *he* did not have money left for gum. *His* dentist saw the effects of *this* three months later.

What do the highlighted words mean? What are their referents? What cues you that "he" and "his" refer to John? Several cues exists, some concern candy and others stem from the act of purchase. How did you assign a meaning to "effects?" Redundancy is a built-in characteristic of the language. It works across and within sentences. In mathematics, such redundancy cues are reduced to a minimum.

The other aspect of learning algebraic concepts and skills relative to what children know about arithmetic is that the algebraic understandings are at the same time the motivation for learning more mathematics. The child who learns to use the algebraic generalization to describe different situations in terms of their commonality recognizes the power of algebra. Suppose a child has worked several problems finding the perimeters of rectangles that have a length of one unit more than the width. The child might construct a table of the numerical relationships as shown in Table 13-5. Initially, the child will make oral statements describing the relationship in the table. (We are jumping over the

TABLE 13-5
Perimeters of Rectangles with width one unit more than their length

Length	Width	Perimeter
5	5 + 1	$2(5) + 2(5 + 1) = 22$
3	3 + 1	$2(3) + 2(4)$
11	12	$22 + 24 =$
8.5	9.5	$17 + 19 =$
105	106	$2(211)$

learning to use parentheses instead of multiplication signs.) A verbal description of "take a side, double it, and add it to the other side doubled to get the perimeter" is a perfectly good generalization that should be acceptable to the teacher. It is an important step toward using variables.

The child may need to deal with several problems at this level. Each row in the table represents a different situation. The child may need to create more lines in the table—more situations—before being ready to recognize the commonality across the situations and to make the oral statement of the rule describing how to compute the perimeter.

The final step of the process is to give children another row to complete in Table 13–5:

X		

They complete the table to look like this:

X	$X + 1$	$2X + 2(X + 1)$

The final statement on the right comes to be appreciated as more efficient than the oral statement of doubling both sides and adding. The child appreciates the efficiency and finds it motivating to use variables for the sake of this efficiency.

As children encounter different problem situations that can be captured in tables, they move back and forth between the oral language version of the generalization and its rendering with the symbols of algebra (Osborne, Leitzel, & Demana, 1985). Some seventh graders must encounter several such tabling situations. The learning is not all or none; rather it develops over several weeks of experience. According to our observations of many classrooms, the teacher who keeps a constant, gentle expectation of use of the variable to summarize the oral rule or generalization makes faster progress with seventh graders than one who continually insists on the use of the variable summary of the rule. That is, give children an opportunity to use variables but back off if the children do not avail themselves of the opportunity.

Gaining control and appreciation of the symboling process is one of the more difficult aspects of learning mathematics. Teachers must be patient and realize most individual children will use variables at times and oral generalization at other times before consistently exhibiting the use of variables. We are convinced children do not learn to use variables consistently and with regularity unless they have encountered many situations in which they make oral generalizations.

Substitution and "Another Name For"

Replacement of one mathematical phrase with its equivalent is a major stumbling block for many children in learning mathematics. This aspect of the register for handling mathematical concepts is encountered frequently and early in elementary school. For example, some texts approach instruction about the addition algorithm as follows:

$$28 = 2 \text{ tens} + 8$$
$$17 = 1 \text{ ten} + 7$$
$$3 \text{ tens} + 15 = 3 \text{ tens} + 1 \text{ ten} + 5$$
$$= 4 \text{ tens} + 5$$
$$= 45$$

This approach serves to structure the explanation of why the regrouping algorithm works, organize the conversation that develops understanding, and guide the use of manipulative materials.

A number of obvious equalities are indicated with a symbol of equality. Each time one is encountered the attention of the learner is supposed to shift to the right or down in order to operate or justify the next step of the algorithm. There are also the equalities, which are not so obvious to the children, that are used for substitutions. Among these are 15 = 1 ten and 5 ones, and 3 tens + 1 ten = 4 tens.

These substitutions are critical to making the explanation flow. Many teachers use chip-trading activities to strengthen the explanation. Others use perceptual highlights to focus attention on what is happening. Note, for example, the double underlining:

$$3 \text{ tens} + \underline{\underline{15}} = 3 \text{ tens} + \underline{\underline{1 \text{ ten} + 5}}$$
$$= 4 \text{ tens} + 5$$

And consider the boxed phrases and arrow as a means of focusing attention on the substitution:

$$3 \text{ tens} + 15 = \boxed{3 \text{ tens} + 1 \text{ ten}} + 5$$
$$\uparrow$$
$$\downarrow$$
$$= \boxed{4 \text{ tens}} + 5$$

Use of chip trading and supporting perceptual highlights improve the explanatory power of this place value-driven approach to the addition algorithm. Without attention to the verbal aspects of the substitution, however, all is for nought for many children. Evidence provided in previous sections indicates that many children have a different concept of equality than mature, experienced adults. Simply to say in the last example that "Because 3 tens plus 1 ten equals 4 tens allows us to write 4 tens + 5" glosses over the problem by ignoring children's differing interpretations of equality.

The teacher who uses this approach to teaching the regrouping algorithm is relying on substitution being meaningful and sensible for children. For inexperienced first or second graders with a limited mathematical register, it is neither meaningful nor sensible. Thus, in addition to providing a base of meaning in the manipulative activities and perceptual cues, the teacher must attend to the language of substitution.

Explanation, activities, and discussion should use many different words and phrases to describe the substitutions and the equalities at the base of the substitutions. One construct many teachers find particularly useful is the phrase "another name for." After discussing the idea of nicknames, talking about children in the class who use nicknames—the James who goes by Jimmy, the Catherine known as Kate—and helping the children realize that whether the given name or the nickname is used, the reference is to the same person, then children are receptive to the notion that 4 tens "is another name for" 3 tens plus 1. Words like "replace" or "substitute" can now be tied to the idea of "another name for," the manipulative activities, and the modifications in the symbol string. By saying the same thing many different but equivalent ways and providing a base of manipulative activities while symboling the mathematics, the mathematical register of words and concepts surrounding substitution is built.

Substitution is a key process in advanced mathematics. Moreover, substitution is relied on throughout elementary mathematics in explaining computation. Children must acquire the substitution concept and control of the associated mathematical register in order to talk about what they are doing with numbers and to listen to others talk.

More is at stake in teaching the initial computational algorithms than simply computational proficiency. They provide a learning situation for mathematical language which profoundly affects learning yet to come. Specifically, the concept of substitution is exceedingly critical to success in algebra. Children's ability to generalize is profoundly affected by whether they have acquired the ability to talk about, and to listen to others talk about, mathematics. Gelman and Gallistel (1978) conclude that early number experience determines algebraic thought patterns.

ORDER OF OPERATIONS, PARENTHESES, AND CALCULATORS

Mathematics ultimately becomes a game of symbols. The symbol strings are meaningful if they are in a particular order. The string $67 + - \times = 31 \times . (\div >$ is meaningless. The rules of order are in some senses analogous to the grammatical rules of language. Preschoolers acquire a sense of appropriate language and a grammar of their own by participating in the ordinary discourse of conversation with family, peers, and other individuals. School experience further refines this language sense and extends it to written discourse.

Most children do not have enough preschool experience in the language of mathematics to provide them a base for talking and listening. That is to say, to the extent that learning mathematics is similar to learning a language, curricular activities must provide the experiential base for talking and listening in mathematics. An important element of this learning is the grammar of mathematics and, in particular, order of operations.

The mathematical phrase $\frac{6 + 12}{4}$ can be interpreted or calculated in at least two different ways that appear sensible to learners. One is to think in terms of computing $12 \div 4$ then adding 6 to give 9. Another is to first add the 6 and the 12, then divide the sum by 4 to give 4.5. The answer 4.5 is the preferred answer consistent with current usage.

The learner progressing through the elementary school curriculum encounters many such choices. Typically there is a mathematical justification or explanation available to the teacher consistent with the mathematics the child has already learned. This does not mean a great deal to the child in much the same way that talking with a three-year-old child about agreement of the plurality of subject and verb is meaningless. A more timely rationale is to focus attention on the appropriateness of making a choice that allows talking with others. If the choice fits the usage of other people, it allows communication. This appears to be a compelling argument for most students by the time they reach the upper grades.

An extension of this idea is to approach order of operations from the standpoint of communicating with your calculator. We have used calculators in numerical problem solving with several seventh-grade classes. Every calculator has its own logic that governs which computations are done first, second, and so on. The calculators we use have an algebraic logic and parentheses to indicate grouping. Children are asked to diagnose their calculator to see what operation is performed first in an expression like $2 \times 3 + 7$. They are savvy enough to see that multiplication before addition gives 13 but addition before multiplication gives 20. Each time a new operation key is introduced, the problem of diagnosing where the operation fits into the calculator's order hierarchy is posed. Parentheses and other symbols of grouping or grammar are introduced to tell the calculator what you mean or intend. One exercise asks the child to tell the calculator to do the computations $\frac{6 + 12}{4}$ and $6 + 12 \div 4$ and to compare the results. Communicating these two computations to the calculator makes the order of operations and the grouping symbols assume significance and importance for the typical learner. Such diagnostic activities are also good problem-solving activities.

We have found that to differentiate between a mathematical phrase and the keying sequence used for computing that phrase helps students learn both the mathematics and the use of the calculator (Osborne, Lietzel, & Demana, 1985). For the phrase $2 \times (12 + 17)$, we indicate the keying sequence by placing boxes around the symbols of operation and grouping as shown:

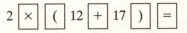

This differentiation introduces an element of control into the discussion about the mathematics and the use of the calculator so that children can be precise.

We have found that this element of mathematical precision is also useful in communication. Although it takes a bit of practice to become used to drawing boxes around the symbols, the contrast between a keying sequence and a mathematical phrase makes it worthwhile. Algebra teachers will differentiate between a mathematical phrase and a mathematical sentence because they need to talk more precisely about what an equation is and about performing operations on one side of the equals symbol. The word "phrase" allows them to identify precisely where the operations are to be applied.

The use of the calculator allows the teacher to introduce an element of precision into mathematical talk in a natural way. This extension of mathematical register allows a more complete appreciation of the power and use of symbols. As a consequence, children acquire understandings to aid them in making generalizations and solving problems.

PRECISION AND INFORMALITY

Mathematics teachers find a constant tension between wanting to use language informally and talking mathematics precisely and accurately. It is easy to err in each direction. Nitpicking precision can drive students up the wall. Informal language can miss nuances of meaning crucial to acquiring a concept or skill. Generally, you can use informal language if you are sure children have a well-developed register for that concept. But in a single lesson it is well to use several different levels of precision in talking mathematics. By varying the level of precision, you increase the probability of communicating with students. Register is a characteristic of the individual that differs from student to student. By using different ways of expressing the same thought, you provide for individual differences.

Children acquire the "official" language of mathematics by using it, both in speaking and in listening. Only by talking and discussing mathematics can children negotiate and shape meanings and understandings. Listening to children talk mathematics gives the teacher information about misconceptions above and beyond what is in written work. This allows the fine-tuning of understandings needed for learning more advanced mathematics.

CHAPTER 13 SUMMARY

This chapter has two major themes. Each is significant in moving children from thinking in arithmetic to thinking in algebraic thought. One theme concerns children's development of a concept of variable. The other theme examines features of children's acquiring control of the language of mathematics. Each is significant in a child's success in secondary school mathematics. The language issue is obviously crucial throughout the school years.

The concept of variable is critical to generalization because it allows the description of many different cases in a single statement. It is a complex concept subject to many different levels of understanding. These evolve in a predictable order as children acquire mathematical experience. The research is conclusive that children, indeed learners at any level of maturity, do not learn about variables overnight. Rather, learning and instruction must span an extended period of time with repeated and varied encounters with the concept.

This chapter was designed to exhibit repeated encounters with the concept of variable. Several examples based on rule-oriented problem situations were presented in an order corresponding to increments in the teaching about variable the authors have found effective. As you think about teaching the idea of variable and helping children acquire the power of generalization, think of providing repeated encounters expanding the breadth and depth of the child's understanding with each encounter.

The case was made that learning about variables is complicated by the limitations of children's understanding of equality and equations. Table-building activities based on rule-based problems highlight the concept of variable as a summary of many cases. We were concerned with decreasing the interference between equality and variable. Rule-oriented situations provide a means of reducing this interference and at the same time emphasize skills of problem solving and generalization.

The theme of acquiring control of language or saying what you mean in mathematics is not so well-verified by research. A well-researched domain of linguistics has been extended to mathematics teaching and learning. It provides an organizing construct for examining critical aspects of learning and doing mathematics. For example, the idea of substitution is used throughout mathematics. Children need to acquire control of the language associated with substitution in order to (1) communicate their ideas and (2) listen to the ideas of others.

Most teachers of secondary school mathematics expect children to have language under control and do not have the training in teaching language that most elementary teachers have. The typical elementary teacher is better equipped than the typical secondary teacher to teach the language-like aspects of mathematics. Stressing the language aspects of mathematics in elementary school gives the learner a significant advantage in the study of the secondary school mathematics that follow.

REFERENCES

Booth, L. R. 1984. *Algebra: Children's strategies and errors.* Windsor, United Kingdom: NFER-Nelson.

Carpenter, T. P., Corbitt, M. K., Kepner, H. S., Lindquist, M. M., & Reys, R. E. 1981. NAEP note: Problem solving. *Mathematics Teacher,* 73:427–433.

Chronicle of Higher Education, *Text of Report on Excellence in Undergraduate Education.* pp. 35–38, and 40–49. 24 October 1984.

Clement, J. 1982. Algebra word problem solutions: Thought processes underlying a common misconception. *Journal for Research in Mathematics Education,* 11:16–30.

Clement, J., Lockhead, J., & Monk, G. 1981. Translation difficulties in learning mathematics. *American Mathematical Monthly,* 88:286−290.

Denamark, T., Barco, E., & Voran, J. 1976. *Final report: A teaching experiment on equality* (PMDC Technical Report No. 6). Tallahassee, FL: Florida State University.

DeStefano, J. S. 1977. *Language: The learner and the school.* New York: John Wiley.

Gelman, R., & Gallistel, C. R. 1978. *The child's understanding of number.* Cambridge: Harvard University Press.

Ginsberg, H. 1975. Young children's informal knowledge of mathematics. *Journal of Children's Mathematical Behavior,* 1:63−156.

Halliday, M. A. K. 1974. Some aspects of sociolinguistics. In *Interactions between linguistics and mathematical education* (pp. 64−73). Paris: UNESCO.

Halliday, M. A. K., & Hasan, R. 1977. *Cohesion in English.* London: Longman.

Hart, K. M. 1980. *Secondary school children's understanding of mathematics* (Research Monograph). London: Mathematics Education, Centre for Science Education, Chelsea College, London University.

Hart, K. M. 1981. *Children's understanding of mathematics: 11−16.* London: John Murray.

Herscovics, N., & Kieran, C. 1980. Constructing meaning for the concept of equation. *Mathematics Teacher,* 73:572−580.

Kieran, C. 1979. Concepts associated with the equality symbol. *Educational Studies in Mathematics,* 12:317−326.

King, M., & Rentel, V. M. 1981. Conveying meaning in written texts. *Language Arts,* 58:721−728.

Kuchemann, D. E. 1981. Algebra. In K. M. Hart, *Children's understanding of mathematics: 11−16* (pp. 102−119). London: John Murray.

Leitzel, J., Demana, F., & Osborne, A. 1985. Seventh grade units—Approaching algebra numerically project. Columbus, OH: Ohio State University.

Leitzel. J., & Osborne, A. 1985. Mathematical alternatives for college preparatory students. In C. R. Hirsch (Ed.), *The secondary mathematics curriculum, 1985 yearbook* (pp. 150−165). Reston, VA: National Council of Teachers of Mathematics.

Osborne, A., Leitzel, J., & Demana, F. 1985. *Teacher's guide for seventh grade units—Approaching algebra numerically project.* Columbus, OH: Ohio State University.

Rhodes, T. M. 1982. *A study to assess and compare the effects on achievement and attitude of two remediation efforts in mathematics by the Ohio State University.* Unpublished doctoral dissertation, Ohio State University, Columbus.

Rosnick, P. 1981. Some misconceptions concerning the concept of variable. *Mathematics Teacher,* 74:418−420.

UNESCO. 1974. *Interactions between linguistics and mathematical education.* Paris: UNESCO.

Van de Walle, J., & Thompson, C. S. 1981. Let's do it: A poster-board balance helps write equations. *Arithmetic Teacher,* 28:4−8.

Wagner, S. 1981. Conservation of equation and function under transformations of variable. *Journal for Research in Mathematics Education,* 12:107−118.

Wagner, S. 1983. What are these things called variables? *Mathematics Teacher,* 76: 474−479.

14 Girls, Boys, and Mathematics

MARGARET R. MEYER

ELIZABETH FENNEMA

University of Wisconsin-Madison

INTRODUCTION

The role of gender in the learning of mathematics has been a frequent topic in professional publications and the popular press in the past few years. After reading headlines like "Do Males Have a Math Gene?" (*Newsweek,* December 15, 1980) or "Math and Sex: Are Girls Born With Less Ability?" (*Science,* December, 1980), the casual reader may think boys, because they were born male, are somehow better than are girls at mathematics. But is this true? Are there really sex-related differences in the learning of mathematics? If so, is it an important issue for teachers of mathematics? What are the consequences of this conclusion? What is the big deal about females and mathematics, anyway?

This chapter goes beyond the headlines to help the reader understand why gender is an important issue and what research can tell us about boys and girls as learners of mathematics. This chapter is written with certain beliefs at its foundation, which provide a framework for the remainder of the chapter.

1. The learning of mathematics is important for all students. From computation skills to high level problem solving, mathematics is increasingly a prerequisite for full participation in our technical society. Full participation

in that society should not be predetermined by sex, race, socioeconomic status, or other arbitrary factors.

2. There is not an immutable, genetic basis for any sex-related difference in mathematics. Despite what the popular press would have us believe, research evidence does not exist to support any conclusions regarding differential, inherent mathematical ability for boys and girls.

3. There may be some biological factors, like an individual's height, that influence how he or she interacts with the world. This interaction in turn influences the learning of mathematics. However, these interactions can be changed as the importance of learning mathematics by all is recognized.

4. Sex-related differences are the result of complex interactions of many factors in the social environment of learners. Note the three components of this belief: the *multiplicity* of factors, their *interaction,* and their *environmental/societal* origin. Also of critical importance is the fact that unlike immutable genetic characteristics, social forces in the environment can be changed and behaviors resulting from them can be modified.

5. Teachers and schools can, and do, make a difference. This belief is, of course, the reason why a chapter such as this is included. A recognition and understanding of the ways teachers and schools contribute to sex-related differences in mathematics can lead to positive change.

The first section of the chapter will examine the nature of the sex-related differences that exist in mathematics. The second section will present a model that attempts to explain those differences in terms of interactions within the classroom environment. The chapter includes some specific activities to eliminate sex-related differences in mathematics.

SEX-RELATED DIFFERENCES IN MATHEMATICS

There *are* sex-related differences in mathematics. These differences appear to be minimal in the elementary school, increase in the secondary school, and are largest and most evident in post-secondary education and adult life. One has only to think about the number of females in any mathematics-related career to recognize that females do not participate in careers that require mathematics at near the same levels as do males. For example, in 1980, only 9.7% of those who graduated with a degree in engineering were female (Stage, Kreinberg, Eccles, & Becker, 1985).

There are at least two hypotheses to explain why differential participation in mathematics-related careers occurs. One has to do with the learning of mathematics. Perhaps females, as a group, just do not learn enough mathematics to enable them to participate in any advanced education or job that requires mathematics. The other hypothesis has to do with attitudes or feelings that influence the learning of mathematics and the selection of a career. The validity of each of these hypotheses will be explored.

Learning Mathematics

Girls and boys apparently enter elementary school with about the same mathematical knowledge. Few, if any, differences in ability to count are found (Callahan & Clements, 1984). Strategies for solving simple addition and subtraction problems are similar for girls and boys (T. P. Carpenter, personal communication, February 1985). However, it is widely believed that by the time learners graduate from high school, boys have learned more mathematics than have girls. Starting in late elementary school and increasing throughout high school, differences between girls and boys on mathematical tasks are apparent. The best source of empirical data that confirms these differences is the Third Mathematics Assessment of the National Assessment of Educational Progress (NAEP, 1983).

NAEP measured performance of a large stratified random sample of learners, age 9, 13, and 17. These students were tested on mathematical items at four levels of cognitive complexity. At age 9, females perform better than do males at the two lowest cognitive levels. However, as the items become more complex and at older age levels, this advantage disappears. At age 17, males perform better than do females at each of the four cognitive levels. This is accentuated when the performance of 17-year-old girls and boys who have taken the same mathematics courses are compared. Boys performed significantly better than did girls and the difference was greater when the items got more complex. These data, collected in 1982, are basically the same as data reported in 1978.

Some studies report no differences between female and male achievement in mathematics. For example, Smith reported no sex-related differences on the New York State Regents High School mathematics examinations in ninth, tenth, and eleventh grade (Smith, 1980). Senk and Usiskin (1982) reported no sex-related differences in a large-scale study dealing with geometry.

Another measure of learning is grades given by teachers. Because many elementary schools do not give letter grades to children, data are only available about children in grades 7 through 12. Grades reflect teachers' assessment of students' performance on what has been covered during instruction. As such, they are undoubtedly a more direct measure of students' learning of the curriculum taught. Girls receive higher grades in mathematics classes than do boys (Stockard & Wood, 1984). Even when only highly precocious girls' and boys' grades are compared, girls receive slightly better grades than do boys (Benbow & Stanley, 1982).

It appears that while sex-related differences are not always found, boys tend to do better on certain types of tasks and girls tend to get better grades. One interpretation of this is that girls learn what is taught somewhat better than do boys, while boys are better able to transfer their learning to untaught high cognitive level situations. (For a complete review of sex-related differences in mathematics achievement, see Fennema, 1984; Stage et al., 1985.)

The fact that sex-related differences in achievement do not appear to be as strong in the elementary school as in later years does not mean the issue is unimportant for elementary school teachers. What happens in the elementary school provides the basis for what happens later. Mathematics learning is cumulative. New knowledge is learned by relating it to previously acquired knowledge. Small inadequacies in learning become larger as students progress through school. In addition, children leave the elementary school with well-formed beliefs about themselves and mathematics which directly affect subsequent learning.

ATTITUDES TOWARD MATHEMATICS

Attitudes have to do with feelings and beliefs. They are not developed independently of achievement, but they are highly related to the learning of mathematics. Not only do they influence the learning of mathematics, development of positive attitudes also is an important goal of any educational program. While there are many attitudes, at least two should be considered in understanding sex-related differences and each will be discussed.

Confidence – Anxiety

Confidence in learning mathematics is related to general self-esteem. One of the most widely held beliefs is that a child's self-esteem or confidence is a highly important influence on how he or she learns mathematics. And in fact, there is a great amount of data to indicate that confidence is strongly related to achievement at about the same level as is verbal ability (Fennema & Sherman, 1978). High confidence in mathematics appears to be located at one end of a continuum and anxiety toward learning mathematics at the other end. Confidence in mathematics is a belief that one has the ability to learn new mathematics and to perform well on mathematical tasks, while anxiety is just the opposite. Likert-type scale items are often used to measure these attitudes. Examples of such items are: I am sure that I can learn mathematics; I can get good grades in math; I'm no good in math; or Math tests scare me.

There are sex-related differences in how girls and boys respond to such items. In the Fennema-Sherman study (Fennema & Sherman, 1978), at each grade level from 6 through 11, when there were usually no significant differences in mathematics achievement, boys were more confident in their abilities to deal with mathematics than were girls. In most instances, these sex-related differences in confidence also appear in the elementary school. Young girls, much more than young boys, report they doubt their own ability to solve mathematics problems. Maccoby and Jacklin (1974) conclude that females of all ages generally lack confidence more than do males (see Reyes, 1984 for a thorough discussion).

Causal Attributions

A much more complex set of attitudes has to do with what one believes causes successes and failures. This complex set of attitudes has been labeled causal attribution. In research studies of this complex belief system, children or adults are typically asked to perform a task, like making a word out of the letters T, A, M, and H. After they solve the puzzle, or fail to solve it, they are asked why they succeeded or failed. Typically, the answers they give can be placed in four categories: Ability (I solved it because I am smart.); Effort (I tried real hard.); Task (It was an easy set of letters.); or Luck (I was just lucky in how the letters fell.). These four categories can be placed into a two by two matrix (Fig. 14−1) with locus of control (internal−external) along one dimension, and stability (stable−unstable) along the other (Weiner, 1974).

When learners are asked about success or failure on mathematics tasks, their responses can be categorized in the same way. Children say success or failure occurred in mathematics because they are smart or dumb (ability), they tried or did not try (effort), the mathematics was easy or difficult (task), or the teacher did or did not explain the idea well (luck/environment).

One way in which attributions of success or failure influence achievement-oriented behavior is in terms of persistence. In a somewhat simplistic summary, if a student attributes success to an internal, stable dimension (ability), then the student expects success in the future and will continue to strive in that area. If a student attributes success to an unstable or an external cause (for example, the teacher), then the student will not be as confident of success in the future and will be less apt to strive or persist. A somewhat different situation is true of failure attributions. If a student attributes failure to unstable causes such as effort, then the student might work harder the next time and failure could be avoided. With this situation, the tendency to approach or persist at tasks will be encouraged. On the other hand, attribution of failure to a stable cause, such as ability, will lead a student to believe that failure can't be avoided.

A belief that outcomes cannot be controlled is part of a phenomenon labeled learned helplessness (Seligman & Maier, 1967). The learned helpless student tends to attribute failure to the internal/stable factor of ability, and success to the external factors of task and luck/environment. Individuals who are "learned helpless" feel defeated before they begin. Their effort is minimal as they do not believe effort will result in success. And besides, if they failed after extensive effort, their lack of ability would be all the more obvious to others.

If you imagine learned helplessness at one end of a continuum, then mastery orientation is at the other. Individuals who are mastery oriented do not feel they are powerless to succeed. Instead, they see that their success is due to a combination of their ability and consistent effort and that when they fail it is a result of insufficient effort. These students are not defeated by setbacks, instead they try harder.

FIGURE 14−1
Weiner's attribution classification

	Internal	External
Stable	Ability	Task
Unstable	Effort	Luck/ Environment

While we must be careful of overgeneralizing data and concluding that all males behave one way and all females another way, many studies have reported that females and males tend to exhibit different attributional patterns both in mathematics and other achievement areas (Bar-Tal & Frieze, 1977; Deaux, 1976; Wolleat, Pedro, Becker, & Fennema, 1980). Males tend to attribute successes to internal causes, and failures to external or unstable causes. Females tend to attribute successes to external or unstable causes and failures to internal causes. In other words, females, more than males, attribute causation in ways that are associated with learned helpless behavior. It has been suggested that this behavior strongly affects achievement (Bar-Tal, 1978).

The two attitudes, confidence and causal attributions, are closely related. If a student feels in control of learning, he or she is confident learning will occur. On the other hand, if a student's learning is not controlled internally, but results from external factors such as the teacher, then no confidence is felt in being able to learn new material.

In summary, there are sex-related differences in mathematics learning. Boys, more than girls, are able to transfer their learning to solving complex problems, while girls, more than boys, perform better on tasks explicitly taught. Girls, more than boys, have less confidence and exhibit an attributional style that inhibits persistence and other achievement-related behaviors. These sex-related differences indicate to us that girls, more than boys, are not becoming independent in their learning and this dependency is a barrier to their mathematics learning as well as choice of mathematics-related careers. Females, more so than males, are not reaching one of the important goals of mathematics education, that of becoming thinkers who are independent problem solvers and who do well in high level cognitive tasks. Girls, more than boys, fail to become autonomous in mathematics.

Exercises and Activities

These activities and exercises will help teachers gain knowledge about their students. It is as important to know about children's feelings about mathematics as it is to know how well they learn mathematics. Suggested ways to measure several attitudes are listed. Try measuring your students' attitudes to see what you learn.

Exercise 14–1

1. Check your own knowledge about causal attributions by doing the following exercise.
   Using Weiner's two by two model of causal attributions (Fig. 14–1), classify the following statements in terms of success and failure on the four categories.

a. I got part of my math homework wrong because I just can't seem to remember to do the steps.

b. I got a good grade in math this semester because I study every night.

c. I had trouble with math today in class because I had no time to ask the teacher for help before class.

d. I am behind most of the class in math because I don't do the homework.

e. I was able to do my math homework in a short time because the problems were very easy.

f. I was able to understand a difficult topic in math because the teacher presented the material very clearly.

g. I received a low grade on my last math test because there were problems on it that I had never seen before.

h. I pass most math tests with no trouble because I guess I am just talented in math.

ATTITUDES TOWARD MATHEMATICS

Following are three sets of items that will give you some information about your students' confidence in mathematics, autonomy in mathematics, and liking of mathematics. Have your students respond to the scales as directed and then compare those results with what you have observed.

Mathematics Attitude Scales

Directions: Make an answer sheet numbered 1–18. Beside each number, put a smiling face, a neutral face, and a frowning face. Give each child an answer sheet. Have them put their name on it. Read aloud to the students:

I want to find out how you feel about mathematics. I am going to read some sentences to you. If the sentence is true for you, draw a ring around the smiling face. If it is not true for you, draw a ring around the frowning face. If you don't know whether it is true or not, draw a ring around the middle face.

Walk around the room as you read the sentences to make sure the children understand the directions. Don't hesitate to reword the items if children do not understand them.

Read the sentences in the order indicated by the numbers to the left of each sentence.

Confidence Scale (Don't read the title to children)

1. I am good at mathematics.
4. I can figure out the answers to math problems.
7. I can get the right answers.

10. I can learn mathematics.
13. I am sure about mathematics problems.
16. I feel good about mathematics.

Autonomy Scale

2. I don't like to be left alone when I am working math.
5. I think working alone in math is fun.
8. I keep trying if I get stuck in math.
11. I like to work alone in math.
14. I keep trying on hard math problems.
17. I like to try to solve problems my way.

Liking of Mathematics Scale

3. I like mathematics.
6. I like to do hard mathematics.
9. Mathematics is my favorite subject.
12. I enjoy doing mathematics.
15. I think doing mathematics is fun.
18. I think working with numbers is fun.

Scoring: Give 6 points for a smiling face; 3 points for a neutral face; and 0 points for a frowning face. Add up each child's points on the Confidence Scale (#1, 4, 7, 10, 13, 16). Add up each child's points on the Autonomy Scale (#2, 5, 8, 11, 14, 17). Add up each child's points on the Liking Mathematics Scale (#3, 6, 9, 12, 15, 18).

Another way to measure children's feelings about mathematics is to have them complete sentences like the following:

When I am working on mathematics, I feel . . . .
Mathematics makes me feel . . . .
When I get a hard math problem, I . . . .
What I get stuck on a math problem, I want to . . . .

One way to measure causal attributions is to present your students with various success and failure events such as found in Exercise 14−1. Ask them to imagine the event happened to them. For each event, have the students write down the "because" part of the sentence, that is, have them supply their own reason or causal attribution. Use these reasons to lead a discussion about how certain attributions can influence future effort. Encourage the use of success attributions to ability and effort and failure attributions to effort. Discourage (but don't criticize!) success attributions to task ease and the environment (luck) and failure attributions to lack of ability.

THE CAUSES OF SEX-RELATED DIFFERENCES IN MATHEMATICS

What prohibits girls, more than boys, from becoming autonomous learners of mathematics? It would be nice if an answer to this question could be written that could be both accurate and easily understood, but that is not possible. The factors that influence any behavior are many, varied, and interact in a complex way. However, a wide range of factors have been investigated in relation to the development of sex-related differences in mathematics (Fig. 14–2) and we now turn to a consideration of them. In considering these factors, it is helpful to organize them in a model that indicates some possible relationships.

The end box of the model in Fig. 14–2 represents the sex-related differences in mathematics which exist. We believe the learning activities (Box C) in which children participate affect their learning of mathematics and their feelings about themselves in relation to mathematics (Box D). We also believe that what children believe about themselves as learners of mathematics (Box A) determines at least partially the effort they put into learning and to some extent the activities in which they participate. These same internal beliefs affect how teachers and others interact with learners (Box B), which in turn influences internal beliefs and also the learning activities in which learners participate.

Internal Influences

Three types of internal influences need to be considered: biological, cognitive, and affective.

Biological Influences

Any time one attempts to understand sex-related differences in some kind of cognitive functioning, one of the first things that comes to mind is biological

FIGURE 14–2 Development of sex-related differences in mathematics

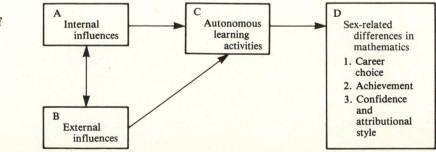

differences. Are there any biological differences to explain the educational differences that are found? Crockett and Peterson (1984) review the literature and divide biological influences into direct effects (x-linked transmission of traits, brain organization, and hormonal influences) and indirect effects. They conclude that the evidence supporting any direct effect as an explanation of sex-related differences in intellectual activities is largely inconclusive. However, some indirect biological factors, such as size and height, influence the educational experience of girls and boys. Adults have greater expectancies for tall children, and size is likely to help determine who is dominant in a peer group. The most important indirect effect is how society responds to the fact that a child is a boy or a girl. Whether a baby is a boy or a girl is of primary importance to parents. By two to three years of age, children know whether they are boys or girls, and whether their peers are girls or boys. One of the first facts adults find out about children is their sex. It is not difficult to believe that much of a child's experience is colored by his or her sex. What parents, peers, and all of society expects of a child is directly related to whether the child is a girl or boy.

By the time children enter school, they have many characteristics that have been developed by the interactions they have had with society, and these interactions have been different for girls and boys. What schools do is to continue selecting experiences for children partially on the basis of sex. This selection of experiences is not done overtly, or even consciously, in most cases. Instead, it is subtle, not recognized, but extremely pervasive. It is done by administrators, custodians, secretaries, teachers, and peers, as well as by the child.

Cognitive Influences

Two cognitive variables, general intelligence and verbal abilities, are highly important in the learning of mathematics. However, these two variables are not helpful as possible explanations of sex-related differences in mathematics. No differences exist between males and females in general intelligence. When differences are found in verbal abilities, they are in favor of females. Therefore, it appears that general intelligence and verbal skills are not helpful in understanding differences in mathematics between females and males.

One cognitive variable that many believe may help to explain sex-related differences in mathematics performance is spatial visualization, a particular subset of spatial skills. Even though the existence of many sex-related differences is being challenged, the evidence is still persuasive that in many cultures, male superiority on tasks that require spatial visualization is evident beginning during adolescence (Fennema, 1975; Maccoby & Jacklin, 1974). Spatial visualization involves visual imagery of objects, movement of the objects, or changes in their properties. In other words, objects or their properties must be manipulated in one's "mind's eye" or mentally. The relationship between mathematics and spatial visualization is logically evident as all spatial visualization tasks are geometric in character. Many teaching materials include spatial visualization components, for example, tangram activities. The number line, which is used extensively to represent whole numbers and operations on them, is a spatial representation. Illustrating the commutativity of multiplication by turning an array 90 degrees involves a direct spatial visualization skill.

While we can build a strong case that spatial visualization skills are a part of mathematics, the way those skills influence the learning of mathematics is unclear. The hypothesis that currently appears valid is that the critical relationship between mathematics and spatial visualization is not direct, but quite indirect. This relationship involves the translation of words and/or mathematical symbols into a form where spatial visualization skills can be utilized. Consider the following problem:

> A pole 12 meters long has been erected near the bank of a lake. Two and a half meters of the pole have been hammered down into the bottom of the lake; one half meter is above the surface of the water. How deep is the lake? (Werdelin, 1961)

For fifth- and sixth-grade children, this is a moderately difficult problem because of the need to remember steps and to sequence them accurately. A student must add the lengths of two pieces of the post and then subtract that length from the total length. Consider the problem from a spatial visualization perspective. If a student can visualize in his or her mind what is involved, a picture like the one shown in Fig. 14–3 might be seen. The solution of the problem then becomes simpler. The child has an image that enables him or her to mentally join the pieces above and below the water; then that length can be subtracted from the total length in order to get the correct answer. Spatial visualization skills can be a major aid in arriving at a solution.

A three-year longitudinal study (Fennema & Tartre, 1985) does give some credibility to the belief that sex-related differences in solving problems may be due to how girls and boys use their spatial visualization skills. Boys and girls

**FIGURE 14–3
Spatial represen-
tation of pole
problem**

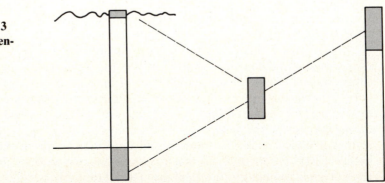

with equivalent spatial visualization skills did not solve the same number of problems, nor did they use the same processes in solving those problems. It also appeared that a low level of spatial visualization skill was more debilitating for girls than for boys.

Attitudinal Influences

Having positive beliefs about oneself in relation to mathematics is not only an important goal of mathematics education, but those same beliefs influence the learning of mathematics by influencing (1) how hard one works at activities, (2) how persistent one is when confronted with an unsolved problem, (3) how independently one works, and (4) whether a certain kind of activity will be done. One internal belief is that mathematics is a male domain. Repeatedly in our society, mathematics and mathematics-related work are seen as masculine. Unfortunately, this perception of mathematics as a male domain is not some archaic view held only by the "older generation" or by males. Osen (1974) notes that "many women in our present culture value mathematical ignorance as if it were a social grace."

Individuals do those things they see as appropriate for their sex. If a girl perceives an activity as feminine, she will be more apt to participate in it. The same influence works on boys. If a boy perceives an activity as appropriate for males, then he will feel more comfortable performing it. Not only do individuals tend to select activities perceived as appropriate for their sex, they fear rejection from others if they do well in opposite-sex stereotyped activities. In relation to mathematics, girls may fear social rejection if they excel in mathematics, while boys' belief that males do well in mathematics pressures them into doing well. What is really being said is that perceived sex role identity acts as a mediator of learning (Huston, 1983; Nash, 1979).

Sex role identity is important to everyone. A portion of that sex role identity is achievement in domains seen as appropriate for one's sex. Mathematics is *not* seen as an appropriate domain for females. Therefore, achievement by a female in mathematics is not seen to be congruent with her sex role identity. She perceives that teachers and peers have lowered expectations of her mathematical success because she is a girl. She also perceives that others see her as somewhat less feminine when she achieves in mathematics, and she becomes increasingly uncomfortable with her achievement. Success is not valued because she thinks others have negative feelings about her success.

External Influences

External influences also affect the learning activities in which children participate. While there are many such influences, two that directly influence learning will be considered: significant others and classrooms.

Significant Others

Girls and boys are not isolated individuals, but rather they live in, interact with, and are influenced by a complex social system. The significant others in a student's life have a profound impact on the learning of mathematics. You have only to watch girls and boys to confirm the idea that peer influence is important. Extremely interested in their peers' opinions, children often tailor their behavior to harmonize with their perception of their peers' expectations. Because boys, much more than girls, stereotype mathematics as a male domain, they no doubt send many subtle, and not-so-subtle, messages that girls who achieve in mathematics are somewhat less feminine. You must not believe girls never stereotype mathematics, and girls also influence other girls.

In many ways, the attitudes and stereotypes parents hold are passed on to their children. A student who receives parental support and encouragement to work hard in mathematics, and who receives parental approval and praise for excelling in mathematics, is much more likely to persist in the subject than a student who does not. Also, a student whose parents view mathematics as useful and who encourage her or him to do well in mathematics will be more likely to do so. Unfortunately, parents are more apt to discuss mathematics with their sons than with their daughters, are more supportive of their sons' mathematical interests, and hold lower educational aspirations for their daughters than for their sons (Fox, 1980).

More so than fathers, mothers often have inadequate mathematics backgrounds and have negative attitudes toward themselves as learners of mathematics. Because daughters often look to the mother as a role model, the mother's feelings about mathematics can be a critical factor. A mother who feels negative about mathematics and lacks mathematics skills is likely to accept her daughter's poor mathematics grades as inevitable. As one seventh grader told the authors, when explaining a girl's negative attitude toward mathematics, "She has it because her mother pretty much has it and . . . it's just been sort of passed down. She just has caught it from her mother."

Classroom Influences

While the entire social milieu influences learning as well as how students feel about mathematics, the most important influences occur within the classroom where mathematics is taught. Learning environments for girls and boys within classrooms, while appearing to be the same, differ a great deal. In addition to peers, the other most important component of the learning environment is the teacher. Part of the teacher's influence is in the learner's development of a sex role identity, which includes definitions of acceptable achievement in the various subjects. What happens if teachers have different standards for boys and girls? The differential standards for mathematics achievement are communicated to boys and girls through differential treatment as well as differential expectations of success. Unfortunately, teachers probably hold many hidden beliefs about what is appropriate learning for boys and girls. In addition, because boys often demand more behavioral attention, teachers spend more time with boys. Teachers often feel that if they can control the boys and keep them on task, the entire class will learn. All too often, quiet, conforming girls receive less than their share of the teacher's time and attention. What does research tell us about this? To start with, there is a great deal of evidence that teachers interact more with boys than they do with girls (Brophy, 1985). Boys generally receive more criticism for their behavior than do girls, and boys also receive more praise and positive feedback than do girls. Boys just seem to be more salient in the teacher's view than are girls. Boys who are high in confidence interact more with mathematics teachers than any other group of students (Fennema, Reyes, Perl, & Konsin, 1980). Interestingly enough, girls who are high in confidence interact with teachers less than any other group. Many girls don't interact with their teacher about mathematics at all on many days.

Many people feel that differential treatment of girls and boys is a result partially of differential teacher expectation of success or failure by girls and boys. The relevant discussion goes something like this. Because of societal beliefs that males are better at mathematics than are females, teachers expect that boys will understand high-level mathematics better and girls will do better on low-level mathematics tasks such as computation. This belief is communicated in a variety of subtle and not-so-subtle ways to both boys and girls. For example, a teacher might encourage boys more than girls to stick with hard mathematical tasks until solutions are found. The teacher might, with good intentions about preventing failure, assist girls more than boys to find the solution to hard problems. Teachers might call on boys more often to respond to problem-solving questions and call on girls more often to respond to low-level tasks. When this behavior occurs, boys and girls could intuit that boys were better at high-level cognitive tasks and girls were better at low-level cognitive tasks. Not only could students conclude that high-level tasks are easier for boys, they could also conclude that such mathematics was more important for boys because teachers encouraged boys more than girls to succeed in such tasks. In addition to these subtle messages, boys would actually be practicing high-level cognitive tasks more than would girls. Because students learn what they practice, boys would learn to do the problem-solving activities better than would girls.

The problem of differential treatment of male and female students by teachers is well documented, and there is no doubt that it strongly influences learning. The longer the problem is studied, the more complex it becomes. Most overt behavior by teachers appears to be nonsexist and fair to most students. In many cases, teachers interact more with boys because they feel they must to maintain control. Many negative interactions occur between boys and teachers. On the surface, teachers' interactions with girls are more positive and are what have been considered to be good educational practice. However, the end result appears to be negative. At least a partial result of differential treatment is that boys become more independent. They learn to depend on themselves and to feel they are in control of their own learning. As evidence of this, consider their attributional style. Boys, more than girls, attribute successes to ability, which is an indication of personal control. Boys are more confident than girls that they can learn new mathematics. Failure is seen by boys as caused by lack of effort, and they believe they can succeed if they work harder. Girls, on the other hand, often believe their success is due to the teacher and their failure is due to lack of ability. As a result, they come to depend on the teacher.

Teachers also appear to structure their classes in such a way that boys learn. For example, boys appear to learn better in a competitive environment while girls learn better in cooperative situations (Peterson & Fennema, 1985). It appears more teachers use competitive games in mathematics than use cooperative activities. Teachers plan activities to keep boys on task, and often don't consider what is best for girls.

Another classroom influence is the relation that exists between girls and boys and the differential roles girls and boys assume—and are expected to assume. Lockheed says that "Two principal sex-related inequities are characteristics of co-educational elementary school classrooms: sex segregation and male preeminence" (Lockheed, 1984, p. 17). Certainly overt sex segregation is not officially sanctioned by schools. Girls and boys are assigned to the same classrooms, taught by the same teachers, and use the same curriculum materials. When, then, does this segregation take place? It appears that voluntarily, boys and girls do not "sit with one another, help one another, or talk with one another as frequently as they interact with same sex peers" (Lockheed, 1984, p. 121). This apparently voluntary choice is approved by teachers because choice, when possible, is believed to be important. We would not disagree. But we question whether the end result of sex segregation is desirable. Within the United States, the danger of segregation by race is well recognized. Such segregation has led to inferior education for ethnic minorities. Many scholars also believe that informal segregation by sex also leads to inferior education. Children are not allowed to make other choices when the choice would interfere with their education. We question if they should be allowed to choose to work only with same sex peers.

Boys are also preeminent in classrooms. They tend to be both the leaders in small group work and to be perceived to be the leader quite often when they are not. Girls are not learning to be leaders, nor are boys learning to regard girls as leaders. The relation of leadership to mathematics learning has not been investigated but certainly being a leader and being autonomous, as is necessary for high cognitive performance, are related. The effect of not being a leader increases females' dependence.

CHAPTER 14 SUMMARY

The first half of this chapter looked at the nature of the sex-related differences in mathematics. The second half has considered several possible causes of these differences. Influences internal and external to the learner have been discussed.

Classrooms are not providing the opportunities, stimulation, or expectations girls need (as much as boys) in order to participate in activities that lead to being independent learners who are able to do high cognitive level mathematics. Girls' own internal belief systems encourage peers and teachers to interact with them in such a way as to encourage dependency. In addition, internal belief systems of teachers and peers accept dependency as appropriate for girls and reinforce dependent behavior. Teachers do not do this consciously, but their overt behavior confirms that it occurs.

Exercises and Activities

One of the beliefs stated early in this chapter was that, if teachers had knowledge, they would work to eliminate sex-related differences in mathematics. In addition to the knowledge already presented in this chapter, teachers' knowledge about their own belief systems, curriculum materials, and overt behaviors is important. These exercises will help a teacher gain knowledge about his or her personal beliefs, behaviors, and curriculum materials.

Exercise 14—2

The following is a list of adjectives that could describe good students:

active	considerate	enterprising	persistent
adventurous	cooperative	frank	poised
aggressive	curious	independent	punctual
appreciative	dependable	inventive	obliging
assertive	efficient	mannerly	sensitive
conscientious	energetic	mature	thorough

From the list, pick those adjectives that describe Mary, a good mathematics student. Now pick those adjectives that describe John, a good mathematics student. Compare the two lists of adjectives and evaluate the differences.

Exercise 14—3

How does your textbook measure up? Find 25 story problems in a mathematics textbook commonly used. Count how many problems depict only males, only females, or both females and males, and list the activity of each story problem. Then consider the following questions:

a. Was the number of "male" problems equal to the number of "female" problems?
b. Were the activities the same for both "male" and "female" problems or were the activities stereotyped for each sex?
c. In the activities of the "both female and male" problems, is one sex more active? independent? knowledgeable?

Exercise 14—4

What are some everyday things that you as a teacher can do to:
   a. Increase a student's confidence?
   b. Encourage the attitude that math is for everyone, not just for boys?

Exercise 14—5

Observe a classroom (or videotape yourself teaching) in which the students are doing seatwork and the teacher is available for questions and/or help. Try to answer the following questions:

   a. Does one sex seem to ask more questions than the other or do they seem to ask questions equally often?
   b. Does the teacher respond to questions and/or requests for help the same for girls as for boys?
   c. Does the teacher do anything in response to requests for help to encourage independence? dependence?

Exercise 14—6

Observe a classroom in which the students are engaged in a competitive math activity. Try to answer the following questions:

   a. Are boys and girls equally involved in the activity?
   b. Do boys and girls seem equally eager to participate in the activity?
   c. Does one sex seem to "win" most often?
   d. Is aggressive behavior rewarded in the activity?
   e. Could the activity be changed so that the same material was practiced without it being competitive?

EQUITY RESOURCES

Downie, D., Slesnick, T., & Stenmark, J. K. 1981. *Math for girls and other problem solvers.* Math/Science Network, Lawrence Hall of Science, University of California, Berkeley, CA. (Copies from Lawrence Hall of Science for $7.50. Send to Careers, Lawrence Hall of Science, University of California, Berkeley, CA 94720.) *This teacher's guide presents curriculum ideas for eight days worth of classes. The material/activities are divided into five different strands focused on four problem-solving skills and a career component. It has two goals: improve attitudes and develop skills. Each day could serve as an independent 90-minute or two-hour workshop, or activities could be organized by strand.*

Fennema, E., Becker, A. D., Wolleat, P. L., & Pedro, J. D. 1981. *Multiplying options*

and subtracting bias (videotapes). Reston, VA: National Council of Teachers of Mathematics.
This intervention program for middle/secondary school students consists of four videotapes, one each for teachers, students, counselors, and parents. A 192-page facilitator's guide is included. Available for purchase from National Council of Teachers of Mathematics, 1906 Association Drive, Reston, VA 22091. Cost: $125 each videotape and guide; $375 for all four videotapes and guide. Also available for rental from Women and Mathematics Education, c/o Education Department, George Mason University, 4400 University Drive, Fairfax, VA 22030.

Fox, L. H. 1980. *The problem of women and mathematics.* A report to the Ford Foundation. New York: Ford Foundation.

Menard, S. L. 1979. *How high the sky? How far the moon?: An educational program for girls and women in math and science.* Newton, MA: WEEA Publishing Center.
This resource provides a way to integrate mathematics science and equity into a K−12 curriculum. It contains activities to help develop scientific and mathematical skills and show the relevance of these to technical jobs. It also contains sections on careers, role models, and an annotated list of resource materials.

National Council of Teachers of Mathematics 1984. *Handbook for conducting equity activities in mathematics education.* Helen Neely Cheek (Ed.). Reston, VA: NCTM.
This handbook contains extensive information and ideas regarding intervention programs and workshops aimed at promoting educational equity. The appendices contain several articles on women and minorities in mathematics.

Osen, L. M. 1974. *Women and mathematics.* Cambridge, MA: The MIT Press.
This book contains the biographies of eight women in history over the period 370 to 1935. The stated goals of the author were to "trace the impact women have had on the development of mathematical thought, to profile the lives of these women, and to explore the social context within which they worked."

Perl, T. 1978. *Math equals: Biographies of women mathematicians and related activities.* Menlo Park, CA: Addison-Wesley Publishing Company.
This book contains nine biographies of women mathematicians. Following each biography is an introduction to the area of mathematics in which the woman worked. The activities are very intriguing, and they provide an accessible entry into nontraditional mathematics.

Sadker, M. P., & Sadker, D. M. 1982. *Sex equity handbook for schools.* New York: Longman, Inc.
The handbook includes, among other things, discussion and guidelines regarding overcoming sex bias in classroom interaction and confronting sex bias in instructional materials, 22 lesson plans that deal with a variety of sex equity issues, and a resource directory.

Women's Educational Equity Act Publishing Center. *216 resources for educational equity.* Current catalog available from EDC/NEEA Publishing Center, 55 Chapel Street, Suite 215, Newton, MA 02160.

ASSOCIATIONS

Lawrence Hall of Science, University of California, Berkeley, CA 94720.

National Council of Teachers of Mathematics, 1906 Association Drive, Reston, VA 22091.

Women and Mathematics Education, c/o Education Department, George Mason University, 4400 University Drive, Fairfax, VA 22030.

REFERENCES

Bar-Tal, D. 1978. Attributional analysis of achievement-related behavior. *Review of Educational Research,* 48:259−271.

Bar-Tal, D., & Frieze, J. H. 1977. Achievement motivation for males and females as a determinant of attributions for success and failure. *Sex Roles,* 3:301−313.

Benbow, C. P., & Stanley, J. C. 1982. Consequences in high school and college of sex differences in mathematical reasoning ability: A longitudinal perspective. *American Educational Research Journal,* 19(4):598−622.

Brophy, J. E. 1985. Interactions of male and female students with male and female teachers. In L. C. Wilkinson & C. B. Marrett (Eds.), *Gender-related differences in the classroom.* New York: Academic Press.

Callahan, L. G., & Clements, D. H. 1984. Sex differences in rote-counting ability on entry to first grade: Some observations. *Journal for Research in Mathematics Education,* 15(5):378−382.

Crockett, L, J., & Peterson, A. C. 1984. Biology: Its role in gender-related educational experiences. In E. Fennema & M. J. Ayer (Eds.), *Women and education: Equity or equality?* Berkeley: McCutchan Publishing Corporation.

Deaux, D. 1976. A perspective on the attributional process. In J. Harvey, W. Ickes, & R. Kidd (Eds.), *New directions in attribution research* (Vol. 1). Hillsdale, NJ: Lawrence Erlbaum Associates.

Fennema, E. 1975. Spatial ability, mathematics, and the sexes. In E. Fennema (Ed.), *Mathematics learning: What research says about sex differences* (pp. 33−45). ERIC Center for Science, Mathematics, and Environmental Education, The Ohio State University.

Fennema, E. 1984. Girls, women, and mathematics. In E. Fennema & M. J. Ayer (Eds.), *Women and education: Equity or equality?* Berkeley: McCutchan Publishing Corporation.

Fennema, E., Reyes, L. H., Perl, T. H., & Konsin, M. A. 1980, April. *Cognitive and affective influences on the development of sex-related differences in mathematics.* Paper presented at the annual meeting of the American Educational Research Association, Boston, MA.

Fennema, E., & Sherman, J. A. 1978. Sex-related differences in mathematics achievement and related factors: A further study. *Journal for Research in Mathematics Education,* 9(3):189−203.

Fennema, E., & Tartre, L. A. 1985. The use of spatial skills in mathematics by girls and boys. *Journal for Research in Mathematics Education,* 16(3):184−206.

Fox, L. H. 1980. *The problem of women and mathematics.* A report to the Ford Foundation. New York: Ford Foundation.

Huston, A. C. 1983. Sex typing. In P. H. Mussen & E. M. Hetherington (Eds.), *Handbook of child psychology: Vol. 4. Socialization, personality, and social development* (4th ed.) (pp. 388−467). New York: Wiley.

Lockheed, M. E. 1984. Sex segregation and male pre-eminence in elementary classrooms. In E. Fennema & M. J. Ayer (Eds.), *Women and eduation: Equity or equality?* Berkeley: McCutchan Publishing Corporation.

Maccoby, E. E., & Jacklin, C. N. 1974. *The psychology of sex differences.* Stanford, CA: Stanford University Press.

Nash, S. C. 1979. Sex role as a mediator of intellectual functioning. In M. A. Peterson & A. C. Peterson (Eds.), *Sex-related differences in cognitive functioning: Developmental issues.* New York: Academic Press.

National Assessment of Educational Progress 1983. *The Third National Mathematics Assessment: Results, trends, and issues* (Report No. 13-MA-01). Denver: Education Commission of the States.

Osen, L. M. 1974. *Women and mathematics.* Cambridge, MA: The MIT Press.

Peterson, P. L., & Fennema, E. 1985. Effective teaching, student engagement in classroom activities, and sex-related differences in learning mathematics. *American Educational Research Journal,* 22(3):309–335.

Reyes, L. H. 1984. Affective variables and mathematics education. *The Elementary School Journal,* 84(5):558–581.

Seligman, M. E. P., & Maier, S. F. 1967. Failure to escape traumatic shock. *Journal of Experimental Psychology,* 74:1–9.

Senk, S., & Usiskin, Z. 1982. *Geometry proof writing: A new view of sex differences in mathematics ability.* Unpublished manuscript, University of Chicago.

Smith, S. E. 1980, October. *Enrollment and achievement by sex in mathematics and science for five 1978 regents samples.* Paper presented at Northeast Educational Research Association Convention, Ellenville, New York.

Stage, E. K., Kreinberg, N., Eccles (Parsons), J., & Becker, J. R. 1985. Women in mathematics, science, and engineering. In S. S. Klein (Ed.), *Handbook for achieving sex equity through education.* Baltimore, MD: The Johns Hopkins University Press.

Stockard, J., & Wood, J. W. 1984. The myth of female underachievement: A re-examination of sex differences in academic underachievement. *American Educational Research Journal,* 21(4):825–838.

Weiner, B. 1974. *Achievement motivation and attribution theory.* Morristown, NJ: General Learning Press.

Werdelin, I. 1961. *Geometrical ability and the space factor in boys and girls.* Lund, Sweden: C. W. K. Gleerup.

Wolleat, P. L., Pedro, J. D., Becker, A. D., & Fennema, E. 1980. Sex differences in high school students' causal attributions of performance in mathematics. *Journal for Research in Mathematics Education,* 11(5):356–366.

15 Mathematical Evaluation and Remediation

ROBERT UNDERHILL

Virginia Tech.

INTRODUCTION

Evaluation is, or should be, an important part of any school curriculum program. By evaluation we determine whether what we are doing is successful or something less than that. If it is not successful an effective program of evaluation can often provide general directions as well as specific steps for improvements.

Evaluation is much more than a mechanism for determining grades in mathematics. In fact, evaluation and grading are generally considered as related but very different concepts. Evaluation tends to deal with rates of progress and diagnosis of errors in thinking and learning. Grading often is little more than labeling that progress as excellent, satisfactory, needs improvement, or A, B, C, or according to some other system. As a result of being subjective in nature, various grading practices have undergone rather substantial criticism in recent years.

Evaluation on the other hand has always been and will continue to be a pivotal process in helping individual teachers, schools, and districts to improve the ways in which we attempt to educate our children.

The goal of this chapter is to provide a rationale and to develop guidelines for constructing specific evaluation and remediation skills. Primary emphasis is placed on the conceptualization of diagnostic and achievement tests of skills and understandings. Sample work is presented to help analyze content and develop tests of your own design. Remediation, retention activities, needs of slow learners, and the modification of student misconceptions or error patterns are also considered. Several activities are presented to help you amplify the ideas discussed.

THE ROLE OF EVALUATION IN THE SCHOOL MATHEMATICS PROGRAM

Evaluation is an aspect of teaching disliked by many teachers. Teachers readily remember when they were students and recognize familiar feelings of anxiety or discomfort. They do not like to be evaluated; they prefer not to evaluate.

Evaluation settings that tend to create learner feelings of discomfort and anxiety are those on which decisions are made such as grades and college entrance. These are referred to as *summative* evaluations; they have a sense of finality about them.

While teachers must make decisions with this sense of finality, there are times when the teacher's main purpose is to help learners; these are *formative* evaluations. Formative evaluations include formal diagnostic tests and informal assessments such as checking homework and observing learners. Formative evaluation is frequently limited by many teachers to helping learners with mathematical content, but valuable information about students' attitudes, anxiety, vision, hearing, home settings, and so on can also be gathered.

To teach effectively, you will need to evaluate your students. There are several questions you need to answer.

1. Why do I need information?
2. What type of information do I need?
3. How much of the information can I collect myself?
4. How can I collect the information?
5. Do I need any special instruments?
6. What do I do with the information after I gather it?

The answers to these questions may prove helpful in making important teaching decisions.

Why Do I Need Evaluation Information?

You need information to make decisions. Many decisions relate to questions *internal* to learners such as "What do they know at this time?" or "Why are they having difficulty?" These are *formative* needs. Others are related to questions *external* to the learner such as "How does she compare with other students?" or "What grade will he receive this grading period?" These are usually *summative*. In both situations, you need such information to do your job well.

What Type of Information Do I Need?

Teachers usually begin the school year with a need for more information about their students' mathematics performance. Thus, they often begin with a group test of mathematics achievement (summative) or some type of diagnostic instrument (formative). The former usually helps teachers get a feel for the makeup of a class; the latter usually yields more detail to help teachers plan instruction. Once instruction begins, teachers usually get considerable support from the objectives and tests that accompany most elementary school textbook series. While group tests can be used in most cases, sometimes teachers want more detail. This is available only by studying more closely the behavior of a single student.

Within mathematics, there are different types of learning and different levels of learning. These might be classified as:

	Understanding	Use
Concepts	a	b
Skills	c	d
Algorithms	e	f

The ability to *identify* a circle (a) is very different from the ability to *use* a circle to solve a design problem (b). Understanding how place value interacts with addition to permit us to add large numbers (c) is very different from solving problems that require a *decision* to add large numbers (d). And knowing how to regroup (carry and borrow) (e) is very different from using addition and subtraction algorithms efficiently (f). Learning and evaluation should rarely stop with *remembering;* they must also focus on *understanding* and *problem solving.*

Sometimes work samples do not provide the teacher with enough information to proceed. At these times the teacher may need to talk with parents, talk with the student, observe the student in class to discern possible vision or hearing impairments, and so on.

How Much Evaluation Data Can I Collect On My Own?

Teachers collect at least 95% of their own formative and summative information. They can also collect nearly all the other information needed to gain a better view of learner needs.

Observation is a powerful tool. When teachers teach, they receive a constant flow of student verbal and nonverbal information. One of the challenges of teaching is to sort this information. There is no perfect way to do it. When one child gazes out the window, he may be bored and have a poor attitude. However, this may also reflect thoughtfulness, fatigue, or an interesting event in the school yard! It is only by knowing students as unique persons and by being sensitive and aware that specific events become clearly understood: Is there a reason to think that Maria cannot hear in the back of the room? Is it possible that Mack worked the wrong problems because he couldn't read the assignment on the chalkboard? Are there problems in Frank's home that make him listless and fatigued and help explain why he often fails to finish his homework? Could it be that Ann is inattentive because she sometimes takes drugs?

How Can I Collect Information?

Informal observation is the strongest and most frequently used source of information. Observation takes place in the classroom; it also occurs in the halls, the playground, at school activities, and in the community at large. It even takes place when the students are not present! For example, teachers collect homework to see if students have completed their work and to spot check for certain types of errors or to discern whether students have grasped a concept or skill.

In addition to observations, there are evaluation instruments. They are generally of two varieties, teacher-made and commercial. Teacher-made tests are very common in the evaluation of daily, weekly, and unit instruction.

Do I Need Any Special Evaluation Instruments?

While observations and teacher-made tests supply nearly all of the information, sometimes special tools are needed. These evaluation tools might be categorized into the following types: Administration, Group, Individual, Cognitive, Affective, and Physical.

There are special tests to evaluate mathematics learning of groups (such as the Stanford Achievement Test) or for individuals (such as KeyMath). There are also instruments for measuring attitudes and anxiety (such as the Fennema-Sherman, see Chapter 14) and physical characteristics (such as charts for vision screening). Some individuals can be screened by classroom teachers; sometimes, because of available time and level of expertise required, individual tests are administered by physicians, or by school nurses, counselors, or psychologists.

What Do I Do With The Information?

Most information you gather will be used to help your students. However, you will also make decisions that are external to the learners. For example, you may need to assign grades or you may need to recommend "pass" or "no pass" to the next grade; you may use it to help recommend tracking into high, medium, or low ability groups; you may use it to help recommend that a child be admitted to a gifted program or a class for special learners.

Diagnostic tests are used to help you help learners. You may use them to help you decide on individual needs such as special work with manipulatives, a useful microcomputer program, or a game. You may also use the results to group learners for a series of lessons or a unit based on common needs. You may also need to make referrals or engage in consultations with others who possess greater skill than you related to vexing problems.

Evaluation is a major part of teaching. While some (summative) tend to give evaluation a bad name, most evaluation is designed to *help* learners (formative). By focusing on the "helping" uses, both teachers and learners can develop positive attitudes toward evaluation.

On the basis of several types of data, you may identify problems such as poor achievement, bad attitudes, poor self-concepts, visual impairments, or anxiety. On the basis of your observations, you can act. You may need to make referrals to specialists.

In this chapter, you will become familiar with information to help you evaluate successfully. You will also develop some evaluation skills, be introduced to some common commercial instruments, and review some remediation strategies.

Exercises

1. When will you need *formative* evaluation data?
2. When will you need *summative* evaluation data?
3. How can you help your students develop positive feelings about evaluation?

RESEARCH RELATED TO EVALUATION AND REMEDIATION

The 1980s has been the decade of broadly defined basic skills. The National Council of Teachers of Mathematics (NCTM) has provided strong leadership in the movement to redefine the basic skills. At the beginning of the decade, Denmark and Kepner (1980) surveyed 1600 members of NCTM to codify their beliefs about skills in mathematics. Selected results of their survey are reported in this section.

Diagnosis: The Cognitive Component

Two questions can be raised concerning the cognitive part of diagnosis: (1) What content is most important to diagnose and remediate, and (2) How do cognitive theories impact diagnosis? The study cited in the previous paragraph helps answer the first question. Following is a paraphrased list of outcomes believed to be important by the 1600 people surveyed (Denmark & Kepner, 1980). At least 75% of those surveyed agreed each of these is a basic skill:

1. Whole number computations
2. Reading and writing multidigit numerals
3. Memorizing basic facts
4. Decimal and percentage computation
5. Fraction computation
6. Conversions among percents, decimals, and fractions
7. Reading symbols
8. Using ratios and proportions
9. Using shortcuts and mental computations
10. Solving consumer and other practical problems
11. Reading maps
12. Solving unfamiliar problems
13. Finding the value of money, coins, and bills
14. Using estimates to check reasonableness
15. Estimating results of practical problems
16. Estimating lengths, distances, and weights
17. Using metric measures
18. Using English measures
19. Determining perimeters, areas, and volumes
20. Using formulas
21. Explaining place value
22. Reasoning logically
23. Solving problems with manipulatives
24. Recalling geometric properties of simple figures
25. Constructing simple figures
26. Interpreting tables, charts, and graphs
27. Remembering properties of operations
28. Using a hand calculator

The preceding list gives you a good idea *what* content to diagnose. *How* you diagnose seems straightforward, but it isn't. How you diagnose depends on the outcomes you are measuring. For example the following question could be used to evaluate a student's competence in addition computation.

$$
\begin{array}{r}
236 \\
+\ 497 \\
\hline
\end{array}
$$

This question evaluates Objective 1 in the preceding list at the level of accurate and efficient computation. However, at the level of *understanding* it is inadequate because learners can compute with memorized procedures. To evaluate understanding, refer to Objective 23 in the list; if the learner can use manipulatives to demonstrate sums, the statement that he or she *understands* can be made much more confidently.

Cognitive Products

What does the learner know? We will call the elements that comprise the answer to this question *cognitive products*. Here are some examples: (1) how to add, (2) how to construct a rectangle, (3) how to compute percents. Considerable work has been done on the evaluation of abstract cognitive products. Gagne (1962, 1965) demonstrated that even though concepts and their prerequisites can be learned in many different sequences, some pathways through the curriculum are more efficient than others. Of special interest is the work of White and Gagne (1978) in which they concluded that structures of learning and retention are identical. This important finding was used by Underhill, Uprichard, and Heddens (1980) when they presented clinical and group diagnostic models that reflected this finding. Textbook authors apply Gagne's ideas when they sequence concepts and skills; test designers apply White and Gagne's research findings when they construct diagnostic tests. The research results are important because they allow you to proceed from evaluation of simple to complex concepts and skills with some assurance that difficulties identified will, when remediated, produce benefits that extend to later concepts and skills.

The cognitive products considered so far are often mastered by learners by learning rote procedures. Bruner's (1966) proposal that humans have three ways of knowing, was used by Underhill (1972) to rationalize three ways to measure understanding or meaningfulness; he proposed evaluating learners' knowledge of relationships by evaluating procedures and objects, procedures and pictures, and procedures by themselves.

Another dimension of cognitive products is the *extent* to which a learner possesses a concept. A learner who recognizes a right triangle in the common upright position may not recognize a right triangle when the long side is used for the base. Similarly, Novillis (1976) found that learners possess many ideas related to "fraction" including parts of circular regions, parts of rectangles, parts of line segments, parts of sets, rectangles partitioned with oblique lines, and so on. She found that learners who have a "good" concept when presented with "usual" models often cannot respond correctly to rectangles such as the one presented in Fig. 15–1.

When you write an evaluation question, it represents only a sample of what a learner may know. If you ask two simple questions, you may get two positive learner responses. If you ask two difficult questions, you may get two negative responses. Be sure to decide in advance at what level you wish your students to

FIGURE 15–1
Four equal parts in a nonstandard arrangement

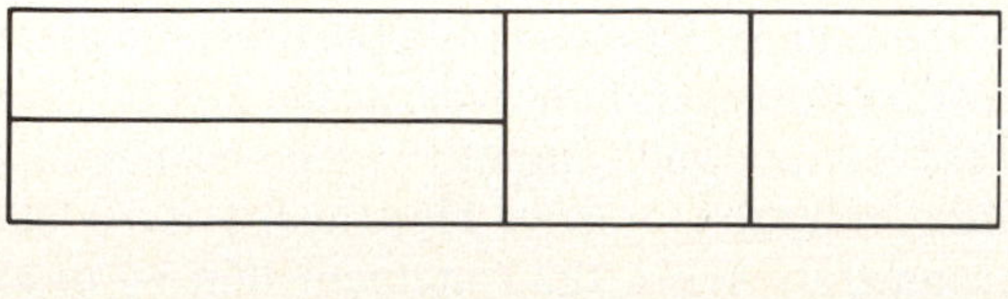

perform. Clearly, learner success is a function of teacher evaluation decisions *and* learner knowledge.

Nearly all group tests measure cognitive products. Some groups tests are successful at exploring mathematical processes or actions such as take-away subtraction or regrouping tens and ones. Individual or clinical evaluations are often needed to evaluate cognitive processes.

Cognitive Processes

When mathematical processes are evaluated and the learner responds, correct or incorrect cognitive processes can be inferred. However, when the learner is not correct, little is known about the cognitive processes. Sometimes inferences can be made from written work using error analysis techniques. If group methods do not produce adequate data, a clinical interview is the best way to proceed.

A Note of Caution

Sometimes wrong responses indicate a lack of a skill or concept; sometimes they do not. Studies by Casey (1979) and Clements (1982) indicate that between 20% and 40% of children's errors are careless errors. Students who are most prone to careless errors are "weak students who do not know that they do not know" and "mathematically competent and confident children, who know that they know." One simple way to reduce incorrect diagnoses is to *use more than one question to evaluate a given concept or skill*. If learners miss two questions, you can be more confident they lack the concept or skill than if they miss only one.

Diagnosis: The Affective Component

While there have been many studies of attitudes and anxiety over the past 30 years, there is fairly common agreement that attitudes and anxiety are difficult to measure in young learners (Aiken, 1976). There is a rather widely held view that affective traits in young learners are fairly unstable and yield low agreement when administered two or more times. Aiken (1976) reported that the two best scales for measuring attitudes of children as low as grade three are the Dutton-Likert (Dutton, 1954) and the Antonnen-revised Hoyt (Antonnen, 1969) scales. Most classroom teachers simply use observational data to evaluate affect. While it is reasonable to assume that attitudes and learning outcomes are related, there is insufficient research evidence to conclude that the relationship is cause–effect. Many children with poor attitudes do learn mathematics and vice versa.

REMEDIATION

A discussion of remediation can be helped by stating some beliefs about learning and knowing. Knowledge has traditionally been presented by an authority. The job of the teacher was to "give" mathematics to learners.

A Piagetian viewpoint that has greatly influenced educators is that there are only "inner realities." You and your friend have different realities; to the extent that you communicate successfully, they agree. To the extent that your realities differ, your communications are faulty. In this view, each person constructs his own reality. When he is aware of conflict or dissonance, he modifies his reality. In this view, the role of the teacher is different; instead of "giving" mathematics to the learner, the teacher helps learners (1) become aware that their beliefs are different, and (2) resolve the differences. For example when the learner believes that $3 + 4 = 7$ but also believes that two collections of three and four are more than a collection of seven, there is *potential* dissonance. Because these two beliefs are typical of children who do not conserve number, the example is a very common one. The task of the teacher is to use experiences and peer interaction to facilitate learner awareness of the conflicting beliefs. *Simply pointing out differences is of little value.* Under the traditional conception of teaching, the teacher points out that they are the same, gets the child to state that they are the same, and moves on. Under the newer conception, teachers realize the old approach had very limited value: while it is indeed possible to get children to make statements that are "correct" (the *teacher's* reality), questioning quickly reveals the learner doesn't really *believe* it (the *child's* reality)!

This conception of learning as an internal constructing activity has given rise to explorations of the teacher's role. If the teacher doesn't *give* knowledge, how does the teacher teach?

Several researchers in New York, Canada, England, and Pennsylvania are working on new models of teaching, which seem to be supportive of this view of learning. Bergeron and Herscovics (1981, 1982, 1984) have been developing a model for several years. They believe children start with *intuitive conceptions* based on their experiences. To these, learners add *procedural understandings* and then, through *reflection,* develop *mathematical abstractions.* Here is an example relating to early addition concepts:

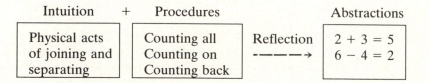

The job of the teacher is threefold: (1) help the learner develop intuitive knowledge for new concepts, (2) help the learner develop procedures, and (3) stimulate the learner to reflect about relationships between intuitions and procedures. From these reflections, the learner slowly develops abstractions.

Confrey (1984) suggests three ways to promote reflection. One way is to create a resource-rich environment in which the learner must make decisions and choices. These experiences are designed to make learners aware of their own mental activity: this is reflection. A second way is to promote learner interactions; this activity stimulates learner awareness of different points of view; the result is dissonance. And the third way is to teach learners to be reflective. To do this the teacher must help learners become more aware of themselves: their feelings, their thoughts, their actions.

In a remedial subtraction study, Omanson (1982) and Resnick (1984) examined two ways to help children. In one group children worked 25 problems with a "human robot" who wouldn't let them proceed if they were making errors; errors had to be corrected as they went along. In the second group, students did a one-to-one sequence of objects and steps in the problems, step by step. The purpose was to compare an error analysis approach (former) with an understanding approach (latter). They found the understanding group made immediate gains but went back to faulty computation after a few weeks. Is there nothing that works?

In England, Bell (1983) and Swan (1983) reported considerable work on diagnostic teaching with 14-year-old students. In treatments spanning about eight hours of teaching, Swan compared two remedial teaching styles. In the "positive only" group, he taught the misconceptions to alleviate them. In the "conflicting teaching," he used a strategy that forced students to become aware of and to reflect about their errors. Both groups made significant short-term gains and the gains held up over time. Further, the conflict group gains were greater (35.9% compared with 24.2%). From this work, a four-step teaching strategy was devised (Bell, 1984):

1. The teacher, in preparation for the conflict teaching, conducts a brief error analysis of faulty work to see which misconceptions need to be included in the lesson.
2. Students work math problems likely to expose the misconceptions.
3. A discussion is held to draw out all answers and discuss them. Students explain their incorrect answers. The teacher may put forward faulty arguments to force students to reflect.
4. Students work more math problems in writing.

There seems to be a strong connection between the amount of conflict induced and student gains. This is probably due to high levels of *reflective activity*.

Other Remediation Strategies

In addition to the conflict model, two other major points are helpful in designing remedial instruction. The first has to do with prerequisites. Is the order of instruction important, or can one just as easily teach the whole and parts simultaneously? Carnine (1980) examined this question in relation to the subskills of computing multiplication facts with 15 below-average first grade students. He found the part-then-whole approach to be much more efficient.

Finally, there is a concept of *metalearning*. Because reflective thinking has already been considered, it should come as no surprise that *learning* to *learn* is also an important outcome from a remedial point of view. Diagnoses and remediation of study skills and learning how to learn can enhance the global impact of the instructional program. One fine set of resources for helping achieve this goal is listed at the end of this chapter (Tobin, 1980).

Some Remediation Dos and Don'ts

Gather as much information as you need to be successful.
Appeal to children's intuitive knowledge.
Use manipulatives.
Use pictures and diagrams.
Use activities that promote peer interaction.
Check progress frequently.
Ask questions that promote reflection.
Allow time for reflection.
Increase wait-time when you ask questions.
Try another approach.
Use leading questions to help learners build their own meaning.
Use games when possible.
Look outside the classroom for remediation—home, counseling, medical specialists, and so forth.
Relate content to out-of-school experiences.
Stress concept development and problem solving.
Interact with learners daily, one on one.
Conduct mini-interviews in troublesome cases.
Be very patient.

Don't stress pencil and paper.
Don't allow students to practice errors.
Don't hurry.
Don't jump into symbol manipulation.
Don't overemphasize computation.
Don't emphasize isolated, single student activity.

Exercises

1. Which basic skills in the list presented do you think should be mastered by the end of third grade?
2. Write five questions to measure *understanding* of fraction concepts. Rank them from easiest to hardest. Exchange your set with a partner. Do you agree?

3. What observational data would lead you to conclude that your student likes math? Dislikes?

4. Examine the homework of a group of learners. Use their errors as the basis for a conflict lesson.

PROVISIONS FOR INDIVIDUAL DIFFERENCES

Two topics are presented in this section that impact the success of diagnostic/remedial activities. They are (1) characteristics of slow learners and (2) memory.

Slow Learners

Since World War II, mathematics has been an important outcome of schooling for every person. In 1972, the need to address instructional concerns of the lower ability range was recognized by the National Council of Teachers of Mathematics when it published a yearbook entitled *The Slow Learner in Mathematics* (NCTM, 1972). This trend was underscored by the 1975 passage of PL 94-142, the Education for All Handicapped Children Act.

What are some of the characteristics of slow learners? How can they be met?

1. Because of histories of failure, slow learners often need a high proportion of success experiences. *Implication:* Present mathematics content in small increments with plenty of practice. Several brief periods of learning and practice are more effective than one or two longer periods.

2. Slow learners often need immediate rather than deferred gratification. *Implication:* Try to provide feedback on tests the day they are administered.

3. Slow learners often have incorrect procedures which should *not* be rehearsed. *Implication:* When you make assignments, allow time for in-class work. Informally observe students and review a couple problems at the beginning of the assignment before students leave for the day.

4. Slow learners often have poor attitudes and low motivation. *Implication:* Use games and activities which permit students to get up and move about; allow students to work in pairs; bring in topics and projects of interest to the age group.

5. Slow learners often have more difficulty remembering concepts and skills. *Implication:* Provide more than the usual amount of practice, preferably through games.

6. Slow learners often are poor readers. *Implication:* Try to use audiotapes, working in pairs, and heterogeneous grouping.

7. Slow learners often develop abstractions more slowly. *Implication:* Permit slow learners to use objects, pictures, and diagrams such as number lines or tables until they seem ready to cease using them.

8. Slow learners tend to forget concepts and skills more readily than their faster peers. *Implication:* Implement periodic practice of important concepts and skills on a 5-minute-each-day or half-hour-each-week basis.

Memory

Short-term memory (STM) (measured in seconds) and long-term memory (LTM) (measured in minutes, hours, days, or weeks) play a vital role in learning mathematics. Learners retain mathematical knowledge in long-term memory (LTM). The following strategies and principles can be used by teachers to help learners store knowledge in LTM:

1. *Verbal rehearsal.* Repeating information orally helps the transition from STM to LTM. When a visual, such as a flash card, is provided, multisensory data are available to enhance LTM storage. Verbalization is crucial to LTM.
2. *Meaningfulness.* Meaningful material is remembered because it allows the learner to make logical connections with other knowledge. Meaning is often provided by social contexts which are familiar to the learner, building upon learners' intuitive knowledge, presenting new information as extensions of existing ideas, and through the use of manipulatives, which help establish relationships between "real-world" knowledge and "mathematical" knowledge.
3. *Attention.* If one is intently concentrating on a task, one is obviously more likely to remember it. You can enhance attention by making activities interesting and motivational (see attitudes and motivation, earlier).
4. *Involvement.* Passivity tends to foster inattention; involvement fosters attention. Games, group activities, manipulatives, and lab exercises promote attention.

Sensory data are stored in STM while solving mathematical tasks. Actually, tasks draw upon LTM, STM, and external storage (see Fig. 15–2). For example, when you add 346 + 429, you write the problem on a piece of paper (external storage), call on the procedure or algorithm from LTM, and process the steps of the algorithm in STM. Because STM storage is quite small (about the size of a telephone number!), enhancing its effective use is *quite* important.

FIGURE 15–2

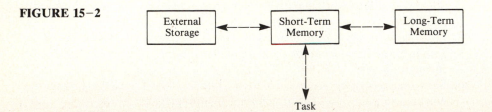

One way is for STM to draw upon some of the contents of LTM "automatically," that is, with little attention or thought (Gagne, 1983). This is a powerful argument for practicing LTM skills such as addition and multiplication until performing them requires hardly any mental effort.

Exercises

1. Work with a partner to choose a concept or skill. Describe one or more activities you can use with slow learners to meet their special needs.
2. Select a unit in a grade level of your choice. What can you do in teaching this unit to help your students retain the concepts and skills?

DIAGNOSTIC PROCEDURES

In this section you will learn some specific diagnostic strategies. After an overview of some important factors, you will learn how to make your own tests. The main focus of this section is on the needs of the classroom teacher. While textbooks often provide error analysis sections as part of specific lessons, classroom teachers usually rely on group tests for formal diagnostic information. Routine observations and homework are the main sources of information about individuals. For a detailed treatment of clinical diagnostic models and strategies, you may wish to refer to Underhill et al. (1980), Reisman (1982), and Fennell (1981), whose works emphasize teacher-made tests. A list of common commercial tests is presented at the end of this chapter.

Mathematical Content

The fundamental question to answer is, "What content do I evaluate?" While most textbooks provide objectives and even chapter tests, the answer to this question is still ambiguous: while on the one hand teachers simply evaluate what they teach, they must also successfully sort out and emphasize ideas according to their importance. There are several major sources to help answer the question:

1. School district curriculum guides
2. Textbook coverage
3. Recommendations of professional organizations
4. Local school board guidelines
5. The information in this book

Given these sources, each teacher must balance different expectations and specify some objectives, especially in small school districts where there are no curriculum guides and no subject-matter supervisors. A sample sequence will now be presented based on some assumptions that, for discussion purposes, are assumed to have been developed by examining 1, 2, 3, and 4 preceding. The following goals will be assumed. (This list is a modification of lists first presented by Underhill (1975).)

Learners in the K−6 whole number addition curriculum will

1. Compute with whole numbers
2. Use calculators
3. Acquire meaningful concepts and skills
4. Commit to memory the basic addition facts
5. Use rounding and estimation to establish reasonableness of results

Once the main goals are specified, the textbook and curriculum guide can be used to develop a list of important skills and concepts that account for prerequisites and that cover the objectives. For discussion purposes, here is such a list relating to calculation.

	Content	Sample Evaluation Items
1.	Sums, 0−5	$1 + 3 =$
2.	Sums, 6−9	$4 + 3 =$
3.	Count to 10	1, 2, 3, 4, 5, _, _, _, _, _
4.	Groups of 4, 5, 6	How many groups of five fingers have you?
5.	Group tens and concepts of 11−20	One ten and three ones = _____
6.	Sums > 9	$7 + 8 =$
7.	Three addends, sums < 20	$6 + 3 + 5 =$
8.	Counting by tens	10, 20, _, _, 50, _
9.	Tens ones = One ten	How many ones in 23?
10.	Add tens	$20 + 30 =$
11.	Regroup tens and ones	4 tens 13 ones =
12.	Numbers through 99	46, 47, 48, _, _, _
13.	Add tens and ones, no regrouping	$34 + 21 =$
14.	Add tens and ones, with regrouping	$47 + 25 =$
15.	Estimate reasonableness of answers by using upper and lower limits, for example, $40 < 24 + 19 < 50$	Round both numbers up and add; then round both numbers down and add: $27 + 36 =$
16.	Three two-digit addends, sum < 100	$13 + 53 + 19 =$
17.	Remember the basic facts through 10	(Administer a three-minute timed test.)

	Content	*Sample Evaluation Items*
18.	Counting by 100s	400, 500, 600, ___, ___, ___
19.	Counting to 1000	595, 596, 597, ___, ___, ___
20.	Three-digit addends, no regrouping	234 + 425 =
21.	Regroup tens and hundreds	2 hundreds 13 tens 7 ones =
22.	Three-digit addends with regrouping	249 + 372 =
23.	Remember all 100 addition facts	(Administer 5-minuted timed test.)
24.	Three three-digit addends	216 + 492 + 185 =
25.	Use a calculator to add one-, two-, and three-digit addends	(Use calculator.)
26.	Ten 100s = One 1000	1 thousand 24 hundreds =
27.	Estimate large sums by using averaging	6842 4213 + 8940
28.	Estimate sums using front-end estimates	6845 319 1200 + 645
29.	Estimate sums using the rule of five	Round and add using the rule of five: 37 + 42 =

Because curricula can be organized many ways, a particular framework is merely an example. The main task is to encompass the school goals within the framework. Here is a sample framework:

1. Whole number operations
2. Rational number operations
3. Measurement
4. Geometry
5. Problem solving
6. Preoperational and number theory concepts

The labels are not as important as the *organization* within categories and the inclusion of all important outcomes. For example, some schemes do not include problem solving as a separate category. This is to emphasize that problem solving should cut across *all* areas of the curriculum rather than be treated as a separate topic. Some school districts mention it separately for emphasis; they want to call attention to its great importance. Thus, the sample framework above might yield several sequence lists. In the third grade, for example, you might establish the following major curriculum units:

Whole number addition
Whole number subtraction
Measurement
Geometry and graphing
Whole number multiplication
Whole number division
Problem solving
Rational number addition

After you develop unit sequences, you can use them to design evaluations. At the third-grade level you might develop the following sequences:

Whole number addition, Grade 3
For most classrooms, #9 through #25 in the preceding list encompasses the performance of most learners.

Whole number subtraction, Grade 3

1. Subtracts tens and ones without regrouping
2. Subtract tens and ones with regrouping
3. Estimation
4. Remember facts
5. Subtract hundreds and tens without regrouping
6. Three-digit subtraction with regrouping
7. Use a calculator for subtraction

Whole number multiplication, Grade 3

1. Skip counting
2. Products < 20
3. Products > 20
4. Tens and ones times ones without regrouping
5. Tens and ones times ones with regrouping
6. Tens and ones times tens
7. Hundreds, tens and ones times ones
8. Remember multiplication facts
9. Estimation
10. Use a calculator for multiplication

Whole number division, Grade 3

1. Repeated subtraction (readiness)
2. Quotients using numbers < 20
3. Quotients using facts through 45
4. Division by 0 and 1
5. Meaning of *all* facts
6. Tens and ones divided by ones, no remainder

7. Tens and ones divided by ones, with remainder
8. Hundreds, tens, ones divided by ones

Fraction addition

1. Fraction concepts
2. More than, less than—same denominator
3. More than, less than—same numerator
4. Sums, same denominator, no regrouping
5. Mixed numerals and regrouping
6. Sums, same denominator, with regrouping

Fraction subtraction

1. Differences, same denominator, no regrouping
2. Differences, same denominator, with regrouping

Measurement

1. Length—inch, millimeter, centimeter, foot—measuring and regrouping (no conversions)
2. Weight—pound, ounce, kilogram (no conversions)
3. Volume—pint, cup, teaspoon, tablespoon (with regrouping)
4. Length—estimation—yards, meters, inches, centimeters
5. Weight—estimation—ounces, pounds, kilograms
6. Volume—estimation—quarts, liters, cups
7. Time—estimation—seconds
8. Money—adding, subtracting, and making change to $1.00

Geometry and graphing

1. Classification of simple shapes in two dimensions
2. Free-hand drawing of simple shapes in two dimensions
3. Using common two-dimensional shapes to construct figures
4. Classification of simple three-dimensional shapes
5. Cardboard construction of simple three-dimensional shapes
6. Construct two-dimensional and three-dimensional patterns

Problem solving

1. Traditional story problems ($+$, $-$, $\times$, $\div$)
2. Games and puzzles
3. Real-world problem situations
4. Problems with extraneous information
5. Interdisciplinary problems
6. Multistep problems
7. Using simple heuristics
8. Solving nonroutine problems

When available, such sequences define the outline of the curriculum with a fair amount of detail. When you begin the year, you can review for a short time and then administer a *survey* test to help you plan your work for the year. *A survey test evaluates performance on a broad range of content at the abstract or symbolic level.* For example, you might prepare a survey test that covers all the whole number operations. Study the following example.

You are the third-grade teacher; the first two weeks you work on lab-type activities, drill and practice games, and whole class review to rebuild whole number skills, which have gotten "rusty" over the summer. After the review, you have a "feel" for the class so you prepare a survey test to establish a mosaic of class performance and diagnose the needs of each student in the class. Based on your work of the first two weeks, you decide the following ranges in the sequence lists stated earlier will encompass the whole number performances of all your students at this time:

Topic	Range	Number To Be Tested	Number of Questions
Addition	9–22	14, including facts	26
Subtraction	1–5	5, including facts	8
Multiplication	2–4	3	6
Division	2	1	2

First, you administer timed tests on the addition and subtraction facts. Based on the results, you assign certain students to work on the facts they have not retained. Next, you construct a survey test. The survey test is constructed by using two questions for each topic. Thus, there are 13 addition categories (excluding facts) evaluated by 26 questions. Similarly, there will be eight subtraction questions, six multiplication questions, and two division questions. Study the sample test in Fig. 15–3.

FIGURE 15–3

<u>Sample Survey Test</u>

<u>Directions:</u> Please answer as many of these questions as you can. If the problems are too hard, go on to the next part.

<u>Part I.   Addition</u>

1. How many ones in 13?   ___13___

2. How many ones in 20?   ___20___

(Continued)

3. 20
   + 30
   ‾‾‾‾
    50

4. 50
   + 40
   ‾‾‾‾
    90

5. 4 tens 13 ones = ___53___
6. 6 tens 12 ones = ___72___

Complete 7 and 8.

7. 46, 47, 48, 49, 50, 51
8. 27, 28, 29, 30, 31, 32

9. 34
   + 21
   ‾‾‾‾
    55

10. 81
    + 12
    ‾‾‾‾
     93

11. ¹47
    + 25
    ‾‾‾‾
     72

12. ¹27
    + 18
    ‾‾‾‾
     45

Estimate results in 13 and 14 by rounding up and rounding down.

13. 36   30   40
    + 42 +40 +50
    ‾‾‾‾ ‾‾‾ ‾‾‾
          70   90

14. 55   50   60
    + 37 +30 +40
    ‾‾‾‾ ‾‾‾ ‾‾‾
          80   100

15. ¹21
     47
    + 18
    ‾‾‾‾
     86

16. ¹49
     12
    + 17
    ‾‾‾‾
     78

Complete the following:

17. 100, 200, 300, 400, 500
18. 600, 700, 800, 900, 1000
19. 277, 278, 279, 280, 281, 282
20. 595, 596, 597, 598, 599, 600, 601

21. 234
    + 425
    ‾‾‾‾‾
     659

22. 613
    + 145
    ‾‾‾‾‾
     758

23. 2 hundreds 13 tens 7 ones = ___337___
24. 3 hundreds 15 tens 0 ones = ___450___

25. ¹¹249
    + 372
    ‾‾‾‾‾
     621

26. ¹¹157
    + 675
    ‾‾‾‾‾
     832

Part II.   Subtraction

1. 57
   − 22
   ‾‾‾‾
    35

2. 87
   − 24
   ‾‾‾‾
    63

3. ⁶7̷1
   − 34
   ‾‾‾‾
    37

4. ⁵6̷5
   − 28
   ‾‾‾‾
    37

5 and 6. Round up/down and down/up.

5. 62   60   70
   − 34 −40 −30
   ‾‾‾‾ ‾‾‾ ‾‾‾
         20   40

6. 84   80   90
   − 66 −70 −60
   ‾‾‾‾ ‾‾‾ ‾‾‾
         10   30

7. 840
   − 310
   ‾‾‾‾‾
    530

8. 762
   − 441
   ‾‾‾‾‾
    321

Part III.   Multiplication

1. 4
   ×3
   ‾‾
   12

2. 2
   ×6
   ‾‾
   12

3. 6
   ×7
   ‾‾
   42

4. 8
   ×4
   ‾‾
   32

5. 12
   × 3
   ‾‾‾
   36

6. 34
   × 2
   ‾‾‾
   68

Part IV.   Division

1. 18 ÷ 3 = ___6___

2. 12 ÷ 4 = ___3___

By recording only the number of items missed in such a test, you can see at a glance how the group performed. By looking down a single column of the evaluation table you can see how a given learner performed. By looking across a single row, you can see the group performance on a given concept or skill.

Of the five objectives identified earlier, this survey test has provided diagnostic data on the following:

1. Compute with whole numbers
5. Use rounding and estimation to establish reasonableness of results.

With the use of a timed test, 4, "Commit to memory the basic addition facts," was also considered. Information was *not* collected on the use of calculators but will be later in the year after it has been taught. That leaves only 3, "Acquire meaningful concepts and skills"; the survey test by design will not evaluate this objective.

	Marcie	Tony	Alice	Frank	....
Addition					
Tens and ones	2	1			
Adding tens					
Regrouping ones	2	2	2	2	
2D* counting					
2D w/o regrouping					
2D w/ regrouping	1	1	2	2	
Estimation	2	2	1	1	
2D column		2			
Counting 100s					
3D* counting					
3D w/o regrouping					
Reg. 10s					
3D w/ regrouping	1	2	2	2	
Subtraction					
2D w/o regrouping					
2D w/ regrouping	1	1	2	2	
Estimation	2	2	1	1	
3D w/o regrouping					
Multiplication					
Facts < 20					
Facts ≥ 20					
2D × 1D w/o reg.	1			1	
Division					
Concept	2	2	2	2	

*2D = two-digit; 3D = three-digit.

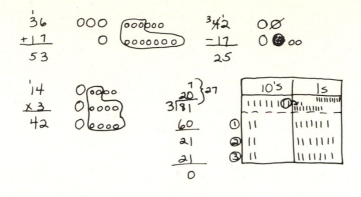

FIGURE 15–4

MEANINGFULNESS

As has been noted throughout this book, meaningfulness of concepts and skills generally means the learner can relate his or her learning to objects, pictures, and diagrams. This knowledge requires evaluation by some means other than survey tests.

Informal methods such as observation and studying homework allow you to evaluate meaningfulness when the class activities and homework are designed to teach and provide practice for meaningful learning. When you want a more formal evaluation, you can administer a second type of test, the *analytical test*. *An analytical test evaluates a much narrower range of mathematical content and evaluates for meaningfulness*. A group test to evaluate meaningfulness usually uses pictures and diagrams.

A teacher can evaluate meaningfulness of measurement, fractions, and tens and ones because pictures of these topics are quite common. However, there are many concepts and skills for which some common or standard pictures do not exist. This requires that you be more resourceful. Four examples are presented in Fig. 15–4, one for each whole number operation.

Analytic tests are usually administered at the end of a unit to determine the extent to which learners have meaningfully learned the content. Students can use the same kinds of pictures and diagrams on the test they used in class and homework. One major reason why it is important to measure meaningful learning is because evaluation is often the engine that runs learning. Because most students will be content to learn only those skills you choose to evaluate, *they will simply memorize procedures if you do not evaluate meaningful learning*.

SUMMING UP

Begin with a list of important outcomes. These are available from most publishers of text series. If one is not available you can construct one by using the textbook your school district has adopted. Once you have the list, use it to: (1) plan curriculum, (2) conduct a survey diagnosis of the class in the fall or a new pupil any time during the year, (3) plan meaningful instruction, and (4) conduct periodic analytical testing.

If you wish to use a commercial test, consult the list of the most commonly used commercial survey tests at the end of this chapter. If you wish to conduct a clinical (individual) appraisal, either use the same list but conduct the evaluation as an interview *with manipulatives* or use a commercial clinical instrument such as KeyMath.

Exercises

1. Write a sample sequence of five subconcepts or skills for one of these:
   a. Addition facts
   b. Area measurement
   c. Subtraction of fractions
   d. Multiplication of whole numbers
2. Prepare a survey test for subtraction of fractions, whole number multiplication, or some other unit with at least five subconcepts or skills.
3. Write a five-item sequence for a unit and prepare an analytical test to evaluate meaningful learning of these five topics in a *group setting*.
4. Administer, score, tabulate, and interpret the results of a survey for at least three students.
5. Administer, score, tabulate, and interpret the results of an analytical test for at least one student.
6. Select a standardized test. Administer it to at least one learner. Score and interpret the results.

SUMMARY CHAPTER 15

This chapter developed the case for evaluation as an important component of any mathematics program. The connection between evaluation and remediation was articulated. Resources were identified and suggestions for the classroom teacher were made.

There are two types of evaluation: Evaluations that collect information to *help* learners (formative), and evaluations that collect information to make decisions other than helping decisions (summative). Formative evaluations are diagnostic and include information that is physical (for example, vision), cognitive (for examples, skills, concepts), and affective (for example, attitudes, anxiety, interests). Summative evaluations are usually cognitive only and are often used to make decisions about the efficiency of lessons, units, and programs and ultimately about grades and placement of students.

Cognitive evaluations can be carried out informally through observations, discussions, and the interpretation of homework. They can also be formal as in the use of teacher-made and commercial tests. Sound evaluation instruments are based on teaching objectives and seek to evaluate abstract outcomes (survey tests) and understanding (analytical tests). Measuring learner understanding requires the use of questions that extend beyond the use of procedures that can be rotely applied. Understanding can be evaluated by manipulating objects, demonstrating relations between symbols and pictures and diagrams, explaining, and solving nonroutine problems. Conversations and interviews with children often provide the most detailed assessment of mathematical understanding.

When learners do not learn or do not remember, some form of remediation is necessary. Techniques to help learners with original learning and with remembering were presented. The conflict model of teaching was presented to help with the unlearning of incorrect knowledge and skills.

By applying the information and skills of this chapter, you can be a more effective teacher. Remember, special care in planning and delivering the initial instruction is your main vehicle for minimizing the need for remedial instruction.

DIAGNOSTIC INSTRUMENTS*

Mathematical Content

Adston Mathematics Skill Series 1979. *Readiness for Operations; Working with Whole Numbers; Common Fractions; Decimal Numbers*. Adston Educational Enterprises, Inc.

Brueckner Diagnostic Test in Decimals. 1942. Educational Test Bureau of Educational Publishers, Inc.

Brueckner Diagnostic Test in Fractions. 1942. Educational Test Bureau of Educational Publishers, Inc.

Brueckner Diagnostic Test in Whole Numbers. 1942. Educational Test Bureau of Educational Publishers, Inc.

Buswell-John Fundamental Processes in Arithmetic. 1925. Bobbs-Merrill Co., Inc.

Diagnostics Mathematics Inventory. 1975. CTB/McGraw-Hill.

Iowa Test of Preschool Development. GO-MO.

KeyMath Diagnostic Arithmetic Test. 1971. American Guidance Service, Inc.

Kraner Preschool Math Inventory. Learning Concepts.

Mann-Suiter Developmental Arithmetic Inventory. Allyn and Bacon, Inc.

Stanford Diagnostic Arithmetic Test. 1976. Harcourt, Brace, Jovanovich, Inc.

Stanford Early School Achievement Test. 1969. Harcourt, Brace, Jovanovich, Inc.

Mathematical Affect

Arithmetic Attitude Scale. 1961. In *Arithmetic for Teachers*. Englewood Cliffs, NJ: Prentice-Hall.

*The interested reader can locate the appropriate publisher's addresses or locate the actual test bureau in *Handbook of Mental Tests and Mental Measurements*.

Attitude Toward Arithmetic Scale. 1968, February. *The Elementary School Journal*, 68.

Attitude Toward Mathematics Scale. 1974. In M. Suydam (Ed.), *Evaluation in the Mathematics Classroom: From What and Why to How and Where*. ERIC.

Mathematics Attitude Scale. 1972, March. *Arithmetic Teacher*, 19.

Survey of School Attitudes. 1975. Harcourt, Brace, Jovanovich, Inc.

Representative General Instruments

Illinois Test of Psycholinguistic Abilities. 1968. University of Illinois Press.

Keystone Visual Survey Tests. 1961. Mast/Keystone.

Marianne Frostig Developmental Test of Visual Perception. 1964. Consulting Psychologists Press.

McCarthy Scales of Children's Abilities. 1972. Psychological Corp.

Memory for Designs Test. 1973. Psychological Test Specialists.

Slossen Intelligence Test for Children and Adults. 1963. Slossen Educational Publications.

Wechsler Intelligence Scale for Children. (WISCR). 1949. Psychological Corp.

REFERENCES

Aiken, L. 1976. Update on attitudes and other affective variables on learning mathematics. *Review of Educational Research*, 46:293–311.

Antonnen, R. 1969. A longitudinal study in mathematics attitude. *Journal of Educational Research*, 62:467–471.

Bell, A. 1983. Diagnostic teaching of additive and multiplicative problems. In R. Herschkowitz (Ed.), *Proceedings of the Seventh International Conference for the Psychology of Mathematics Education*. Rehovat, Israel: Weizmann Institute of Science.

Bell, A. 1984. Short and long term learning—experiments in diagnostic teaching design. In *Proceedings of the Eighth International Conference for the Psychology of Mathematics Education*. Darlinghurst NSW, Australia: Mathematical Association of NSW.

Bergeron, J., & Herscovics, N. 1981. Problems related to the application of a model of understanding to elementary school mathematics. In T. Post and M. Roberts (eds.), *Proceedings of the Third Annual Meeting of PME-NA*. Minneapolis: U. of Minnesota.

Bergeron, J., & Herscovics, N. 1982. A constructivist model of understanding. In S. Wagner (Ed.), *Proceedings of the Fourth Annual Meeting of PME-NA*. Athens, GA: University of Georgia.

Bruner, J. 1966. *Toward a theory of instruction*. New York: Norton.

Carnine, D. 1980. Preteaching versus concurrent teaching of the component skills of a multiplication algorithm. *Journal for Research in Mathematics Education*, 11:375–378.

Casey, D. 1979. *An analysis of errors made by junior secondary pupils on written mathematical tasks*. Unpublished master's thesis. Quebec: Monash University.

Clements, M. 1982. Careless errors made by sixth-grade children on written mathematical tasks. *Journal for Research in Mathematics Education*, 13:136–144.

Confrey, J. 1984. *Towards a framework for constructionist instruction*. A paper presented at the Annual Meeting of the North American Chapter of the International Group for the Psychology of Mathematics Education, Madison, WI.

Denmark, T., & Kepner, H. 1980. Basic skills in mathematics: a survey. *Journal for Research in Mathematics Education,* 11:104–123.

Dutton, W. 1954. Measuring attitudes toward arithmetic. *Elementary School Journal,* 55:24–31.

Fennel, F. 1981. *Elementary mathematics diagnosis and correction kit.* West Nyack, NY: Center for Applied Research in Education.

Gagne, R. 1962. The acquisition of knowledge. *Psychological Review,* 62:355–365.

Gagne, R. 1965. *The conditions of learning.* New York: Holt, Rinehart & Winston.

Gagne, R. 1983. . . . Some issues in the psychology of mathematics instruction. *Journal for Research in Mathematics Education,* 14:7–18.

National Council of Teachers of Mathematics. 1972. *The slow learner in mathematics.* 35th Yearbook. Reston, VA: NCTM.

Novillis, C. 1976. An analysis of the fraction concept into a hierarchy of selected subcomponents and the testing of the hierarchical dependencies. *Journal for Research in Mathematics Education,* 7:131–144.

Omanson, S. 1982. Instruction by mapping: Its effects on understanding and skill in subtraction. Unpublished master's thesis, University of Pittsburgh, Pittsburgh, PA.

Reisman, F. 1982. *A guide to the diagnostic teaching of arithmetic* (3rd ed.). Columbus, OH: Charles E. Merrill.

Resnick, L. 1984. Beyond error analysis: The role of understanding in elementary school mathematics. In H. Cheek (Ed.), *Diagnostic and prescriptive mathematics: Issues, ideas and insights.* Kent, OH: Research Council for Diagnostic and Prescriptive Mathematics.

Swan, M. 1983. Teaching decimal place value—A comparative study of "conflict" and "positive only" approaches. In R. Herschkowitz (Ed.), *Proceedings of the Seventh International Conference for the Psychology of Mathematics Education.* Rehovat, Israel: Weizmann Institute of Science.

Tobin, C. 1980. *Math study skills program.* Reston, VA: National Council of Teachers of Mathematics and the National Association of Secondary School Principals.

Underhill, R. 1975. *Methods of teaching elementary school mathematics.* Columbus, OH: Charles E. Merrill.

Underhill, R. 1981. *Teaching elementary school mathematics* (3rd ed.) Columbus, OH: Charles E. Merrill.

Underhill, R., Uprichard, A., & Heddens, J. 1980. *Diagnosing mathematical difficulties.* Columbus, OH: Charles E. Merrill.

White, R., & Gagne, R. 1978. Formative evaluation applied to a learning hierarchy. *Contemporary Educational Psychology,* 3:87–94.

Epilogue

You have undoubtedly noticed several themes recurring throughout this book. Keep in mind that the authors wrote their chapters independently. They were asked only to present their topic in a format usable by teachers and from a point of view that best represents state of the art thinking in the area. So these recurring themes must suggest that there is widespread agreement among the experts about the ways in which mathematics should be taught to young people.

The recurring themes are:

1. Mathematics must be taught in a meaningful way. Rote approaches, techniques, and procedures are short-sighted and do not serve the students' best interests over the long run.
2. Learning occurs best when it proceeds from the simple to the complex and from the concrete to the abstract. A variety of actual real-world situations, manipulative materials, and laboratory experiences can be used to enhance the quality of any mathematics program by developing the foundations upon which later abstraction can be based.
3. The scope of the mathematics program must be expanded to include topics not included in traditional programs.
4. Many concepts are complex and require extended time periods and repeated exposures. Successive experiences should expand both breadth and depth.
5. Symbolic algorithms should be delayed until students have developed intuitive understandings of the topics involved. Premature abstraction will lead to future difficulties.

6. Calculator usage can add a dimension to the mathematics program never before possible. It frees up time, allows the consideration of more realistic programs, and releases many students from the burden of tedious, time-consuming, and rote manipulations. It should be a constant presence in the mathematics classroom.

7. The stereotypical model of students working alone at their desks working problem sets needs to be expanded to include small group discussions, project work, and students working cooperatively rather than competitively. Students must talk about mathematical ideas and concepts.

These themes if implemented will immeasurably improve the quality of your mathematics program. The challenges are great but so are the opportunities. Good teaching!!

T.R.P.

About the Authors

THOMAS R. POST is currently professor of mathematics education at the University of Minnesota at Minneapolis. He has taught mathematics in public schools in New York State and a wide variety of undergraduate and graduate courses in mathematics education at Minnesota. These courses have focused on methods, research, manipulative materials, remedial instruction, and the psychology of mathematical conceptual development. He has conducted research dealing with mathematical learning and concept development. He is interested in the implications which psychologically related findings have for the development of instructional activities particularly those which utilize manipulative materials.

Dr. Post has served as national co-chairperson of the Special Interest Group—Research in Mathematics Education of the AERA, as chairperson of The North American Chapter of the International Group for the Psychology of Mathematics Education (NA-PME), and on the editorial board of the *Journal for Research in Mathematics Education.* He has been co-principal investigator of the National Science Foundation supported Rational Number Project, designed to gain information on the nature of the cognitive structures employed in children's learning of rational number concepts and to investigate the role of these concepts in the development of proportional reasoning skills. In April 1987 the fourth cooperative NSF grant was received. This effort will deal with assessment of elementary teachers conceptions of mathematics and the subsequent development of leadership teams within the Minneapolis Public Schools.

Dr. Post has co-authored two other texts, one related to the mathematics laboratory, the other to interdisciplinary approaches to curriculum. His publications also include 13 book chapters and over 50 journal articles, technical reports and papers currently under review. He has given more than sixty research related presentations at state, national, and international meetings.

He has been to England several times and has been influenced by the philosophy and organization of the British Primary School. He considers the coauthors of this book to be personal friends as well as professional colleagues.

JULIE ANGHILERI is Senior Lecturer of Mathematical Education at the Froebel Institute College, Roehampton Institute of Higher Education, London, England. She has two degrees from the University of London and has done extensive work in schools with children and teachers relating to all aspects of primary school mathematics. She has been involved in both initial training and in-service training for undergraduate and graduate students.

MERLYN BEHR is Professor of Mathematical Sciences and Education at Northern Illinois University and has been a teacher educator for more than 20 years. His experience in teacher education includes work with undergraduate pre-service elementary and secondary mathematics teachers, and work with teachers at the graduate level.

Professor Behr has been involved extensively in research concerned with how children learn mathematics. His early interests were with children's learning of computational algorithms. For the past 10 years his research has been directed at investigations of how children learn fraction and rational number concepts, with more recent attention given to the development of proportional reasoning ability in children. Through his research work, Professor Behr has had extensive experience teaching children mathematics concepts.

ARTHUR ELLIS recently became professor of education at Seattle Pacific-University. Prior to his move to the west coast, he was a professor of elementary education at the University of Minnesota and a close colleague of A. Humphreys and T. Post. Dr. Ellis is the author of seven books and many research and practical articles for teachers. His major area of expertise is social science but he also specializes in the practical aspects of effective instruction and planning and in interdisciplinary approaches to curriculum. He has taught elementary school, has five children, plays a great game of tennis, and generally enjoys thinking about ways to improve educational experiences for children.

ELIZABETH FENNEMA is a professor in the Department of Curriculum and Instruction at the University of Wisconsin—Madison. Her specialty is in mathematics education and she works intensively with pre-service and in-service elementary teachers. Since about 1974, her main area of scholarly work has been gender-related differences in mathematics. She has received many grants to do research within this area and to develop intervention programs. She has a national and international reputation as a scholar and change-agent in the area of women and mathematics.

ALAN HOFFER is a Professor of Mathematics, and a Professor of Mathematics and Computer Education at Boston University. He has degrees in mathematics from UCLA (B.A.), & Notre Dame (M.S.), and the University of Michigan (Ph.D). At this writing, he is on leave to the National Science Foundation in the Division of Teacher Preparation and Enhancement.

Professor Hoffer has taught mathematics from the second grade level through graduate school. He initiated the mathematics resource center at the University of Oregon and also directed a project to develop resource materials for middle school mathematics teachers. He is a member of the advisory board the Logo and Geometry Project (Kent State University), the Middle Grades Assessment Project (University of North Carolina), the Earth Lab Project (Bank Street College), the Intelligent Tutorial Project (Carnegie-Mellon University), and has been Chairman of the Commission on the Education of Teachers of Mathematics (NCTM).

Dr. Hoffer initiated, conducted, or was consultant to research projects dealing with the van Hiele thought levels at the University of Oregon, Brooklyn College, and the University of Chicago. He has analyzed the Soviet mathematics curriculum and served as Chairman of the task force to analyze the mathematics program in the Boston public schools. He is the author of a modern geometry book and has published numerous articles for teachers and research articles. He has been the invited speaker at numerous conferences of teachers and research organizations, including The International Congress on Mathematics Education, and the study group on the Psychology of Mathematics Education.

ALAN HUMPHREYS began his career at the University of Texas, completing a Ph.D. in 1961. He has worked closely with schools, as a staff member for several national science projects, and has published several books and many papers relating to science teaching.

He retired after 25 years at the University of Minnesota and now spends his summers on the Snake River in central Minnesota and his winters in Guadalajara, Mexico.

DAVID C. JOHNSON currently holds the Shell Professorship in Mathematics Education at Kings College, London, one of only three or four such endowed professorships in the entire UK. For 20 years he has written extensively in the area of computer-related materials and has conducted research in this domain.

His career began at the University of Minnesota. Where he became the first editor of the *Journal for Research in Mathematics Education* and was instrumental in making Minnesota a national leader in the implementation of school-related educational computing, a trend that continues to this day. His wide range of interests and expertise and continued productivity contribute to the international visibility which he currently enjoys.

RICHARD LESH has been a professor of Mathematics and Psychology at Northwestern University. He is currently the Mathematics and Science Education Director at the World Institute for Computer Assisted Teacher (WICAT). WICAT has produced complete computer-based courses for IBM and for CDC (PLATO) in the following areas: Primary School Math, Middle School Math, Algebra I and II, Geometry, Calculus, Chemistry, SAT preparation, Adult Basic Skills, and others.

Dr. Lesh's research projects have been in the areas of: rational number concept development, proportional reasoning processes, problem solving, and mathematics teacher training. He has written textbooks for both children and adults, in addition to computer-based software. He is currently focusing on problem solving, teacher training, and the role of computer utilities and computer representations in mathematics learning and problem solving.

MARGARET R. MEYER is an assistant professor at the University of Wisconsin–Madison. She is involved in the training of pre-service secondary mathematics teachers. Her research interests are in the area of affective variables as they related to problem-solving performance and sex-related differences in mathematics. Before returning to obtain her Ph.D., she taught high school mathematics and computer science for ten years.

JAMES MOSER is currently a mathematics curriculum consultant for the Wisconsin Department of Public Instruction. Previously he was an active researcher at the Wisconsin Center for Education Research where his interests were in the early problem solving behaviors of primary age students. While at the Wisconsin Center, he also acted as Project Coordinator for the Developing Mathematical Processes (DMP) program which produced a complete, manipulative-based elementary curriculum. Dr. Moser has taught both mathematics and pre-service mathematics methods courses at the elementary and secondary level at the University of Wisconsin and at the University of Colorado. He has been active in both national and international organizations dealing with mathematics education research. He has taught overseas and has spent time in France as a visiting researcher with an agency of the French government.

ALAN OSBORNE has been a professor in mathematics education at The Ohio State University since 1966. His interests have included examining children's learning of measurement concepts and the acquisition of concepts that facilitate the learning of algebra. Most recently he has been co-director of the Approaching Algebra Numerically Project that has resulted in instructional materials designed to establish the concept of variables before children encounter the formalities of algebra. His work includes studies of how graphing skills are acquired. He was the director of the Priorities in School Mathematics Project of the National Council of Teachers of Mathematics which provided foundational information for the NCTM's *Agenda for Action*.

BARBARA REYS is an assistant professor of mathematics education at the University of Missouri–Columbia. She has taught secondary, junior high, and elementary mathematics in several Missouri school districts.

Her current research interest are in the teaching and learning of mental computation and estimation as well as the effective and appropriate use of calculators in mathematics instruction. She has participated in several major grants dealing with the clarification of the estimation processes used by good estimators and developing instructional materials to help develop those processes in school-age children.

RICHARD SHUMWAY is a professor of mathematics education specializing in mathematical concept learning and computers. He has major responsibility for training mathematics educators and conducting research, both in the United States and Mexico. He has published over 50 articles and books, has conducted major research projects on concept learning and calculators and computers, and has the experience, over a 20-year period, of teaching children mathematics with computers and calculators as well as training teachers. He is a co-author of eight books for elementary children, co-author of a text for pre-calculus mathematics, co-editor of a book on the psychological foundations for learning and teaching mathematics, editor of a leading research reference for mathematics education, and author of a major book designed to teach the learning of mathematics through programming computers. He has five children and is recognized for his practical, approach to using research to improve the teaching of mathematics.

ROBERT G. UNDERHILL has been active in mathematics education for over 25 years. He has taught mathematics in public schools and in a technical college and has trained mathematics teachers, especially for grades K-9, at four universities.

Dr. Underhill has written extensively, including three editions of a text for teaching elementary school mathematics, has developed a comprehensive slide-tape mathematics teacher training series, and has worked extensively as a special consultant to the Republic of China Ministry of Education and the Taiwan Department of Education.

One of his major written works has been a co-authored text on mathematical diagnosis. He is a recognized leader in this field, having served as the President of the Research Council for Diagnostic and Prescriptive Mathematics. His research areas have been in mathematical diagnosis and the development of place value and problem solving concepts.

PATRICIA S. WILSON is currently an assistant professor at the University of Georgia. She received her B.S. in Mathematics from Ohio University and her M.A. and Ph.D. in Mathematics Education from The Ohio State University. She has worked as a classroom teacher, tutor, and curriculum developer teaching mathematics to children in grades K-12. Her interests in measurement and pre-algebra have developed from classroom experience with student difficulties and research related to how students process examples. Her research in how children learn mathematical concepts has led to numerous presentations and workshops in the United States, Canada, and Mexico. At the college level, she has taught both pre-service and in-service courses for elementary, middle school, and secondary teachers.

JUDITH ZAWOJEWSKI was a mathematics teacher of fifth through eighth grade students over a period of nine years in the suburbs of Chicago. She now works with pre-service and in-service elementary school teachers in her position at the National College of Education in Evanston, Illinois. The Chicago metropolitan area has provided her with numerous opportunities to work in both inner-city and suburban settings. A great deal of her work is field-based with in-service occurring in the schools during the school day.

Dr. Zawojewski's recent research interests involve mathematics topics that middle school students can use in everyday settings: applied problem solving, estimation, and statistics. Her work with Richard Lesh on The Applied Problem Solving Project at Northwestern University initiated her integrated interest in problem solving and statistics. Dr. Zawojewski also worked with Robert Reys, Paul Trafton and Barbara Reys on a National Science Foundation project that supported the development of estimation materials for the middle grades.

Index

NAMES

A

Abelson, H., 364, 365
Abramowitz, S., 311
Aiken, L., 433
Al-Khowarizmi, 154n
Anderson, N. H., 90, 103, 104
Anghileri, Julie, 146–188
Anick, C. M., 117
Antonnen, R., 433

B

Bailey, J. H., 90
Baratta-Lorton, M., 331
Barco, E., 392
Barody, A. J., 116
Bar-Tal, D., 411
Beattie, I. D., 116
Bebout, H. C., 137
Becker, A. D., 411
Becker, J. R., 407, 408
Begle, E. G., 48
Behr, Meryln J., 16, 64, 190–229
Beilin, H., 91, 95
Bell, A., 435
Bell, M. S., 41, 42
Benbow, C. P., 408
Bergeron, J., 434
Bestgen, B. J., 265, 266, 378
Bidwell, J., 187
Billstein, R., 254
Bloom, B., 27, 35, 36, 37, 49, 51

Blume, G., 117
Boe, B., 243
Booth, R., 386
Bossert, S., 25
Bosstick, M., 331
Briars, D. J., 120
Bright, G., 193
Brophy, J. E., 419
Brown, J. S., 118, 140
Brown, M., 151, 152, 153, 155, 157
Brown, S., 41, 61
Brownell, W. A., 116, 187
Bruner, Jerome, 4, 6, 7, 8, 11–16, 21, 432
Budd-Rowe, M. B., 27, 59, 319
Burger, W., 240, 245
Burkhardt, H., 41
Burns, M., 331
Burton, L., 41
Butts, T., 41

C

Cable, J. L., 331
Caldwell, J., 49
Callahan, L. G., 408
Cardozo, P., 331
Carlton, R. A., 264
Carnine, D., 435
Carpenter, T. P., 40, 64, 90, 91, 92, 114, 117, 119, 137, 191, 223, 274, 392, 408
Carroll, Lewis, 187

Casey, D., 433
Channell, D. W., 336, 348
Clason, R., 187
Clement, J., 392
Clements, D. H., 408
Clements, M., 433
Cleveland, R., 311
Coburn, T. G., 92, 337, 338, 378
Conference Board for the Mathematical Sciences, 112n, 343
Confrey, J., 435
Cooney, T., 40
Corbitt, M. K., 40, 64, 191, 223, 274, 392
Cox, L. S., 154
Crockett, L. J., 415
Crosswhite, J., 40
Cuneo, D. O., 90, 103, 104

D

Davis, E., 243, 258
Deaux, D., 411
Deichmann, J. W., 116
Dekkers, J., 316
de la Rocha, O., 65
Demana, F., 384, 399, 402
Denmark, T., 392, 430, 431
Deri, M., 155, 227
DeStefano, J. S., 397
Dienes, Zoltan P., 6, 7, 8–9, 10–11, 13, 16, 116, 162
diSessa, A., 365